Hertfordshire

Cambs.
14/9/09

7/12

Please renew/return this item by the last date shown.

So that your telephone call is charged at local rate, please call the numbers as set out below:

	From Area codes 01923 or 020:	From the rest of Herts:
Renewals:	01923 471373	01438 737373
Enquiries:	01923 471333	01438 737333
Textphone:	01923 471599	01438 737599

L32   www.hertsdirect.org/librarycatalogue

Maude Royden: A Life

To
Helen Blackstone, Gill Sutherland and Pamela Hawker,
who in different ways enabled me to write this book
and to the memory of
Emil Oberholzer

Maude Royden: A Life

Sheila Fletcher

Basil Blackwell

Copyright © Sheila Fletcher 1989

First published 1989

Basil Blackwell Ltd
108 Cowley Road, Oxford, OX4 1JF, UK

Basil Blackwell, Inc.
3 Cambridge Center
Cambridge, Massachusetts 02142, USA

British Library Cataloguing in Publication Data

A CIP catalogue record for this book is available from the British Library.

Library of Congress Cataloging-in-Publication Data

Fletcher, Sheila.
Maude Royden.

Bibliography: p.
1. Royden, Maude. 2. Anglicans – England
–Biography. I. Title.
BX5199.R778F54 1989   283'.092'4 [B] 88–35067
ISBN 0–631–15422–1

Typeset 10 on 11½ pt. Bembo
by Vera-Reyes, Inc. (Philippines)
Printed in Great Britain by
The Camelot Press, Southampton

Contents

Acknowledgements

My greatest debt in connection with this book is one which cannot easily be assessed or acknowledged. In 1962 Dr Emil Oberholzer Jr, an American church historian whose many fields of interest included the status of women in the world-wide Anglican community, started to research the life of Maude Royden. He worked on this project over the years until his sudden death at the age of fifty-four on 6 January 1981. He had done an enormous amount of research at the time he died. Concerned that his work should not be wasted, his great friend Dr Richard Henshaw of Colgate Rochester Divinity School set out to find someone to carry on the project. It was my good fortune to be asked to do so.

Naturally this is not the book that Emil Oberholzer would have written. Apart from differences of style and emphasis (he might well, for instance, have given more weight to Maude Royden's influence in the USA and less to the detail of her suffrage work) our lines of research have differed somewhat. An important source – the letters now at Lady Margaret Hall which Maude Royden wrote to Kathleen Courtney – was not available to him; and in addition, he started work before the development of women's studies transformed the history of feminism. Emil Oberholzer spotted his subject when she was still more or less 'hidden from history' and I wish most warmly to express my gratitude at having fallen heir to his scholarship.

Very many people have helped and encouraged me, among them another friend of Emil Oberholzer, Professor Martha Vogeler, who has shown great interest. At the Fawcett Library Catherine Ireland, David Doughan and Sue Cross have been unstintingly helpful and patient, while early on I had generous assistance from Ruth Dipple, librarian at Lady Margaret Hall and from Dr Hough, of Church House Archives. Professor Stuart Marriott assisted me greatly with expert knowledge of Hudson Shaw, Professor Adrian Hastings gave up time to discuss aspects of church history and Monica Furlong to put me in touch with the women's movement in the church today. I am much indebted to Dr Gillian Sutherland for critical comments on the final draft, to Dr Brian Harrison for comments and references and to Dr David Rubinstein, whose sustaining letters, full of relevant information, are almost worth publishing on their own. Cecily Blackley, Pamela Hawker, Emily White and Robert Green, who have given me good advice on chapter after chapter over the years, know how grateful I am to them. My thanks go also to Felicity Hunt for much encouragement and practical help and to Charlie Hunt for some expert photography.

I would like finally to acknowledge the help I have had from Maude Royden's adopted daughter, Mrs Helen Blackstone, and from her nieces Mrs Joan Batten and Mrs Mary Laird; also to thank Lady Richardson of Duntisbourne for lending me letters Maude Royden wrote to her father, Dick Sheppard, and Miss Christine Anson for talking to me about her father, Harold Anson.

Abbreviations

CC	Common Cause
CLWS	Church League for Women's Suffrage
COS	Charity Organisation Society
ECU	English Church Union
FOR	Fellowhip of Reconciliation
ILP	Independent Labour Party
LCM	League of the Church Militant
LMH	Lady Margaret Hall
NCW	National Council of Women
NU	National Union. This is used alone to refer to NUSEC National Union of Societies for Equal Citizenship or NUWSS National Union of Women's Suffrage Societies
PPU	Peace Pledge Union
SCM	Student Christian Movement
WEA	Worker's Educational Association
WIL	Women's International League
WSPU	Women's Social and Political Union
YWCA	Young Women's Christian Association

1

The Really Famous Maude Royden

I was born a woman and I can't get over it.

Maude Royden (1922).

When Maude Royden arrived in Australia in the course of a speaking tour in 1928 reporters were surprised by her unassuming manner. 'You could talk to her for some time without realising that she was the really famous Maude Royden, England's first woman preacher and described by one considerable person as England's greatest woman,' said the *Sydney Daily Guardian*. The judgement itself, which came from Jane Addams, the American suffragist and social reformer – seems to have been picked up in the 1920s by almost everyone who wrote on Maude Royden, then at the height of her career.

'I should hesitate to say that she is either the wisest or the greatest woman in England,' said A. G. Gardiner, the literary man, 'even though the present generation of Englishwomen is not rich in personalities of conspicuous gifts. But she holds the most individual position among the public women of the time.'[1] It is this *individual* position which has kept Maude Royden 'hidden from history'; or at least substantially unexamined.[2] It is not just that she is idiosyncratic but that her idiosyncrasy lies in a mixture of feminism and religion – a mixture likely to arouse mistrust if not hostility in both camps.

The *Church Times*, commenting in 1913 on a conference called to discuss 'The Religious Aspect of the Women's Movement', ventured to doubt that there was such a thing. And this, one feels, would be the reaction of a great many church people today. Church historians have paid little regard to the impact on the churches of the women's movement,[3] while studies of that movement have paid equally little to the influence of religion on what

---

[1]A. G. Gardiner, *Certain People of Importance* (1926) 240. Gardiner edited the *Daily News* 1902–19.

[2]There are useful references in Martin Ceadel, *Pacifism in Britain 1914–1945* (1980); Sybil Oldfield, *Spinsters of this Parish* (1984); Anne Wiltsher, *Most Dangerous Women* (1985) and Brian Heeney, *The Women's Movement in the Church of England* (1988).

[3]Heeney's recent study opens up the subject.

Maude Royden herself considered 'the most profoundly moral movement since the foundation of the Christian Church'.

Feminist suspicions have obvious roots. What has been called the feminist case against God relates to the profound alienation of women for whom Christianity 'proclaims, endorses and affirms a male-centred universe.'[4] Faced with the fact that through its traditions, structure and theology the Church has been a most powerful mediator of the idea that the male is norm, these women see God as 'a tyrannical male deity, erected by a patriarchal society with the aim of giving injustice to women a divine seal of approval'. 'Even the God we no longer believe in is still envisaged as male,' says one.

This is not new. No modern feminist has made the case against God more fully, or more bitterly, than it was made in 1893 by Mathilda Joslyn Gage, a leader of the American women's rights movement and colleague of the better-known Elizabeth Cady Stanton and Susan B. Anthony. *Woman, Church and State* is an angry indictment, extending over nearly 600 pages, of women's oppression under Christianity. 'As I look backward through history I see the Church everywhere stepping upon advancing civilisation, hurling woman from the plane of "natural rights" where the fact of her humanity had placed her.' 'The whole theory regarding woman, under Christianity, has been based upon the conception that she had no right to live for herself alone.'[5] She lost this right with the sin of Eve and in consequence of her impurity is to be for ever subject to man, as man himself is subject to God. So the Church supplies through the centuries the rationale for patriarchy, the development of which Gage follows minutely, recording among 'its most degenerate forms' the burning of hundreds of thousands of witches. Men were very rarely punished for magic. 'When for "witches" we read "women" we gain fuller comprehension of the cruelties inflicted by the Church upon this portion of humanity.' Gage emphatically rejects the view that the Church's misogyny belongs to the past; seeing on the one hand plenty of evidence of its oppression of women in her own day; and convinced that however its power had waned, its values were largely reproduced in the Christian culture of secular society.

Woman will gain nothing by a compromising attitude, by excusing the Church's 'great wrong towards her sex or by palliation of its motives', she states. Presumably she would have had little to say to those Christian feminists of the present day whom one writer calls 'house revolutionaries'; women who see much wrong with the Church yet remain to make their protest inside it, since 'our own sympathies and fervent energies anchor us to the Christian faith.'[6]

---

[4]Elaine Storkey, 'The Feminist Case Against God' in Kathy Keay (ed.), *Men Women and God* (1987).
   [5]Mathilda Joslyn Gage, *Woman, Church and State* (1893) 544, 530–1.
   [6]Judith L. Weidman (ed.) *Christian Feminism* (1984), Introduction; Susan Dowell and Linda Hurcombe, *Dispossessed Daughters of Eve* (1981, 1987) 67.

Maude Royden was the prototype house revolutionary. Conscious that 'history has always . . . been written from the point of view of the possessing classes,' and that the major possessing class is men, she too arraigns the Church's historic role in the subordination of women.[7] But her own work *The Church and Woman* has very little in common with Gage's (which there is no sign that she ever read). She writes from inside. She is in the tradition of another insider, Josephine Butler; and what they would have seen in the American book is the effective absence of Christ. Search through the Gospel, Butler says,

> and observe His conduct in regard to women, and it will be found that the word liberation expresses, above all others, the act which changed the whole life and character and position of the women dealt with, and which ought to have changed the character of men's treatment of women from that time forward.[8]

She speaks elsewhere of the need for women preaching and calls it 'an astonishing and melancholy thing' that the churches have virtually ignored this aspect of the first Pentecost – hailed by St Peter as fulfilling the promise of the prophet Joel: 'Your sons and your *daughters* shall prophesy.' 'Is it possible,' Butler asks, 'that the Church has ever fully believed this?' 'The most stupendous announcement ever made to the world' (of the Resurrection) Christ made to a woman. Yet those who write about woman's position nearly always refer to St Paul and seldom to the higher authority. They choose to be guided by early adaptations of the principles announced by Christ 'rather than by the pure principles themselves'.

This was exactly Maude Royden's position. For her, as for Butler, the appeal rests with Christ.

> It is part of the amazing originality of Christ that there is to be found in his teaching no word whatever which suggests a difference in the spiritual ideals, the spheres, or the potentialities of men and women. There is no classification of virtues assigning some to men . . . and others to women. There is no limitation of sphere . . . . If the words of Christ were isolated from their context and read to one to whom the gospels were not familiar it would be absolutely impossible for him to guess whether any special word or phrase was addressed to a woman or to a man.[9]

'No other great religion,' she says, 'has thus ignored the differences between men and women.'

For her, then, Christ is the first feminist: recognising women's humanity before the attribute of sex. 'Who else considered them first as human beings

---

[7]Maude Royden, *The Church and Woman* (1924) 9.

[8]This and the other Butler passages are quoted in the *Church Militant*, (July 1919) 37–40. Josephine Butler (1828–1906), whose Christian convictions drove her into social reform, is best known for her campaign against the Contagious Diseases Acts.

[9]Royden *The Church and Woman* 167.

and afterwards as women?' she asks. This is what she brings to the suffrage struggle; and what gives meaning to a later tribute that she was 'truly the heart and soul of the Feminist Movement of her day – yes, the *soul* of it'.[10] Her charge against the Church (the Church of England, 'my spiritual home') is that while subscribing to that spiritual equality which was the essence of Christ's teaching, by its practice it 'sets an example and gives an object lesson to men in contempt for women'.[11] While women were excluded not only from the priesthood and from the pulpit but from coming near the altar, singing in the choir – even taking the collection, how could it be otherwise?

Her struggle with the Church is not simply of interest as the start of a struggle which continues today. It is of course a page in feminist history but it is also a particular case of individual against institution. Because of the nature of what it represents the Church does not see itself as an institution in the ordinary sense of the word. There is always the spiritual element, the mystery which it exists to proclaim and which has meant, for instance, that women's admission to professions in England in the twentieth century has not been held to constitute a precedent for admitting them to the Anglican priesthood. But while it does not perceive itself in ordinary institutional terms, when it comes to such questions the Church behaves like any other professional body. It is exclusive. And the effect of exclusion – absolute, total – is what it would be (indeed once was) in the secular professions: first, a great difficulty for a woman to imagine she could have a vocation at all; then, as the exclusion persists over years (and the Church offers no means of testing whether her call 'is of God or not') a fading, if not a failing of vocation, because there is no space in which it can be exercised. Maude Royden's life gives unusual insight into this because she took things as far as she did; working for many years as a minister with her own congregation and her own 'church'. She would not herself have felt that inverted commas made it right to call the Guildhouse a church. She never did so, knowing only too well what a church was and what a priest was and feeling herself defeated in the end by the fact that both it and she were disqualified.

How relevant is such experience to most women, or even to most feminists today? Things have moved on in the seventy or so years since these issues were first thrashed out. For one thing, the Church's influence has waned and it counts for less as a pattern for society. For another, some women who hope for ordination see it now less as a single goal than as 'the narrow end' of a great debate, of which 'the broad end is the full evaluation of women within the Christian community and maybe within society as a whole.' Indeed, the broad end gets ever broader. Some Christian feminists make a link between the Church's failure to wean itself from traditional

---

[10]'*Memorial Address for Maude Royden preached 5 Aug. 1956 by Rev. Claude Coltman at Kings Weigh House Church, London.*'

[11]Royden *The Church and Woman* 233.

patterns of domination and the macho spirit of today's society, with its violence and abuse of the helpless, of which women and children are prime victims.[12]

None of this would have surprised Maude Royden, whose feminism was a demonstration of her belief in moral law. The women's movement, as she saw it, could only ever be based on this. For if the appeal were to physical force, women, who were physically weak, were nowhere. Feminism and pacifism alike were aspects of the need to harness spiritual power before the world rushed on its own destruction. She was responding to troubled times.

In view of this, it is almost a shock to be reminded by one of her contemporaries that 'Maude Royden saw twenty-five years of the nineteenth century and therefore will be counted as a Victorian.[13] She was born in 1876 and passed through childhood, schooldays and Oxford in late-Victorian comfort and stability. Her father was a shipowner, Thomas Royden, who in fact was also the last exemplar of Liverpool's once-famous shipbuilding industry. She was very fond and very admiring of the man she nicknamed the Breadwinner; and he seems to have had great ability, winning an enormous amount of bread, for he was a millionaire when he died. Maude and others of his large family (she was the youngest of eight, and sixth daughter) inherited his brains and his charm of manner. One cannot read the comments of later years on the warm appeal of her smile without remembering that her father's smile was said to be the Tories' best asset in Liverpool. 'Smiling Tom' and 'Sir Tom O'Smiles' he was nicknamed by the *Porcupine* – satirist of Liverpool's political scene. Unquestionably a tough politician, he was also a Tory with the common touch, as the paper noted in 1904. 'During a recent procession he was recognised by an Irish lady in the crowd, with the greeting: "There goes Tommy Royden – bless his owld whiskers!"'

The assertiveness which had led him, at thirty, to go against his father's old-fashioned judgement and insist that Thomas Royden & Sons should at last take orders for iron ships, brought him into politics in 1873 as a member of the city council. In 1878 he was Lord Mayor of Liverpool and served from 1885–92 as Member of Parliament for West Toxteth. Forced out of politics for a time by ill health, he was active again at the turn of the century; was appointed High Sheriff of Cheshire, and in 1905 received the reward of a baronetcy.

There is very much less to say of Maude's mother. 'She once said to me,'

[12]Monica Furlong, quoted in *Dispossessed Daughters of Eve* xviii. Also Furlong 'A Sense of Rejection', *The Tablet* (10 Oct. 1987).
[13]Lord Pethick Lawrence, memorial tribute, Fawcett 223.

Plate 1   Maude Royden (seated second from right) with her sisters and brothers in the late 1880s. *Reproduced by permission of Mrs Helen Blackstone.* (Photograph: Mary Evans/Fawcett Library)

Maude wrote to one of her friends in 1903, 'that she "often thought" how curious it was that I was so much younger than she, and yet had seen so much more of life and people.'

It is rather pathetic, I think. Of couse being married and having babies is a world in itself. But in other ways, my mother is just *ignorant*. It is not fair – is it? – to keep women boxed up, and then complain that they are foolish.[14]

Such other scraps of evidence as exist do nothing to alter this impression that Alice Royden lived through her husband and children, that she was a rather clinging person and not a particularly clever one. She was evidently kind, but also fussy, and, as she grew older, 'rather a weeper'. Maude seems to have felt tenderly towards her, but given that she herself was bright and impatient and found it hard to suffer fools gladly, it seems unlikely that her mother inspired the kind of respect she gave to her father. Lady Royden had no public life, beyond the duties of a village philanthropy typified at length

[14]Maude to Kathleen Courtney (24 July 1903) LMH archives (henceforth Maude to KC).

by her coffin borne into church on the shoulders of the villagers through a lane formed by the Mothers' Union. Some of Maude's talent for attracting service very probably came from her, for a local reporter doing a series on 'The Stately Homes of Merseyside' in 1929 was struck that so many had worked so long at the family home near Birkenhead.

> A year or so ago, one who had been for 63 years a member of the household died in harness. Another followed her, with a record of 53 years, and two more had been members of the staff for 40 years. The butler has been in Lady Royden's servce for 40 years and the head housemaid, a daughter of one of those just mentioned, has also been at Frankby Hall for 40 years. Everyone loves her.[15]

The reporter was also staggered by his tour of Lady Royden's household treasures, and went away to write about the Ming vases and cabinets of beautiful English china, the Turner and other watercolours jostling each other on the dining room walls. Some of them were lovely, Maude said in her youth, but so crowded no one could really see them. 'I am amazed at the way people (I mean my mother) spends weeks in hanging up pictures. Why have so many?'[16]

Even in this rich and well-staffed household spending so much time hanging pictures was probably an indulgence of later years. When Maude was born there were eight children under ten and her feeling against large families, which lasted throughout her life, began with the experience that her own parents never had enough time to go round. 'As one of a perfectly charming and affectionate family of eight, I affirm with conviction, 'she wrote much later, 'that my parents were practically strangers, at least to the younger ones.'

> They had no time to be anything else. We were far from poor but eight children take a lot of time and money. Our mother was exhausted. As for our father, a joke in an ancient *Punch* describes the situation:
> Child: 'Mother, who is that kind man who comes to cut the beef on Sunday?'[17]

To a younger friend whose family was increasing in the 1940s she took the same line, 'there is so little leisure when it has to be spread out over so many.'[18] As for herself, she did not like being the youngest ('The sixth daughter and eighth child doesn't feel very necessary'); she did not like her name ('Yes, please do call me by my ugly name and I you by your beautiful one,' she told Vera Brittain later on); and as a child she did not like it that she was unable to sit cross-legged. Though nobody understood at the time – indeed, her lameness was not even noticed in babyhood till she started to walk – she had been born with both hips dislocated.

[15] *Liverpool Evening Express* (4 Nov. 1929).
[16] Maude to KC (2 Oct. 1905).
[17] Maude Royden, *Sex and Common Sense* (1922) 99.
[18] Maude to Betty Tucker (22 Feb. 1946) lent by Mrs Tucker.

Though the condition was known to Hippocrates and some treatment was attempted in the nineteenth century, effective and early diagnosis of dislocated hips was to depend on X-ray; and the X-ray itself was not discovered till twenty years after Maude was born. What her condition meant in the seventies was a lame child crying with pain – until the moment when her parents nerved themselves, after many visits to conventional doctors, to take her to a well-known bonesetter. This man, of the celebrated Hutton family, evidently broke down some adhesions. At any rate, he stopped the pain.[19]

After that, she seems to have been free to enter into the dangerous games which the Royden children devised for themselves and their friends among the families of the butler and coachman. They did not use gunpowder or fight with swords, as Maude's fellow campaigner for women's ordination, Edith Picton-Turbervill, relates of her youth. But the grounds contained ponds deep enough to drown in, a disused quarry and a railway cutting. This cutting was marvellous – made on a curve round which rushed the fast trains from London to Liverpool – and the great thing was to lie on the track with your ear to the rail and listen for them coming. Maude admits to having been frightened by this – but not by walking on the quarry wall, above a sheer drop, and taking her turn to rock on the flat stone that moved at the end.[20]

It was some time, she says, before she realised that her physical defects were other than those which naturally attached to being the youngest. 'My brothers and sisters must have been very kind to me or of course I should have minded much more.' In adult life she played down her lameness. Yet one gets the feeling it was never quite banished, either by success or friendship or love, for she took great pleasure in physical things. In childhood it seems to have been her lameness that led her first to think hard about God. She was, she says, not at all inclined to question the religious side of her upbringing: going to church at least twice on Sunday, becoming confirmed as a matter of course and taking a vengeful God for granted. 'That children who called Elisha "baldhead" should immediately be devoured by two bears was. . . received by me without any sense of shock.'[21] The Bible was, in fact, 'out of real life'. But when her parents said God had sent her lameness this was something she could not accept. It did not tie in with her own idea of any God that she would want to worship and the seed was sown for her later belief that illness and disease were of human making, and for her search for spiritual healing when it came to her own old age.

---

[19] Maude seems to have been treated by Robert Hutton, who came of a northern family of bonesetters who had exercised their art from time immemorial and achieved remarkable results.
[20] Margot Oxford (ed.), *Myself When Young* (1938) 319-20; BBC broadcast by Maude Royden, (7 Oct. 1952).
[21] Oxford (ed.), *Myself When Young* 362.

She herself wondered, looking back, whether it was her lameness in the first place that gave her a feeling for the underdog – a feeling which seems to have been reinforced by little things of a domestic kind, for her childhood was very far removed from the Liverpool slums that she knew well later. 'Countenances haggard with distress and hunger . . . children with scarcely rags to cover them' were not seen in the village of Frankby.[22] Some things puzzled her nonetheless. Why, when Christ preferred the poor to the rich, did people prefer the rich to the poor? Why, when she was taken once by her nurse to visit Hutton the bonesetter and sat in a crowded waiting room for hours until her nurse at last made a fuss, was she received then with soup and apologies and the receptionist very much blamed, though the crowd of poor people outside was still waiting? Why, when she accompanied an elder sister to buy flannel for their own petticoats and her sister asked for a cheaper quality, did the shop assistant reply 'Oh, if it is for *charitable purposes* –' and produce something coarse and hard?[23]

She describes herself as a late developer who did not make the leap from this kind of thing to an embryonic social critique for years. She was in fact only two at the time when her father found himself involved as lord mayor with the Liverpool dock strike of 1879. The strike was called to resist wage cuts which the shipowners made to protect themselves against the effects of the long depression. 'Very few of the voyages of the large steamers sailing from Liverpool have been even moderately profitable,' it was said. The labourer's wage was docked sixpence a day. But 'in these hard times,' one labourer asked 'who wants it worse – they who have a good meal to go home to, or us who have none? Sixpence a day means a loaf less for our little ones.' There were huge mass meetings and fear of riots. Royden, as mayor, made a proclamation calling on people to assist the authorities in the maintenance of public order. Also – reluctantly, it was said – he telegraphed to Manchester for troops and it was arranged to have marines and blue jackets from HMS *Resistance*, the guardship in the river. As it turned out, there was no clash with troops and when the strike ended the Mayor was praised for his cool handling of the situation – which was even held to have been eased somewhat by his popularity as an employer.

Many years later she asked her father why depressions could not be provided for.

His answer was that these things came in cycles and no one could possibly prevent them: but he added that 'the system' demanded a surplus of men so that, when the boom came, the industry could draw them in, although unfortunately this meant

---

[22]*Liverpool Daily Post* account of scenes in the dock strike, 1879. The Roydens were benevolent patrons of Frankby.

[23]These anecdotes are drawn from Oxford (ed.), *Myself When Young*; Sir James Marchant (ed.), *If I Had My Time Again* (1951); autobiographical articles in *Homes and Gardens* (Sept.- Dec. 1950); broadcasts by Maude Royden and other autobiographical fragments, including the typescript 'Bid Me Discourse', Fawcett 224.

that when the depression came, they were squeezed out. This bothered me for years. In fact, it made me a Socialist in the end.[24]

For all that, she could not forget where she came from. Active as she was through the 1920s in defending the miners' case she would not condemn capitalists as a class and was always proud to think of her father and her brother as model employers. How unworthy the mine owners seemed by comparison! Speaking about the events which followed the decontrol of mines in 1921 she said, 'There is not – I belong to business people, and I say it with pride – there is not another industry in the country where such a devastating situation could have arisen and have been met as the mine owners met it.' They had refused to discuss with the men. 'The miners were ready to forgive their grievances: the owners could not forget their class.'[25]

Among her siblings, she felt special affection always for her elder brother Tom, chairman of Cunard and at length Lord Royden, a breadwinner on the grandest scale, though as a young woman she was often impatient of his conventional, Tory style.

> I dined alone with my brother last night and I couldn't talk about horses, and I suppose he didn't want to talk about books; so we talked gossip, which is degrading and boring both. Isn't it sad to see a young mind grown old? Tom used to be – or *tended* to be – a Liberal. Now he is the most convinced Tory . . . that exists![26]

But despite their contrasting views and life styles (Tom Royden, apart from his business interests, took great pleasure in polo and hunting and offering good sport to his friends) they were always fond of each other. He gave her his backing for what, by most standards, was an eccentric enterprise: the Guildhouse. His letters into old age are loving: 'Darling Minnie', he writes, or 'My beloved Sister'; signing, 'All my love and gratitude, Timkey' or 'Your completely adoring brother, Tom.'

Tom and her other brother, Ernest, went to Winchester. 'When they came home it seemed natural to receive them with rejoicing and to regard them with respect.' Not because they were boys but because they were older. Apart from a fleeting sense of disquiet that Adam should have put the blame on Eve (for she had been taught by her siblings that to give someone away was not done) Maude grew up, by her own account, 'as unconscious as a Quaker of sex antagonism'. When she found later that the world at large put boys above girls it made her angry. 'I was a born feminist and thought myself as good as anyone.' That was the start. The Royden parents

---

[24]Oxford (ed.), *Myself When Young* 376.

[25]*Human Nature and Industrial Disputes*, pamphlet (n.d.) of sermon preached at the Guildhouse, 7.

[26]Maude to KC (2 Oct. 1905).

do not seem to have been advocates of sex equality but there is no sign that their daughters suffered from that shameless favouring of sons so bitterly recalled by Helena Swanwick, one of Maudes's colleagues in suffrage days. Nor, to judge by their escapades, was genteel behaviour enforced upon them. 'How savagely,' says Swanwick, 'I resented being told that boys might romp and get red in the face, and tear their clothes, but that a girl should be quiet and tidy.'[27] The Roydens were kept on an easy rein – so easy that Maude was incredulous later to meet the theory of penis envy. 'I was one of rather a crowd of children . . . several other families playing with us . . . and we constantly saw each other naked and I can't remember that any of us ever gave the matter a thought!'[28]

The vigour of life outdoors was matched by argument round the dining table. How to squeeze themselves into the debate of so many confident, articulate people exercised some of Maude's friends who came. 'I never witnessed such a sharpening of wits as I did in her home,' wrote one. 'It was incessant – like a game of ping-pong.'[29] Maude learnt very well to keep her end up but as she grew older she felt increasingly that she was the odd one out in the family. 'There seems to me,' she told her sister Mary, in their old age, 'to be an underlying and much deeper difference between me and the rest which makes me feel a "sport".'[30] She was always a Royden (and that counted for much with the Royden clan) but she had no kindred spirit in the family before the birth in 1894 of her eldest sister's second son, Ralph. Ralph Rooper was a brilliant young man, later to be killed in World War I, whose own poor health matched her disability. Apart from that, she says, 'We were both "freaks" in our political and other views, and though no freaks can ever have been more kindly treated by their families, we could not help feeling drawn . . . together.'[31]

It says something for the Roydens that they took to a 'freak'. 'I know full well she has the true foundations which must tell for good in any walk of life,' her mother wrote to one of Maude's Oxford friends in the summer of 1903. But she could never have reckoned then on walks of life such as suffrage, socialism, pacifism, preaching (in defiance of a bishop). By 1903 Maude had done nothing more freakish than insist on going to Oxford, and

[27]'Daughters' *Common Cause* (2 Oct. 1914) 462. Also see Swanwick's autobiography *I Have Been Young*, (1935) and Royden 'The Ministry of Women', *Guildhouse Monthly* (Feb 1919) 'Every boy who grows up thinking that his sisters are of less importance than himself is . . . put into the position of one who has a right to exploit them.'

[28]Maude to Ursula Roberts (21 March 1934).

[29]'Women of the Day', *Yorkshire Post* (12 Nov. 1923).

[30]Maude to Mary Royden (17 Oct. 1950) Fawcett 222. Maude goes on, 'I have also felt that you might have been a "sport" too, if circumstances hadn't enforced a kind of conformity on you – as it would on me if I had had to live at home.'

[31]A. Maude Royden, 'Ralph Bonfoy Rooper: A Memoir' (n.d.) Fawcett 380, illustrates the depth of their friendship. The typescript 'Ralph Rooper', Fawcett 223, contains a lively critique of public schools written by Ralph as a schoolboy at Charterhouse, together with sundry 'freakish' proposals to improve the relations of rich and poor.

before that, on going to school. In none of this was she following her sisters. Her parents allowed her to choose a school and after a short spell at Belvedere High School she chose the best-known: Cheltenham Ladies' College. The relative importance of girls and boys did not dawn on her, Maude recalled, until her mother informed her one day that her education 'cost as much as a boy's'.

> I realised by the tone of her voice that this was a surprising and rather shocking thing. . . . *Why shouldn't* it cost as much as a boy's? I could not understand. . . . But I was furious.[32]

---

[32]Royden 'Bid Me Discourse'.

2

Oxford and After

This is an "I" letter, isn't it?
                    Maude to Kathleen Courtney (29 November 1902).

In retrospect Maude speaks of herself as 'grateful for being sent to so great a school' and all her comments on Cheltenham express the satisfaction of a strong personality moving out into the mainstream. 'I do love things done on a large scale!' she said with pride on discovering later that the number of pupils had reached 1,000. Even in her day there had been 600, which was huge for girls' school then. When she arrived in 1893 Cheltenham, in fact, had just embarked on its grandest period of Victorian expansion. The principal's house was being built, and the new library and the long corridor with its black and white marble paving – still an imposing sight today – and the Oxford and Cambridge Rooms. It was thought that the stately rooms, stained glass and pictures, 'contribute much to the teaching power of our college.' And Maude, for whom beauty became a subject for many sermons in after years, no doubt admired it all – pondering also upon the statues of noble women and upon the portentous inscription in one window of the Oxford Room: 'Long tarries destiny but comes to those who pray.'

  A great school with a great headmistress: Miss Beale by now was known throughout England, her school a model, her opinion sought by royal commissions on education. Though she taught less than in her pioneer days the ethos of Cheltenham was very much hers: rigorous educational standards with high religious and social ideals. After an earlier building phase she had commented, 'Some say our school is churchlike. I am glad, for churches are built to remind us that God is not far away, but very near to us . . . . May His presence be seen in this house.'[1] But the school's religious life seems to have made little impact on Maude. What she recalled later was the experience of worshipping sometimes at All Saints, Cheltenham. 'I was a born ritualist.' And here for the first time she discovered what ritual could be. 'It appealed to my sense of beauty so strongly that I worshipped. That

[1]*Cheltenham Ladies' College Magazine* (1893) 267.

was, I think, my first real religius experience.'[2]

Viewed more broadly, the religious experience of girls at Cheltenham embraced the Guild. The Guild, established, in 1884, was meant by Miss Beale to be something more than an ordinary old students' body, and she herself chose its emblem, the daisy, ('the single eye . . . the real heliotrope, that stands ever gazing upward . . . burning towards heaven') with full regard to its symbolic value. Membership of the Guild implied a real commitment to serve the poor. By the time that Maude was admitted it had established an East End mission, and many old students, including herself, later on turned to settlement work.

Her main occupation as a schoolgirl, however, outside the schoolroom, was enjoying herself, generally by amusing her friends. Assured, courteous, sociable, spendthrift, comical and clever, as one recalled, she took with extreme delight to dancing, which was less tiring than walking, for her; took up acting with enormous verve ('I never expect to see a better Mrs Malaprop, nor a more versatile producer of charades') and when she could not act ('after closing hours') entertained them with scenes from Shakespeare which she was able to recite at will.[3]

She came out near the top of Cheltenham's list for the Cambridge Higher Local examination but does not appear among those senior girls who, in the autumn of 1895, went to Oxford University Extension lectures given in the town by one of the great men of Oxford's Extension teaching at the time, the Rev. G. W. Hudson Shaw. He, as it turned out, was to have more influence on Maude's life than anyone else; and they married, eventually. But her immediate future was Oxford. In 1896 she was accepted as a history student at Lady Margaret Hall.

Her parents evidently raised no objection. It is true that by 1896 the idea of women going to college was less freakish than it had been in the 1870s when such colleges were founded. But it was very far from widely accepted. The women students had no standing at either Oxford or Cambridge University. They were admitted on sufferance to lectures and were not permitted to take degrees. Apart from that there was the social factor. The hard, bright edge of the 'college woman' was thought to frighten off prospective husbands. Miss Wordsworth, Principal of Lady Margaret Hall, was even said to have warned one mother 'you know, our girls do not marry well'. Possibly the Roydens did not think Maude would marry and saw higher education as a makeweight for lameness. At any rate, once they had taken the plunge, Lady Margaret Hall was the obvious choice for Anglican, Tory parents like these. It had been founded in the High Church tradition, in marked contrast to its rival, Somerville, the boldly undenominational place where Maude's contemporary was Eleanor Rath-

---

[2]Oxford (ed.), *Myself When Young* 366.
[3]'Women of the Day' *Yorkshire Post* (12 Nov. 1923).

bone, daughter of Liverpool Liberalism.

For one who liked things done on a large scale Lady Margaret Hall in the 1890s could only have been a disappointment. Though it had outgrown the original villa, it was modest, compared with Cheltenham, having fewer than fifty students – the most so far; and far too many, in the eyes of its principal, Elizabeth Wordsworth, who, unlike Maude, had no love whatever for things done on a large scale. Her scale, for girls, was the scale of the family; and though she became resigned to expansion, she also always gave the impression that the original intake (nine) when the college started, had been just about right.

Even now her college was run like a family. Miss Wordsworth cared about the social arts, expecting students not only to study but to know how to make conversation, attend her tea parties, read aloud to her, accompany her on walks and afternoon calls. It is true that she was no ordinary lady. She had a quick and original wit. She was also a scholar, gifted enough to have picked up her Latin, Greek and Hebrew almost informally from her father, Christopher Wordsworth, Bishop of Lincoln, whom she had assisted with his biblical commentary. The Wordsworth name (she was a great niece of the poet) her father's elevated reputation, her own personality and brilliant talk opened many doors to her in Oxford. And that was how she thought doors should be opened. Beating against them, breaking them down through any sort of movement was quite alien to her.

> In my younger days, if I had been told at a party that a young lady belonged to a Ladies' College I should have preferred occupying the stiffest of upright chairs, in a thorough draught, to sitting by her on the most comfortable of sofas.[4]

It was thus no sense of women's rights in education, no passionate desire that they should take degrees (such, for instance, as drove Emily Davies, founder of Girton College, Cambridge) which brought her to be head of Lady Margaret Hall, but a deep religious sense – and the fact that she was asked.

She never really took to students like Maude – distrustful always of immoderate enthusiasm – and perhaps not quite at ease with an industrial background. Miss Wordsworth belonged, on her own admission, to that class of society 'which was recruited from . . . our universities, our cathedrals and our country parsonages'.[5] With this world she was superbly au fait. But the world of Liverpool shipowners was different. She did not warm to Maude; and had not, earlier, warmed to Gertrude Bell (the future explorer), daughter of a great ironmaster of Durham. Possibly such backgrounds tended to foster more independence than she cared for in girls; or a

---

[4]Georgina Battiscombe, *Reluctant Pioneer* (1978) 101; and see Miss Wordsworth's own memoir *Glimpses of the Past* (1912).
[5]Wordsworth, *Glimpses* 28.

type of personality that seemed in need of St Paul's advice, which she once suggested should be carved above a college mantelpiece: 'Study to be quiet.' (St Paul, she observed, showed here his wonderful and customary insight into human nature; especially women's.)

Maude, for her part, felt she owed little to this 'daughter of a thousand bishops'. She could not, for all the celebrated wit (though she loved wit) forgive Miss Wordsworth's lack of interest in the cause of women and reckoned her a most unsuitable person to have had the charge of a women's college.[6] Religion – which might have made a bond between them – does not seem to have worked that way. Miss Wordsworth's first care when the college started had been to set aside a room for a chapel. By Maude's day a real chapel had been built, adorned with stained glass, marble pavement, candlesticks and altar plate. The eloquent addresses Miss Wordsworth gave here show her at her most direct. It could be Maude in a pulpit, later, talking of the fearlessness of Christianity, of a faith which 'does not fear to face truth . . . loves to face inquiry'. Here was common ground, surely; a bridge that could have linked the one personality, with its touch of the eighteenth century, to the other, impatient for the twentieth. But Maude says nothing about chapel addresses. Her recollection is of sceptics at Oxford, with no very strong influence the other way; of LMH as churchy and of churchiness as something which tended to inhibit the pioneers of women's education. In her letters of the Oxford period there is certainly a lot about religion, but her remarks about religion at college are few and flippant. 'Are you late for chapel?' she writes to a friend. 'Well, you'll have to sit next to Miss Wordsworth. Heigh-ho.'

She thought she might have liked Somerville better. But she would not there have escaped the restrictions common in those days to every women's college: the peremptory evening bell that broke up so many cocoa parties, the chaperonage still insisted upon if a solitary woman attended a lecture (though chaperonage for groups of women had gone), the rule about not going alone into the town. However, against those restrictions was the freedom – novel, then, to girls – to dispose of their time without being expected to account for it to someone; and, equally delightful, the room of one's own. 'To know one was safe from the intrusion of friends, relatives and housemaids was freedom', wrote one near contemporary.[7] And Maude felt this keenly, writing back from Frankby to the friend still at college, 'Oh Kathleen, I would like to be there, with a room to hide in and work to do and "engaged" to keep out the cold world!'[8]

It was easy enough to hanker after work when the burden of it had been left behind. The signs are that she found it quite difficult to get down to

---

[6]Marchant (ed.), *If I Had My Time Again* 150.
[7]Winifred Peck, *A Little Learning* (1952) 156.
[8]Maude to KC (17 Oct. 1899).

work when she first came to Oxford. For one thing, she was naturally lazy. For another, it seems that Cheltenham and its large scale had tired her so much that she wasted her first term. Work had become a serious matter by this time for Oxford women. Though they were actually there on sufferance examinations had been opened to them, and almost all lectures, while a system of coaching had developed which brought them into contact with some of the best minds in the university. As a history student Maude was coached by the brilliant and unorthodox A. L. Smith. Whether, as recorded of Eglantyne Jebb, she wanted to *dance* back to LMH after his coaching we do not know; nor whether he was one of those tutors who encouraged her to hope for a first, but she kept to the end the little note he sent her in 1916 in response to her congratulations on his becoming master of Balliol.

> I thank you very much for your kind letter . . . Now, when I boast that you were once my pupil, I find people a little sceptical, as when I make the same claim as to Herbert Fisher or C. G. Lang.[9]

By this time she was a well-known speaker, but her apprenticeship to speaking, at Oxford, seems to have started very slowly. Though she was interested in social questions there is nothing to suggest that she discussed them systematically, as Eleanor Rathbone did at Somerville with her group of 'Associated Prigs'.[10] And though she loved argument she did not, at first, figure prominently in the debates of the Oxford Students' Debating Society, the women's modest counterpart to the Union (a body from which they were, of course, excluded). Diffidence and vanity perhaps held her back; the desire to shine, and the dread of failing, were certainly at war within her in the years before she had fully developed her powers. As for the lighter side of things, at LMH hockey was the ruling passion; but, of course, she did not play. More luckily, there was scope for histrionic talent: in 'Sociable' (where students sang, recited or offered other forms of entertainment), in the Shakespeare Society, and especially in the play which was written by Miss Wordsworth every year to be performed by students just before Christmas. The play was a highlight. But beyond all doubt for Maude the highlight was her first experience of close friendship.

'I do not think that there is anyone . . . who desired friends more than I did when I was a girl, or had them less,' she said years later; and at that time it must have sounded like a rich man afraid of poverty, for she had great numbers of friends – close friends – and never ceased to make them. She had an unusual talent for friendship. Nonetheless, throughout her life she had a fear of being separate from people. By her own account she lacked friends as a girl 'because I was more concerned with my desire to be loved, my desire to be wanted than I was conscious of other people's desire to be loved

[9]A. L. Smith to Maude Royden (10 May 1916) Fawcett Library, Box 221.
[10]Mary Stocks, *Eleanor Rathbone* (1948) 43–7.

and to be wanted.' Later on she evokes the experience of stepping out into the sunlight of friendship, a thing 'so intoxicating and joyful and absorbing that you feel you are in the seventh heaven because at last you have found a kindred spirit.'[11]

Her kindred spirit now was Evelyn Gunter, a third year student whom she claimed as such despite the elaborate unwritten rules which governed the behaviour of freshers and seniors. Their backgrounds were not particularly similar. The Gunters were retired army people; conventional, perhaps, though not too conventional to send two daughters to LMH, Evelyn and a young sister. They were a warm and devoted family but without the panache of the Roydens; or the Royden wealth (though this trickled down to Maude in very measured allocations; she was often overspent and always having to nerve herself to ask 'the Breadwinner' for something or other). One can easily see the basis of attraction: Evelyn was a warm and modest person, by no means lacking a critical faculty, yet very ready to think other people more talented and interesting than herself; Maude, although she struggled against it, was often tempted to think herself more talented and interesting than other people. Evelyn had a maternal bent, which, in later years, was to have full play in her relationship with Maude's adopted daughter. At Oxford, it was Maude, with her mental turmoil, her headaches, her lameness, whom she wanted to protect.

Evelyn left LMH in 1897, having got a third, which in Maude's opinion did less than justice to her abilities. She started work in Oxford as assistant secretary to the University Extension Delegacy, a post in which her hard work, administrative flair and steady temper came to be valued, but one which, as a woman, she was lucky to get then; and most probably would not have got without the backing of Miss Wordsworth. Evelyn's view of her was different from Maude's. She kept Miss Wordsworth's photograph in her room and saw her from time to time. 'The dear old thing,' as she told a friend, had been 'charming and affectionate' and read Browning to her at a little tête-à-tête lunch they had. So she was not cut off from the Hall; nor from Maude, who, in what Evelyn looked back on as 'a quite extraordinarily generous way', drew her first friend within the radius of her own new friendship with Kathleen Courtney. Such generosity was typical enough, for Maude was intense but not exclusive in her friendships.

Kathleen came to LMH in Maude's second term, a daughter of the Anglo-Irish gentry, beautiful (though she did not think so) with the fine-boned looks that were not to be destroyed by age or even by the strains and chagrin of a life's work for international peace. When, in her nineties, she looked back to Oxford, it was to a college life 'new and exciting' and especially to friendship and the endless discussion of 'fundamental questions': except one, it seems. 'There was very little talk of sex.' Why, she

---

[11]*Church Militant* supplement, (Sept. 1922), Guildhouse sermon on 'Friendship'.

wondered, was the current generation of young people so obsessed with that?

> We made great and lasting friendships but they were not lesbian. (Of course, we did not know the word in those days.) Our friendships were founded on some sort of affinity, a community of mind – admiration, too; that was essential. My greatest discovery was Maude Royden.[12]

She kept the letters both Maude and Evelyn wrote in the first years after she met them, and they project vividly an Oxford friendship between young women at the turn of the century. Underneath Maude's patter about clothes and plays and her earnest arguing over religion there is a bedrock of shared assumptions that make what Kathleen called community of mind: a belief in goodness and the need to pursue it; a wish to live life worthily, at least; a spirit ready to account for itself. She admires George Eliot, Maude declares, because 'she has such a determination to face things . . . she never lets you off the personal responsibility which is yours if you make a mess of your life.'[13] That is the spirit of their correspondence. They do not sound like people who have not got a vote.

The letters are loving, full of terms of endearment. 'I hear the very tones of your voice,' writes Evelyn. 'I simply crave to see you again.' 'Dearest Kathleen,' Maude writes. 'Kathleen mavourneen'. 'Dear little Kafleen'. 'Dear, dear friend'. 'Do you remember that Sunday we walked round the Parks hand in hand and smiled insanely?'[14] They were not lesbian, Kathleen said. They were exceedingly romantic, however, in a manner so commonplace then and so uncommonplace seventy years later that there seemed to be a need to defend it. They were in a sense the last pre-Freudians.

It would be hard to imagine an environment more favourable to romantic love than Oxford. Maude, in those days, hardly uttered the name without some encomium on the spire of St Mary's, or the Cherwell, or even the sky. Naturally, in this wonderful place, they were ready to make wonderful friends. And did so, with that sense of discovery, that almost incredulous gradual perception of the qualities of the beloved characteristic of romantic love and very different from their steady affection for the all-too-predictable people at home. When they were parted – and for less than a year were they ever all together at Lady Margaret Hall – they sustained each other by letters saying everything that might have been said over cocoa at night, meeting when they could – though no such meetings ever assuaged their yearning to meet – affirming their love and doing everything possible – which in

---

[12]Francesca Wilson, 'Dame Kathleen Courtney'; typescript, LMH archives.
[13]Maude to KC (8 March 1901).
[14]Maude to KC (19 Jan. 1900). In the early 1970s when two California high school girls, as a piece of practical research, walked round the campus holding hands as Maude and Kathleen walked round the Parks, they provoked abuse and derision. See Lilian Faderman, *Surpassing the Love of Men* (1981) 312.

Maude's letters is quite a lot – to re-create a sense of physical contact. 'I can't write tonight, though I feel the more. Can you hear me without words at this distance, Kathleen? Listen and you will know that I love you.' 'Where really are you?' she asks, from Italy, where she is on holiday with her sister.

> 9.30 pm Sunday evening. Perhaps at a cocoa party? No, you eschew them on the Sabbath, I know. Then by your fire? I will sit with you. Or in bed? But not crying, I hope. Let us talk.[15]

And they 'talked' to such purpose that, at the end of a year's separation, Maude felt they were actually closer than ever. In spite of that, she often asked for reassurance. 'When you find someone you love much much better than me, you will only love him more and not me less, won't you?[16]

High on friendship, she seems to have branched out more in her later years at LMH, taking plum parts, (Romeo, Shylock) in the college's play-reading group, and beginning to make herself heard in the Oxford Students' Debating Society. Indeed, in February 1898, with hands that shook so badly that she could not read the pages on which she had carefully inscribed every word, Maude spoke to oppose the motion 'That the attitude of the men in the late Strike has dealt a blow to the cause of Trade Unionism.'[17] (Her father, no doubt, would have been interested to learn how earnestly she took up the workers' case.) This experience, though the motion was carried, seems to have taught her something about speaking, for when she came to oppose another, ('That England should declare a protectorate over Egypt') she was quick to catch the mood of her audience. Her opponent, she recalled, had been very conscientious.

> Rightly supposing that very few indeed of us knew anything at all about the matter, she was careful to preface her argument by a short history of Egypt and had not got beyond Rameses II before her time was up and she was compelled to sit down . . . . After this, my own deep ignorance of the whole subject and my assurance that 'it is unnecessary to do more than remind the House of such beneficent work as the Barrage' were received with loud applause . . . the House voted with enthusiasm on the side of the shorter speech.[18]

She and Kathleen helped to revive 'sharp practice' at LMH, a form of debating in which the proposer of a motion had only five minutes to make her case and the general debate was hard-hitting and speedy, with members trying to shout each other down and even jumping onto chairs and tables in

[15]Maude to KC (29 Oct. 1899); and from Rome, early spring 1900.
[16]Maude to KC (14 Nov. 1899).
[17]*Fritillary* (No. 13, March 1898) 216.
[18]Oxford (ed.), *Myself When Young* 378–9.

their anxiety to get a word in. It is possible that Kathleen and Maude found it good training for their suffrage days.

By the end of her second year Maude was supposed to be taking seriously the prospect of 'Schools', the final exams, on which the women were classed, like the men, though they were not entitled to degrees. She hoped for a first, but whether she worked for it seems doubtful for, in Kathleen's recollection, plays and acting distracted her a lot.[19] 'I'm having such a good time! Twelve times to the theatre!' she writes in her second long vacation. Her tutor has been pressing her, however.

> Mr. Armstrong has been writing me such sweet letters. Urging me to get a 1st etc. etc. and all sorts of wild projects. Isn't it *awfully* sweet of him? But Oh Kathleen, I wish the sky might fall before I go in for Schools![20]

But concern gave way to theatricals again. A few weeks before her finals she wrote

> No theatres this vac! Oh yes, one. Benson in *Richard II*. Very good indeed. I do like that man. Oh Kathleen, isn't it interesting. A man we know has written a play, and my married sister (Daisy) thinks of bringing it out, with herself for the villainess, and me for the 'ingénue'. Wouldn't it be amusing?

She had stuck at her books till the comings and goings for another sister's wedding made it difficult.

> 'You see the house was full for the wedding and dance, when I got home; and no sooner empty than full again for the races. . . . As for Schools, I should faint at the mere thought of them but for the fact that I am now desperate. And so Come Death, etc. I haven't even heard from Mr Armstrong, the toad.

Of the pre-exam weeks back in Oxford she recalled, with a mixture of shame and gratitude, her own 'unbearable irritability' and Kathleen's 'marvellous patience'. For her 'Schools weekend' they hired a pony cart and went off to Tetsworth where they spent an idyllic few days, indulged with hot weather and chocolate noisettes. Schools was lived through somehow, in the end. 'I never seriously believed that I should present myself for examination – always thought I should die, or the sky would fall, or the process of manufacturing paper and pens fall into disuse, or something of that sort.' Then came the news of her second class. 'I was absolutely certain that I had a 2nd and yet when the fatal list was read – such a pang of disappointment!' But before her viva was out of the way she was caught up in her sister's project of putting on a play – *The Chequer-Board* – which they were to act in local theatres. The ingénue part was second-best, she told Kathleen, 'But anything for a chance of acting.' And, as it turned out,

[19]Dame Kathleen Courtney, interviewed 19 April 1966 by Emil Oberholzer.
[20]Maude to KC (19 Sept. 1898).

acting with professionals, for two members of Benson's company were to
be involved in the play, one of them taking the part of her father, which
made her rather nervous. She was also doubtful what her mother's reaction
would be, 'but fortunately she regards it as "less embarrassing" than "any
stray young man" – so that's all right'. She was ecstatic over the clothes.

> I've just been to Liverpool theatrically shopping. Did I tell you my first frock is a
> white silk with tiny pink rosebuds? . . . This is the skirt, [she wrote, sketching
> it]. The bodice is chiefly a white fichu . . . fastened in front with a cluster of
> roses . . . . Do say you think it's pretty, and *young!*

On a small stage her lameness did not show, whereas it did prevent her
from going to dances 'except occasionally'; and, 'at home, if you don't go
much to dances you get more or less left out of it.'[21] On the stage she was
never left out.

For all the excitement of *The Chequer-Board*, Maude found it hard to settle
down at Frankby. For her and many other college women of her day, the
point when three years came to an end and they had to leave university was
dismal. It meant not only parting with friends; with Oxford, perhaps, and a
pleasant life of intellectual stimulus and no responsibility – the men might
easily have felt all that – but a kind of blank wall; the end of a road. There
was no obvious way forward for women. 'It must be a horrid thing to feel a
dreadful door with "No Road" posted on it across your life', Eglantyne
Jebb had written from Oxford to the aunt whose payment of her college
fees she felt would allow her to escape that fate.[22] The movement for
women's higher education had certainly arisen in part from a desire to
remove the 'No Road' sign which blocked the path of girls at eighteen, but
to some of them it seemed as if the sign had only been moved further on: or
that after college they came to a fork. At LMH, recalled a near contemporary of Maude, 'we divided ourselves into two classes: those who meant to
earn their living, and those we described . . . as Home Sunbeams.'[23] For
the daughter of a wealthy home to earn her living raised not only the usual
questions about how this should be done and whether one's parents could
be persuaded to consent (Maude was twenty-three now but still assuming a
need to seek the Breadwinner's approval) but, to a scrupulous mind like
hers, the question whether a girl with an allowance had the right to take a
job from someone less fortunate. Evelyn, from a less affluent background,
was earning £125 a year at her post with the Extension Delegacy. Maude
agonised about 'taking the bread out of someone else's mouth' if she did a
little coaching. Naively, she hoped to get round the problem by taking girls

[21]ibid. (22 Dec. 1899); (6 Oct. 1901).
[22]Francesca Wilson, *Rebel Daughter of a Country House* (1967) 57.
[23]Peck, *A Little Learning* 163.

'honestly unable to pay'. But then another problem presented itself: 'Do you object to unpaid work on principle?' she enquired of Kathleen.

If not work, then a 'Home Sunbeam'? Anyone less suited to that than Maude it would have been difficult to discover. She was bursting to get her teeth into something, as her letters show; to make some impact on the world. Evelyn was more cut out to be a 'Sunbeam'. 'What to do with one's Mother!' cried Maude, after about a month of it.

> Mine is developing positive hysteria in the belief that everyone is or wishes to be unkind to her. You know the feeling? It was not unknown at LMH but in Mother's boudoir it is permanent. Oughtn't self-respect to prevent such a belief? Oh Kathleen, the pit-falls of old age![24]

There were, of course, diversions: her singing lessons, and seeing Irving and Ellen Terry, and having Evelyn to stay ('my people all fell in love with her'); but she missed Oxford dreadfully. At one time she had tried to persuade her father to allow her an extra year. 'I would give much to be there with you,' she wrote in the autumn of 1899 as Kathleen returned to college again. And, a page later, 'Who is in my room? I forbid you to love her as much as me!' Her first weeks at Frankby had caused her to reflect 'how very few things one has to do at Oxford that one doesn't want to', and she was overjoyed when everything was fixed for an early visit.

> Oh Kathleen! 3 cheers! I am so glad. Providence is kind indeed. Beautiful, beautiful Oxford. Do arrange for the pale blue sky to last; I like St Mary's spire just so . . . . Yes, by all means let us go to Cowley (or anywhere so it is together).[25]

Home again, she found herself 'irritable and horrid'. The great success of *The Chequer-Board* did not drive out nostalgic longings which came to the fore when Kathleen went back to LMH in January 1900. 'Oh I wish I were with you. Who will hold the chair and embrace your knees as you ascend the rocking pile in order to cope with your electric light? Do you remember?' She had hatched with Evelyn 'a *lovely* plan' for a reading party for the three of them, after Kathleen's finals. Meanwhile,

> I wish I were sitting by your fire with a prospect of cocoa and biscuits in the near future and much much talk . . . . These things . . . cannot be, but talking about them makes me feel as if I were in your dear room again, talking to you. Dear, dear Kathleen, don't forget me, will you? even when I'm in far Italy.[26]

The holiday in Italy with her sister Mary occupied the early spring of that year. Returning, Maude was ready to devote herself to Kathleen's prospects in the final exams. 'Kathleen mavourneen, don't overwork, will you? But

[24]Maude to KC (17 July 1899).
[25]ibid. (17 Oct. 1899).
[26]ibid. (19 Jan. 1900).

do – Oh you will – get a first. I know you will, because I've wished it every time I've seen the new moon or 3 stars on a piebald horse!' 'Dear, dear Kathleen, *don't* work too hard at that loathsome task of revision.'[27] But for all her wishing, in the event, Kathleen was placed in the second class also.

The letters of sympathy she had from her friends display their characteristic style. Both were acutely disappointed. Evelyn, who had wired the news, begins, quietly:

> I hesitated much as to whether to put congratulations. At first I *could* not, for I had always looked for a first for you, knowing your work was first rate, but then I felt a second class was so good too, that I added the congratulations, and the telegram then read 'Second class congratulations' which must have made you laugh if you thought about it, but which not inaptly expressed my meaning.[28]

Maude, as usual, went over the top.

> 'Dear heart, I am so sorry – so very sorry, I would have given anything for you to have had the first you deserved. I *can't* be satisfied, even if you are. I had so set your heart on it – what *have* I put? *My* heart, I mean. And you did so deserve it, and your brain is worth it, and examiners are simply detestable and examinations loathsome and let us never go in for them again. Oh but I am so disappointed . . . Anyhow, you *know* we will be together in that 2nd class which is the ultimate goal of all the wit and wisdom of the 'Varsity. Oh but Kathleen mavourneen I would have liked a first for you.'[29]

There can be no doubt which style Miss Wordsworth would have approved as ladylike. As for Maude, though at twenty-three she was still inclined to admire her own rhetoric, she was conscious, too, of a need to pull back: not so much in writing as in life; and not to be ladylike but to be disciplined. 'It's *awful* to have no self control,' she wrote to Kathleen, in regard to an acquaintance, 'sometimes I feel that I too shall wreck for lack of it.' But for all that, when her passion was roused – which happened all the time – she was carried away, as she herself put it, 'like that Old Testamentarian whose heart burned within him . . . and he spake with his tongue.'

Kathleen's departure from LMH in June 1900 was felt by them all. Evelyn wrote from Oxford, 'I miss you horribly and feel such a blank at the Hall now your dear friendly face has gone.' Maude wrote,

> Isn't it tomorrow you go down? Your letter, dear Kathleen, makes me feel as if we were saying Goodbye again in your room at LMH. You will be sorry to go and I sorry to think that 'all of me' has left the hall, now you have gone too. One always has a place there so long as one has a friend. And no longer, I think.[30]

[27] ibid. (22 April, 2 May 1900).
[28] Evelyn Gunter to Kathleen Courtney (henceforth Evelyn to KC) (1 July 1900).
[29] Maude to KC (29 June 1900).
[30] Evelyn to KC (1 July 1900): Maude to KC (24 June 1900).

But thinking had taken her round in circles on the subject of work and her own future. Kathleen planned settlement work in London and for a time Maude had hoped to join her. Now she decided she must stay at home. 'Would you believe that the duty which I have been looking for in London and Central Africa, lies as near as my own Mother?' Mrs Royden was subject to depression. Her sisters, Maude wrote, had got more or less used to it and didn't seem to think they could make an improvement.

> I have been away from home so much that I don't think the little Mother dislikes me quite so badly as the rest of her family . . . So it looks as if I ought to try some sort of way of getting her out of her Slough of Despond . . . Heaven knows how it is to be done.

For the moment, then, however much it chafed her, she had settled for the 'sunbeam' role; or, as she put it, adopted the principle of 'doing the thing that's nearest'. But was this right?

> Is it a lazy way of deciding? A sort of shifting the responsibility on to the shoulders of the Deity who put a small duty near you; and a large one far away? People always assume that you should do the nearest thing – is that laziness or resignation?[31]

'Isn't this a selfish letter?' she adds, 'I must always be talking about myself.' In contrast, she saw Kathleen as 'perfectly unselfish'. 'I have always a sense of restfulness when I am with you,' she writes elsewhere, 'a feeling that I can be just myself as myself comes.' But if it came, as she often thought it did, as rather second-rate in moral terms – as vain, self-centred, excitable, irritable, indolent, unworthy – she looked to Kathleen to help her on the road to higher things. It is very easy to see why Kathleen, in her old age, marked 'admiration' as an essential of Oxford friendships. Maude had no doubt that her friend stood morally, head and shoulders above herself. It was hard in conversation to bare one's soul, even to an intimate friend, she said, but, 'you . . . will understand that you cannot help me more than by expecting from me the very most and best that I am able (as you see me) to give.'[32]

The admiration was by no means one-sided. Evelyn recalled having criticised Maude once, and Kathleen's having answered, 'I admire Maude so enormously that I can't even see that she is so and so.' They were both attracted by her gaiety and humour, her quick response to people and capacity for loving. But what they admired was something different. It was not so much a Joan of Arc quality (though Evelyn wrote to Kathleen in 1901, 'She is the sort of person who could head a movement') as the quality which Evelyn called 'the ardency of her longing to do right'. It might be said that they all longed to do right; that it was the thing with college

[31]Maude to KC (19 June 1900).
[32]ibid. (21 Oct. 1900).

women then, in those years of the awakened conscience of the rich. 'We were all of us serious,' Kathleen remembered, 'and thought we ought to do some good in the world.' Certainly the letters show all three balancing the good of the world against the good of their families. But her friends discerned more than this in Maude: a more ardent and a more spiritual longing. 'I have never met anyone before,' said Evelyn, *'forced*, as she is, by an internal craving to do not less than the very highest she knows . . . . She is a living rebuke to easy going Christians.'[33]

In 1901, when this was written, Maude was a very new Christian indeed, in her own view, for she did not count the formal allegiance of childhood days. The road led back to All Saints, Cheltenham, and her first perception of God as beauty. It had been a glimpse, a lifting of the curtain, but hardly faith. Indeed, at Oxford she entered on a period of great uncertainty: High Anglican in practice, agnostic in spirit, deeply committed to Christ's moral teaching, yet needing still to justify his claim to her exclusive commitment by reflecting that while Buddha's teaching might be equally lofty it was Christ who had moulded the western world.[34] It amazed her, later, to look back on this phase when, unbelieving, she had sought belief in all the places where it might be found.

Even in the nineties the air of Oxford pre-eminently favoured such an endeavour. The great Tractarians, it is true, were dead. Newman's passing in 1890 had turned the last page of that extraordinary tale. But then, for Maude, as for every generation who could not know the man, there was the *Apologia*; and she plunged in and was enraptured by it. How could she not be? Henry Scott Holland, himself of Oxford's later Anglican tradition, stressed that every word written by Newman 'seems to have in it a human gesture'. Through it all the reader feels the touch of his nature, 'and the look of his face, and the light of his eyes, and the magic of his voice. You can't get away from him.'[35] How could a temperament such as Maude's fail to idolise a man whose motto was *Cor ad cor loquitur* – heart speaks to heart? She was eager for Kathleen to read the *Apologia*, 'for I want you to sympathise . . . in my hero worship of this saint of God'. She cycled out to Littlemore like a pilgrim; and of course she pondered the implications of the *Apologia* for her own faith. Could a man who wrote such English be mistaken?

Her search for faith at Oxford impelled her, also, through all five volumes of Liddon's *Life of Pusey*, which took months to read. 'I read them when I should have been reading Stubbs' *Charters* or Green's *History of England*,' she recalled. They were not stuff to inspire idolatry; nor could she easily have warmed to a man who resolved not to smile but in the presence

[33]Evelyn to KC (2 Oct. 1901).
[34]Oxford (ed.), *Myself When Young* 372.
[35]Henry Scott Holland, *A Bundle of Memories* (1915) 112.

of children. Nonetheless, to read this unreadable work was to penetrate the heart of Tractarianism. Maude read Pusey. And her favourite church in Oxford was Puseyite: the church of the Cowley Fathers.

The Cowley Fathers were the embodiment of the new high concept of Anglican priesthood. Their church, though austere and not yet completed, seemed exceedingly beautiful to Maude. She had never heard plainsong before. And the Fathers, she said, were saints, 'in spite of grime and curious profiles'.[36] The church lay well beyond Magdalen Bridge, a good two miles from Lady Margaret Hall and tiring to get to because of her lameness, as Sunday cycling was not allowed. She did not always go there but she always came back to it. 'I do love that church,' she wrote to Kathleen; reminded, on a visit after leaving Oxford, of all she owed it. Seeing it again, 'I felt as if my soul had been *born* there!' Though in fact it hadn't; or not, she explained, in any sense that could be called conversion. She had never felt any such inrush of the Spirit.[37] It was the church, though, of her first confession; the one where she found herself at home.

A home of iniquity, it seemed to some. For Oxford was in the thick of the battle raging then between the ritualists and the Protestant end of the English Church. The 'bell, book and candlepower of the priesthood' provoked strong letters in the Oxford Times and while confessions were heard at Cowley, speakers for the National Protestant League demanded in other Oxford churches whether the teaching of auricular confession was to be found in the word of God, and addressed public meetings on such topics as 'Secret Societies of the Ritualists'. Maude, of course, championed the ritualists. 'Isn't it melancholy about incense and lights?' she wrote to Kathleen in 1899, the year that incense and reservation were declared illegal in the Church of England. 'No, perhaps you don't think so. But I do, and you will sympathise at least. I hear they have been obedient at Cowley. On the whole, don't you think we Ritualists have behaved rather well?'

Her experience of ritual was dramatically enlarged a few months later on the visit to Italy made with her sister in the spring of 1900. There she found ritual so glorious, so uplifting, that it took her breath away. They stepped into Milan cathedral from the sunlight.

It is very dark. We could see only a grove of pillars growing up and up – far away and high up the light fell on the great crucifix. That was all. It was one vast shrine built round that Christ. Afterwards a long procession wound in and out of the pillars, with banners and crosses and chanting, and clouds of incense rising into those dark vaults . . . . It carried one away in a flood of worship.

In Rome, the superstition dismayed her. Seven thousand years' indulgence

[36]Maude to KC (16 April 1903). Founded by Pusey's disciple, Richard Benson, the Society of St John the Evangelist at Cowley was devoted to missionary work and to the teaching of the spiritual life by means of confession, retreats and direction.
[37]Maude to KC (6 April 1903).

for climbing on your knees up the Santa Scala! But then, the expressions on the faces of the faithful! The crowds who moved familiarly round St Peter's,

> just walking about, kneeling down anywhere on the marble floor or perhaps at their favourite altars, or behind a pillar or anywhere – praying, or confessing, or reading or kissing St Peter's toe. They seemed to feel quite at home and happy. . . . I can't tell you. I had no conception of the hold Roman Catholicism had even here in Italy. Surely it is not a worn-out religion.[38]

Earlier in the same letter she said, 'I shall turn Roman Catholic'; but in the next, 'I'm not going to join the Church of Rome.' She had written, meanwhile, to Evelyn on the subject, 'mostly, I believe, for the relief of making things clear to myself. *C'est passé, enfin.*' But it was not finished, really.

The end of the Italian holiday was clouded by news of the death of Evelyn's brother, fighting in South Africa. 'Poor, poor Evelyn. She is so devoted to her people and must feel it terribly. . . . It makes me ache to think of her. Isn't it terrible, dear Kathleen, how *absolutely* alone we are?'[39] She returned from Italy still preoccupied with trains of thought that had arisen there. 'I want to know your views about the Roman Catholic Church, and whether you entirely reprobate my sympathy with it – or can forgive me.' She was reading the Bible and 'considerably surprised' at what she found in it. 'I suppose most people are, when they read it with a view to acting on the advice they receive. It never occurred to me to do so before.' 'No,' she hastens to add, a week later, 'I'm not putting into practice what I find in the Bible. I'm only considering the question.' And it seemed to boil down to this: 'If it is possible, should we not do it? If it is impossible, should we believe it?'[40]

Once back at Frankby she had to face the fact that her immediate future, at least, held nothing more earnest than a plan to study the social history and conditions of England, against the day when she was free to do more. Though she had decided to stay with her mother it was still disappointing to give up the prospect of joining Kathleen in settlement work. 'Do you know,' she wrote, 'I envy you most your opportunity of doing something to cure the social ills of the England you and I have talked so much about.' The England they had talked about was 'Darkest England'; they, like others, were consumed with shame at the thought of the 'submerged tenth'.[41] 'This horrible life that is led in the slums must corrupt a nation

[38] ibid. (5 April 1900).
[39] ibid. (5 April 1900).
[40] ibid. (2 May 1900).
[41] ibid. (19 June 1900). *In Darkest England and the Way Out,* by General William Booth of the Salvation Army, was published in 1899. Booth reckoned that a 'submerged tenth' of the population consisted of paupers, the homeless, the starving, the very poor and the inmates of prisons.

which cannot, at least in part, solve the problem of pauperism,' Maude wrote; and in these early days, before she worked in one, she thought, like many of her class and generation, that settlements might provide an answer.

The settlement movement had begun with Canon Barnett, who opened Toynbee Hall in 1884 as a centre where privileged people would actually live amongst the poor – not as purveyors of religion or charity, but as friends. So strong was the appeal to idealistic young men that it soon became common to go to Whitechapel after coming down from Oxford or Cambridge. Involvement there in the local community came especially through cultural activities: those who had so much brought to those who had nothing the benefits of art, literature and music. Women's settlements soon emerged, but from a different root. The practical philanthropy of Octavia Hill and the Charity Organisation Society appealed very strongly to girls' schools and colleges – especially those which tended to stress (as did Cheltenham and Lady Margaret Hall) the feminine virtues of public life. Cheltenham had its mission in Bethnal Green. Lady Margaret Hall, to the joy of Miss Wordsworth, began its own settlement in 1897. Whether or not Maude and Kathleen were active in the college's weekly working party, sewing flannelette garments for the poor, Kathleen soon began to think seriously of settlements.

'For selfish reasons, I can't help grudging you. . . . Do tell me, if you go again,' wrote Maude, 'what are your impressions . . . . One hears so much that is good, bad, and indifferent. And yet it seems to be the most hopeful of all the methods that have been tried.' If indeed it reached the 'submerged tenth' and did not stop short at the 'comparatively respectable'.[42] Kathleen began work at the Daisy Club, a girls' club in Lambeth, in July 1900, just after her finals. The other two fussed about possible exhaustion through taking such demanding work so soon after Schools. Evelyn pressed for an assurance that she would always have a proper lunch. Maude was relieved she would be living at home, 'and not starving yourself in the somewhat squalid atmosphere of settlements as they are, or seem to me. That may be necessary eventually but now you do need to be looked after.' It was good news, though, and 'sounds just the thing for you'. Her letter closed with a valedictory flourish: 'Good-bye dear Kathleen of Lady Margaret Hall and welcome dear Kathleen of the world in general and humanity in particular.'[43]

Her own prospects looked brighter now, for she had come across a settlement in Liverpool at which she might be able to work from home. Her mother's health had improved sufficiently for there to be talk of going to Aix. 'If she goes, I rather hope she will take me with her, but this is of the vaguest . . . . Mother's arrangements or lack of arrangements are driving

[42]Maude to KC (20 July 1899).
[43]ibid (29 June 1900).

me nearly mad,' wrote Maude. In fact, she spent the summer of 1900 in a delightful rush of holidays in England: Cheltenham in July for the Guild reunion (where, she told Kathleen, she was living at the rate of 'more than 24 hours to the day'), the Lakes in August and September with her friends, at the family house in Ambleside.

Evelyn joined her first and Kathleen in September. Between these two, in anticipation, there was some debate about what to wear. 'I think you must have a *dress*,' advised Evelyn, 'it gives one a solid feeling, which blouses and skirts never do, and one must go with a fairly free mind to pay visits.' As she had stayed with the Roydens before she could assure Kathleen 'they are awfully nice and simple, and you will feel at home with them at once, I know.' However, she admitted they were very smart on Sundays.

In fact, they dress a good deal, especially in the evening i.e. they don't mind having no sleeves – don't pass on my definition to Maude but you know what I mean, and I am always so grateful for tips myself that I send one to you.

However, for herself, 'I go on stolidly in the same evening frock night after night and pretend I don't mind, which I do, but it is no good worrying, and wicked to have frocks you can't afford.' She had just invested in a black and white foulard, 'such as elderly ladies of 60 wear up and down the aisle in church . . . . The consolation is that I can wear this dress when I am forty. It had a train, though, 'and I am still baby enough to love a train and to peacock before the glass in it when no one is looking.'

She had never been to the Lakes before and wrote ecstatically to Kathleen of the marvellous excursions they had made.

The Roydens are splendid people to stay with, they are so very sporting, and as none of the elder members of the family are here there is no limit to energy beyond our own feelings. Maude has a fishing mania on, and last night we were torn in half by desire to fish and to see the sunset.[44]

'I thought you would find the Royden family as deeply interesting as I did,' she comments, after her return. 'Their frankness charms me . . . . By the way, Kathleen, I am 25! and I feel I have passed a most important milestone, after which I can no longer be called a girl, so next time when you refer to me say 'a woman I know'.[45]

With her full-time job for the Extension Delegacy (a job she was to carry on for twenty years) Evelyn was differently placed from the others, and in her letters there is none of that sense of the world as a great stage waiting for her entrance which we get in Maude's; though Maude, it must be said, as often thinks of Kathleen's debut as of her own and has high hopes for her, as she affirms whenever there seems need of encouragement.

[44]Evelyn to KC (16 July, 26 Aug. 1900).
[45]ibid. (26 Sept. 1900).

You will do good work before you die, dear friend, that will be good to look back upon. 'I have fought a good fight; I have finished my course,' Oh Kathleen, you are right. They're the grandest words ever spoken. Shall we be able to say that, do you think?[46]

Some of the impediments to *starting* the course, in her own case, seemed to yield, that autumn. First, the tangled question of belief: in October 1900 she conveyed to Kathleen ('because you know more of my religious life – it is far too high a phrase – than any other of my friends') that she had at last resolved that struggle.

To me, Christ is God, and it is to Him that I must look for strength. If I have ever said anything, dear heart, which has in the slightest degree influenced you to a contrary belief, I beseech you to give it no weight, as being the argument of one now believing.

The other new departure for Maude that autumn was that she started settlement work. Having long envied Kathleen, from a distance ('the depressing details disappear in the glorious prospect of having something to do') she began at the Victoria Women's Settlement in Liverpool at the end of October; living at home. 'The Breadwinner seems quite calm about this slumming,' she told Kathleen in her first account; and she too seems quite calm, considering she had never had such contact before with the Scotland Road area of Liverpool. The district assigned to her for provident collecting had 'one short street of respectable people and one long slum street,' she explained; 'cellars, you know, and all sorts of horrors'.

These slum dwellings were often divided between Irish Catholics and Irish Protestants. 'A deal of stabbing goes on there,' a policeman told her; but, writing to Kathleen, she chose to focus on her first impressions – hardly flattering – of her fellow workers ('They dress badly, crack foolish jokes and eat apples with steel knives') and her impressions of the poor, who amazed her by their warmth and seeming lack of resentment. Some even seemed grateful to be visited. '*I* shouldn't be grateful if Lady Warwick e.g. came to see me every week, to get me to put a few shillings into a provident fund. I should be mad . . . . It seems to me quite extraordinary.'[47]

Being improvident herself, she hit it off with her 'improvident women'. Those who struck lucky, like the dock labourer's wife who got £300 for his death, were not afraid to tell her they had blued it all. 'I bought the children everything they asked for and then I began to get something for myself.' 'How grand that, just for once, she had the chance to do so!' Maude reflected, many years on. 'She told me some of the things she had bought and we laughed like anything.' She liked the street. She liked being given

[46]Maude to KC (24 June 1900).
[47]ibid. (2 Nov. 1900). See also Maude's account of the Liverpool slums in 'Apprenticeship for Life', *Homes and Gardens* (Oct. 1950).

cups of tea and sweets and winkles. She was very touched when one woman said she had a merry heart and that she would pray Heaven to send her a good husband. ('Considering that her two daughters are both *stone*-blind from having their heads bashed about by their respective husbands, I thought she showed considerable faith in that she still believed in the existence of good husbands!')[48] She liked the Irish and their gift of the gab. Probably both she and they responded to the histrionic quality in the other. Perhaps her lameness made her seem less privileged. Or it was simply that she laughed a lot. 'Not what we give but what we share, For the gift without the giver is bare,' ran the Victoria Settlement's motto. Maude was very good at this kind of sharing. It had its limitations, though, in settlement work. She was, she admitted, 'an idiot at grasping the difference between the deserving and the un-!' That is, she was hopeless at assessing need according to the priciples laid down by the Charity Organisation Society.

> I do not feel the least competent to distinguish between genuine and pretended distress. I wish I had some sort of a training. They all look to me *unspeakably* poor, and I believe they drink like fiends! What is one to do? Poor, poor dears! *I* should drink if I lived in Lancaster Street.[49]

Meanwhile, she was feeling rather guilty at having got caught up in theatricals again,

> trying not to be wholly absorbed in a perfectly delightful part, and to remember that districts and the visitation of the sick are the really important things of life, which will still be with me, when theatricals are a thing of the past. Such a jolly 'past', dear Kathleen!'

She felt flat and depressed when the excitement was over.

> We had three performances and two suppers which I enjoyed hugely, and a surfeit of praise, compliments and pretty speeches – no, not a surfeit, for that sort of things always leaves me hungry for more! Do you sympathise with me or despise me horribly? . . . . Heigh-ho! . . . . I wish I were on the stage – I wish I were strong-minded – I wish I were you . . . . instead of your imbecile weak-minded and generally unsatisfactory friend.[50]

She and Kathleen had kept up their habit of being concerned about each other's health. 'I am so afraid of this slummy work being too much for you,' wrote Maude. In fact, she sometimes found it too much herself, and welcomed the approaching Christmas holiday, even while outlining plans to introduce provident collecting in the village of Frankby, and asking Kathleen's advice on reading.

---

[48]Maude to KC (5 Dec. 1900).
[49]ibid. (29 Jan. 1901); (5 Dec. 1900).
[50]ibid. (28 Nov., 5 Dec 1900).

Three things interest me.
1 Housing of the poor.
2 Migration from country to town.
3 Position of women. (I put that last but it comes first!)
One is enough for a lifetime. Which?[51]

The one that sparked a flare-up was housing. Kathleen said that it made little difference to give slum dwellers better conditions. Maude scrawled back on the 29th December:

It does make a difference – it must make a difference – Are you to blot out the result of a whole life of filth and squalor by a week in a clean house? No. Of course they are filthy. Isn't that our fault? It has taken generations of unspeakable poverty . . . to create every slum child that crawls in the gutter. Very well. Then let us not complain if it takes generations to make that slum child clean again!

Then, quickly repenting of her passion, 'here is a tirade if you talk of tirades! Forgive, dear. Indeed you . . . don't deserve this shout. Only dear Kathleen, do let us look at it – it is a holy war. We can't stand out of it for fear of making mistakes.' She quoted Newman. Then wished her friend all that was best for the new century. 'Just imagine,' she entreated Kathleen, 'a whole new century to do something with!'[52]

[51]ibid. (22 Dec. 1900).
[52]ibid. (29 Dec. 1900).

3

Difficult Questions

'But we are tired of philanthropy,' men say . . . .'Things are better than they were, and even if the evil in the world is terrible, God bears it, and so can we.'

Hudson Shaw, sermon (1901).

Maude's perception of 'a whole new century' was somewhat dimmed by her eighteen months with the Victoria Women's Settlement. She had longed to start, but in time she longed to finish, subdued by frustration, physical exhaustion and continued spiritual debate. Her lifeline was the correspondence with her friends. On one difficult occasion, it seems, she stuffed a letter from Kathleen in one pocket and a letter from Evelyn in the other, 'and felt as if each of you were holding a hand!'[1] Kathleen's experience at the Daisy Club had something in common with her own and they discussed the problems created by unruly slum girls and difficult colleagues. The books they were reading, the plays they were acting in, plans to organise a reading party or set up house together absorbed them. Naturally, too, they discussed their feelings. 'I feel so horrid and lonely tonight. Do love me. I like to think you are loving me all the time,' Maude wrote.[2] These bouts of depression were not provoked by her encounters with improvident women; rather, it seems that such encounters were the invigorating part of the job. What dragged her down was a growing doubt of the value of the undertaking, coupled with a sense that things were badly run.

The Victoria Settlement, typical enough of women's settlements at this time, had been conceived as 'a bridge of personal service' across the chasm between rich and poor.

> We want to make our less fortunate fellow countrymen feel . . . that they are not really outcast, because we refuse to cast them out; that they are not uncared for, because we care for them – care for them enough to live among them.[3]

[1]Maude to KC (n.d.)
[2]ibid. (29 Jan. 1901).
[3]Victoria Settlement, *First Annual Report* (1898). The Settlement had been started by Dr Lilias Hamilton and Miss Edith Sing, both old students of Cheltenham Ladies' College.

The Settlement, of course, was not luxurious. A shabby private house had been cheaply converted to take five residents on its upper floors. Classes and dispensary were held in the basement and the ill-lit, stuffy dispensary waiting room had to double as a club room for girls. Money was tight. Though cast-off furniture and similar gifts covered the basic needs, subscription income from the Rathbones and others never reached the annual £400 needed. Frequent staff changes were also a problem. When Maude came a new warden had just been appointed, the sixth in the three years since the settlement began. Miss Dolphin's 'great experience of work amongst the poor' aroused high hopes, but she seems, in fact, to have been yet another in the line of ladies who, whatever their general competence, had no special training in settlement work nor a professional conception of it. She failed, at all events, to attract enough residents to put the place on a stable footing, and the period of her failing was the period Maude was there.

Maude's own work – Monday morning 'provident collecting' and afternoon visits to the workhouse infirmary – was only part of an undertaking that involved numerous part-time workers, engaged on different days in similar tasks; or, it might be, reading to tailors, helping with the girls' clubs and the crippled children or assisting the resident woman doctor with the ever-growing load of the dispensary. How the poor rated these various services is hard to say, but in the eyes of the Settlement, provident collecting stood very near the top, exemplifying the essential nature of that bridge across the chasm between rich and poor. No one could undertake the work without being made aware of this. 'The house-to-house collecting of small savings', it was claimed,

> apart from the direct object of inculcating thrift, gives us an *entrée* into the homes of the people. In this way we come across girls for our clubs . . . hear of others who want situations . . . and find chronic invalids, who, perhaps will like regular visits, and in fact become generally so well acquainted with our depositors that in times of distress we know whether they are deserving of help or not.[4]

This concept of 'deserving' and 'undeserving' was the fulcrum on which all else turned and a great difficulty to Maude. At first she seems to have judged her inability to appraise the deserts of the exceedingly poor as a personal failure, susceptible to training. 'I hate to do the thing badly,' she wrote, 'and I cannot do it well.' In London, the Women's University Settlement and the settlement started by Lady Margaret Hall already offered training under the auspices of the Charity Organisation Society. 'I wish I could train under the COS, but there is no COS in Liverpool.'[5] Whether she would have fared much better in the era of 'efficient' social work training about to dawn there, may be doubted. She had quick – indeed

---

[4]Victoria Settlement, *Fourth Annual Report* (1901).
[5]Maude to KC (5 Dec. 1900).

agonising – apprehension of the social dilemma but could not address it with Eleanor Rathbone's cool spirit of inquiry or flair for systematic research. No one more easily made friends in the slums, but she felt defeated by the iron logic at the heart of the prevailing social work philosophy.

> I can think of nothing but the dangers of 'giving'. They appear to me so great as to be almost paralysing. You musn't give money; or clothes. If you help them to get work, wouldn't it be better for their independence of character if they got it for themselves? It seems to me that the only people worth helping are the ones who don't need it.

She hoped to understand more, 'but in the meantime, that is where I stick.'[6]

A brighter prospect was offered by the girls' club. She was more than pleased to be asked by Miss Dolphin to coach the girls in theatricals. 'This would amuse me, and give me a chance of seeing how I can get on with girls – my real interest.' Soon she was extending her Mondays at the Settlement to stay overnight and work with the club, which had sunk so low with frequent changes of leader that only seven came the first time she went, though there were thirty-three on the books.

> They sang for a little while; then danced for about ten minutes, then played games; then got bored. Anything more flat, you can hardly imagine. Had I the choice, I would infinitely prefer to loaf in the streets with a (presumably) attractive young man. Most of them do.

She consulted Kathleen on how 'to put a little more spirit into it'. Miss Dolphin had told her that the girls wouldn't come, or wouldn't apply themselves if they came, 'but your club contrives to make a success of itself, why shouldn't ours?'

She pressed Kathleen also on a very different matter, prompted perhaps by the beginning of Lent:

> Do you think it a duty to fast . . . ? I don't mean strictly in an ecclesiastical sense, because I think it would make one very conspicuous, and probably enrage one's parents! But at all? It seems to me that to abstain from something one liked might be a sort of training in self-control.

Kathleen seems not to have approved the idea. And Maude agreed that there was something absurd in deliberately making oneself uncomfortable.

> Still I cannot persuade myself that is the view taken by the New Testament . . . . It seems to me that we are told to [fast]; that the primitive Church certainly did so; and that the Roman Church does so now. Why don't we? Can you argue me out of that position?

But Kathleen's arguments didn't convince her. Alms giving, prayer and

[6]ibid. (29 Jan. 1901).

fasting were mentioned in the same way in the Sermon on the Mount. 'If alms and prayers are duties, why not fasting? If fasting were enjoined then 'we must obey; though in doing so, as you say, we ought to try and see why. What I hold is, that even if we can't, we must still obey. There I think you join issue.'[7]

Kathleen joined issue, so it would seem, on one doctrinal point after another. Maude was drawn to the Roman Catholic Church and whatever else she wrote about – settlement work, or her brother's wedding, or her new bicycle with a freewheel – she nearly always came back to that, sometimes seeming nearer Rome, sometimes further off. At one of the further points she dilated on the forged decretals of Isidore and on Mariolatry which, reading Pusey, she saw as a major stumbling block. Yet a few weeks later, in a different mood, she was not pleased to find that Kathleen had taken her remarks as an indictment of the Church. 'I said (or should have said if I didn't) "*it seems to me* an invention". It is more than possible that I am wholly mistaken. I speak too dogmatically, because in a letter it is hard to put on the brake.' Her thoughts had turned now to the crucial words: 'Thou art Peter and on this rock I will build My Church.' But was it Rome, or was it all the churches of the apostolic succession; the church of the baptised, or of all believers? 'I will not rest till I . . . know,' Maude said. 'And when I do – if ever I do – I will become a member of the Church, if I am not one already. Till then, dear Kathleen, will you forgive me if I argue and puzzle and contradict myself?'[8]

One way and another she drove herself hard.

If I stop worrying about my religion, I begin worrying about my duties. The only alternative is to work so hard that I have no time to think at all, and then I get overtired and morbid and find the world a hollow place.

'What slaves we are to our bodies,' she adds. And hers was certainly exigent; for apart from the fatigue brought on by lameness she was subject to headaches and menstrual pain – indeed the letters make many allusions to her own and Kathleen's discomfort with 'the fiend'.

You poor poor dear! I am . . . glad you . . . went on Saturday, for travelling on Monday with the fiend . . . would have been appalling. You will get this . . . tomorrow, and *your* more immediate troubles will be over. I got yours on my return from Liverpool. I had come up from the station in the cart, which seemed more than usually 'joggy', so that at last, in sheer desperation, I had to lift myself off the seat with my hands and balance myself so!! It really was torture, and I got beyond caring a dump if the groom was thinking I had gone mad![9]

---

[7]ibid., (21 Feb., 30 March, 21 April 1901). Fasting and other ascetic practices were much in vogue among earnest young High Anglicans.
[8]ibid. (3 Sept. 1901).
[9]ibid. (1 Oct. 1901).

Lack of stamina forced her to give up her work with the girls' club on Monday nights. 'I was always such a corpse . . . after district and hospital, that at last Miss Dolphin refused to let me go.' However, she hoped to start a club of her own, but for a rougher type of girl. 'I want girls who have not got decent homes to go to. Do you think it possible to get them?' The present girls often had 'charming homes' and skipped club night to go to Philharmonic concerts 'or other refined and edifying entertainment. Now I simply don't call that worthwhile. But do give me the benefit of your experience.' A few weeks later, Maude reported: 'Miss Dolphin says she can't get a room for girls' club.' Indeed, by April 1901, she had a sad sense of underachievement. No club work, and on top of that, 'my district is to be taken from me!' Miss Dolphin wanted to put her in charge of another district close to the Settlement, '"that we may be strongest near the centre" – which I must regard as a compliment, but rather a woeful one!' For, as she said, 'I had got so fond of my dear people, and some of them were fond of me, I think.'[10]

Possibly all this chopping and changing contributed to her growing conviction that Miss Dolphin was not right for the job, a feeling which became more insistent from the autumn of 1901 when Maude at last went to live in the Settlement. For a long time she had planned to 'settle' properly, but had to feel her way with her parents. To Kathleen, also caught between conflicting duties, she might assert that, 'as a family, we do have more liberty, perhaps, than most girls to develop our own "ego's".' But there were limits. Her mother, for instance, opposed the idea of her staying at the Settlement over Lent; and she resided there on Monday nights only – till October 1901, when she was able to write,

My father has given me permission to 'settle' for 6 months. It makes me smile – but also it makes me blush – to think how I salved my conscience for not offering to go before, because I felt sure he wouldn't hear of it!! What a coward I am – and how appallingly easy to persuade that the smooth paths are the right ones.

Her mother, too, had risen to the occasion.

Instead of regarding this new departure as a device for escaping from home (as at one time she certainly would have done) she has taken it into her head to be pleased and proud. She did nothing all last week but press gifts into my hand – boxes of chocolate and hot-water bottles! It is too quaint for words, but it makes me absurdly happy.[11]

As for her two friends, Kathleen was anxious to be reassured about conditions at the Settlement. 'Have no anxiety about me,' wrote Maude.

[10]ibid. (8 March, 21 April 1901).
[11]ibid. (16 Oct. 1901). Mrs Royden's interest in the Settlement expressed itself in a two-guinea subscription once Maude became involved. Unlike the Rathbones, who appear on every list, the Roydens do not seem to have supported it till then.

installed now in Netherfield Road North, 'I am quite happy and quite comfortable. This place is a palace compared to the Daisy Club, and we all have rooms to ourselves!' Evelyn, for her part, welcomed the change because Maude would have less time to worry about religion. As a good broad Anglican herself she had become extremely unhappy about the preoccupation with Rome which was manifest in every letter, and still more unhappy about the strain, mental and physical, which it imposed. 'I want her to leave the matter . . . for a while. I think the strife will wear her out physically.' 'I simply dare not say what is best for her,' she wrote to Kathleen in September.

> I dare not even pray that she may not go to Rome. I dread her doing it because of the awful suffering she will have to go [through], and oh, I dread lest it may not bring her the peace and satisfaction she craves, but if it will be best for her, I cannot feel that it matters, though the church of Rome seems to me quite quite wrong.

She was glad that Kathleen could argue the case.

> It is useless for me to do it. I am so ignorant . . . and in any case I have less power of argument than anyone I have ever met . . . .[Maude] says such unanswerable things – at least, they seem to me unanswerable, but all I can say is, 'cannot you try first to carry out every ideal of our church and you will find enough there to last, surely!'[12]

Evelyn, as usual, undervalued herself. No doubt she was only too glad to leave Kathleen to cope with papal infallibility, but her picture of herself as a helpless bystander watching a shipwreck is quite misleading. She was very practical and, that summer, had taken the very practical step of sending Maude, when she came to stay, to discuss her problems with the man whose name stood highest in her own world of Extension teaching: the Reverend George William Hudson Shaw, who was then in Oxford, taking part in the Extensionists' Summer Meeting. 'I was terrified,' Maude told Kathleen. And not surprisingly. It is unlikely that Evelyn had worked for four years at the Delegacy without in some way conveying the impression that Shaw was a giant. 'I was terrified, of course, but I did so unspeakably want to be helped.'[13]

Decades later, when she set this meeting in the context of a lifetime's love for Shaw, she recalled arriving early at his lodgings and looking out into Merton Street and then listening to his footsteps on the stairs. 'I hear them still,' she wrote, thinking of what Maeterlinck had said about listening to footsteps with awe, 'for one knows not who is coming into one's life.' In the Oxford days she had adored Maerterlinck. However, all she wrote to Kathleen at the time was that they had a long discussion about Rome, and Shaw had said, 'I think you will go.'

[12]Evelyn to KC (8 Sept. 1901).
[13]Maude to KC (3 Sept. 1901).

That made me see, more or less, where I was and what a long way I had come. It was a relief too, in a way . . . . He is the most understanding soul alive. I suppose because the difficulty presented itself to him in much the same terms as to me. There are many things which lead people to Rome. But it is the same thing which attracted him, which is now influencing me. After all [she added] he has not gone.[14]

Evelyn must have been relieved by Shaw's counsel to 'let the Eternal Problem rest a while.'[15] Burdened as she was herself that August by the weight of the Summer Meeting arrangements (a thousand visiting Extension students were lodged, lectured to and entertained) she had clearly been at her wits' end trying to cope with theology as well. Yet her heart overflowed with pity for Maude ('Poor darling, she is indeed having a fiery trial') and her friend's great qualities had never seemed more striking. 'I feel just as you do about Maude,' she told Kathleen, 'she is a true saint of the medieval type in the wholeness of her desire for self-sacrifice, and in the ardency of her longing to do right.' Shaw had perceived it. ('Mr Shaw, dear man, divined at once, and said to me "she's splendid".') But for all that Evelyn thought she was wrong. 'Wrong about the ideals and wrong in thinking the ascetic life necessarily the highest.' 'I sometimes think – anything to make her happy, and to give her peace . . . . But would Rome make her happy? One so dreads utter disillusionment.' Meanwhile work seemed to be best solution. 'I do not say that it would prevent her from becoming an RC but it might.' What about elementary teaching, she asked Kathleen. 'Anything rather than that she should end in a convent, or even in a working sisterhood.'[16]

Shaw had also stressed the importance of work. It was not, he admitted, 'the sovereign remedy that Carlyle thought, but it settles many problems.[17] The hope they had of work as a salvation was fulfilled in the sense that Maude, as a resident 'settler', had much more to do. She was busy preparing lectures on the Poor Law and made a start with her rough girls' club. The girls were younger than she had expected, but 'as good as anyone else, I suppose. Certainly they are as *bad*, in that they come from some horrible streets.' But the challenge was obviously exhilarating and she told Kathleen that the new club members were 'as wild and as jolly as possible'. The Poor Law lectures were highly praised and her initial nervousness passed quickly. ('I am a brazen-faced woman really; and I can't altogether regret it, as it does make things so much easier!')[18] Now she had in mind to give a lantern lecture on 'Shakespeare and the Sea' at the Seamen's Institute, unintimi-

[14]Maude Royden, *A Threefold Cord* (1947) (henceforth TFC) 9; Maude to KC (3 Sept. 1901).
[15]TFC 10.
[16]Evelyn to KC (8 Sept., 2 Oct. 1901). Elementary school teaching as a form of social service seems to have appealed to a number of upper-class girls at this time.
[17]TFC 10.
[18]Maude to KC (2 Nov. 1901).

dated by the knowledge that the men would simply walk out if they were bored. All in all, as she wrote to Kathleen, 'I am really getting under way at last.' But there was Miss Dolphin. 'I don't think Miss Dolphin is the right woman in the right place, and I rather think she will sooner or later, probably sooner, give up the post.'[19] She was inclined to cast cold water on any flame of enthusiasm. 'What is more disastrous is that people won't work with her, and this (I believe) is why we can't get residents.' So they achieved little. 'We beat the air . . . And there is so much to be done.' Miss Dolphin hung on. And Maude, who found herself workers' representative on the committee, worried that she ought to take some sort of action.

What probably worried Kathleen and Evelyn was that Miss Dolphin had been added to Rome as a source of tension in Maude's life. Whether the proposal Kathleen came up with was to rescue Maude or herself is not clear. She had her own problems at the club in London, with unruly elements and with colleagues; and was also unsure about the future. Now she proposed that in a few months' time, when they finished 'settling', they should live together. It was not exactly a new idea. The thought that they might share their work and a household – like the pleasant notion of a reading party – was part of the Oxford baggage they clung to; all the more because neither had yet found anything substantial to take its place. 'I long for our little *ménage à deux* of the future,' wrote Maude, when she first went to the Settlement. But their dream had never had a practical context. Now Kathleen supplied one. Her idea, it seems, was that she should keep house and Maude should run a school.

What school? Where? With training or without? Kathleen usually had her feet on the ground but whether or not she had worked out any of the details in this case there is no means of knowing. The proposal seems to have been a bombshell to Maude, who wrote:

I know you want something to *do* . . . . You think, I gather, that to house-keep for me and undertake various duties in the parish we lived in, and assist me in my school, would be a 'duty' sufficient for you. Dear Kathleen, I cannot bring myself to think so. I look for something more . . . likely to give scope to your abilities than that.

She was overwhelmed with conflicting emotions – begging, on the one hand to be convinced ('I can't bear to think that I could lose such a happiness . . . And *what* a happiness it would be I realise more intensely every day I am here'), yet already certain it would not do. Her thoughts might be confused, she admitted, but

I do know how I *feel* – and that is, intensely reluctant to allow you to subordinate yourself in any way to me or my comfort or my advancement . . . . To work side by side in the slums or anywhere, that would be different. Though even that I

[19] ibid. (15 Nov. 1901).

should hesitate long about, as fearing to snatch so great a happiness for myself. But this . . . I cannot feel I ought to let it be.[20]

So many of Maude's letters convey her sense of taking more from Kathleen and others than she is able to return, and her own rueful acceptance of this. 'Somehow I don't mind as perhaps I ought to. I think I'm not proud with my friends,' she had said. But her letter now conveys something like shock at having attracted such an offer. And just as talking to Hudson Shaw had shown her where she was 'and what a long way I had come', so Kathleen's proposal seems to bring home to her this aspect of her nature, and she recoils. 'I am not a prophet that my friends should sacrifice themselves for me. How much less you who are to do much more valuable work in the world than I shall ever deram of.'[21]

Her friends, however, remained determined to rescue her. Evelyn suggested another clergyman whom Maude could consult if she wished. 'I am glad I did so for she seemed pleased . . . and without my asking she offered me a promise that she would see no Roman priest until she had heard the last word of the English Church.' 'But alas,' wrote Evelyn, 'Maude has now become friends with a pious Roman Catholic lady,'

> I dread this lady, who Maude admires with all the power of her nature, far more than a Roman priest for I can see her influence is likely to be strong and I have urged Maude to include her in the promise so far as conversations on religion extend . . . . Oh Kathleen . . . though I have not given up the struggle, and will hope on and pray on . . . I dread the end. If it is Rome, God grant that she may find her peace there, for sometimes I believe when Rome attracts people strongly, go they must and will.[22]

She was afraid to argue lest it drive Maude along the road to Rome faster. Maude, though, seemed preoccupied with Miss Dolphin, with whom her relationship had become strained since the warden told the other residents, and even the president of the Committee, 'that I was the most unwilling worker she had ever had!' The injustice of it all was conveyed to Kathleen in a miserable letter ending, 'Ought I to stay here?'[23] In the same letter she felt bound to admit that all was not well with the 'Ruffian Club'. Where she had once talked with spirit and affection of 'my little demons' and had seemed undaunted when things occasionally got out of hand ('I rather like a battle') she now thought the club was unlikely to succeed; confessing, with 'any amount of cruelly punctured vanity', that clubs would not figure in her future programme. She had no difficulty keeping order. But – and for somebody of her temperament it was the most damaging 'but' of all – 'I don't think they like me.'

[20]ibid. (2 and 15 Nov. 1901).
[21]ibid. (2 Nov. 1901).
[22]Evelyn to KC (5 Jan. 1902).
[23]Maude to KC (20 Jan. 1902).

In the depths of uncertainty whether to remain at the Settlement or not, she once again turned to Hudson Shaw. 'He has been unspeakably kind,' she told the others, 'and has corresponded with me at some length.' More – they had met and discussed the problem and Shaw had made a practical suggestion.

Last Thursday evening I got a letter . . . to say would I meet him at the Walker Art Gallery . . . . Of course I went and we talked and talked, and this is what we settled. He wants help in [his parish] South Luffenham. I want a job. So I am to go to him for three months this summer to see how I like it.

She went on to explain that Shaw's wife was an invalid; so there was no one to do any parish work in South Luffenham during the week, when he was away from home, lecturing. She would take charge then.

I am to have a 'free hand' . . . especially with the girls . . . I offered to go and train as an elementary teacher. He says, 'No, come at once. I will see that you take any classes you like in the school.' Now, my dear friends, what am I to do? Will you, . . . remembering all my faults, tell me what you would decide if I were not your friend?[24]

Maude wrote this letter to the other two jointly, knowing that they were to be together, but as she sent it to the wrong address it did not reach Evelyn till Kathleen had left. Evelyn sent it on to her with a covering letter absolutely overflowing with relief.

Read it, and then tell me if it is not the most wonderful answer to prayer you have ever had, and if it does not make you feel as if you can never worry and lack in trust again. For I feel no doubt of your answer to Maude, that you will feel it is the opening God has deliberately been preparing for her while we have been fumbling in our poor human way, and that you will say 'in God's name' do it.

She was glad, though, the arrangement was only for three months and thought it would be better, in the first instance, if Maude did not go and live with the Shaws.

I do not feel sure that they would be a comfortable household. Mrs is very invalidish, and I do not see why Maude should turn into sick nurse . . . . I am certain it will not all be a bed of roses, so she can satisfy her soul with dis-ease.

'I *wish* her letter had come here,' she adds, seized by 'sudden terror' lest Kathleen should take a very different view of it from her own. 'But I do not think you will. I *hope* I have not been hasty, but I do think this must be what we asked for her.'[25]

It was never what Mrs Royden asked – and Maude says nothing about how she persuaded her mother, who had once objected to her acting with

[24]ibid. (1 Feb. 1902.)
[25]Evelyn to KC (4 Feb. 1902).

'any stray young man', to let her go to South Luffenham. Shaw was not young, of course, nor stray; but an invalid wife who was a ghost in the parish must have seemed the opposite of reassuring. Nor did it turn out much better when they met. 'Hudson and my mother shouted to each other across a wide, wide gulf' in Maude's account of their formal visit to the rectory – which again is silent on significant matters such as whether Mrs Royden, who thought Gladstone was Anti-Christ, knew she was meeting a radical Liberal.[26] In spite of everything the matter was settled. Maude was to go to South Luffenham in May.

In fact, she did not go till September, for she suffered a breakdown – provoked, she wrote later, by medical advice that her lameness was hysterical. 'I was told I could walk quite well if I chose.' Shocked by the implication, she tried to do so and drove herself to the point of collapse. Though her account is vague as to dates it seems to have been not long after this that a true diagnosis was made with X-ray by Sir Robert Jones, the pioneer of orthopaedics, and she was relieved from her mental anguish. Indeed, the relief was so immense that it almost obscured the fact that nothing could be done. She had to live with lameness. That she did so, in her twenties, without conceding one iota of her love of fashionable clothes, or of acting, is clear from the letters. Indeed, to Kathleen she once alleged that she was rather glad to be lame since otherwise she would have succumbed to the temptation, which she felt strongly, to be idle and frivolous, 'a regular society girl'. 'The "world" is so attractive to me, I often think I should have given myself up to it, if it would have had me.'[27]

To be obliged now to postpone South Luffenham left her disappointed, though relieved as well, 'because I feel so slack and weary, and long to be stupid and bored for a while. On the other hand, I feel rebellious and resentful that my body should play me such a trick.'[28] Ominous signs had been building up during the various social visits she allowed herself after leaving Liverpool. For all her gaiety on shopping sprees, Evelyn was worried by her frequent headaches, while her next hosts, the Diggle family (Canon Diggle was the priest of her childhood and an old friend) insisted on her spending most of her visit lying on a sofa. Evelyn approved of their taking such care and found the Roydens deficient in this. 'They never dream of lying down at home. Are they not a queer family?' she wrote to Kathleen.

> They seem to me to be detached units, living in a community, and to have a clannish feeling rather than affection, except in pairs here and there! But I do wish they would look after Maude or that we could look after her.[29]

[26]TFC 14.
[27]Maude to KC (16 Oct. 1901).
[28]ibid. (25 May 1902).
[29]Evelyn to KC (2 June 1902).

But even Evelyn could not have complained of the invalid's regime at Frankby that summer: breakfast in bed, rest after lunch, bed again at 9.30. 'I feel like a cauliflower!' wrote Maude, distracted with boredom after a week, and compensating with enormous letters. Kathleen, in Italy with relations, was begged to see this fresco and that, pressed to say if she herself did not feel the attraction of Rome and if she had reformed her uncle's views on women. Mr Diggle's had been insulting: 'the sort of imbecile-angel type'. Discussion of the Pharisees filled some pages in her old controversial style; but mostly she was pleased to lie in the garden, soaking up the heat of a perfect June and at intervals, thanking God, guiltily, that she was not in Netherfield Road. 'I have become all body and no soul.'[30] She didn't miss work and didn't want to be ascetic ('how . . . one gets accustomed to fleshpots again!') And to reassure Kathleen, who deplored her cold baths, she added that her mother ran the bath after breakfast and insisted on taking the chill off so that it was hardly cold at all. As to the progress of her physical health – for all the summer ecstasy, she had to admit, 'I don't feel just exactly like Goliath.' But in Ambleside she regained her vitality: bathing, cycling and – novel pleasure – learning to drive a four-in-hand. ('Wasn't it jolly? Four dear brown hot horses!')[31] Kathleen came to join her in August and in September Maude went to South Luffenham.

There must have been times, in the garden at Frankby, or in the Lakes that indolent summer, when Shaw and South Luffenham seemed as distant as Miss Dolphin and Netherfield Road. Evelyn had delighted her in mid-July by reporting that she had seen Shaw in Oxford and writing 'rather enthusiastically' about him. 'You don't know what balm this is to my feelings,' Maude told Kathleen,

> for no one here knows him except my Mother who doesn't like him! And none of my other friends know him, except yourself and that hardly. And sometimes I quite long to hear of him from someone who does know him really well, and appreciates him. By the way, I am looking forward with confidence to the next Summer Meeting, when you are to see a *lot* of him, and forgive the untidy garments, which I admit to be a drawback![32]

In the handsome group photographs taken at the Summer Meetings of Extension students, Shaw does not look especially untidy – indeed, he bears a considerable resemblance to a key figure on these occasions: John (later Sir John) Marriott, Secretary to the Delegacy. With the same broad features, full moustache, solid build and academic dress; of the same age (forty-three in 1902), they could well be related. Shaw's background, however, had been considerably the more precarious.

[30]Maude to KC (11 June, 14 July 1902).
[31]ibid. (27 Aug. 1902).
[32]ibid (14 July 1902).

Plate 2 Hudson Shaw among his colleagues, 1909. *Reproduced by permission of Oxford University Archives.*

He was born in Leeds in 1859.[33] His father, a civil engineer, formerly borough surveyor to Bradford, had drifted from one post to another, in

[33]The details of Shaw's life which follow are derived from Stuart Marriott's article on Shaw in J. E. Thomas and B. Elsey (eds.), *International Biography of Adult Education* (1985); Stuart Marriott, *University Extension Lecturers: The Organisation of Extra-Mural Employment in England, 1873–1914*, (1985) and from discussion with Professor Marriott at Leeds University.

consequence, it seems, of a progressive mental illness, and died when Shaw was twelve years old. His mother then kept the family afloat by means of a shop and a boarding house, while he, the eldest child, left school and worked for a time as a grammar school usher. From this, however, he was rescued by an aunt. In 1877, when his mother (now remarried) decided to emigrate to Australia, Shaw was informally adopted by her sister, a prosperous widow living in Ilkley, and sent by her to Bradford Grammar School. Here his outstanding ability was seen and the way opened for him to Balliol College, Oxford; though, typically (Shaw's life was never straightforward) he arrived indirectly, by the poor man's route as a noncollegiate student before he was spotted and raised up to that Olympus of talent. Balliol offered him an exhibition. In 1882 he fulfilled all hopes by winning the Stanhope Prize for history – only to disappoint them later when he was placed in the second class. But in that last year he was president of the Union and his studies may (as he said of Maude's, later) have been marked 'more by brilliance . . . than assiduity'.

Balliol was famous not only for talent but as a focus of Oxfords's concern with social crisis in the world outside, strongly linked with Toynbee Hall and full of 'men of moral inspiration.' (A. L. Smith, Shaw's history tutor – and later, Maude's – was one of them.) For a young man who felt passionately committed, as Shaw did, to serve the poor, Balliol was uplifting. He planned to be ordained in the Anglican priesthood and work in the cities. But he had no money; and, rashly, had got himself engaged to be married as soon as he left Oxford. At this juncture it seemed that emigration was the only hope and Shaw had given up thought of the priesthood when, quite suddenly, everything changed. Out of the blue came a lawyer's letter on behalf of an 'unknown benefactor' who offered to make him a steady allowance to stay and carry on his work in England. 'I was in despair,' he wrote in response to this liberal, anonymous person who offered 'independence, a career and hope'. 'Without your help I should have been compelled, from the circumstances in which I am placed, to go out to Australia to a work for which I had little heart.' Now he could devote himself to the poor.

> I have not the slightest notion who you are. This only I know, that you wish me to try to do good. You have given me happiness. I can only promise that with God's help, I will spend my life in trying to make others happy.[34]

Many years on, when Maude looked back to her first impressions of Hudson Shaw, she recalled her tendency to hero-worship and put it down partly to the difference in their ages. In fact, by the time she came into his life, Shaw's heroic quality was felt by many. The unknown benefactor, for instance (who later emerged as Bolton King, a Balliol contemporary) had subsidised Shaw to prevent the loss to England of a valiant fighter in the

---

[34]Hudson Shaw to Bolton King (21 Dec. 1883) Fawcett Library, Box 222.

social cause. King himself, a man of talent and conscience, the very exemplar of the Balliol ideal, wrote to Shaw many years later to explain that he had felt he had done something worth doing, 'if I kept you and your voice for the country'.[35] He had wanted Shaw's voice to speak for the poor. And Shaw spoke for them, landing in trouble in his very first curacy, in Horsham, by preaching 'not what folks wanted me to preach but what I believed in re the question of Christianity, Poverty & Wealth.' The town was outraged, he told another Oxford friend. 'I am accused of Radicalism, Communism . . . inciting the poor to revolution &c. The majority have sent me to Coventry . . . . Whether I shall retain my Orders in this respectability-ridden, comfortable, damnable Establishment is more than I can say.'[36] To gain funds for the poor, he and his wife had left their house and gone to live in a labourer's cottage.

Michael Sadler, to whom Shaw wrote this, was to bring him his next piece of luck. Sadler, another radical Liberal, had recently been appointed secretary to the Oxford University Extension Delegacy (the body responsible for Oxford's programme of adult education) and was eager to recruit new lecturers with his own commitment to mass education. He wrote to Shaw in 1886 and urged him to consider Extension teaching, now at a crucial stage of its development.

> If we can only seize the moment it seems as though the University might provide a national education for masses of men . . . . In so doing it justifies its own existence and brings help to hundreds . . . who are debarred from access to higher education.

Knowing that his friend was not well-off (with a child now as well as a wife to support) and that the income from Extension teaching was poor, Sadler had actually persuaded the delegates to break all precedents and offer Shaw a three-year salaried lectureship. But his strongest card was the nature of the work. So great was the desire for education, he wrote, that in one place working men walked three miles to and from the lectures; while in another the class was only ended at 10 p.m. by turning off the gas. It was missionary work. 'And rather than that you should . . . decline I will take train to Horsham and talk to you for 12 hours!'[37] Shaw did not decline. He was a missionary by nature. And the mission that he now made his own for life embodied everything understood by that article of Liberal faith, 'the education of the democracy'.

He left Horsham and went back north where he worked as an unpaid

[35]King to Shaw (11 Oct. 1909) Fawcett 222. King pursued the line of a practical idealist from his Oxford days, living for a time at Toynbee Hall, a model landlord in Warwickshire (and later Director of Education for that county) a scholar and historian of Italian unity. See R. Bolton King, J. D. Browne and E. M. H. Ibbotson, *Bolton King, Pratical Idealist* (1978).
[36]Michael Sadleir, *Sir Michael Sadler: A Memoir by his Son* (1949) 86.
[37]Sadler to Shaw (1 Feb. 1886) Fawcett 222.

curate and threw himself into Extension teaching in Lancashire and the West Riding. Sadler, it soon became clear, had chosen an exceptional teacher of ordinary people, a scholar-showman who could hold huge numbers by his intellectual and moral force. Those who derided the Extension movement as a kind of educational Salvation Army would certainly have said that Shaw's capacity to draw 1,000 working men in Oldham into classes on Imperial Rome or Ruskin, was simply 'tickling the ears of the mob'.[38] He made it a vocation. But this success was accompanied by misfortune in his private life. His first wife died in 1888. The care of the household (including his small son) was taken over by his widowed aunt, Ada Ringrose, whose daughter Effie came with her to Thornthwaite, where Shaw was now vicar. Two years later Shaw married his cousin – an unsurprising turn of events, though Sadler was rather doubtful about it. Visiting the Shaws in their Yorkshire vicarage a year after the marriage he found a strange household. 'He and his wife live in this house almost as visitors might,' he wrote home.

> They take the ends of the table but all is prepared for them by Mrs Ringrose. She is really the lady of the house; plans the meals; arranges with the servants; is down in time for breakfast; keeps them to their appointments; looks for them when wanted; trims the lamps; makes the jam; pour out coffee in the m'g and then, when Mrs Shaw appears, slips into a side chair, like a Prime Minister might before the constitutional sovereign, & never forgets to jog Mrs Shaw's elbow when someone's cup is empty or a hostess' duties have to be performed . . . . It is queer, isn't it?[39]

It was evidently queerer than Sadler knew. Maude's account of the marriage, looking back – and one that fits with other impressions of Shaw's impulsive, self-destructive style – was that Effie and her mother had been left without means and he married her in order to be able to support them. Effie certainly needed support, and not just materially. She had great charm but also, as he knew then, was mentally unstable and a prey to pathological fears. Could he not have helped her, outside marriage? This was a question Maude asked later, given the way that things turned out.

> But I know the answer – No, he could not. No relation, no cousin, however kind, could have done for her what a husband could. No one . . . could altogether save her from fear, but all that was possible he did.[40]

In 1891, when Sadler met her Effie was less strange than she became later on, and he told his wife,

> I feel a good deal reassured. Mrs Shaw has lots in her but no administrative

[38]Quoted in Stuart Marriott, 'Extensionalia: The Fugitive Literature of Early University Adult Education', *Studies in Adult Education*, (10) 1978, 50–72.
[39]Michael Sadler to his wife (22 Aug. 1891) quoted Sadleir *Sir Michael Sadler*, 134.
[40]TFC 103.

ability, I fear. She is stimulating to him in rather a dreamy preoccupied way. By no means a mere admirer but rather exciting to him on his generous side without being a remedy to his weaker.

As to that, a more robust wife than Effie might have been defeated by the bouts of depression which in Shaw's case often succeeded the pressures and glories of the lecture round. To a French academic who came to hear him he seemed bursting with animal spirits, more than equal to the life of 'un missionaire d'Oxford'.[41] Extension courses, in any case, occupied only six months of the year. But six months of weekdays in railway carriages, travelling from one centre to another and usually correcting essays en route; six months of addressing enormous classes, of summoning every talent to bring the Renaissance or Ruskin's philosophy to working men; six months of always eating in a hurry and always rushing back to his parish at weekends, might be expected to leave some mark. Shaw was physically very strong but his mental heredity, like Effie's, was not; and he suffered from exhaustion and gloom.

Yet teaching working men was his life. When Oxford friends, concerned for his health, gained him the offer of a wealthy living, Shaw declined it because of his commitment, first and foremost, to Extension work. Aware that he could ill afford such a gesture, Balliol combed its statutes and found a way to elect him to a fellowship – a thing unheard-of for a man who was not teaching within the University. Unhappily, the fellowship stipend was too small to allow him to reduce his teaching load, but that did not change his attitude. When Michael Sadler refused a post with the *Manchester Guardian* because it would have meant deserting 'the Extension', Shaw wrote warmly,

> I have no doubt from the wordly point of view that you *have* done the foolish thing; but I am very proud that you have been 'foolish'. This is a tremendous sacrifice to make, but *you have saved* the Extension![42]

And with the Extension (whether the problems of his private life) Shaw went from strength to strength in the nineties.

When Evelyn started to work for the Delegacy one of her first impressions must have been that everybody wanted lectures from Shaw and that he was a lion at the Summer Meeting – that highlight of the Extension year when ordinary people poured into Oxford ready for an intellectual feast. In 1901, when Maude sought his advice, Shaw had chanced to be the Summer Meeting preacher and she probably heard his opening sermon preached in the University Church. Summer Meeting preachers were chosen with care as men who had rapport with this special congregation,

---

[41] In *Le Rôle Social des Universités* (1892) 28–31, Max Leclerc describes hearing Shaw give an Extension lecture with superlative command of his audience.

[42] Sadleir, *Sir Michael Sadler*, III. The living Shaw declined was worth £1300 p.a.

and Shaw preached movingly on 'Christian Ambition', proclaiming that 'Greatness . . . is service . . . . There is only one lawful ambition . . . to serve.'

'But we are tired of philanthropy,' men say. 'We are sick of the poor, and the working classes, and social problems. Temperance, missions, the housing question, old age pensions – would that we might never hear the dreary names again! Give us leave to possess our own souls in peace. Things are better than they were, and even if the evil in the world is terrible, God bears it and so can we.'[43]

This ebb-tide of the spirit marked the new century. 'All the good causes are stricken with languor . . . . The money power . . . day by day threatens . . . a new tyranny . . . . It will not last,' he said, 'No, it will not.' The only Christian ambition was service: at home, and in the world of preventible suffering 'crying to us for . . . deliverance', beyond. Of such service Carlyle had written, 'it is great . . . and there is no other greatness.'

Maude could not have listened to this without responding, like those Balliol men whose energies were kindled by Arnold Toynbee's 'prophetic power' or the 'prophetic zeal' of Canon Barnett. 'I am not a prophet,' she had said to Kathleen, 'that my friends should sacrifice themselves for me' – using the word as it was often used, to describe 'men of moral inspiration'. 'The prophet' was her nickname later for Shaw and no doubt later she became attuned to the note of pain in his preaching. 'Religion is Service and . . . it must begin at home,' he had told the Summer Meeting that day. 'No beneficent activities outside will compensate for failure there.' And when he said 'It is in his home that a man is tested and tried,' no doubt he meant it, for his marriage was a failure.

It was now ten years since Sadler had wondered at the strange, abstracted quality of Effie and nine since her one experience of childbirth had driven her temporarily out of her mind. Effie had been afraid to have children and they tried to prevent it. When she conceived she was mad with fear, and insane for two years after the birth. For the rest of her life there were always times when she needed a mental nurse and even at her best she depended on Shaw (with whom she had ceased to have sexual relations) to exorcise the nameless dread which pursued her. 'Dear, strange enchanting Effie!' wrote Maude, much later, when she strove to convey a likeness of someone so important to her. 'With all her gifts, there was a strange spell on her – a shyness almost frantic . . . a fear of life which lay on her like frost upon a flower.'[44]

But of course she knew nothing of that when she came to South Luffenham in 1902. True to form, she took the first opportunity to write to

[43]*Christian Ambition: A Sermon preached in the Church of St Mary-the-Virgin, Oxford, on Sunday, August 18th, 1901, before the Summer Meeting of University Extension Students by the Rev. W. Hudson Shaw, MA.*
[44]TFC 15.

her friends describing the household. Shaw had come to meet her at the station 'and we had our first encounter about who should pay the cab. I *regret* to say that he won.'[45] Evelyn was relieved by her cheerful tone. 'It does seem, dear Kathleen, don't you think, as if she had found her niche in a wonderful way, and even if she is uprooted from South Luffenham I am sure we can trust that something else will follow.'[46]

[45]Maude to KC (12 Sept. 1902).
[46]Evelyn to KC (21 Oct. 1902).

4

Hudson Shaw

We ought to be one shriek of horror at the sadness of life, if it were not that happiness makes us strong.

Maude to Kathleen Courtney (16 December 1903).

Nothing that she knew in Oxford or in Liverpool could have prepared Maude for South Luffenham exactly. Oxford was full of people like herself, eagerly debating the choices before them; Liverpool, of people who had no choices, yet were habituated, nonetheless, to the upheavals of the Irish ghetto and the uncertainties of work at the docks. South Luffenham was static: three hundred people, farmhouses dating back to Elizabeth, labourers earning twelve shillings a week, pagan customs, Shaw said, 'pagan village feasts and Biblical gleanings in the harvest fields'.[1] In a letter to his future parishioners before he went there in 1899, he had assured them of his wish to serve, 'to share your life – if you will allow me, your joys and your sorrows, to care for your children, to support every movement which may tend to your benefit, whether in this life or the life to come.'[2] They would strive together to make South Luffenham into a little 'City of God'. What did the villagers make of this? Most were 'as hard as nails religiously', he admitted later. It was uphill work.

For Maude, as it turned out, provident collecting was not a bad apprenticeship to village life and in no time at all she formed in the cottages the same warm and easy relationships which she had enjoyed with improvident women. 'Enjoyed' is the right word. Shaw, looking back, spoke of her as the 'one true democrat' he had ever known and compared her with St Francis.[3] We can allow something to the eye of love; it is unlikely that St Francis would have marked down the other Settlement workers, as Maude did, for eating apples with steel knives. She was not unaware of class. But her frank response to people as people in slums and cottages was rare all the same.

[1] Hudson Shaw, 'Maude Royden 1901–1920', *International Women's Suffrage News* (May–June 1920).
[2] Hudson Shaw, 'To the Parishioners of South Luffenham' (Nov. 1898).
[3] Shaw, 'Maude Royden, 1901–1920'.

Yesterday we went into one of the cottages and Mr Shaw sat down and barked at them, till I nearly screamed aloud with suppressed merriment; but no one else saw how comic it was, and for the 1000th time, [she told Kathleen] I wished you were here to laugh with me. But I talked to one woman, and she took me into another room and showed me herself in her wedding dress (I mean a photograph) and said she didn't see much of her husband and I said she might be thankful she had one at all, and we screamed with laughter and were merry. And Mr Shaw went on barking in the other room all the time. In between the barks, an old woman described her internal economy and how she had eaten an egg and it had stopped just *there* and she had asked the doctor to give her something to fetch it up again.[4]

'I have visited nearly everyone in the village,' she wrote a little later, 'they are so nice.' Shaw, it seems, had been nervous at first of asking her to do things she might not like, but her programme soon acquired a routine. Every fortnight she took the Mothers' Meeting ('I buy flannelette in large quantities and they buy it off me in small; and pay me in smaller, and the result is complicated accounts which I know I shall get wrong.') She took a weekly girls' class for sewing, Shakespeare and games, and a girls' night school in domestic economy ('out of a book!!!'), and Sunday school ('I hate it. Began yesterday, and bored them all to tears, including myself!') She was also to give some lantern lectures and 'get up an entertainment of sorts'.

At the time Maude arrived the rectory household included (apart from Hudson and Effie) Arnold, Shaw's son by his first marriage, 'a nice but not wildly interesting youth' of seventeen, and the younger one, nine-year-old Bernard, whose birth had been so traumatic for Effie. 'He is an intelligent little creature, and reminds me of my small nephew Ralph. Not so much brain, though,' Maude told Kathleen. Bernard had taken a great fancy to her, ran errands for her and attended her classes, while she played with him at ping-pong and croquet. 'It always gives me such an absurd pleasure when children like me,' she admitted. As for the practical running of the household, Effie's mother, who was once 'Prime Minister', had since remarried and that role was filled by a family friend. Of Effie, Maude wrote: 'Mrs Shaw has a sense of humour that is rather like mine, and that is such a bond, isn't it?'[5]

Her bond with Effie, as well as with Shaw, was to be the theme of *A Threefold Cord*, the memoir she wrote more than forty years later. 'I fell in love with her, too, at first sight.' But in fact it had not been so simple. She had at first reported to Kathleen, 'Mrs Shaw . . . rather terrifies me. I try to talk in a low voice and be what my mother calls "gentle"! I *hope* we shall get on all right. I feared we should not but now I think we shall – with care!' And in another letter she admits, 'I don't get any nearer to Mrs Shaw.' However, in October Evelyn noted that the two 'had suddenly found each

[4]Maude to KC (12 Sept. 1902).
[5]ibid. (10 Nov. 1902).

other out, and seemed on the borders of a friendship',[6] while Maude told Kathleen, 'I have taught her to smoke!' The success of the whole thing was left in no doubt by her next letter, where she wrote delightedly that the Shaws both hoped she would accompany them if they moved to another parish (which seemed possible at that time). Her cup overflowed. She was surprised and flattered that they wanted her – an outsider – to be with them. The question had been put to her by Shaw one Sunday breakfast, and he greeted Effie, when she came down, with 'Miss Royden says she will. There's a happy day for you!' 'Am I awfully vain? Yes, I am,' wrote Maude, out of the fullness of her own pleasure and the confidence of being vindicated. For after all, when she had joined the Shaws, 'so many people shook their heads at me for trying such a risky experiment; and shook their heads at Effie as well. 'She tells me her friends all thought her mad.'[7]

Who, one wonders, were Effie's friends? She was never seen in streets or shops. An 'almost frenzied shyness' blocked her off from people. Even when surrounded by those she loved, she would leave the piano if anyone was listening, and often retreat to 'an island of silence'.[8] Lines of communication were lost with even a few days' separation. Then it was a triumph, as Maude discovered, to be able to get through to her again. 'I found Effie well and cheerful,' she wrote to Kathleen after one such break, 'and got right *to* her at once.'

> You will, I feel sure, be pleased to hear this; for generally, the briefest absence finds us miles apart . . . and it takes so long to come together again, I say us, because I know Effie thinks she does some of the 'coming'. Otherwise . . . I am of opinion that I have the whole journey to myself![9]

Maude wrote this after a year with the Shaws; knowing then – surely – that Effie was unbalanced, but enjoying the wit and the 'critical amazement' that was sometimes directed towards herself. They lent each other books and admired each other's clothes. 'The reason why I like you so much,' said Effie, in the spring of that first year, 'is because your clothes are so entirely satisfactory.' At thirty-three, for all her dependence, there were times when she played the elder sister. 'Don't laugh!' wrote Maude, recounting to Kathleen how an attempt to fast one Sunday had resulted in a violent headache and collapse. 'Mrs Shaw found me in this state, and was absolutely angelic, and I hung on to her hand and gasped and cried and behaved like a perfect idiot.'[10] Well before the end of the three-month period which had been agreed for Maude's trial run, she and Effie had become attached. 'What a comfort they now love each other,' wrote Evelyn.

[6]Evelyn to KC (31 Oct. 1902).
[7]Maude to KC (29 Nov. 1902).
[8]TFC 18–19.
[9]Maude to KC (16 Dec. 1903).
[10]ibid. (6 Oct. 1902).

The tone of Maude's relationship with Shaw had been set by their argument at the railway station. It continued to be adversarial, a kind of mental guerilla warfare, which she revelled in, though glad of respites playing a dominoes game called 'Smiff'. Immortality, the housing question, the education bill, the rights of women – 'We fight all the time,' she wrote to Kathleen. 'It is most exhilarating. Only we generally end by finding that we really think alike, which is flat.' They did not think alike, though, on 'the Woman question'; which might have been expected, for he idolised Ruskin, and Ruskin's view of women she had spurned long ago. Now, however, she was disappointed to find that, whatever he professed in theory, some of Shaw's off-the-cuff reactions were little in advance of Mr Diggle's.

> Mr Shaw put forward such admirable views on the subject of the sexes yesterday. He said that there was *no* generality to be made about either sex, except perhaps that on the whole women were better. Imagine my annoyance on discovering that these admirable sentiments did not prevent him from assuming without hesitation a moment later that certain ridiculous anonymous communications with which he is bored must certainly emanate from a woman 'because no man would take the trouble'. Positively Mr Shaw talked about 'she' and 'the good lady', till at last I said in surprise 'Do you know who it is, then?' 'No' 'Then why "she"?' 'Oh, of course it must be a "she".'[11]

'This from the logical sex!' wrote Maude. When they got onto women's suffrage and Shaw produced the conventional argument that women could not vote because they could not bear arms, she felt bound to allow it; lacking, in those days, sufficient expertise to knock it down. But she was dismayed by signs of his adherence to a cloistered, Ruskinite ideal of womanhood.

> The prophet found Mrs Shaw reading one of my books – Webster's *Duchess of Malfi* – and was *furious* – said women had no business to read such things. Personally, I should think a woman who had read and understood [Tolstoy's] *Resurrection* would not have much to learn. But what simply amazed me was Mr Shaw's having such ideas about women. To hear him talk, you would imagine he couldn't be guilty of absurd and unjust generalisations like that![12]

Yet, she said later, he escaped the vanity of the revered Victorian male. He was inherently a humble man. A biblical scholar, who not only went deep but could engross his village congregation in the finer points of the Book of Deuteronomy, Shaw felt the defects of his early schooling and was unspoilt by the adulation of some of his female relatives. His sister, for instance, who was sometimes at South Luffenham, could not bear that he should ever be criticised. His aunt – Effie's mother – though a characterful lady with a

[11]ibid. (12 Sept. 1902).
[12]ibid. (29 Nov. 1902).

strong mind and opinions of her own, once checked a conversation between Maude and Effie with, 'Hush, Hudson is going to speak!' 'After this, whenever Hudson opened his mouth, Effie and I were liable to raise our hands in admonition and say to each other, "Hush! Hudson is going to speak!"'[13]

Effie, as Sadler had discovered way back, was certainly no 'mere admirer' of her husband. 'Who is Miss Hale?' she enquires of Maude during one of the Summer Schools, her customary irony heightened a little by the use of Hudson's pet name, 'the Man'. 'Why has the Man lost his heart to her? Does she wear "shirtwaists"? It seems she has written, "For *me*, you are Oxford!" Can homage go further?'[14]

Maude seems to bring out the youngness in Effie. Sometimes they behave like schoolgirls struggling not to laugh at a favourite teacher who, even off duty, cannot discard the ingrained habit of being instructive. ('He would gaze . . . at a plough and urge us . . . to realise that ploughs . . . "just that shape" had been used . . . for centuries'). At other times they combined to indulge him – for all the world like those 'ideal' women the one fell short of and the other disliked. For Effie, who was so far from fulfilling the social and sexual role of a wife, and Maude, so impatient of stereotypes, often displayed the conventional indulgence of 'thorough women' to the man in their life ('the Man', or 'Man'). They involved themselves in whatever was his latest passion – and Shaw had many. The purchase of an organ – a new organ for the village church, very largely paid for by money that he raised lecturing in America – absorbed him for months. He talks constantly, says Effie, 'of "tubular pneumatics", "eliptic pins", "composition pedal-action" and the "balanced principle" and wonders if he might invite the 2 workmen to dinner. I suggest Wed, to meet Miss Alice from North Luffenham.'[15]

With the Shaws, then, Maude had found her niche. But if it had ever seemed that South Luffenham would provide quick answers to the problems that beset her, a month or two was enough to disprove it. Rutland was a far cry from Netherfield Road yet she was soon asking the same old questions: 'Is this my work?' 'If it is not, should I do it because it needs doing?' Very soon she admitted to Kathleen that it was easier to worship God than to love His creatures, and that she doubted if the three of them had sufficient zeal for their fellow men. 'I know I haven't and that makes all my work wrong.'[16] Village work anyway began to seem cramped. 'But it wants doing – badly.'

She was torn in two between her craving for intellectual life and the work

[13]TFC 21.
[14]Effie to Maude (25 Aug. 1903). Effie's letters were evidently in Fawcett Library Box 222 at one time but I cannot trace them there and have used Emil Oberholzer's photocopies.
[15]ibid. (25 Aug. 1903).
[16]Maude to KC (6 Oct. 1902).

which 'does seem to have been sent straight to me', and which surely ought
to be fulfilling 'if I were enough of a Christian'. After much debate, she
decided to 'try to make my religion everything, and give up intellectual
ambitions, for a time.' Shaw thought otherwise. However much inclined to
spend himself in crazes of his own, where her religion and her future were
concerned, he dedicated his mind to her entirely. His advice now was that
she try her hand at lecturing, and combine it with parish work. 'He does
understand her,' Evelyn admitted, despite some doubts of the benefit to
Maude of her and Shaw being so much alike, 'both eating their hearts out,
both burning with passionate zeal, both subject to ups and downs, and
continually strung up to the highest pitch of nervous tension.' As for
lecturing, 'the only thing is for her to try it. I am afraid it will be too much
for her, but she can but try, and it seems to be a relief she positively must
have.'[17]

From Evelyn's standpoint, the move to South Luffenham, which she had
hailed as an answer to prayer, had not yet lived up to expectations. At the
start it had seemed such a deliverance she felt she could never worry again.
Yet by November she was worrying ceaselessly. Maude's letters to her,
though less frequent than before, were full and long.

> But oh! Kathleen, I am sometimes so possessed with fear for her that I must hear
> every day. Fear that she is eating her heart out with hopes, fears, plans, doubts,
> agonies of all sorts; and I know that she has had a hard time lately which I do trust
> has been succeeded by peace. Will she ever have peace, do you think?[18]

And would peace mean Rome? She had not mentioned *that* 'and I do *hope* it
is in abeyance, but I know she worries . . . . I wish you were here.'
Kathleen, however, was at home in Ireland, and the thought of Ireland did
nothing to brighten Evelyn's view of 'the RC question'. She wrote of her
distaste for Mariolatry and of the increase of bigotry in England, 'wherever
the High Church doctrines flourish – and where do they not flourish
nowadays?' She could not have written thus to Maude; nor could she have
admitted what was hardest to bear: that Shaw had promised to write and
tell her how Maude was, and had not done so. 'That letter never comes and
keeps on never coming and I know how busy he is and yet just *pine* for it.'
To make things worse, Maude had cancelled a visit already arranged
because of a meeting Shaw fixed later.

> I have intreated her to give herself intervals of . . . commonsense unthinking
> work and relaxation. I mean, to *force* herself to take them for I fear so greatly that
> the nervous strain must be telling on her and that a breakdown may come.
> Sometimes I am in absolute *terror* about her, which is very wrong, but I do not
> see how a frame like hers can bear the wear and tear.

[17]Evelyn to KC (7 Dec. 1902).
[18]ibid. (14 Nov. 1902).

And as she had feared, 'the RC question' was only dormant. 'She says in her last letter that she must turn to a deliberate effort to find out the truth, and I suppose that is what it means. Dear Kathleen, how long can this go on?'[19]

It certainly went on throughout the autumn, absorbing any mental energy left from the girls' class and the Mothers' Meetings and argued out perpetually with Shaw when he returned to the parish at weekends. 'No words can say,' Maude wrote to Kathleen, 'how marvellously patient and sympathetic he is with me.'[20] She took ten pages to set out their argument about confession. Was the meaning of *John* 20. 23 that there should be auricular confession to a priest?[21] She thought yes and Shaw thought no. Thinking yes took her practically to Rome; thinking no reflected his view of the dangers of building on isolated texts. He spoke to her about the early Church, when penitents confessed to the whole congregation, in which was vested the power to absolve. Maude rejected this Protestant view, satisfied that, for ordinary purposes, absolution appertained to the priesthood. And so on and so on. What it came to, in practice, was that Shaw did not go to confession, and she did, though it involved a special journey to an Anglican convent some miles away. He only insisted that she take a cab.

The appeal of Rome, as she acknowledged later, was partly temperamental. But Shaw insisted that she must never let herself swallow what she did not accept as true. So they thrashed out *John* 20. 23. and the rest. And she marvelled at his even-handedness, at his being able to say, without pressure, 'If you feel you must go, God be with you.'[22] This was more detachment, perhaps, than he felt. He later spoke of saving Maude from 'that atrophy of the mind, R.C.' That he saw the Roman Church like this is not strange. While Maude herself seems quite unaware of the temper of Rome at this time, Shaw could not have been. He was up at Oxford when the reactionary Leo XIII forbade Roman Catholics to study there; he had been a priest of ten years' standing when this same Pope condemned Anglican Orders; he was a liberal, in church and out, and one who struck Mrs Humphry Ward as the very type of the rebel clergyman she had depicted in *Richard Meynell*.[23] How could he have talked of Rome without reference to the battle then joined with the Modernists? Yet there is no hint of such things in Maude's letters. Perhaps he feared they might be counter

[19] ibid. (7 Dec. 1902).

[20] Maude to KC (29 Nov. 1902).

[21] ibid. (31 Oct. 1902). *John* 20.23 'Whose soever sins ye remit, they are remitted unto them; and whose soever sins ye retain, they are retained.'

[22] TFC 11.

[23] Mrs Humphry Ward, who was deeply interested in the struggle of the Catholic Modernists, wrote *The Case of Richard Meynell* (1911) about the similar struggle of an Anglican clergyman. Not long before the book came out she was staying at Alderley Edge in Cheshire (where Shaw became rector in 1907) and wrote, 'on Sunday I heard Meynell preach! – in Alderley church, in the person of Mr Hudson Shaw. An astonishing sermon and a crowded congregation.' (J.P. Trevelyan, *Mrs Humprhy Ward* (1923)).

productive, perversely giving a rightward tilt to that balance between Protestant and Catholic which was a fundamental part of her nature. She was continually pulled two ways. An independent and courageous spirit, a wish to act, to change things, especially for women, drew her in a Protestant direction, while the Catholic longed for beauty in worship – for God as Beauty – for spiritual repose and glad submission to authority. She had for some time – since Oxford, anyway – been moving away from conservatism. 'There must be an answer somewhere,' she wrote, brooding on the poor, 'is it socialism?'[24] But if Shaw had asked 'Can *you* be allied to a Church that is allied to reaction – a Church un-sickened, or so it seems, by all that sickened you over Dreyfus, for instance?' She might well have answered, 'It is God's Church.'

No wonder Evelyn said, 'How long can this go on?' For ever, if it were a matter of debate. But then there was *feeling* with its well-known tendency to settle things somehow, in the end. For instance, though Maude was a long way yet from regarding herself as in love with Shaw, when she told him at some point that autumn that it would now be harder to 'go over', she did not mean because of arguments advanced in the interpretation of *John* 20. 23.

Shaw was due to go on a lecture tour in America at the end of December and Evelyn, who knew this, and must also have known his dilatoriness as a correspondent, still waited, on pins, for the letter he had promised.

> Mr Shaw has not written to me and I am not surprised but I do want to hear. Do you not think, dear Kathleen, that I might write to him after Maude has left and ask for an account of her and his opinion? I do not like to do it while she is there but I can make Xmas wishes an excuse.[25]

But she did not write then, and Shaw did not either. She wrote to Kathleen on December 23, almost too depressed to send Christmas greetings. Maude had now told her that 'if it must be Rome' the Shaws had offered her their house as a shelter. 'What will the end be?' To Evelyn, by this time, the question was rhetorical. All they could pray for was that Maude would find peace of mind. 'But oh Kathleen dear will it ever be the same? . . . . Will there not always be some shadow between us and how shall we bear it? . . . . My heart is sore . . . and I can feel no Xmas joy, but only sadness.'[26] That night she wrote to Shaw.

The post next day (which was Christmas Eve) brought Evelyn a note he had managed to scribble on his way to board the *SS Umbria*. It had crossed hers; and she sent it on to Kathleen with a postscript saying, 'Mr Shaw gives me hope.' It was certainly all she could have wished for. '*I have not met*

[24] Maude to KC (n.d., probably Dec. 1903).
[25] Evelyn to KC (7 Dec. 1902).
[26] ibid. (23 Dec. 1902).

anyone like her,' he wrote. (Nowhere in the letter did he feel the need to name the person they were talking about.) 'We are *all* her devoted slaves, my Wife especially.' And further on, 'She has made my Wife another person, and the whole village loves her.' Then, as to Rome: 'Don't think it inevitable, or let her think so either. She said to me that it would be harder now to go over. I believe –' and this belief may already have meant as much to him as it did to Evelyn –' she may be saved yet from that atrophy of the mind, RC.'

> What we have to work for is *delay*, and to provide engrossing work. I am trying all I can. Village + Extension, or other lecturing, is the ideal programme . . . . I have asked her today to come to S[outh] L[uffenham] for three years. More later, I must go. A glad New Year to you.

And the final words of reassurance, 'Have hope for your noble friend.'[27]

The question of Rome fades from Evelyn's letters after Christmas 1902 and she busies herself, for the time being, with her own affairs, wandering if Kathleen could take her post for a month or two at the Delegacy as she is needed to look after her mother. This was arranged to the delight of them all. 'How lovely it is to be friends!' wrote Maude, in the midst of a round of New Year visits to Evelyn, to the Diggles, and others. Her letters are lighthearted. ('How are you, dears? I am having another red coat and skirt! . . . A little short straight coat . . . long in the front'). To be back at Frankby was a strain, though, in some ways. Her earlier scruples about taking paid work were melting in 'the fierce heat of family life' and she longed to be independent. 'I *wish* I could get some lecturing.' Her tone overall is unusually relaxed, though, and Evelyn was delighted when she came to stay.

> She was really merry, and I do not wonder at the relief she finds in knowing the Shaws are a refuge for her always, and the pleasure in knowing she is a real help and inspiration to him – it is truly marvellous how they fit, I think.[28]

Now she had gone. 'But when Maude goes she does not go away completely . . . does she? She never seems to me very far away – yet you know the blank she leaves too!'

The one who felt the blank after Christmas was Effie. Maude had delighted her by sending flowers from Frankby and she wrote

> Why are you such a Darling to me? I can't understand it! Either you are guilty of . . . perjury . . . or else you love me a little for myself which is very strange and quite unexpected . . . I read your letter many many times to make sure I haven't dreamed it.[29]

[27]Shaw to Evelyn (27 Dec. 1902) Fawcett 222.
[28]Evelyn to KC (1 Feb. 1903).
[29]Effie to Maude (22 Dec. 1902).

Shaw had been packing for his American trip.

> Won't you write to him please before he goes? I think he misses you – he doesn't
> enthuse about many people nowadays. A very very happy Christmas to you who
> do so much to make others happy, and every loving wish for 1903. Will it bring
> you back to us? Please say yes!

Later, she wrote about parish business, which she now seems to have had to
get involved in, aided by a neighbouring vicar. 'I'm in charge of the Poor
Fund as Mr Nevinson's pride does not allow him to make friends by the
means of the mammon of unrighteousness.' This was not the worst,
however.

> How could you leave me those terrible Mother's Meetings! They all come and we
> don't even pretend not to be bored! Mr Nevinson comes to 'help' and you know
> what that means. He asked to open the Meetings with Prayer but was sternly
> refused and made to shake hands all round instead. I have disgraced myself
> absolutely by not knowing what 5¼ yds at 3¾ was and I don't know now, and
> Mr N. thinks I'm not fit to be in charge of a Parish and I entirely agree with him.[30]

These few letters, loving and ironic, which mark the earliest days of the
relationship between Maude and the Shaws, are almost all we have to bring
us anywhere near to Effie. Though she was to be the essential strand in their
'threefold cord', it is hard to imagine her; and especially, to imagine the line
between her 'normal' and 'abnormal' self. 'Did Evelyn succeed in conveying to you any impression of Effie's appearance and personality?' Maude
asked Kathleen, after Evelyn's first visit to the rectory. 'It is a difficult one
to convey.' And forty years on she still found it difficult. Of Effie she writes
in *A Threefold Cord*, 'I heap words on words and none find her.' To find her
now is virtually impossible. How can we, reading Effie's letters, enter into
her intimidating silence? It may be that Effie of the letters is the 'real' one;
free, on paper, from whatever it was that kept her silent habitually. The 'real'
one, then, is the ironic observer of Mr Nevinson and the parish; the 'real'
one is confident enough to assert that the idea of the poor being healthy
must have been invented to teach people contentment; 'it can never have
been suggested by observation'. The 'real' one can even admit that she is
lonely. 'You and the Man spoil one so dreadfully for ordinary folk!' she
wrote to Maude.[31] 'Dearest Mytts. Where are you? You seem so far away! I
begin to wonder if you really ever were here. . . . Tell me you are not
vanished utterly!' Shaw, too, was anxious to have news of her.

> He does speak of you so beautifully it just does me good to hear him! He has such
> reverence for your goodness and says you give him new inspiration. It is so lovely
> to think you will never disappoint him.[32]

[30]ibid. (no month 1903).
[31]ibid. (21 Jan. 1903).
[32]ibid. (n.d., probably March 1903).

Effie's precarious mental state was something Maude only grasped by degrees. 'I try to talk in a low voice,' she had written early on, as if from a sick room. Her voice, in fact, was naturally low. What was not low was her personality, but this does not seem to have bothered Effie. On the contrary, the irruption on the scene of an offbeat, dynamic young woman – the transformation of the dinner table by banter and debate and a kind of conflict – seems to have amused her. 'It's as good as a play!' She may not actually have used the words, but that is how it seems to have struck her. Maude and Hudson were the players, she the spectator. And sometimes, even, it really was a play; for Maude, along with her passion for acting, had a remarkable verbal memory. On winter evenings she recited Shakespeare. You asked for *Hamlet* and you got it, as Shaw remembered proudly, later; followed by *Lear*, perhaps, the next night.[33] All this brought new life to a household suffering, like any country parsonage, from its cultural isolation among what Effie called 'ordinary folk'. But Maude's capacity as entertainer was gravely limited when Shaw was not there, for then there was no one to argue with, no one 'perpetually dragging his coat-tail for me to step on'; just the spectator. And it was some time before she realised that this was Effie's role; that she would simply be there, waiting, silent, for her to begin.

> The idea that conversation cannot be a monologue was one [Effie] never got hold of. It was, she held, easy for me to talk and difficult for her. Why then did I not talk, whether Hudson was there or not? It could only be that I thought her not worth talking to![34]

Then would come the desperate search for topics, and the often futile struggle to get through. All this Maude recalled sharply, later; conscious, then, that her own immaturity had laid her open to the worst of it. She had loved Effie and could not bear to fail her; nor to fall down on her trust to Shaw. But, 'I am sure Effie never knew what I suffered, and only a very immature young woman could have suffered in just that way.' 'I adored her but I hardly knew her.' Certainly, she had not understood in those days the extent to which Effie was possessed by fear.

'An overwhelming fear of life,' is how Maude puts it in *A Threefold Cord*. She does not say when she gained this insight but it must have been new territory to someone who, so far from fearing life herself, advanced upon it, whatever her doubts, with the high courage of the little girl who liked to balanced on the quarry wall, or the young woman who seized the reins of the four-in-hand up in Ambleside. Here was the opposite. Effie fled. By the time Maude came on the scene, her flight was usually into silence. In earlier days, though, she had fled to her room, locked the door and refused to

[33]Shaw, 'Maude Royden, 1901–1920'.
[34]TFC 17.

come down if the house was invaded by strangers.[35] Still less had she borne
the invasion of herself. From sex and childbirth she had fled into madness.
'Effie was repelled by passion,' wrote Maude, so many years on that she had
probably forgotten how long it took to piece the whole thing together and
how confusing it seemed at the start. What had Effie, for instance, tried to
convey by asking her to read Tolstoy's *Resurrection*? 'It is the weirdest
world,' she told Kathleen.

> Mrs Shaw has just lent me a book of extraordinary filthiness. After I had read a
> few chapters, I said, 'Is it necessary to read this book?' She said doubtfully, 'No,
> not necessary; but advisable.' I said I found it perfectly repulsive; to which she
> answered nothing.[36]

In her memoir Maude wrote that 'from her very nature' Effie could not
understand what she was asking in forcing upon Hudson a completely
celibate life. 'That was an integral part of her problem.'[37] And he at last
perceived it as such. 'They really are quite separate people', she told
Kathleen, long before she knew how separate.[38] Indeed, what struck her
when Shaw was away was Effie's utter dependence on him. For all her own
efforts, Maude came to understand that only he could provide Effie's
security. 'Without him, no one, however loved, could save her from that
strange terror of which she once said to me that "if she only knew what she
was afraid of she wouldn't be afraid."' She clung to his strength.

> His very muscle was a joy to her. Once, when in one of her acute accesses of fear,
> she asked him 'what would he do if a policeman came to take her away?' 'Smash
> his face in', was the prompt reply, and even in her misery Effie could not help
> laughing. She was so sure he could.[39]

His return from the American lecture tour in the spring of 1903 was a
matter for rejoicing. Conversation flowed again and Effie listened. 'She
used to laugh at us or perhaps it would be more true to say that she and I
together laughed at Hudson and she and he together laughed at me.'[40] Shaw
now turned his mind purposefully to getting Maude into Extension teaching – which was easier said than done. For despite the fact that the
movement had developed out of the movement for women's education,
that many of its most influential figures were sympathetic to the women's
cause, and that at least two thirds of its students were women, there had
always been strong resistance to appointing women as lecturers. One

[35] TFC 26.
[36] Maude to KC (29 Nov. 1902). Tolstoy claimed that this study of seduction was written to
express his horror of lust, but to some the book seemed to wallow in it.
[37] TFC 103.
[38] Maude to KC (31 March 1903).
[39] TFC 18; 44.
[40] TFC 18.

argument was that the lecture circuit was too physically exhausting for women; another that the local committees would not want them.

The idea that Maude should attempt this work came to Shaw through the Shakespeare evenings. He had been impressed then by her scholarship and by her power to hold an audience. She had 'a most attractive and lovely voice, perfect delivery, teaching capacity, enthusiasm and . . . no nerves'.[41] At this time, of course, he had himself been active in Extension teaching for seventeen years. He was still strongly committed to it, but the glad, bright day of the beginning was past. Certainly the movement's ideology was not yet under explicit challenge; but Sadler had moved to other work and problems of structure and finance were apparent which had not been obvious at the beginning. This was the context in which he had told Maude, when they first met, 'I have lived so long now with the jog-trot and the ordinary, the cool, practical folk, that it was absolutely refreshing to meet someone burnt up with enthusiasm and not ashamed of it.'[42] It was still the context two years later when he determined to persuade the Delegates to allow her a trial lecture. Before that issue came to the test, though, he arranged a trial lecture of his own.

Maude would never have agreed that she had no nerves. Her letters to Kathleen often enlarge on the nervous agony of performing, whether in theatricals or at the Settlement when she had to give Poor Law lectures. Now, when she went to Duffield with Shaw to give a lecture-recital on *Hamlet*, she spent the morning in a state of 'sick fright' and had to hide her hands beneath the table at lunch because they were trembling. She began her talk 'in a voice which, I regret to say, *shook* with terror'.[43] As for the rest: as she recalled it, she didn't relax until half way through; then discovered she was running out of time, skipped a large piece, lost the peroration, invented a new one (badly) and sat down. There were sixty-eight people present and it must have been the kind of audience the anti-Extensionists liked to jeer at, for the woman who proposed the vote of thanks was so moved she burst into tears. ('I had not the faintest intention of being emotional,' Maude told Kathleen, 'though, of course, *Hamlet* is unspeakably sad.') Extravagant compliments were paid; and, what was much more to the point, she received further invitations to lecture. From Derby, the Mothers' Union asked her to talk on introducing Shakespeare to children.

> Ashbourne wants me to go there with Mr Shaw for a sort of fillip to their centre. Best of all, if I am admitted by the Delegates, Duffield wants me to deliver a course on Shakespeare next autumn. I believe they have already applied for someone; but they are prepared to withdraw that, if I become a . . . lecturer.

[41]Shaw, 'Maude Royden, 1901–1920'.
[42]TFC 10.
[43]Maude to KC (23 April 1903). The account which follows comes from this letter.

Euphorically she went on, 'hug me hard, and put a poultice on my swelled head, and remind me how really bad . . . my lecture was . . . I know it . . . but . . . I do feel in my *bones* as if I *could* lecture, in time, with work and self control, and one or two other little additions!' From his seat at the back of the room, Shaw judged her lecture 'quite bad', she said; 'badly arranged, and delivered much too fast . . . but . . . he believes I *obsessed* them all,' and ought to lecture from behind a screen, 'because for his part, he couldn't listen to what I said for looking at my face; and was it I, anyhow, or was I acting, or was it someone else?' Of course, she acknowledged, Mr Shaw was very much influenced by friendship. 'Also he is very responsive by nature; also *Hamlet* is a subject which might well inspire a stone. So we must take off about 70%'

When Shaw raised the matter of a lectureship in Oxford the Delegates' response was what might have been expected. 'Authority scoffed and poured buckets of cold water. Work not fit for a woman, too hard, too much travelling. Had been tried many times and always failed.'[44] He then pushed harder. 'Shaw was like oak,' said Sadler once, in regard to some dispute. He was like oak now. Staking his own reputation on hers, he offered to resign if she proved less than able. On 15 May they agreed to offer her a trial lecture at the Summer Meeting.

So there it was. And its huge importance does not seem to have weighed on her unduly, though now and then she sends a message to Kathleen, begging her to borrow some learned work from the Taylorian Institute in Oxford. 'I am in despair about *Faust*,' she admits once ('The Faust Legend in the Middle Ages' was to be her theme) and, a few weeks later, 'I am rather harassed about my lecture.' But there were other things to think of; some very pleasant, like her first experience of sleeping out all night in a hammock ('Isn't it luck that the Shaws' garden is so completely sheltered from the public gaze?') and the May queen's crowning in the village, and the expedition to see her father, who was then high sheriff of Cheshire, going to cathedral in state with the judges. ('He looked a perfect pet in his court dress. I sat opposite him in cathedral, and felt impelled to step across the aisle and kiss him at intervals. He would have been so surprised.')[45]

One of her greatest pleasures that year was bringing her friends together with the Shaws. 'I begin to think it is the only thing I can do for my friends – give them to one another!' And with such friends as these, it was sufficient, surely. 'The Shaws are lovely, aren't they?' she wrote to Kathleen. 'He is extraordinarily sympathetic. . . . He has something of the *ewig-weibliche* in him, as every really beautiful man's character has.'[46] Evelyn had been the first to visit. 'I don't feel half so cut off now,' wrote Maude. And,

[44]Shaw, 'Maude Royden, 1901–1920'.
[45]Maude to KC (24 July 1903).
[46]loc. cit. *ewig-weibliche* = the eternal feminine (from the famous last line of Goethe's *Faust*).

in spite of initial apprehension, Effie has been so charmed with Evelyn that she actually talked to her. 'I simply must have you here, mavourneen, then it will be complete,' Maude told Kathleen, 'I do so very very much want you to know her.' Unfortunately, there was little chance that Effie would be at the Summer Meeting. 'Her mother is coming here for August. . . .I think she simply worships her mother and won't want to miss a single day of her.'[47] But at least Kathleen met Shaw in Oxford. 'The Prophet fell in love with you and thinks me the most outrageous person ever to suffer from a moment's despondency when I am blessed with such friends,' wrote Maude. He had been intrigued by this 'three-cornered' friendship, and wondered how they shared their affections. She had told him that they never thought of it; just loved one another, and that 'each two were constantly amazed at the virtues of the other one.' So he understood now; and thought it must be lovely. 'Not that anyone has . . . any idea how lovely,' Maude said, 'except ourselves!'[48]

She was trying at this time to buoy up Kathleen, who was suffering from bouts of depression, unable to decide if the needs of her family really required her to be at home. 'I wish you wouldn't think so hardly of yourself. You spur me on to be brave and trustful, and yourself sound so sad.'[49] But exuberance breaks through. 'Best beloved, be happy. Spring has come, and you have a new frock (with silk foundation) and hat with feathers, and life is very beautiful!' Her imagination had been seized by *Faust*. 'I am obsessed by it,' she wrote. On a different level, she prepared for August by taking any opportunity to lecture, even if only to high school girls. Shaw was anxious as a mother hen and Kathleen, who was present on the first occasion, pleased him by sending him a favourable critique. 'I am glad you think I ought to lecture,' wrote Maude, 'I do feel it in my bones . . . The only thing is – will anyone let me lecture to them?'

The Summer Meeting of 1903 – the largest of any recent year – was inaugurated by the American Ambassador, in whose honour the Examination Schools were thronged with a very prestigious crowd, presided over by the Vice Chancellor. The serious business was begun by Marriott, Secretary to the Delegacy, with an introductory lecture on Mediaeval England; and he was followed by Michael Sadler, now a professor at Manchester, whose 'Education and Fiscal Policy', in the words of the *Oxford Chronicle*, 'touched the very heart of the great questions which the British Empire has to solve.' Students came to these Summer Meetings for the pleasure of hearing eminent men and the dozen unfledged lecturers on trial (of whom Maude was the only woman) appear among stars and rising stars: Rashdall on Oxford in the fourteenth century, Dicey on the Cabinet,

[47]ibid. (28 May 1903).
[48]ibid. (16 May 1903).
[49]ibid. (16 May 1903).

Pares on the Tartars, Ralph Vaughan Williams on Medieval folk songs, J. C. Powys on *Henry IV*.[50] Maude was not speaking till the second week, and at the end of the first came the occasion which was a highlight to her and many others: the garden party at Balliol. She had had it in mind for a long time, enquiring six months earlier of Kathleen.

> Shall you like me in a white silk dress, trimmed with much black insertion and a large black chiffon hat with feather? This is my garden party costume, but it isn't made yet, except the hat, which wouldn't be sufficient, though large. In this costume I propose to melt the hearts of any lecturers who regard me as myself and freeze all those who figure to themselves that I am Mr Shaw's Miss Royden.'

That was how Evelyn thought she would be seen, and the idea probably did not displease her. She was not 'Mr Shaw's Miss Royden', however, when she stood up to lecture on Faust. Tracing the legend from its inception, she focused at length on Marlowe's play. But the appeal which the subject made to her could not be concealed by the scholarly treatment. She was not neutral on this great theme of Man and the Devil and does not appear so, even in the lines of the printed summary. The *Oxford Chronicle* praised her paper for content, style, and grace of delivery. Her friends were effusive. Evelyn took pains to send Maude's mother a long report; and Mrs Royden, from St Moritz, expressed deep gratitude for such perception of 'the longing desire which we had to hear from some authentic source an account of dear Maude's initial lecture. Evelyn's letter would be kept, she said, amongst the greatest family treasures.

> I had read sufficiently between the lines of Maude's very modestly expressed version of her lecture to feel quite confident she had been successful and I felt very proud, but I was quite overcome when I read your emphatic account of success . . . . Of the excellence of her matter I felt sure, but I rejoice to know she has the great ability of being able to impart it to others. Her voice and intonation are charming and without the appearance of effort she seems to make it carry – but what delights me most of all is that you say that the strength and beauty of her character will tell in lecturing, for I had not realised *that*.

'Thank you too,' Mrs Royden went on, 'for the little touch you put in about her looks. Appearance is by no means to be despised, and I am so glad to know she wore a large black hat, which is so much the most becoming headdress she can wear.'[51]

Effie, in her usual ironic vein, wrote that the criticisms and opinions of the lectures and lecturers by different people had left her quite confused and giddy.

> Aren't you glad you have a voice and don't mumble into your chin and make

[50]Report of the Summer Meeting 1903, Bodleian Library, DES/M/3/3/10.
[51]Mrs Royden to Evelyn (31 August 1903), Fawcett 222.

jokes into your waistcoat like Mr Smith, who exasperated his audience at the back to frenzy? Why did he look like a 'deserted fisherman' and why did you look like an 'inspired Sybil' and why does appearance matter so much anyway?[52]

She had begun her letter by saying, 'The Man tells me you are coming home this week. I'm so glad, for there isn't a day when I do not sadly want you.'

Maude now saw that she had become indispensable to both the Shaws. 'I have to be a help . . . to these two,' she told Kathleen, at the end of a sad account of gloom and depression in South Luffenham that autumn.[53] She had become familiar with Shaw's tendency to get 'perfectly dispairing about nothing at all'. It was part of his nature, 'and you *can't* help him'. The next year, indeed, his depressive illness was to overwhelm him completely for a time; and domestic worry was intensified by his elder son, Arnold's leaving Oxford abruptly and taking himself off to America. A feeling too, that, whatever he did, he was making no headway in the parish, sometimes seemed insupportable to Shaw. As at Horsham, he would turn his thoughts to striking forms of Christian example, such as going to live in a cottage. Maude, who thought that a better idea would be to share the rectory with the parish, making it into a sort of club, was nonetheless ready to try the cottage, or any measure likely to dent 'the apparent indifference with which this village regards the wild banging of my head, and Mr Shaw's against a stone wall.' She felt 'battered and bruised' by the struggle against apathy. 'Dear, it isn't fair to tell you this,' she wrote in the autumn of 1903, 'but truly I can't bear myself any longer; and can't give way either, because Effie and Mr Shaw are more bruised than I am.' But that she must stand by them she did not doubt. 'With the exception of yourself and Evelyn, I have not two such friends in the world.'[54]

South Luffenham had become her base; and the programme of parish and Extension work that Shaw had sketched for her was now a reality with the Delegates' offer of a lectureship. This, though a triumph in its way, (only four of the twelve who were 'tried' received such offers unconditionally) did not guarantee employment, for that depended on invitations from the local centres. According to Shaw, she swept the country. He recalled 'extraordinary and unbroken success, North or South, East or West . . . with cultivated women or . . . artisans . . . more invitations than she could accept.'[55] This, however, was written many years on. Maude was undoubtedly a great success but not in the whirlwind fashion he suggests. It took time to build a reputation, that was one of the problems of the work. And she was a woman. They knew very well the kind of difficulty that would

[52] Effie to Maude (25 August, no year, but evidently 1903).
[53] Maude to KC (30 Nov. 1903).
[54] ibid. (29 June 1903).
[55] Shaw, 'Maude Royden, 1901–1921'.

bring. 'But for the solitary impediment of sex,' Shaw told the Delegates in his report after a course they shared at the beginning, he prophesied for her a brilliant future.

> From every point of view, scholarship, delivery, *interest and stimulus*, arrangement, conduct of class, Miss Royden's lecturing seems to me *remarkable*. I doubt exceedingly whether there are more than two or three men on our staff who can do better work than this apprentice in Class B.[56]

Extension was a buyers' market, however. Ultimately, it was not what he thought but what the local secretaries thought that counted, and here the picture is not very clear. One of the local reports suggests that numbers on Maude's course were reduced by 'strong prejudice against a woman lecturer'.[57] But in another, the novel experience becomes a matter for congratulation, moving the local secretary to boast, 'we think we have every cause for satisfaction at having (for the first time since our commencement) invited a Lady Lecturer!' Generally, comments are confined to the course. 'Do you think,' Maude had once asked Kathleen, 'I may be able to make any human being care for Shakespeare who didn't care before?' And here, in answer, are notes of the enjoyment and the commitment and interest aroused by 'Selected Plays of Shakespeare', or 'Shakespeare's Women'. 'Miss Royden is a brilliant lecturer and soon got in touch with her audience,' writes one. Another calls her 'a most attractive lecturer'; and that, in the context, suggests more than looks. For though, as her mother said and Maude understood, appearance was by no means to be despised (and she had at this stage a dark kind of beauty, and all through life very beautiful eyes), 'attraction' in her case was also the influence which she was able to exert upon others. She drew them. The French professor who listened to Shaw, and noted how closely he held his audience would certainly have made some comment on this; and on other resemblances, perhaps: her pleasure in give-and-take with the audience; her respect for opinion; her passion for her theme. That was exactly Shaw's style, too; the high style of the Extension lecturer – taking manna to the wilderness.

With it went their sense of the special value of the response of working-class students, their eagerness to match the efforts of those who were starting from a lower base. Shaw always brightened at the thought of Oldham and his class of 1,000 working men and women. In 1905, when he spoke, with Maude, to an audience of 700 at Crompton, he was in great spirits, she said, 'and thinks it will be another Oldham. The audience was mostly men and quite "artizan"'.[58] She herself was particularly conscious,

---

[56]Oxford University Extension Delegacy, Lecturers' and Examiners' Reports, 1903–4, Bodleian Library, DES/R/3.
[57]For this and further comments, see ibid. Examination Reports, DES/R/3/32–39.
[58]Maude to KC (2 Oct. 1905).

when she taught at Bury, of the difficulties faced by inarticulate students in writing essays. There was 'more thought and more knowledge behind the sometimes halting phrases than the writer had been able to set down on paper,' she told the Delegates. Students like that could not do themselves justice in an examination, but 'the real spirit of the student is in them, and . . . real love and understanding of our greatest poet.' 'Your help has been given to those you wished to reach.'[59] Shaw might have said it. For both of them, this was the meaning of Extension work.

When she came to write *A Threefold Cord* Maude gave 1905 as the year that she understood she was in love with Shaw. This understanding was thrust upon her by an older woman who was staying at the rectory; not by Evelyn or Kathleen, it seems. And if, as she reports, she was quite incredulous, no doubt they were incredulous too, because of the immense psychological barriers standing between them and such a possibility. They did not look upon Shaw as an equal; not only because he was so much older, but because of his prestige in the world of Extension, a world with which they were all involved. He was 'the Prophet'. He was also married, which meant that the question of love could not arise. They were all three rather innocent and serious. As Kathleen recalled of their Oxford days, there was 'very little talk of sex'. There is even less in the letters. When Evelyn refers to Maude's 'sensuous' nature, she adds, in brackets, 'I mean it in the good sense.'[60] If Maude talks of flirting, it is only, after all, with Colonel Gunter and an elderly friend − not the sort of thing which is going to find issue in one of those notes which some of her contemporaries write to Miss Wordsworth, announcing their engagement, with proud details of the man in the case: a barrister, a doctor, a master at Eton, a clergyman, a master of the Wharfedale Otter Hounds, an administrator, an Australian, even. One of Maude's year is marrying a captain, 9th Hobson's Horse, and will live in Lahore. Another old student is bound for India as wife to a partner in a firm in Calcutta. All declare themselves radiantly happy. 'I am the happiest person alive.' 'I never dreamed I could be quite *quite* so.' 'I am just absolutely happy'. Everyone knows that in Miss Wordsworth's opinion, this is the crown of a woman's life. 'You will be glad . . . I am engaged,' writes one, 'for you always did approve of that course of action!'[61]

Marriage, when it figures in Maude's leters at all, is mainly the occasion for a bridemaid's dress; in Evelyn's, the spur to rather nervous reflection. At the end of her sister's wedding day Evelyn stands amid the rose petals, struck quite suddenly by her loss.

So strange to think a year ago this week they had never seen each other, and now he has taken her right away. Oh, Kathleen, the sight of her room a few hours after

[59]Bodleian Library, DES/R/3/38.
[60]Evelyn to KC (2 Oct. 1901).
[61]'Letters to Elizabeth Wordsworth from Old Students', LMH.

the wedding – her white silk stockings on the floor as she got out of them – her
dress, her veil, all slipped like a shell, and she gone – right away – for it never will
be the same again in spite of the often times she has told me it will, and it is right
that it should be so.'

'Right', perhaps, but she has reservations.

A palmist has just told me I shall marry before 30, which has put me in a perfect
panic! Fancy only 3 more years of freedom . . . fancy not wanting to be free. I do
desperately at present, it's all owing to my sister's marriage. I went to see them
for the afternoon and he hardly lets her feed herself![62]

Later she writes to Kathleen of a friend whose 'inability to merge her
identity in that of a man . . . has kept her a spinster, and I honour her for it.'
Women who treat men as superior beings invite her scorn (her landlady, for
instance, whose son rules the household for no other reason than that 'he is
of the opposite sex!'). Kathleen agrees. And Maude is derisive about the
prestige which the bare fact of marriage automatically confers on a woman.
'Any *thing* that happens to get married is instantly placed on a lofty pedestal.
Why? And how silly it all is!' (But, illogically, she got some pleasure from
discovering in 1905 when her father was made a baronet, that this gave her
'precedence' over most married women.)

'I don't think we three shall ever have husbands,' Evelyn said. And with
such good friends, were they necessary? she wondered. 'I have never yet felt
the need of one!'[63] In Maude's case, no special argument was called for. Her
self-image was so damaged by her lameness that she was convinced she
would not marry. And since (whatever Evelyn may have thought) she was
sensuous in the 'bad' sense as well as in the 'good', it cannot have been easy
to come to terms with. But she insists that this was her view; and also that it
gave her a sense of immunity, in regard to men, which had made it quite
easy to go to Shaw at South Luffenham.[64] Outwardly, she carried her
lameness well. It was not always immediately obvious, even to doctors; or
not, at least, to the celebrated Mrs Scharlieb, whom she consulted in 1906
on matters relating to her general health.

She was so petrified with astonishment to think that a person with congenital
dislocation of both hips could walk across a room and sit down without her . . .
noticing . . . that I was quite sorry I ever told her . . . . All the same, girls, I shall
get quite stuck-up about my walk, so there![65]

Inwardly, so deep went her sense of defect that nothing ever meant more to

[62]Evelyn to KC (5 July, 24 Aug. 1902).
[63]Evelyn to KC (14 Nov. 1905).
[64]TFC 13–14.
[65]Maude to KC (29 July 1906). Mary Scharlieb was one of the first two women medical
graduates of London University and the first woman to become a consultant at a general
teaching hospital (the Royal Free).

her in love than that Hudson could love her lameness. '"I want you to be cured . . . but, for myself, I should miss it." Could anything more sweet and consoling be said by one human being to another?' wrote Maude.[66]

In the early months, though, of 1905 Maude still seems to inhabit a country where love and friendship are not distinct. 'Oh beloved, rejoice with me!' she writes from South Luffenham to the others with a plan to visit them in Oxford, 'I am so fearfully happy here, but I want you, dears, so badly, and don't ever seem to have had as much as I am hungry for!' She hopes to get the Shaws to come to Oxford too, 'as the Man must in any case (to get himself clothes) and I want Effie to . . . hear Bradley lecture and then I could see more of you, *darlings*, than one night.'[67]

Into this paradise where friends meet friends, comes the serpent with her startling suggestion that Maude is actually *in love* with Shaw. From one point of view – indeed, almost anyone's – what could be more likely? But they think it absurd. Both of them.

'She thinks I'm in love with you,' I roared. And he roared too, for Hudson also a little resembled the china-shop bull. . . .We didn't even trouble to assure each other that we were not in love: the idea still seemed preposterous. We didn't think of it. It could not be.[68]

It is not hard to imagine Shaw with a sense of outrage equal to her own, for he too had the simplicity of those who fix their gaze on the high ground. They were both impulsive, but he the more so – uncalculating to the point of folly. 'Give me leave to be reckless tonight,' he once preached at a Summer Meeting. 'Life is passing. I want to know the truth. Consequences must take care of themselves.' In a just cause, no kind of self-interest ever stopped him going out on a limb, whether that meant 'socialist' preaching in Horsham, or choosing to live in a labourer's cottage or offering to resign to get Maude a trial lecture. To those who loved him, his impetuosity was both exasperating and endearing. Effie comments, 'It's so like the Man to buy a £285 organ and lose it!' It was so like him, too, to invite a young woman whose spirituality and fire he was drawn to, to live at South Luffenham; himself assuming the role of confessor – Pygmalion, even (for Maude said, rightly, that he made her a speaker) – and to suppose it would mean nothing more; or rather, not to put his mind to such things. And when she had set the whole village alight, and Effie too, and they had joked, as they did, about whether she was Mr Shaw's Miss Royden or he Miss Royden's Mr Shaw, it was so like him, and Maude as well, to be furious at being told they were in love. 'We didn't think of it. . . .That was enough.'[69] But it was a mess, in reality.

[66] TFC 13
[67] Maude to KC (18 May 1905).
[68] TFC 24.
[69] TFC 30.

Shaw's tendency to get into difficulties had often been matched by his luck in getting out of them. 'I am in the devil's own mess just now,' he had written from Horsham, twenty years back – and Sadler had offered him Extension teaching. Earlier, he had been raised from despair by the intervention of the benefactor. Later, when he turned down a wealthy living, Balliol had found him a fellowship. On several occasions, the Oxford Delegates subsidised him through bouts of illness. It was as if, when he needed help, his abilities and largeness of spirit secured it. But some situations cannot be helped. Who could step in and remedy his marriage – a marriage which, it seems all too likely, he had contracted impetuously, even quixotically, and which had proved disastrous? By his lights there was no way out. 'I was dead with failure, torture, solitariness, sick of life at forty-five,' he wrote later.[70] He had adapted, after a fashion; subduing his own strong sexuality and living, emotionally, through his faith, and through his commitment to Extension work. The two were not so different, for Extension, to him, was 'in a most real sense religious'. By such means he sustained an equilibrium.

That it was now shattered, they could hardly doubt. Maude describes in *A Threefold Cord* how it proved impossible, whatever they might wish, to put the genie back into the bottle. The earlier relaxed and happy atmosphere had gone. They could not behave as they had done before. Their nerves were on edge. They snapped at each other; yet still, it seems, shutting their eyes to the cause. It was Effie in the end who made them face it. Effie's role, as much as her own and Shaw's, is what Maude writes about. And no wonder; for her reaction was crucial to them all. At this juncture, quite untypically, Effie became the benefactor. Maude describes finding Effie in tears after one of the flare-ups with Shaw. Apparently, she had grasped the situation and wept, not from jealousy or shock or rage, but because she thought that the two of them were spoiling 'one of the loveliest things in the world'. 'I marvel as I write it. Will anyone believe that she was never jealous of our love?' asks Maude, forty years on, addressing the reader on what still seems remarkable to her, and paying very much less attention to what some readers found more remarkable: that the relationship of Hudson and Maude, thus acknowledged and blessed by Effie, should have been both passionate and platonic. 'She did not wish her husband and her friend to transgress their moral standard or hers: she did want us to have all that was possible for us – not love only, but passionate love.'[71]

It was an extraordinary intervention by the woman Sadler had once marked down as a spectator in her own house – the silent third at South

---

[70]TFC 26.

[71]TFC 26–7. 'What seems to me really inexplicable is the assumption that . . . Hudson and I . . . could have had an illicit love and continued with the work that we were doing. . . . We were not only committed to a Christian way of life but we took it upon ourselves to teach others.' TFC 121.

Luffenham, delighting in the quickfire of the other two much as an audience delights in a play! In a sense, they had provided a play; one which brought her close to life, but not too close. Perhaps she could not bear that it should ever end. Or perhaps her feeling when she saw what had happened was mainly of relief; of a dispensation; or gladness, as Maude said, 'that Hudson should have something at least of what he needed'.[72] And Maude too. And herself. For Effie's own life had been transformed by Maude's coming. 'My dearest, my dearest,' she writes, like a lover, in 1904 for Maude's twenty-eighth birthday, 'how does it feel to be so dreadfully old?'

> All my thoughts will go to you tomorrow, loving and blessing you. . . . What can I do but pray that you may be brave and strong and happy, and you are all of these already. Dear, I shall just ask for you to stay always always just what you are now. May I? Why, we have loved each other two years now haven't we? And you have made everything sweeter and easier and lovelier all the time and have given the poor Man new hope and inspiration and have made us all so happy by just being what you are. . . . Can you wonder that I am a little selfish sometimes?
>
> I wish I could have *my* time over again and begin afresh to make fewer mistakes and never to hurt you again. But I do thank you all I can and love you with my soul. Put your arms round me and hold me close.[73]

The outward pattern of their lives was not changed. Shaw had his usual heavy load of lecturing. And not only that. He was deeply involved at this time in Extension politics, leading the move to set up a council of the Oxford lecturers and force the Delegates to change the system of insecure, badly-paid, piece-work employment. Maude was trying to get a foothold in Extension. Her health in the summer of 1905 does not seem to have been too good. 'My face is covered with spots and specks, and my hair stands stiffly away from all the bald corners,' she wrote to Kathleen. 'Do you wonder that I feel inclined to go into a sisterhood?'[74] Because she found it so exhausting to travel to Extension centres from South Luffenham she and Hudson and Effie agreed she ought to look for a more central base. She moved to rooms in Oxford that autumn, joining Evelyn and other friends. But she was often back with the Shaws.

'From the beginning there were three of us. That made possible everything that was impossible.'[75] Years earlier, when someone had scoffed at her 'three-concerned arrangement' with Evelyn and Kathleen, Maude wrote, 'I suppose it does sound "three-cornered" to the laity. But the expression sounds comic to us, doesn't it?' She did not think in terms of corners. 'A threefold cord is not quickly broken.'[76] She had already some experience of

---

[72]TFC 27.
[73]Effie to Maude (n.d. but evidently November 1904).
[74]Maude to KC (17 July 1905).
[75]TFC 28.
[76]This quotation, from *Ecclesiastes* 4.12, appears below the title of *A Threefold Cord*.

that, though possibly, at first, between two such relationships, there were some adjustments to make. She wrote to Kathleen in 1906:

> I am so afraid you will think I am feeling lonely, if I let you see how much I want Mr Shaw sometimes. You see, Beloved, I do want him – often – but hunger is not the same as loneliness, and I think I was vaguely afraid you might feel that they were. Now it is utterly impossible for me to feel *lonely* when I am with you; *utterly*. When I am with the Shaws, I often want you; and when I am with you, I often want them. That must be, with everyone who has more than a single friend, I suppose. . . .But I am never *lonely*, when I am with Mr Shaw; and the very *possibility* of loneliness seems even more remote when I am with you. It is a question of understanding, as well as of love.

'You know I love Effie very dearly' she went on, 'more than I can put into words. But she is not, and cannot be, to me what you and Evelyn are.'

> With Mr Shaw it is different. But I can't put it into words either, without seeming to make distinctions, and speak of less and more, where there is no less or more. Only there is always a difference in the love of men and women, I think. In some ways it is nearer; in others so much further off.[77]

Shaw gave her Dante's *Vita Nuova*; in that, perhaps, reflecting the difference in their years. For whatever insights she came to later, she had not then lived long enough to need a new life, in the sense that he did. Her painful uncertainty was not the same as his painful defeat. When Maude said, 'I do feel in my *bones* . . .' what she felt was the rise of her abilities. 'I do feel in my *bones* as if I *could* lecture.' In his bones he felt nothing new. Consciously or not, she was working towards the time 'when I may have something to say that is worth saying', ('if the time should ever come – and I mean it to').[78] For Shaw, the time had come, but some of his sermons read like a passionate cry, 'To what end!'

> Civilisation! We are not civilised. There is no such thing known yet on the earth. What we have is Industrial Chaos, based on egoism and strife and greed. . . . It is no use hiding the fact. The rich and comfortable fill our churches: the masses are outside. The main cause of their alienation is the monstrous contradiction between Christian ethics and the state of society which Christians tolerate.[79]

And so from public to private failure. 'I believe I have not emphasised enough,' wrote Maude, 'the wound made in his heart by the failure of his married life in what he regarded as its holiest aspect.' Shaw had his own lameness, though it was not visible: the sense that he could not inspire in a woman desire for the physical expression of love.

---

[77]Maude to KC (23 July 1906).
[78]ibid. (2 Nov. 1900).
[79]*Christianity and Riches: A Sermon preached . . . on Sunday, August 4th, 1907 before the Summer Meeting . . . by the Rev. W. Hudson Shaw, MA.*

When Effie asked him to give me something more than friendship, she understood, perhaps without knowing it, his deepest need: she gave him the knowledge that he was one who could be passionately loved.

And this, Maude says, he needed still more than the fulfilment he could not have. They did not even dare to think about *that*. Only Effie was insouciant enough to imagine they might ever be able to marry. 'She made Hudson promise that, if she died, he would marry me "at once", without waiting, "not troubling about what people said of us."' But they knew they could not indulge such thoughts. 'We must be always three. This was our safety.'[80]

So the Vita Nuova was not reflected in any dramatic outward change. To most people, Maude's new life, at this time, was her involvement in women's suffrage.

[80]TFC 28, 29.

5

The Common Cause of Humanity

Ours is not a warfare against men, but against evil; a war in which women and men fight together, side by side, in 'the Common Cause of Humanity'.

Common Cause, (14 November 1913).

There can be no doubt that it was women's suffrage which brought Maude into the mainstream of affairs and very soon made her a public figure. If her private life seems to fade in consequence, that is not because it ceased to exist. Though she moved to Oxford in 1905 to ease the burden of Extension travelling, she was constantly visiting the Shaws, and volunteered the next year to look after Effie while Shaw lectured again in America. But there are now few letters of the kind that give such glimpses of her younger days. None of the hundreds that she and Hudson wrote to each other survive, for instance; and for lack of such personal sources we face what seems like an abrupt transition from the still diffident lecturer-apprentice trying to work up an Extension round, to one of the most compelling speakers in the country. Suffrage transformed her and no later fame ever blunted Maude's sense of good fortune in having been involved in 'the cause' in her prime. With all her tendency to agonise and doubt, the years from 1905 to World War I, her suffrage years, were years of certainty.

We can see now that the suffrage struggle involved a great deal more than the vote: that indeed, in the words of one of its protagonists, 'the movement was not primarily political; it was social, moral, psychological and profoundly religious'.[1] There were, no doubt, women who felt they should vote only because their gardeners could. But the ideal implicit in 'the cause', to militants and nonmilitants alike, was what they hoped the vote would achieve: better conditions for working women, protection for children and – underlying all – an elevated sexual morality replacing the notorious 'double standard' which society adopted towards men and women. Such great hopes were enhanced by a sense that the women's movement was

[1] Helena Swanwick, quoted Susan Kingskey Kent, *Sex and Suffrage in Britain 1860–1914* (1987) 3.

international. Maude and Kathleen were both elated by the experience of attending, in 1913, the congress in Budapest of the International Women's Suffrage Alliance. It was a wonder, Maude wrote afterwards, that women from countries so painfully divided should have come together, united in the fight to sustain peace and combat such evils as prostitution and child neglect. 'Women will be moved by . . . hope of moral reforms or they will not be moved at all.' At about this time, she told a different audience that, in her view, the women's movement was 'the most profoundly moral movement . . . since the foundation of the Christian Church'.[2]

Why, then, was she nearly thirty before becoming actively involved in suffrage? After Oxford, Eleanor Rathbone took a lead in the Liverpool Women's Suffrage Society while Maude seems to have done nothing more than attend the occasional Zenana meeting. Politically she was immature. In any case the suffrage movement was in the doldrums at the turn of the century. Nearly forty years of steady campaigning and countless parliamentary bills had led nowhere. The Pankhursts had yet to sound their clarion call. Suffrage had grown stale, and was crowded out of the public mind by the South African war. And even that, Maude admitted later, 'never . . . touched my intelligence. I heard of strange creatures called "pro-Boers" but I didn't really believe in them.'[3]

What she believed in, in 1900, were her improvident Liverpool women. It was they who started her suffrage education. For, after all, from Netherfield Road, 'the position of women' was all too clear. Very often they housekept in cellars; some drank heavily ('I would drink, if I lived in Lancaster Street!'); some were beaten up by their husbands; some almost crushed in the deathly struggle to support a family on their own. The sense of outrage it inspired in Maude ran through much of what she argued later in the suffragist journal, the Common Cause, and on suffrage platforms. But at the time, her letters, as we know, were full of Miss Dolphin; the front of her mind was taken up with that, and with Rome, and then of course with Shaw. She thought herself a suffragist at South Luffenham. 'I don't believe I shall ever learn not to "rise" to an attack on my sex!'[4] But her real apprenticeship dates from the move back to Oxford in 1905 – the year that suffrage became hot news again when Christabel Pankhurst and Annie Kenney got themselves arrested in Manchester.

The Oxford ambience was certainly propitious. Evelyn's interest in women's suffrage was well-developed before Maude came. In January 1905 she wrote to Kathleen that she meant to go to a suffrage meeting and hoped no one would screech, 'for if they do, it will put up the backs of every

---

[2]Jus Suffragii (15 July 1913) 6; The Religious Aspect of the Women's Movement: Being a series of Addresses delivered at Meetings held at the Queen's Hall, London, on June 19, 1912 (published by the Collegium 1912) 44.
[3]Oxford (ed.), Myself When Young, 375.
[4]Maude to KC (n.d., evidently 1902).

woman there against it, and I believe awfully few women want it.' This sad
conclusion seems to have emerged from research among her own acquaintance. 'I have talked with several people lately about it, and they have all
been against it, but I have not yet heard a single good argument on their
side, most of them being really contemptible.' Miss Bridges, full of interest
in politics, 'has a low opinion of her sex (most anomalous) and "does *not*
want the world to be governed by women"'.

> Here I gently intimate that so it might, if all women would vote one way – but
> they wouldn't – which stumps her for a few moments. But she ends up every
> discussion with – *No*, I do not want women to have it all their own way!! . . .
> Well, I go to Mrs Wells, and to my surprise and pain find her undesirous of the
> Suffrage. Her reason? Because she has a husband!

He is strongly protectionist; she, free trade 'and yet is content for him to
represent her!'

> But she thinks her Mother, a widow, certainly ought to have a vote!! though she
> is not able to take any steps about it, such as going to a meeting, as she "has an
> instinctive dislike to it". Kathleen, I do like Mrs Wells, and think she is just the
> sort of woman who ought to have a vote and it pains me to find this attitude in
> her. It is a vast relief to come straight back and pour it out to you.

Meanwhile, all one could do was to work upon people, Evelyn decided; to
make them think about it. 'For most women never give it a thought.'[5]
   According to Maude's later recollection, she herself began to give it a
thought when the implications of the double standard of sexual morality
came home to her. She was far from unique in this, Helena Swanwick, a
colleague of hers later, remembered the resentment she felt as a girl when
she was not allowed out after dark for fear she might be 'insulted' by men.
Society's solution – 'to shut up the girls instead of the men' – made her boil
with rage. For Maude, a similar trauma was inflicted through the behaviour
of people she knew. It seems that some young man of her acquaintance
turned out to have been seducing girls, and people consoled his parents with
the thought such behaviour was natural to young men and should not be
taken too seriously. A different judgement was made of the girls. How
could this be assimilated? In her search for some sort of context Maude
turned to Lecky's *History of European Morals* where she came on 'that
magnificent and ghastly passage' in which the author accepts prostitution as
the cornerstone of domestic purity. Many times later she recalled her
dismay. That 'a good man, an honest man, even a religious man' such as
Lecky could accept the degradation of some women to preserve the 'virtue'
of others, shocked her deeply. From that moment the suffrage fight became
for her too a passionate revolt against the double moral standard conventional in a 'Christian' society and she was eager to pick up the torch which

[5]Evelyn to KC (21 Jan. 1905).

had first been lit by Josephine Butler in her long Victorian campaign against the Contagious Diseases Acts.[6]

On a more pragmatic level, in 1905, Maude was forced to give thought to an aspect of the position of women which perhaps had not struck her before. The Oxford University Extension Delegates were sufficiently pleased with her performance as a lecturer to wish to put her on a higher grade. The offer was to be made, however, 'with a strong recommendation that it should not be accepted'; and the secretary, Marriot, had the awkward job of writing to her in this sense. There would, he said, be 'a serious risk' in advising her to accept the promotion; meaning that, given the general reluctance of local centres to take a woman, if she were entitled to a higher fee she might well price herself out of a job.

> I think you know how exceedingly anxious I am to obtain employment for women lecturers . . . but do what I will, I seem quite unable to overcome the prejudice which exists in the vast majority of Extension Centres against the engagement of Women Lecturers. I am afraid it is true that *ceteris paribus* there is hardly a centre which would accept a woman in preference to a man.[7]

Years later, when Eleanor Rathbone made a case against equal pay on the grounds that it would mean the ousting of women from many jobs where they earned tolerably well, Maude took her stand on the dishonesty implied in paying for something, not according to its worth, but according to the necessity of the seller. 'I do not believe that either men or women want artificial protection from each other. . . . Would Miss Rathbone, I wonder, have commended me if, in my position as University Extension lecturer, I had taken lower pay than a man in order to get more work?'[8] She had, of course, taken the 'serious risk' Marriott spoke so gravely about, and in the event it had not proved serious. Centres still asked for 'Shakespeare's Women'. 'I feel fairly happy about my work,' she told Kathleen in the summer of 1906, planning a holiday with Ida O'Malley (a friend of LMH days who was active in suffrage) and working up a new lecture on Dante (which Shaw pronounced to be 'much too stiff'). She was less happy about her health, which seemed no better. Alarmed by now at the thought of the coming winter session, she went to see the formidable Mrs Scharlieb – who decided that the trouble was teeth, and sent her off to have four extractions. ('So now I shall be a horrible person with teeth in a tumbler – Oh girls!') After this, though, the headaches went, and she spent the rest of the summer at South Luffenham.

---

[6]'Speech by Miss ROYDEN at the Albert Hall Demonstration, Feb. 14th, 1914', 7–8 (NUWSS pamphlet); also 'Bid Me discourse,' Fawcett 224.
[7]J. A. C. Marriott to Maude Royden (6 Nov. 1905), Secretary's Letter Books, Oxford University Extension Delegacy.
[8]Maude Royden, 'The Economic Position of Married Women', *Common Cause* (henceforth' CC) (11 Jan. 1912) 689.

At the time of anxiety about Maude's health, Kathleen seems to have renewed the offer which she first made when they had just left Oxford – that they should set up house together. Maude again refused; and for the same reason.

> Beloved – I can't thank you – yet I should like to try! Do you know, dear Heart, I am so much *more* touched by your feeling about me, that I know you . . . are ambitious yourself. I wish there were a *good* word for ambition . . . I mean that I always feel you ought to be leading, and have the capacity for it, and therefore must *need* to do it, as one does *need* to exercise a gift. And I am longing to see you doing something . . . that influences people and *lots* of people.

Probably, said Maude, she saw Kathleen as a speaker because speaking was what she was trying to do herself. 'I can't help feeling that anyone who *thinks* so clearly must make a *good* speaker.'

> You *ought not* to spend time waiting on me. I think your reasons for wishing to do so – well, I can't tell you what I think of them. . . .It is the most *utterly* unselfish wish, but I think . . . it would be wrong for you to make even a part of your life mine, in a sense which really means that what you would do independently is of less importance than what I would do.

'I wouldn't think it wrong in some cases,' she added, 'honestly I wouldn't. But in yours – yes I do.'[9]

This sort of interchange belongs, in essence, to that youthful, unresolved period of life which they were in process of leaving behind. They were both moving to more exigent times, when the chance of meeting, and the manner of it – whether for a few days' holiday together or on platforms, committees and deputations – would depend on factors outside their control. Unlike Evelyn, both Maude and Kathleen had sufficient family means to be able to throw themselves into suffrage without having to worry about earning a living. In 1908, Kathleen left Oxford for Manchester to become secretary to the North of England Society for Women's Suffrage. Maude for a time continued in Oxford, combining Extension and suffrage work, but increasingly committed to the women's cause, which seemed to her now to be borne along by 'the developing spirit of the age'.

'This is a time of awakening,' she wrote, in October 1908, 'a time of hope, a time when great causes shall be brought to great issues,'[10] Public interest in women's suffrage had certainly been revived by the tactics of those who were now labelled 'suffragettes' – the Women's Social and Political Union, launched by Mrs Pankhurst a few years back. Though from the first a militant body, 'a suffrage army in the field', as she said, it was not at first violent; and the courage of those who endured rough handling and harsh prison treatment for suffrage disturbances roused the

[9]Maude to KC (2 Aug. 1906).
[10]*The Highway*, (Oct. 1908) 4.

admiration of many more decorous or diffident women. The time came, later, when suffragette violence was regarded by the law-abiding body – the National Union of Women's Suffrage Societies – as almost as great an impediment to progress as Mr Asquith. At the start, however, even the National Union's leader, Mrs Fawcett, allowed that the militants had sparked imagination and given new impetus to the cause for which so many had worked for so long.

The General Election of 1905 provided additional grounds for hope since Labour for the first time managed to achieve a sizeable phalanx in the House of Commons. In view of its commitment to political equality the emergence of Labour as a viable party was welcomed by suffragists, except for those who did not want to be swept into the franchise on the back of some huge democratic tide. A rather different fear was that the tide would sweep in but that women would not be swept in with it. Radical socialists dismissed women's suffrage as essentially a middle-class question. Adult suffrage was their priority and some would certainly have accepted a measure which was limited to adult *men*. To her disappointment, Maude discovered that most of the students she encountered who belonged to that new and dynamic body, the Workers' Educational Association, were committed to the adult vote. 'Naturally, we felt that Women's Suffrage must be a burning question to such an association. To be quite frank, it is not,' she admitted, after the Summer School of 1909.[11] All the same, it was the WEA which seemed to be infusing new life these days into the old Extension system, and Maude was certainly impressed by its faith in 'the education of the democracy' – without any distinction of sex. 'They don't do enough, of course; nobody does enough; but they do put women on equal terms with men.'

In fact, it was the WEA journal, *The Highway,* in its early issues, which first gave her scope for what would now be called consciousness-raising. 'Sisters!' she began, in October 1908, in an article enlarging on the value to the nation of women's 'capacity of intense feeling' – so often dismissed as emotionalism. 'What does the accusation mean? Does it mean that we feel too much? We cannot feel too much! It is because we feel too little that progress is so slow!' But they must have education. Without it 'this magnificent capacity for *caring* – of which let no woman ever be ashamed – becomes a danger and a menace.' Women must therefore take full advantage of the new scheme for tutorial classes now devised by the WEA in conjunction with Oxford University. This was their chance as well as the men's. But, given generations of restriction and shyness, women must be specially encouraged to take part. 'It is no use just *letting* us come!' In another article she introduced them to Fletcher's sequel to *The Taming of the Shrew* where Petrucchio is outclassed by his second wife, Maria, who stands

[11]CC (12 Aug. 1909) 229.

'not only for herself, but for her cause'.[12]

Yet even Maria encounters women with a deficient sense of sisterhood, and Maude was conscious of writing at a time when, if not on education then on other great issues, women were bitterly at odds with one another. July 1908 saw the inauguration of the Women's National Anti-Suffrage League, its members warmly exhorted by the *Times* to fight the suffragists with their own weapons of agitation and argument. Suffragists themselves stood sharply divided now that the militant WSPU had a last turned to violent action. In June 1908 the first stones were thrown through the windows of Downing Street. Hunger striking and forcible feeding were to follow in the coming year. The National Union was faced with a need to distance itself from militancy; to define, and keep on defining, its position as a democratic federation of suffrage societies, opposed to violence. In 1909 it launched its own weekly, with a title – *Common Cause* – chosen by the editor, Helena Swanwick, to show that the women's cause was also the men's.[13] Later, when Maude took on the editorship, the front page heading ran WOMEN'S SUFFRAGE: THE COMMON CAUSE OF HUMANITY. But at first humanity was just implied.

What did it mean, though? The concept of 'humanity' must have been among the most overworked and least-defined in these suffrage years. Everyone claimed it. 'Goodbye, dear Kathleen of Lady Margaret Hall and welcome dear Kathleen of the world in general and humanity in particular!' Maude had written in their salad days – not needing then to be more precise about their plans to do good in the world. And many such broad allusions to humanity were to appear in suffrage speeches. The link between suffrage and social reform was often made in the *Common Cause*, which monitored the progress of social legislation where women were already enfranchised – in New Zealand and some parts of the USA. If the vote was a sword to protect the oppressed, every hour's delay was being paid for in suffering. 'If we believe what we say on a thousand platforms . . . how can we think "there is no need for depression" at the thought that our enfranchisement may be again delayed?' Maude demanded in December 1910. '*Now* – at this hour – women are being sweated in Government employ; girls are being entrapped into a life of vice; wives and mothers are suffering under our iniquitous sex laws. Every day sees fresh victims.'[14]

She spoke of depression, though, without being depressed. Temperamentally, it was not in her, especially in youth, to be truly depressed – that is, despairing – about humanity. Reviewing Masterman's *Condition of England* in 1909 for the *Common Cause*, she challenged his pessimism, not his facts.

[12]*The Highway*, (Oct. 1908) 4–5; (Dec. 1908) 46–7; (Jan. 1909) 61–2; (April 1909) 100–1; (May 1909) 116–18.
[13]H. M. Swanwick, *I Have Been Young* (1935) 207.
[14]CC (15 Dec. 1910) 598–9.

There is only one remedy we can even think of – the spirit of self-devotion, faith and hope. And this spirit we have. It is abroad. The tide of materialism has rolled back. Great causes are stirring our hearts and in great causes it has become possible to believe.

'Humanity' then was the inscription on the banner, and 'human being' the badge of pride. Mary Wollstonecraft's passionate demand that a woman be considered a human being remained the very essence, Maude declared, 'of what is misleadingly called "feminism"'.[15]

H. G. Wells' failure to comprehend this was her main point when she reviewed *Ann Veronica*. Ready to concede his brilliance and wit, she went on to be very scathing about 'that essentially masculine conception, Ann Veronica herself'. The rebellious schoolgirl breaking out for liberty was presented simply as breaking out for love. A travesty, said Maude, of the women's struggle. Let women not be presented as angels; they were animal too, and part of all that was indeed their desire to be allowed sex instincts. But it was not the whole. The whole was their wish 'to be classed – finally – with human beings'.

The critic, St John Ervine, pounced upon her. 'What exactly is it that women want?' he asked in the paper's correspondence column.

I dislike your reviewer's talk about 'being a human being'! A human being is an exceedingly offensive thing, full of loose, splodgy emotions, which drag it down from every ideal . . . and fling it prone on the very earthy earth . . . I hope to heaven women don't want to be like that!

They wanted to be free, said Maude, from serving two masters, 'the God who made us, and the man – husband, father or legislator – who wants to re-make us to a pattern of his own . . . we want freedom to develop our whole humanity.' As to the value of humanity, they differed. To him a human being was 'a rampant animal'. 'To me a human being is a potential Christ.'[16]

From 1909 the pressure of Maude's suffrage work rose steadily. 'It is not easy to keep our cause before the world,' she wrote. And this was specially true for the National Union. The sensational and heroic exploits of the militants attracted enormous attention in the Press; the nation was shocked by forcible feeding. Meanwhile, the constitutionalists pressed on; persuasive, but never persuasive enough. Maude wrote a good deal for the *Common Cause;* sometimes on aspects of suffrage politics but more often pleading for the breadth and balance and justice in society which she urged would follow from the enfranchisement of women. As things stood, 'the mother element is excluded from our legislature and our laws faithfully reflect the exclusion'. Thus, while the soldier was honoured for his service,

[15]CC (5 Aug. 1909) 216–7; (1 June 1911).
[16]CC (18 Nov. 1909) 422; (2 Dec. 1909) 454; (9 Dec. 1909) 472.

there was no recognition of the equally vital and dangerous service of childbearing. On the contrary, as she pointed out in a critique of a government report on infant mortality in 1909, the tendency was always to blame the mother for supposed neglect and inadequacy. 'To judge by this report . . . every man starts on the inquiry with the determination to find that the industrial employment of women is the largest factor in infant mortality.' Yet in some regions with high infant death rates the employment of women in industry was low. If mothers worked as washerwomen nothing was said, though it was cruelty exhausting labour.[17]

The conflict of 'male' and 'female' values was thrown into relief now by the naval arms race, for the spectacular cost of dreadnoughts threatened the government's welfare programme. 'We want Eight, and we won't wait!' was not propitious to the nurturing principle.

'Shall we ever learn that the safety of England depends on the health and strength and character of the average Englishman and Englishwoman? No sir, I think we shall not learn it, as long as by 'the people' so many mean 'the men'.'[18]

The first general election of 1910 plunged Maude into electioneering. 'Few of us go even into a by-election, for the first time, without some shrinking,' she admitted. But she found people quite ready to listen. 'Women come and listen as well as men. . . . "What quarrel have we with Germany, Miss? That's what *I* want to know!"' They were keenly aware that, as women, they had to stand by while life and death matters were decided for them. A cabinet minister might joke and say, he was afraid that when the enemy came, he would not ask whether women had votes! But 'can you protect us from bearing the consequences of what you today decide?' wrote Maude. 'If you make a mistake, will all your chivalry save us from suffering for your mistake? . . . Let us share the choice, since we must abide by it!'[19]

She was beginning to be known in the movement, and her evident skill as a speaker led to her being asked to take speakers' classes. Her own experience of suffrage platforms – at that time – was not extensive. The Albert Hall and Hyde Park came later; as did the grind of ceaseless speaking and ceaseless travelling that sometimes wore her out. However, she was able to live once more with Hudson and Effie, who had moved to Cheshire, where he became rector of Old Alderley. Most of her Extension and suffrage meetings were in the area, and in 1909 they organised a suffrage picnic together in the grounds of Alderley Rectory. He was not, she once said, 'a soundly saved feminist'. Yet he was a suffragist. She liked to recall how her

[17]CC (3 June 1909) 103; (8 Sept. 1909) 352.

[18]CC (7 April, 1910) 731. In 1909 Britain was alarmed to discover that her naval lead was threatened by Germany's progress in constructing the new super-battleship, the dreadnought. Under massive public pressure, the government stepped up its own construction. 'We want Eight' was a music hall refrain.

[19]CC (20 Jan. 1910) 556.

Plate 3 Maude in her thirties. *Reproduced by permission of Mrs Joan Batten.*

own first speech from a suffrage platform had been made standing in for him; and it was he who had recommended Kathleen for the post of organising secretary to the North of England Women's Suffrage Society. The Extension Summer Meeting in 1913 heard a very strong sermon from Hudson on 'Christianity and Womanhood', in which he wound up, 'I am sick and weary of the irrational chatter of our time concerning the inferiority of one sex to the other . . . These controversies should be relegated to Bedlam.'[20] He was also one of the small band of clergy who joined the Church League for Women's Suffrage.

The move to Old Alderley seemed to have been a good one. It was near to the industrial Extension centres. The stipend was better – which meant less pressure to take on excessive Extension work – and Shaw got backing from the patron, Lord Stanley (who as Lyulph Stanley was well known for his interest in adult education). Years later, Alderley people remembered how their new rector had arrived like a whirlwind and thrown himself into all kinds of work. His preaching filled the church every Sunday, while people listened at the windows outside. After the service he took a cab to another village (where he preached a fresh sermon) and many people followed, to hear him again.[21] It was at Alderley, in 1910, that Mrs Humphry Ward heard him preach, and felt she was listening to 'Richard Meynell'.

> An astonishing sermon, and a crowded congregation. 'I shall not in future read the Athanasian Creed, or the cursing psalms or the Ten Commandments, or the Exhortations at the beginning of the Marriage Service – and I shall take the consequences. The Baptismal Service ought to be altered – so ought the Burial Service. And how you, the laity, can tolerate us – the clergy – standing up Sunday after Sunday and saying these things to you, I cannot understand. But I for one will do it no more, happen what may.'[22]

She could hardly have guessed that 'Richard Meynell', the previous year, had suffered a serious mental breakdown.

This time, perhaps, it was something more than the result of overwork, or his bizarre domestic situation. Certainly the breakdown of 1909 followed developments which could be seen as undermining the Extension movement – or at least, as a kind of takeover by the emergent WEA. The WEA scheme for tutorial classes, which was so brilliantly promoted now by its secretary, Albert Mansbridge, met a demand from working people for a

---

[20] Reprinted, *Guildhouse Fellowship* (March 1946).

[21] Mr Whalley Jones of Alderley Edge, interviewed 29 March 1967 by Emil Oberholzer, found no praise high enough for Hudson Shaw who, he said, would have killed himself with work had he stayed at Old Alderley. As at South Luffenham, Shaw not only enlivened the parish but made many improvements to the church.

[22] J. P. Trevelyan, *Life of Mrs Humphry Ward* (1927) 258. In Hudson's own prayer book objectionable passages were struck out 'with heavy indignant pen'. TFC 117.

chance to study in depth, and for a system that was more democratic.[23] It was a breakthrough – applauded by Maude (provided women got their chance) as we know. As for Hudson, his name was great and his inspiration freely acknowledged, but his style did not really suit the new mode. WEA tutors would not be like him – charismatic, larger than life. He may have sensed Mansbridge had no place for him, or been depressed by the realisation – a dismal one, in his fiftieth year – that funds originally subscribed in Oxford to provide salaries and some security for Extension lecturers – a thing he had fought for – were going to support tutorial classes. At any rate, he became very ill.

The breakdown caused desperate concern among his friends. Michael Sadler wrote:

> For more than twenty years you have been one of the great moving forces for good in English life. More than any other man, you have made Ruskin's words . . . bear fruits . . . Let it be a comfort to you in your illness to think what a great part you have been given to play in perhaps the most far-reaching stir in political and economic thought which has been seen in England since 1848 – perhaps since the French Revolution. . . . We all think of you in your illness and are thankful for what you have given us.[24]

To help raise Shaw from his deep depression, the unknown benefactor, Bolton King, was persuaded to reveal his identity. 'I feared it might make things different between us, but now I know it won't.' As to the help which he had given, 'It was the best investment I ever made.'[25] Shaw's parishioners were desolate ('we cannot bear the thought of anybody else taking the services in Alderley Church') and one woman who was not a parishioner wrote to him now, on black-bordered paper:

> I think you understand what it is to suffer. When my dear little son died at the beginning of the year all seemed dark and hopeless there did not seem to be a ray of light anywhere and I felt dreadful almost out of my mind I think. Then I went to your church and you preached a sermon which relieved and comforted me very much for which I thank you from the bottom of my heart.[26]

And Maude? There is no record of what she felt. What she did was to take the Extension classes he was committed to that autumn, nerving herself to face the disappointment of the seventy students at the Cheadle centre and ninety at Ilkley who expected him. 'You have the time to recuperate,'

[23]For accounts of the WEA initiative (in which the prime movers, apart from Mansbridge, were R. H. Tawney and Bishop Gore) see Bernard Jennings, 'The Oxford Report Reconsidered', *Studies in Adult Education* 7 (1975); and especially Stuart Marriott, 'Oxford and Working-class Education: A Foundation Myth Re-examined', *History of Education* 12 (1983).

[24]Sadler to Shaw, (7 Oct. 1909) Fawcett 222.

[25]King to Shaw, (11 Oct. 1909) Fawcett 222. For all King said, it seems that the impression in his family is that he was disappointed in Shaw.

[26]Mabel Walker (3 Oct. 1909) Fawcett 221; Edith E. Beswick (5 Oct. 1909) Fawcett 222.

Sadler had written, hinting at a future when Shaw's influence would be 'greater than ever'. He did recuperate, as was plain from the sermon that attracted Mrs Humphry Ward. He also went back to Extension teaching. But as to influence, one might say that his star was descending as Maude's rose.

'Before long,' he recounted, later, in a loving, admiring but careless little memoir, 'she was, as it were, Mrs Fawcett's right hand.'[27] Mrs Fawcett had many right hands. In 1911, when Maude was first elected to the National Union's Executive Committee, she became one officially, in such company as Eleanor Rathbone, Dorothea Rackham, Chrystal Macmillan, Margaret Ashton, Catherine Marshall, Ida O'Malley – all more or less of her own generation – with Isabella Ford and Nellie Swanwick, who were older; and, of course, Kathleen.

Kathleen by this time really was Mrs Fawcett's right hand, having left Manchester for London to work as secretary to the National Union. The two of them, then, moved into prominence at national level at about the same time; a very disheartening time for the movement, for 1910 had seen the frustration of what had seemed a hopeful all-party attempt to shape a Conciliation Bill which would have enfranchised women householders. In response to this promising initiative, the militants had actually called a truce. However, when the government let the bill drop after a successful second reading the suffrage outlook seemed worse than ever. In the context of the frightful battle between police and militants which marked 'black Friday', and the government's own complete absorption in its battle with the House of Lords, it was easy to lose heart. The journey was so long; the goal so distant, as Maude allowed. They were called fanatics for insisting on the vote. 'Why not take a larger view?' people asked. The larger view, in fact, was what was always before her; the only one that mattered. Their goal, she wrote, in an article entitled 'A Long Journey', was no less than the right of every individual to develop 'to the full extent of God-given powers'. The vote was only one step towards this, 'but it is the step we are able to make now.' Who would refuse to begin a long journey because the first step was so far from the end? 'For all journeys, long as well as short, there is only one step of importance . . . the next.'[28]

Suffrage hopes in 1911 focussed on a new Conciliation Bill which passed its second reading with a good majority. After that, however, the government decided to postpone further action till the following year; which was how things stood when Maude set out on a speaking tour in the USA at the end of October 1911. The tour began officially in Philadelphia, but unofficially almost as soon as the *Mauretania* docked in New York. Her crowded programme (which meant, as she recalled, that 'most of the time that I was

[27]Shaw, 'Maude Royden 1901–1920'.
[28]CC (2 Feb. 1911) 696.

not on a platform I was in a train') combined suffrage engagements with lectures on Shakespeare, the Romantic poets, 'Florence and her Great Men' and other topics taken from her Extension list. The whole was arranged by Hudson's elder son, Arnold, now a young man of twenty-seven, who had left Oxford before taking his degree and gone to America where he worked for the American University Lecturers' Association. Apparently, they did not get on well.

She got on well with her audiences, however. In Philadelphia they were pleasantly surprised to find her voice 'more like that of a trained actress than of a public agitator', and her appearance, 'in direct contrast to that of the suffragette of the comic supplement'.[29] In fact, like Mrs Fawcett and every other speaker for the National Union at this time, she aimed to stress the difference between suffragettes and others. It seemed increasingly urgent to do so. How else could moderates limit the damage they felt was being done to the cause? How could they stem the moral haemorrhage? The militants, said Maude in a New York interview, by using force were 'throwing away one of the great arguments for the cause of women – that government is not based on force.'[30] That it was so based (however discreetly) was now the new weapon, the dreadnought of the 'antis' who urged that woman's physical weakness disqualified her for enfranchisement. Maude found this argument especially repellent.

> All human progress is a denial of this dishonouring belief . . . every advance of civilization – above all, every measure of enfranchisement extended to the poor and the oppressed . . . The fact that it is asserted once more . . . is a call to us to' make the denial final. We claim our freedom, we women, who are physically weak, and in claiming it we claim the spiritual heritage of mankind.[31]

Thus women's suffrage took its place as 'a great moral and human question'.

Maude's ability to lift an audience to the heights of her own intense conviction had been apparent from the time, long past, when she did her trial run for Shaw at Duffield and moved at least one of those present to tears. 'Of course,' she had said then, '*Hamlet* is unspeakably sad.' Now, other kinds of unspeakable sadness pressed upon her. There was stuff for tears in England's five million sweated women workers, the subject of her address in Philadelphia to a meeting of the Equal Suffrage League. Paid around seven and sixpence a week, many were driven to prostitution. 'What is the use of building hospitals and . . . jails . . . and tying up

[29] *Philadelphia Public Ledger* (31 Oct. 1911).

[30] *New York Evening Post* (27 Oct. 1911). Her pamphlet, *Physical Force and Democracy*, was published by the National Union in response to *The Physical Force Argument against Woman Suffrage* by A. MacCallum Scott MP.

[31] *Extracts from May Mission Speeches* Church League for Women's Suffrage (henceforth CLWS) pamphlet no. 3, 6. (Speech in Essex Hall, London, 12 May 1910.)

wounds and binding up sores when the great canker is at the heart of the country?' The Government was the largest sweating employer. 'If we were represented . . . we would refuse to be responsible for the wretched condition of the working women and would demand the enactment of laws for their protection.'[32] Women could no longer plead ignorance, she told them, appealing as one paper said, to the primitive impulse of human sympathy and sisterhood.

Maude spoke later in Boston and New York on the exploitation of working women – their low pay and the obstacles they faced to acquiring any but domestic skills. Along with the sombre facts she related, the American papers stressed her wit. 'A brilliant speaker,' said the *Philadelphia Record,* noting that her discourse on working women was 'full of witty sallies and telling shots'. She had indeed learnt since Duffield days to illuminate the painful through the absurd. What could be more painful, after all, than the wholesale restriction of women's work by men? What more absurd than her hairdresser's comment that women were not suited to his profession ('The curling tongs are exceedingly heavy and it takes a strong man's arm to lift them.'[33]) Her deft response to questions also drew comment. In Boston she visited Wellesley College where she was asked by 'one pretty young girl' if she did not think that women would be more dishonest in selling votes than men. 'Miss Royden,' according to the *Boston Herald,* 'turned to her with surprised eyes. "Are you dishonest?" . . . "Why, no," was the reply. "Are your women friends dishonest?" "No." "Well," answered Miss Royden, "an argument based on the supposition that you are exceptional is on a very weak foundation." '[34]

In Boston she was questioned about 'Premier Asquith's recent statement that a full manhood suffrage bill would be carried in the next Parliament'. All Maude knew was what friends had written of the move which was to go down in suffrage history as leaving an unparalleled sense of betrayal. Asquith had as good as dished the prospects of the promised Conciliation Bill by proposing a Reform Bill to enfranchise adult men. Militant and non-militant reaction to this catastrophe ran true to form. The militants smashed hundreds of windows (feeling , as Maude later wrote to Catherine Marshall, that behind every one stood Lloyd George and Churchill when 'in fact there was nothing . . . but Dickins & Jones') Her own view goes for the National Union: 'We *must* stop thinking how we can best relieve our feelings, and consider what are our real weapons!'[35] Catherine Marshall and Kathleen Courtney, the Union's best political strategists, were indeed giving much thought to that and in due course came up with a scheme for close co-operation with the Labour Party.

[32]*North American* (31 Oct. 1911); *Philadelphia Record* (31 Oct. 1911).
[33]*New York Herald* (12 Dec. 1911).
[34]*Boston Herald* (26 Nov. 1911).
[35]Marshall Papers, (8 April 1912) Cumbria Record office, D/Mar/3/14.

But before she herself could take any part in the National Union's new initiative Maude had to get back from the USA. Before she went she had told Catherine Marshall that she would rather not have gone at that time. Now, to another suffrage contact, she wrote that it had all been exceedingly interesting, but was 'still more exceedingly distracting to me to be out of England these last weeks!'[36] There was obviously much work to be done. 'All the people who, quite honestly if supinely, thought the vote would come without any one assisting but Providence must now surely see that they were mistaken,' she commented to Marshall in April 1912. In the *Common Cause* she urged that they must work harder; go on handing out bills at street corners, though most of them were dropped in the mud. Go on speaking, she might have added; in market places, at tube stations; in drawing rooms and Co-op. halls; at garden meetings and White Elephant sales. And go on travelling.

The railway companies must have done well in 1912 from National Union speakers alone. Maude's programme in the second half of February took her from Sunderland to Southport to Somerset, then north to Eccles, then south to London, then back to Chester.[37] In March, at least, most of her engagements were in London and here by now she had a home, for the Shaws had recently moved from Alderley to the living of St Botolph's, Bishopsgate, and she shared a flat with them in Bedford Square. It was hard, though, – harder than Extension work; for in suffrage there was no closed season, though she made a point of taking August as holiday – going very often to Coverack in Cornwall or on some Italian excursion with Kathleen. And she still managed to act now and then – usually these days with the Campden Guild, which went in for Jacobean comedy. But 1912 was a very tough year: more speaking than ever and no sign of victory. The Conciliation Bill was indeed defeated; the Reform Bill still unsettled at the end of the year. At about this time, as Mrs Fawcett recalled, a sympathetic cabinet minister advised them to try to work up public opinion.

'Why do you not hold a few meetings and get good speakers, like Miss Royden, to address them?' We replied that we had held 4,000 public meetings in the last four months, filling the largest halls again and again, and that Miss Royden, never very robust, had nearly killed herself by fulfilling the constant demands that were made upon her for speeches at our innumerable demonstrations. She had spoken 267 times in the last twelve months.[38]

Though she was always liable to headaches and sometimes the account of a

[36]Maude to Miss Robinson, London Society for Women's Suffrage (4 Dec. 1911) Fawcett 149.
[37]Unless otherwise stated, details of engagements come from the lists in the *Common Cause*. Maude's handicap made travelling arduous and she explained to Catherine Marshall that except in London where transport was easy, her lameness would make her 'a costly nuisance' if it came to electioneering.
[38]M. G. Fawcett, *The Women's Victory and After* (1920) 39.

meeting records that she had to leave early because of fatigue, Maude never tried to cut down her programme. On the contrary, she was even willing to cram speakers' classes into the gaps, as the London Society's Secretary explained to a would-be pupil.

> Miss Royden happens to be stopping in London for a short period and in response to many requests has consented to give such spare moments as she was able to taking a class of speakers. Miss Royden has so many engagements all over the country that we are very thankful to take what we can of her time and I am afraid there will be no other chance of lessons from her in the near future.[39]

The speakers' class in Victoria Street ran from 11.30 till 1.00. Then on to Wandsworth, say, for 2.30, to speak on 'Working Women and the Vote'; then to South Kensington for Mrs Rendel's drawing-room meeting at eight o'clock. On another morning, the speakers' class; then to a mission hall in the East End; then to the Edgeware Road Labour Exchange for a branch meeting of the shop assistants' union. Sometimes her task was to inspire the faithful (as at the London Society's receptions, often addressed by Mrs Fawcett, Kathleen, Maude, and other leaders). But the real audience lay outside – in civic halls, where she often shared a platform with colleagues who were of local standing (Margaret Ashton in Manchester, Dorothea Rackham in Cambridge, for instance) and, above all, at outdoor meetings. Outdoor speaking, she told the Americans, meant you had to start before a meeting existed.

> You must stand up in a chair on a street corner in London and say to two children and a dog, 'People of England!' And, Oh, I do assure you that is a difficult thing to do. But you must do it, for you address two men to every five women in a hall and nine men to every one woman in the street.[40]

Maude did her share of open-air speaking though she always felt her voice did not carry. Trafalgar Square and Hyde Park were the worst. The best thing was to have a wall at your back; and this arrangement had another advantage – that missiles could not come at you unawares. Heckling was no problem – indeed, she enjoyed it. The risk of violence was something else. For her, she once said, the smell of the Underground always evoked the shelter it afforded – or might have afforded – in case of need. (The entrance to Tufnell Park underground station was one such accommodating suffrage pitch.) The risk increased with public resentment at the West End window-smashing raids and subsequent letter-box campaign, but Maude's real brush with violence came later. In suffrage work she met nothing worse than horseplay. (On one occasion, literally: her platform was a waggon and a man in the crowd took the horse's bridle and led it round

---

[39]Philippa Strachey to Miss Hay (31 Oct. 1912) Fawcett 149. In old age Maude wrote a series of articles on the art of public speaking, under the title 'Bid Me Discourse', Fawcett 224.
[40]*Brooklyn Daily Eagle* (19 Nov. 1911).

while she tried to go on speaking. It was, she said, 'exquisitely funny'. 'A small boy threw an ice-cream . . . as I passed, and as it . . . ran down the back of my neck I reflected gloomily on the frenzy of dislike which must have inspired so great a sacrifice.')[41]

In 1913 she did less speaking on the regular suffrage trail. For one thing, from April when she started work as editor of the *Common Cause,* she had to be in London mid-week. As the paper came out on Fridays, Tuesdays and Wednesdays were chaotic.

> Everyone 'rushing' for all she is worth – Press boys dashing in and out for 'copy' – growing conviction that 'we have got too much again' . . . At the last hour, when every line is measured, we get a letter enclosing columns of reports from the local Press about a meeting, with the request to 'kindly write an account of this and insert in *Common Cause,* 'marked' Urgent! . . . My feelings overcame me when I read PS 'Had I more time I would do it myself,' Had I more time –! We go to Press in half an hour![42]

The paper's 'new look' did not please everyone. The bugler girl (oddly Viking in appearance) now bestriding the front page, struck Hitchin Women's Suffrage Society as truculent, to say the least, and they wrote to say they thought it a pity 'that women in their constitutional struggle should . . . perpetuate the use of military symbolism'. Such reactions were not surprising at a time of rising militant violence. Maude had in fact taken on the *Common Cause* at just the moment when the 'Cat and Mouse' Act provoked a new phase of confrontation.[43] Golf greens were ruined, telegraph wires cut, houses and racecourse stands set on fire. The press was full of it. The Oxford Union debated the government's response and Maude was very proud that her nephew, Ralph, in his first term at New College that autumn, made his maiden speech in the debate as one of a minority supporting suffrage. 'If you succeed (as I am sure you will),' wrote the Lancashire suffragists, Ada Nield Chew, 'in making the *Common Cause* a real live human paper, it will be the most powerful propaganda instrument the Women's Suffrage movement can have.'[44]

On militancy, though, is seemed about as powerful as a hand pump against a blazing hayrick. For one thing, it was hard to counter the charge – from the law-abiding – that militancy *paid*. 'It was when they came forward,' wrote one reader, 'that we began to be taken seriously.' On this Maude's editorial comment was, if violence were wrong it could not be expedient; which provoked the answer that the National Union was making itself look rather silly 'by basing a limited temporal demand on a semi-

[41]Royden, 'Bid Me Discourse'.
[42]CC (4 July 1913) 207.
[43]Under this measure hunger–striking suffragettes were conditionally released from prison and brought back again when their health was restored. Between April 1913 and July 1914 Mrs Pankhurst was imprisoned and released ten times.
[44]CC (5 Sept. 1913) 372.

religious ground'.[45] Maude believed utterly in what she said: that the moral
argument was always the strongest. But like others who drew inspiration
from that great militant, Joan of Arc, she was not immune to the appeal of
danger. 'I was often attracted and almost seduced,' she said of militancy
later on. She had been stung, in 1912, to receive a white feather for refusing
to participate in public debate with Gladys Pott of the National League for
Opposing Woman Suffrage.[46] Now she wrote proudly in the *Common
Cause* of the courage shown by law-abiding suffragists who were molested
as public rowdyism grew in response to militant outrage. Near Oxford, for
instance, the burning of a woodshed (allegedly by the suffragettes) led to all
suffrage meetings being threatened with riot.

> We believe that no one who has not undergone the strain can fully realise what it
> means. To canvas day after day for a meeting, and hear perpetually that it 'will be
> broken up'; to go, notwithstanding, to the meeting, and endure the expected
> 'baiting', conscious that you have done nothing to provoke it, and must not
> retaliate; to do all this again and again, as part of your day's work, without
> advertisement, without fame, without recognition; this it is to be a Constitutional
> Suffragist – that cowardly and timid thing! We salute all those who thus 'fight
> with wild beasts at Ephesus' – and not wholly without envy at the privilege of
> suffering that is theirs.[47]

So far as the National Union was concerned, after the fiasco of the
government Reform Bill the process which Mrs Fawcett once likened to
beavers rebuilding a dam began again. There was now no parliamentary bill
to work for, but by April 1913 they were making plans for a suffrage
pilgrimage, nationwide, to reach its climax in London in July. 'The Pilgrimage of Grace', Maude called it , in 'Notes and Comments', that section
of the paper where she ranged broadly – from the marriage bar in teaching
to prostitution and the white slave traffic; from Miss Bebb's fight to become
a solicitor to the threatened sacking of pitbrow lasses; from the first stirrings
of suffrage in India to the odd case of the American wife who could not vote
but whose signature was needed to validate the vote of her illiterate
spouse.[48] Whether the pilgrims were Christian or not, she said, their call was
'a moving, living sense of the deep spiritual meaning of the Suffrage
movement' – a movement which, like Christianity itself, had come 'to turn
the world upside down'. They would set out to bring the world to their
fellowship 'with something of the gaiety of the early Franciscans'. 'The

---

[45]CC (7 Nov. 1913) 546.

[46]Pott challenged the statistical basis of Maude's pamphlet *Votes and Wages*. Pro- and anti-
debates were common (Kathleen certainly debated with Pott) but Maude held that it would not
be productive simply to argue matters of fact. Later she regretted her decision.

[47]CC(11 July 1913) 225.

[48]Like most regular features in the *Common Cause* 'Notes and Comments' is unsigned, but
Maude evidently wrote it: the NUWSS Executive minutes for 5 June 1913 show her asking for
someone to take on 'In Parliament' and 'Notes and Comments' while she is away.

scarlet, green and white of the Union should be known from Land's End to John of Groats by the time pilgrims gather in St Paul's for the final act of dedication.'

With bands playing and colours flying the women walked to London along five main routes, laid out for *Common Cause* readers on a map. The paper carried photographs and vivid reports of some of the hundreds of meetings held. Circulation rose. As the pilgrims neared London Maude was appealing for volunteer sellers and for motors and carts to carry supplies. The vehicles themselves were to be an advertisement, all decked out with posters and the colours. She noted leaders who had joined the pilgrimage. 'Mrs Fawcett has been walking for weeks. Mis Margaret Ashton rushes to and fro, walking and speaking and going back to Manchester at intervals . . . Miss Courtney and Miss Marshall have been on the road, and Mrs Harley and Miss Eleanor Rathbone.'[49] Pilgrims had already raised £6,000. 'Who would pay tribute for not marching?' she asked. Maude did not march, for obvious reasons, though as rowdyism became more and more of a problem, she was one of a flying corps of speakers who went by train to various places to draw hostile fire before the pilgrims arrived. Later she expressed the gratitude of those 'who could not take the road' to all those who did. As the pilgrims streamed into London her part was to address them at open-air meetings at Stratford Broadway and Tower Hill; and, of course, the following day in Hyde Park, from one of the nineteen speakers' platforms. From another, Kathleen spoke, beside Mrs Fawcett and the American leader, Mrs Chapman Catt.

On the Sunday 1,000 pilgrims attended the service in St Paul's. As the *Common Cause* noted,

A woman might not preach [there] but was allowed to do so in the Ethical Church, by the great kindness of Dr Stanton Coit. The Church was crowded, the ordinary congregation, the 'Spiritual Militants' and many Pilgrims being there. Mrs Fawcett was present and Miss Royden spoke on 'The Pilgrim Spirit'.[50]

It had been a reminder that joy and adventure and romance, she said, 'were truly a part of the Suffrage work, indeed the very heart of it'. In such a long struggle there were times when machinery and compromise and politics seemed more real than the vision that inspired it. The pilgrimage had given this back to them.

What it achieved in practical terms seems to have been mainly a meeting with Asquith. In August the prime minister received a deputation from the National Union which, besides the officers (Mrs Fawcett, Catherine Marshall and Kathleen) comprised Helena Swanwick, Dorothea Rackham, Margaret Harley, Margaret Robertson and Maude. He was told of the

---

[49]CC (9 May 1913) 67; (16 May 1913) 81; (25 July 1913) 265.
[50]CC (1 Aug. 1913) 294.

noticeable change in attitude of working men towards women's suffrage, as evinced during the pilgrimage. He was taken to task by Mrs Fawcett for spoiling the Conciliation Bill and told by Kathleen that his unwillingness to meet them when the Reform Bill was under discussion showed how badly they needed the vote. Maude countered the argument that women's needs were already well looked after. In the last suffrage debate, she said, she had heard him say that the interests of women had not been 'unduly neglected' by the Commons. She went on, 'It would be tactless to ask what degree of neglect was "due"', (here, according to the *Common Cause,* Asquith began to leaf through *Hansard,* as if attempting to disown the phrase) 'but . . . women think there has been much neglect.' She gave as one example the failure of the Truck Act in its application to women workers.

> But rather than run through a list of grievances I should prefer to argue as you, sir, would in another case have argued, that good government is no substitute for self-government. Women have become politically conscious, and when that happens to any class it can never be sent to sleep again.[51]

All this read well in the *Common Cause.* But, as indeed they must have known by now, given the political balance at the time, and Asquith at the top, it meant less than nothing. 'It is a queer adjustment of relative values that fills these papers with the Rugby match and records that "Miss Royden also spoke"', complained the author of a lyrical account of one of Maude's speeches the following year. In the outside world it was the normal adjustment. The Rugby match was very important, an international between England and Ireland. And suffrage? When the Reform Bill was withdrawn amid some shouts of 'Resign! Resign!' Asquith looked amused and said, 'On Woman's Suffrage?'[52]

The only political card they held had been acquired in 1912: co-operation with the Labour Party. Before that, their by-election policy had been to back the candidate most friendly to suffrage. It was in the context of extreme disenchantment with many such 'friends' and with the Liberal government that Catherine Marshall and Kathleen Courtney urged the Union to negotiate with Labour as being the only political party which actually had women's suffrage in its programme. They launched an Election Fighting Fund to back Labour candidates in three-cornered contests, while Labour shook off its years of ambivalence and explicitly pledged opposition to any reform bill which did not include women. It was an important political step – more than political, Maude insisted. She had always been conscious of a natural affinity between women as a disfranchised group and working people who had fought the same battle. 'The working classes,' said Arthur Taylor, future Labour MP for Lincoln, 'had learned much from

[51]CC (15 Aug. 1913) 319–22.
[52]CC (20 Feb. 1914) 879; David Morgan *Suffragists and Liberals* (1975) 117.

Plate 4 Kathleen Courtney, 1914. Drawing by Sybil Ashmore. *Reproduced by permission of the Principal and Fellows of Lady Margaret Hall, Oxford.*

some of the writings of Miss Royden.'[53] He was introducing her at a local meeting not long after the 'entente' was established, with Labour well-represented on the platform. Whether or not every trades unionist present liked what she had written (and what she told them) about giving women the same wage as men for the same work, they backed her on suffrage.

[53]*Lincolnshire Chronicle* (19 July 1912).

The alliance of Labour and the suffragists was sealed in February 1914 at a joint demonstration in the Albert Hall unprecedented in the history of the movement, as Mrs Fawcett said from the chair. Speakers included Arthur Henderson, deputy leader of the Labour party, Robert Smillie of the Miners' Federation, Fenner Brockway of the *Labour Leader*, as well as Lord Lytton, the Conservative suffragist, Mrs Louise Creighton and Maude. Behind them on the platform were hundreds of trades unionists; before them, an audience packed to the roof. That it included some suffragettes who tried (but failed) to shout Henderson down, did not impair 'the extraordinary sense of a great spiritual force through it all'. The audience was with him and clapped and sang 'For he's a jolly good fellow!' when he finished and roared at the news that over £6,000 had been raise to press for suffrage at the next general election.[54]

Then Maude spoke. The *Common Cause* reporter focuses almost entirely on her:

> one heard, during the bursts of applause which punctuated her speech, hearty cries from men, 'That's right! You've got it! True!' And from women, 'Oh, it's right!' It must be good for her to feel that in uttering what was noble and witty and true in her own mind she was striking notes which thrilled response from so many other minds and hearts of men and women.

Maude had had plenty of experience by now of public speaking in all kinds of conditions, and this huge audience in the Albert Hall, warmed and aroused by Henderson's performance, was quite evidently hers for the taking. Though she thought her voice did not carry out-of-doors it carried to perfection to the thousands here. Many years later, Fenner Brockway (who followed her as a speaker that night) said of her that it wasn't rhetoric or gesture but 'the sheer conviction of her personality' that got through to people. 'She could pack the Albert Hall and no one would leave until they had heard her.'[55] Her principal theme that evening was plain. In a sense it was her only theme: that women were part of humanity. The very presence of so many men at a women's meeting emphasised that, she said – making them laugh by mocking the debates that sometimes went on in the House of Commons as to whether or not a woman was person 'within the meaning of the Act'. 'The governing class has never allowed to the governed equal humanity with itself.' Long ago this was the attitude of kings; later, of the ruling classes towards the poor. 'And when government passed . . . from a class to a sex, the same feeling persisted. When a man says "human being", he is generally thinking "man".' 'Women then are now claiming that they are human, and that their humanity is a greater and deeper thing than their

[54]CC (20 Feb. 1914) 878–9. The militants' attitude to Labour, by this time, is summed up in Christabel Pankhurst's view that 'a man-made Socialism is not less dangerous to women than a man-made Capitalism.'

[55]Quoted by Sybil Oldfield, *Spinsters of this Parish* (1984) 304.

sex.' For was any derogation of humanity worse than the exploitation of women by men? Men ('yes, even working men') were guilty of this, she said; quoting Lecky on the prostitute's function as a kind of safety valve for society. 'Such a dogma is impossible to those . . . who believe that women are human beings.'

By now she was actively involved in the campaign for social purity, that fight to revolutionise sexual standards which was germane to the women's movement for militants and constitutionalists alike. Their patron saint was Josephine Butler who in crusading, a generation back, for outcast women, had secured the repeal of the Contagious Diseases Acts. Now the reformers hoped to put more teeth into the Criminal Law Amendment Act, another product of the earlier campaign, and both Maude and Mrs Fawcett were on the committee which pressed for the raising the age of consent. At many suffrage meetings – certainly at those where her theme was 'Working Women and the Vote' – Maude spoke of what she had termed in Philadelphia 'the great canker at the heart of the country', making much of the abominable link between poverty, sweating and prostitution. Her fame as a speaker on moral issues really began though in 1912 when she contributed to a symposium at the Queen's Hall which took for its theme, 'The Religious Aspect of the Women's Movement'. In retrospect she saw this occasion as her 'first stepping stone out of a little suffrage circle'. It was certainly the first time she addressed a large audience in the company of leaders of the Anglican Church (the much-revered Bishop Gore of Oxford among them) and a rare opportunity, at that date, to speak as a *Christian* for the movement she regarded as 'the direct development of the spirit of Christ.' To her, as she told them, the women's movement was 'the most profoundly moral movement . . . perhaps with the exception of the movement against slavery . . . since the foundation of the Christian Church.' Most of her address concerned its ethical aspects for, in her eyes, the double moral standard affronted not only the humanity of women but the humanity of Christ himself.

> Christ said to us 'Be ye perfect.' He spoke not only to the Apostles, nor only to a nation, nor only to a sex. He said to every man and woman in the world, 'Be ye perfect.' In what sense did he say it? Did he say, 'In those virtues which become your class,' or 'your sex'? He said 'be ye perfect, even as your Father which is in heaven is perfect.'

Yet the world had chosen to modify its view of necessary virtues according to sex, regarding the virtue of chastity, for instance, as the most essential of all in a woman and as the least essential in a man. 'In whose name shall we receive dispensation from any of the virtues which Christ set before us?'

> We stand here to affirm the whole ideal of Christ for every human being, man or woman. This is not, as it has been called, a *feminist* movement, but more rightly a humanist movement, because we ask for the whole human ideal for all, for purity

and gentleness and self-sacrifice in men; for courage, judgment and wisdom in women . . . The franchise that we ask is the franchise of the Kingdom of God. We ask for the freedom of all the virtues.[56]

Though she rightly disclaimed having been the first woman to talk publicly about prostitution and other aspects of sexual abuse, the Queen's Hall meeting gave her a new audience 'and made it . . . much easier for other women to be asked to speak on the same question.'[57] For herself, other invitations followed. In 1913 she was asked to speak on the white slave traffic to Oxford undergraduates. This was with the backing of the vice chancellor. Leading undergraduates (the president of the Union, the captain of cricket and other grandees) appeared on the platform, while the chair was taken by the regius professor of divinity, Scott Holland, in whom she sensed 'rock-like strength and support'. It was bold, said the *Oxford Magazine*, to hold a meeting on the subject at all, and the risks were intensified by the fact that a woman had been invited to speak. Maude felt nervous, as she recalled, though less of the subject than of the audience; some of whom, she learned later on, had come to make fun of the whole thing. In fact, they did not: deflated perhaps, like the Dauphin's courtiers in the face of St Joan, by the 'sheer conviction of personality' which Fenner Brockway so well remembered. The *Oxford Magazine* found the risk was justified by 'Miss Royden's truly great speech'. ('No one who heard [it] will forget either it or the burning words of Canon Scott Holland.') Her audience was not spared the vision of 'multitudes of quite little girls, broken by force in body and soul in order to serve the ends of their procurers.' But nor was it allowed to take refuge in attitudes of horror and indignation.

> She pressed home the lesson of what is implied in the common acceptance of a double standard of chastity for men and for women. She laid bare a little of the real heart of the Women's Movement, namely the intolerable sense among . . . sheltered women that their own honour and immunity are secured . . . at the cost of the degradation . . . of others.[58]

Maude said later, 'I believe that God . . . enabled me to speak to the purpose.' But at the time she spent a sleepless night, having, as she fancied, failed completely.

Shortly after this the Bishop of Winchester, Edward Talbot, wrote begging her to speak on the same theme at the Church Congress, to be held the following September in Southampton. Talbot in his young days had taken a lead in promoting women's education at Oxford and especially in the founding of Lady Margaret Hall. Now nearly seventy, he was still

---

[56]'The Ethical Aspect of the Women's Movement' in *The Religious Aspect of the Women's Movement*.

[57]Maude to Mrs Schairer (15 May, 1937) Fawcett 221. For her memories of social purity meetings see also Royden, 'Bid Me Discourse.'

[58]*Oxford Magazine* (27 Feb. 1913).

sufficiently sympathetic to the women's cause to propose 'The Kingdom of God and the Sexes' as one of the main themes for this Congress, and stick to it in spite of pressure from Lord Curzon, president of the National League for Opposing Woman Suffrage. He wanted Maude to speak before the Congress began – first of all, at a women's meeting.

> My wife and I are equally anxious to secure your help for that. She feels very strongly how desirable it is that the matters with which the White Slave horrors are connected should be put rightly and powerfully before *Women* as well as before men . . . Will you, *please*, help us in this way.

Two months later he approached her again.

> I don't know how far it is right to tax your strength and time. You have most kindly agreed to address the Women's Meeting . . . We are to have that night a great meeting of Men, which will be addressed by the Bishop of London. Knowing what I do of the way in which you spoke to Oxford undergraduates in the Schools there, I should feel it a very great advantage to my men in Southampton if I could obtain from you something of the same kind that night. I know so well how such a thing will appeal to you, that I don't weaken the claim by any particular words about it. You will do what you know to be right.[59]

That summer, the fifth International Congress on the White Slave Traffic was held in London, so the public could hardly be called unprepared. Talbot was strongly criticised, though, for asking Maude to speak and she offered to withdraw. He would not have it. 'If she does half as much good . . . at Southampton as she apparently did to her Oxford audience I shall be satisfied,' he wrote in August. 'She will justify me and discomfit her critics if she rises to her moral and spiritual Oxford level, and leaves suffrage for the moment aside.'[60] An unusual sense of drama and excitement hung round Southampton in Congress week. The town itself was buzzing with suffrage activity and a suffragist lantern procession with a piper added to the glamour of September 29th, the day appointed for social purity.

Southampton's coliseum was packed to bursting for the women's meeting in the afternoon, and the speakers had to do a repeat performance at an overflow meeting in a Baptist chapel. The audience listened first to Mary Sumner, aged foundress of the Mother's Union; then to Canon Ivens on such threats to home life as the alluring picture palace; then to Maude on purity. 'No words of mine,' ran one account, 'can at all adequately express the impression created by the intense earnestness, sympathy and spirituality with which she treated the subject.'[61] Her main theme was that sex was not shameful.

It has become a kind of convention with women to speak of the instincts of sex as

[59]Edward Talbot to Maude (2 March, 10 May 1913). Fawcett 222.
[60]Edward Talbot letter beginning 'My dear Emily,' (17 Aug. 1913) Fawcett 222.
[61]CC (3 Oct. 1913) 434.

though they were not beautiful. They speak of motherhood as though it were the noblest thing on earth, but they despise that which created motherhood. They speak even to their children of the instincts of sex as though there were something in them that was shameful.

How then could they expect their children to regard the body as 'the temple of the Holy Spirit' and chastity as something worth striving for?[62] At times, apparently, listening to this 'the audience was hushed to almost painful tension'.

In the evening, this same coliseum, seating over 2,000, was packed with men. 'One woman facing 2,000 men,' said one account, omitting to add that, in addition to 2,000 in front, there were nine others with Maude on the platform: the Archbishop of Canterbury, the Bishops of London, Willesden, Guildford and, of course, Winchester; Bishop Welldon, Canon Scott Holland, the Archdeacon of Birmingham, and the Chaplain-General of the Forces. As she joined them Winnington-Ingram, Bishop of London, a kindly man, had taken her by the hands and said 'God will be with you every moment of the time', but she felt nervous as she had done at Oxford – not of the subject but of the audience; also a little thrown by an encounter just before the meeting with Mrs Talbot, who had reservations about her dress. It was a nice dress – black, said Maude, but not 'up to the chin and down to the wrists'. It seems unlikely that the dowdiest dress could have done much to reduce the impact of seeing a woman up there with the bishops, and thirty years younger than most of them. At this time Maude was thirty-six. 'One little woman among all us rough men', said Talbot, introducing her. The whole thing was striking, and would have been so if her theme had been the culture of geraniums, said one man. As it was, he was staggered to think of her handling such a theme as the white slave traffic, 'rehearsing . . . such appalling abominations as two male friends could only mention with awe between themselves'.[63]

In substance, she said what she had said at Oxford, citing data on the scale of the traffic, pressing to the end the implications of the double standard, 'at the heart of which, there is a deep-seated irreverence for that which God had made, the human body and human personality.' There were certainly those who doubted the wisdom of having invited a woman to speak. But word got round that she had made a great impression, and all agreed on her 'fearless courage' and delicate handling of the 'beastialities'. The special correspondent of the *Church Times* wrote, 'Miss Maude Royden's speech . . . stands by itself. I should think that so plain-spoken a speech by a woman to a vast assembly of men has never before been delivered.' He stressed that

[62]Report of the Church Congress, Southampton (1913).
[63]*Church Times* (3 Oct. 1913). Maude recalled in 'Bid Me Discourse' 'People thought it very difficult or "very brave" to tackle sex injustice at all, and especially on a public platform . . . . But for my part I never felt it either difficult or frightening: the fire burnt too hot within me.'

her style of delivery had been very low-key her voice only rarely touched by emotion: 'the voice of one who has a message to deliver.'[64]

To possess such a voice would have seemed beyond her in the days when she used to talk to Kathleen about the problem of self-control ('Sometimes I fear I too shall wreck for lack of it'). To feel intensely, and convey that feeling, yet never to let emotion slop over; to be able to use, as this man noted, 'calm, deliberate and earnest language' in a great cause, would have been her dream. At the Church Congress she seems to have attained it, for he ended, 'It was good to have heard her speak; it was good to go away and think. We had listened to a Prophetess of Purity.' In a different manner, the woman who wrote for the *Southampton Times* also tried to convey a certain sense of otherworldliness.

> Perhaps it is her gentleness, her perfect mental poise, her aloofness from heated argument and freedom from prejudice of any kind that have made her, not a conspicuous figure, but a penetrating influence throughout the week. Miss Royden is curiously above the clang and dust of the Suffrage movement – by which I do not of course mean that she is not taking a very large part in the struggle on the level plains. But her spirit, so it seems to me, dwells on the heights.[65]

So this speech also passed into the canon. One clergyman speaking later in the week called it 'historic', and the Bishop of Lichfield, the following year, looked back upon it as 'epoch-making'. Neither, strangely, made the obvious comparison with the pioneer of purity, Ellice Hopkins, who had spoken to an audience of men on this theme at the Church Congress thirty years earlier. Hopkins' address *was* epoch-making, in that it led to the formation of the Church of England Purity Society, and the White Cross Army, that bold experiment which enlisted men in the purity crusade. Purity leagues sprang up all over England. Innumerable purity pamphlets were written. Maude said herself that no honour could be greater than that of following Ellice Hopkins.[66] She did not follow her, though, in the sense of being ready to distribute blame. 'It is not ours to apportion the guilt,' she told the women's meeting in Southampton. Ellice Hopkins had been more hard-hitting.

> I know . . . it is often the woman who tempts; these poor creatures must tempt or starve. But . . . it is men who endow the degradation of women; it is men who, making the demand, create the supply. Stop the money of men, and the whole thing would be starved out in three months' time.[67]

---

[64] *Church Times* (3 Oct. 1913).
[65] *Southampton Times* (4 Oct. 1913).
[66] CC (21 Nov. 1913) 592. For the work of Ellice Hopkins, see Sheila Jeffries, *The Spinster and Her Enemies* (1985) and F. K. Prochaska, *Women and Philanthropy in 19th-Century England* (1980).
[67] Jeffries, *The Spinster and her Enemies* 14.

'Men may be more guilty in act,' said Maude, 'but I sometimes think that women are less beautiful in thought', and from this she enlarged on the tendency of women to disparage sexual relations. Not that she set out to exonerate men. Like every fighter for social purity, from Ellice Hopkins to Christabel Pankhurst, she began with the assumption that the male sex instinct could not be accepted as 'uncontrollable' and therefore an excuse for the abuse of women. For Christians, she told them, there was no solution 'but that you should accept an equal standard of morals for yourselves and for us.'

> *There is no other solution.* That is the thing which I want to bring home . . . If men say that to be chaste is impossible because it injures a man's health, though I am not here to discuss that outworn lie, I will go further and say that *if it were true* you have no right to use another human being's body for such a purpose.

But, 'I do not pretend . . . the fault has all been with men. God forbid.'

'The old old story,' wrote the militant leader Christabel Pankhurst, in another context, 'the woman is to blame.'[68] That was not Maude's view. Nonetheless, to compare her speeches with Pankhurst's writing on venereal disease at this time in *The Suffragette* is to become aware of the range of feminist response to the sexual dilemma. Not that they lack a common ground. Maude might well have said, 'Sexual intercourse without spiritual love is beneath human dignity'; or, 'standards of morality made by men only, do wrong to women'. The Pankhurst slogan that aroused such fury, 'Votes for Women and Chastity for Men', after all encapsulates the two main arguments put less roughly but quite plainly by Maude: that women's political and economic weakness was a prime factor in prostitution, and that men – like women – should aspire to be chaste. But the difference of tone is significant. Pankhurst is separatist; anti-men. Maude could not be. She would not have disputed that their re-education on sexual matters was 'one of the most urgent needs of the day',[69] but she did not – and would not have – come out with such statements as that 80 per cent of them had gonorrhea: on one level inhibited, no doubt, by the knowledge that precise statistics to back such a claim did not exist in England; on another, by religion – she could not have regarded any of God's work with such distaste; on yet another by her liking for men and tendency to romanticise sex; above all, by her relationship with Shaw.

It would be hard to read her speeches without being constantly aware of that, as she must have been herself. Her Christian view of what was possible for men was fortified by what was possible for him; her reaction to women's disparagement of sex heightened by her knowledge of his married life; her view of 'suffering worth bearing for . . . chastity', based on experience. Maude's own dilemma was far from being 'sexual slavery in

[68] *The Suffragette (3 Oct. 1913) 883.*
[69] ibid. (15 Aug. 1913) 759.

marriage' (that question closely allied to prostitution which preoccupied more radical feminists). And the solution some of them found in the idea of 'psychic love' could have had only a limited appeal for one who felt deprived of the physical kind.[70] Of herself and Hudson, she once remarked that they were both physically passionate, 'and nothing could make it easy for us'. At one stage they even parted for a time. Then resumed the old pattern. 'We went on working.'[71] In this hard school she may well have learned 'the perfect mental poise' that was admired so much.

[70]See Jeffries, *The Spinster and Her Enemies* chapter 2 for the ideas of Elizabeth Wolsten-holme- Elmy and Francis Swiney on psychic (i.e. intellectual, spiritual, non-genital) love as an advance on the usual kind. Towards the end of *Woman and Labour* (1911) Olive Schreiner looks forward to the New Woman and the New Man sharing a love 'more largely psychic and intellectual than crudely and purely physical'.
[71]TFC 101, 31–2.

6

Peace and War

I hear of working men who will not shoot down their fellow-
workers, and Socialists who refuse to fight with Socialists. I hear of
no Christians who refuse to shoot down Christians.

Maude Royden (21 August 1914)

It is a commonplace that Britain's entry into war with Germany in 1914
took the nation by surprise; and that whether you look in parish magazines
or the national press or even cabinet papers, there is nothing to suggest that
the Archduke's murder struck anybody as the first step to hell. People did
not cancel holiday bookings nor leading churchmen their plans to discuss
Christianity and Peace with churchmen from Germany, nor the International Women's Suffrage Alliance their meeting organised for London
that July. As to this last occasion, it is true that a key figure was Rosika
Schwimmer, the Hungarian feminist, whose fear that the conflict would
spread throughout Europe impelled her to seek a special meeting with
Lloyd George.[1] He was not convinced, but her fears were soon realised in a
nightmare sequence from 28 July: Austria-Hungary declared war on Serbia;
Russia mobilised and Germany then declared war on Russia and her ally,
France. Schwimmer, Catherine Marshall and others struggled against the
tide of events, organising a public meeting to urge the British government
to mediate. They also – 'women of 26 countries in the International
Women's Suffrage Alliance' drew up an appeal for mediation which
Schwimmer, Mrs Fawcett and Chrystal Macmillan delivered by hand to the
Foreign Office and all the European embassies in London.

Of course it was hopeless. By 4 August, the date for which their public
meeting was planned, the situation from the British standpoint had been
changed by Germany's invasion of Belgium. In London, as ministers
awaited a response to Britain's ultimatum to Berlin, the women gathered in
the Kingsway Hall knowing that mediation was dead. 'Whilst the child was
alive I fasted and wept,'Mrs Fawcett told them in characteristic style. But
the time for fasting and weeping had gone, and they would have to meet the

[1] *Ann Wiltsher, Most Dangerous Women* (1985) – a study of feminist peace campaigners of the
Great War – deals at length with the efforts of Schwimmer.

calamity, she said, and alleviate the suffering which must ensue. This did not quite hit the mood of the audience, many of whom, from the Women's Labour League, the National Federation of Women Workers and the Women's Co-operative Guild, responded more warmly when the Guild's president said working people must refuse to have war. According to the *Common Cause* report,

> All the enthusiasm and response of the meeting was for those who denounced the war, and called on the women of Europe, even at the eleventh hour, to fling themselves between the combatants. 'Down tools!' called some of the audience, and interjections as to the capitalist origin of wars were frequent.[2]

They passed a resolution calling on governments to support every effort to restore peace, and another one concerning relief work. The meeting ended at 10.00 p.m., and an hour later, as Big Ben struck and the British ultimatum to Germany expired, people started shouting 'War is declared!'

Kathleen was in London in the midst of all this, but Maude was not. As she remembers:

> I was in Oxford staying in rooms at that particular part in the curve of the High Street from which one can see the spire of St Mary the Virgin on the right and the tower of Magdalen College on the left. It was a lovely day. I sat in the window seat and looked out. Soldiers were already on the march. They went marching up the High and people stood on the kerb, laughing and cheering. Other men were carrying mattresses into the Examination Schools just opposite. It was to be a hospital – for those men who were now being cheered. The spire of St Mary's stood up against a blue and cloudless sky – St Mary the Virgin, the Mother of the Lord. No one seemed to be hurt by the sight.[3]

Like a lot of other people she had to admit that she had never expected war, never believed what was happening could happen; or thought out what she would do if it did. The Boer War had hardly impinged upon her, apart from the death of Evelyn's brother and the pain of watching Evelyn submerge her grief 'in the common sorrow of England'. Anyway, in those days, as she said later on, '"My country right or wrong" was still my simple creed.' Certainly her letters at the time suggest it. 'We must continue to exist as a nation and as a great nation, for the sake of civilisation,' she had written to Kathleen in 1900. 'I believe that as firmly as I believe anything; don't you? If we are rotten, who is to colonise? And if it is to be Germany or France, God help the world.'[4]

The fear of war touched her for the first time in 1913 when she attended the Budapest congress of the International Women's Suffrage Alliance. For

[2]CC (7 Aug. 1914) 377.
[3]'Bid Me Discourse' Fawcett 224. Maude wrote this memoir in the 1950's. Because there is more than one draft version it is not possible to give page references.
[4]Maude to KC (22 April 1900).

whereas the English delegates had come preoccupied with social aspects of the women's cause, many on the continent could think of nothing but that women should unite against war. 'La guerre contre la guerre!' – the thrilling cry of Marie Vérone, the French delegate, and the great storm of clapping it aroused, haunted Maude yet in no way prepared her for the trauma of 1914.

True, her 'simple creed' had given way by now to an abrasive view of British foreign policy. 'I well believe Sir Edward Grey strove to avert war,' she wrote to the liberal Church weekly, *The Challenge*. But a glance at the map showed that Britain's aim for years had been to isolate Germany. 'Look at Germany, wedged between hostile France and the countless millions of Russia, and let us ask ourselves whether we in her place might not have been more militarist than we are.' As for Britain as the champion of the little peoples, 'Do we expect to be taken seriously after the example we set in South Africa?'[5]

The question of the little peoples was crucial. That was how the Government presented the case, and for many who were not laughing and cheering that was what settled the whole thing: Belgium. To defend Belgium was a matter of honour, of resistance to the principle that might was right. But to some – including suffragists like Maude who had set themselves to resist that principle when they rejected militancy – to deny force by exerting force offered no escape from the moral dilemma. For her indeed it led straight to the question: what was the Christian attitude to war?

The marching soldiers and Browning's Christ 'Whose sad face on the cross sees only this / After the passion of a thousand years' filled her mind. Maude recalled later how she waited for someone – some Christian body or newpaper or person – to speak and condemn 'not only war in general but *this* war'. When no one did so she wrote to *The Challenge* 'We are all agreed . . . that war is an evil; but to what purpose, if we justify each war as it arises?' Both England and Germany thought themselves forced now to take up arms in self-defence. What should be the Christian response to this? 'I hear of no Christians who refuse to shoot down Christians.' Yet after all, 'taking war at its best – are Christians allowed to fight in self-defence? By disarming St Peter Christ disarmed every soldier. 'I search the New Testament . . . for any assurance that I am wrong and all my fellow-Christians right.'

Her fellow-Christians' response was hostile. Such traitorous stuff was not fit reading for loyal English people, wrote one. With casualty lists coming in, said another, it was hardly the time for the abstract question of the moral justification of war. Other writers became involved in debating the meaning of Christ's teaching. He had never attacked institutions as such (war, slavery, prostitution). There was a relativity in moral questions which Maude overlooked, according to one clergyman. Slavery had now

[5] *The Challenge* (21 Aug. 1914) 509.

been rejected by humanity; war would be, one day. But as things stood, war was not wrong *per se* in 1914. Indeed, he thought it the only way – faced with the threat of German militarism.

It might be – perhaps it was the case, said Maude 'that the cause of Peace demands a martyr nation.'

> Sir, is it not clear that we cannot end war except by refusing to make war? It is useless to wait till we find a war we can condemn, for we justify each as it arises . . . Even now it is contended that the present conflict is 'a war to end war' and those who hate war most persuade themselves that *this* time at least war is justified for the sake of peace. So do we perpetually assume that Satan can be induced to cast out Satan. No illusion is more common, no hope more undying.[6]

The correspondence went on and on. A dreadful sense of loneliness assailed her. In a letter written in October to Professor Gilbert Murray she speaks of being 'very much troubled and perplexed' by the weight of opinion on the other side. 'The weight is so great that a thousand times I have thought. . . . that I *must* be mistaken.' The letter makes clear that Murray's own view had increased her confusion and disappointment. Here was a man of immense prestige; one who, himself, had been execrated during the Boer War for his stand against it. Now he was the author of a pamphlet signed by himself and other well-known writers backing the British government's line 'with a full conviction of its righteousness'. 'When Belgium in her dire need appealed to Great Britain to carry out her pledges, this country's course was clear.' That was the statesman's view, no doubt. But Maude insisted,

> I am only interested to know what the teaching of Christ is. If I thought this teaching might be wrong, I should cease to be a Christian and should begin to argue the question afresh, from the point of view you support.[7]

Murray, apparently, detected arrogance in her sense of being guided by divine revelation. It did not mean, she said, that there was 'no more difficulty'; just that there was a different kind.

> Your difficulty is 'Is war ever right? Is this war right? Were we bound in honour to make war?' Mine is, 'What is the teaching of Christ about war?' I do not know whether I am again sounding horribly insolent, because I am assuming that you do not argue the case from a Christian point of view? If so, forgive me, I have read your pamphlet with great care, and I do not find in it any question of the teaching of Christ on the subject of war. This is why I make the assumption that it would not be for you the final word.

If the sense of isolation made her sound self-righteous, she asked him to

---

[6]ibid. (2 Oct. 1914) 616.

[7]Maude to Gilbert Murray (17 Oct. 1914) Bodleian Library, Gilbert Murray MSS, 25 ff 79–81. I am grateful to Brian Harrison for drawing my attention to these letters.

understand 'how hard it is to find the exactly right words to express an overwhelmingly unpopular opinion.'

There was very little to comfort Maude in the reactions of most church leaders. 'My belief,' wrote Winnington-Ingram, Bishop of London, in a letter to her a few days after war broke out,

> is that this is the last Armageddon of the world, and that when the great storm cloud has burst and spent itself, the great sun of Love which has been growing in intensity behind it, will shine out in its permanent strength.[8]

'I keep on preaching to everyone, 'he said,' that we are not fighting the German people but seeking to crush the military clique.' Before very long, though, he was a by-word for the crudest kind of recruiting sermon. It was a holy war, he told men, and to fight in a holy war was an honour. 'War is right,' wrote Canon Scott Holland, 'when it is fought on behalf of Peace.' And Maude's beloved Cowley Fathers proffered an eschatalogical acceptance:

> We recognise a great day of God, a time of reckoning with the Eternal Justice, a time of testing and transition. For the Day of God when it comes and passes, leaves nothing as it was before. . . . Already . . . we have died the saving death . . . all littleness . . . is burned in the furnace of affliction.[9]

Edward Talbot, Bishop of Winchester, who shared this sense of a judgement on the nation, urged repentance for England's part in precipitating war but did not doubt the cause was righteous. A Church of England Peace League had been formed in 1910 to work for international friendship, but its membership was tiny. Its president, Bishop Hicks of Lincoln, had been dubbed pro-Boer but his view that war was a sport for bankers and armament makers did not make him a pacifist now; any more than similar views made pacifists of many peace-lovers in the Labour Movement. They could not swallow the thought of Belgium.

So in the end, for all Maude said, there were not many socialists who refused to fight socialists. On 2 August a great Labour rally had been held in Trafalgar Square at which Keir Hardy, Arthur Henderson, Margaret Bondfield, Mary Macarthur, George Lansbury and others spoke against the war. And as we saw, many of the Labour women who came to the meeting in the Kingsway Hall applauded the idea of downing tools or even trying to separate the combatants. But neither from the Church nor from the Labour movement was there an effective pacifist reaction to the shock of August 1914.

Shaw's son Bernard joined up from Balliol. Maude's nephew Ralph was rejected as unfit but felt desolate in what his friend Victor Gollancz stigma-

[8]Winnington-Ingram to Maude (13 Aug. 1913) Fawcett 221.
[9]Alan Wilkinson, *The Church of England and the First World War* (1978) 17.

tised as 'a bogus Oxford'. His elder brother Jack had volunteered straight off and the younger one went into the Flying Corps. 'I did not become a pacifist at once,' wrote Maude.

> I could not want to cut myself off from the great torrent of my country's suffering and aspiration. I had not a relative in the world who did not share that aspiration. I had not one who did not regard Pacifists with horror. I longed to be convinced that I was wrong. As one of my friends said to me, 'I can stand aside from my countrymen when they are happy but I can't stand aside when they are suffering.' This is the real agony of pacifism.[10]

What broke down her sense of isolation was contact with those who by the end of the year had formed the Fellowship of Reconciliation.

The initiative was Nonconformist and Quaker. The Quakers alone of all denominations had a corporate pacifist tradition and in sharp contrast to the drumming for recruits in Anglican pulpits at this time, had insisted in every leading paper that war was the outcome of unchristian conditions and that it was for Christians now to show courage 'in the cause of love and in the hate of hate'. Attempts to shape a Christian pacifist philosophy were presented at a conference held in Cambridge at the end of December 1914.[11] Richard Roberts, a Presbyterian minister, dissected the anatomy of doubt that faced them: the sense that this was a 'righteous' war, that they had to choose between war and dishonour; the feeling that they could not divest themselves of a sense of corporateness with the nation; their own involvement in the nation's sin. Against this he reminded them, 'The Church stands or falls by its loyalty to the Christian ethic.' War was the product of a way of life which the Church existed to transform. His appeal to reject 'pessimistic acceptance' is reminiscent of Maude's to reject the sexual mores of untold ages. And when she came to speak in her turn there were echoes of that other theme in her use of the word 'perfect'. 'Christ said to us "Be ye perfect"' she had told the meeting in the Queen's Hall. Now she said Christ had not waited to come until the world was sufficiently advanced not to crucify him; he did not tell his disciples 'that some day, when good was stronger . . . it would be their duty to rely . . . on love and put aside earthly weapons of defence'. They were to be 'perfect' not in the future, when other people also were better, 'but now'.

For those who took part in the Cambridge conference the sense of being no longer alone brought a feeling of light emerging from darkness. In those few days they constructed the basis of a Christian pacifist philosophy which did not rely on selective texts (Christ disarming St Peter, for instance) but on the fundamental Christian principle that only love can overcome evil. 'He told them to overcome evil with good now,' Maude said in her own

---

[10]'Bid Me Discourse'.
[11]See Vera Brittain, *The Rebel Passion* (1964). The papers given at the FOR conference in Cambridge, Dec. 1914, were published in Joan Fry (ed.), *Christ and Peace* (1915)

address, 'and in this command there was surely . . . a promise that good is
really stronger than evil.' The five-point 'basis' they drew up assumed this,
but also assumed that the world did not accept it; that there would be grave
risks in living it out and that, as Christians, they would take those risks. But
the idea of 'reconciliation' meant much more than rejecting war. They were
called to work 'for the enthronement of Love in personal, social, commercial and national life', and parted to consider its implications.

Maude was appointed travelling secretary to the Fellowship in 1915. In
January she had been one of the signatories of an open letter from British
women pacifists to the women of Germany and Austria, but naturally she
could not push pacifist views from the editorial desk of the *Common Cause*,
though peace and war questions filled its pages. She had not in fact been
working as editor at the very moment war broke out, having been on sick
leave (for what cause it is not clear) from the end of April 1914. With some
difficulty a substitute was found, and when she came back the landscape had
changed. Suffrage agitation had been suspended. The National Union was
committed to relief work, its London office a labour bureau set up to help
the many women who had lost their jobs with the dislocation of normal
business and closing down of luxury trades. Help for refugees was another
undertaking. In one issue of the *Common Cause* the Union appears as a
symbolic female leading a haggard mother and her children away from a
land marked 'Starvation and War'.

But it was not long before the question was raised whether women
should just go on 'picking up the pieces'. What were they going to do,
asked one correspondent, to promote the Kingsway Hall resolution urging
governments to try to restore peace? In the same issue, in 'Notes and
Comments' in a paragraph headed 'The Women's Peace Movement',
Maude urged the need to make people understand 'the great permanent
causes of war' so that when peace came it was not used merely as a period of
preparation for another war.[12] However, some readers disliked what they
saw as 'a feminine agitation for a premature peace'. 'Let us talk of peace
when Germany and all the horror it stands for, is defeated.' One wanted
German 'abasement to the dust'. And there were fears that, if women
pressed for peace it would seem to prove that the 'Antis' were right in
thinking them unfit to judge Imperial matters.

There were some voices on the other side. Against the view that such
'thoughtless tomfoolery' would spoil women's chances of getting the vote,
one writer said that some men at least would respect them for not being
carried away 'by the unreason which now threatens us no less than Prussian
militarism itself'. 'Have we any guarantee,' asked another, 'that when we
have gone on to the bitter end we shall have actually achieved a lasting
peace?' But such fears could not dim the confidence that stated 'This present

[12]CC (18 Sept. 1914) 437.

war has acted like a tonic; you can see it in the very way people walk now.'

In practical terms, apart from relief work, the National Union was very much concerned to protect working women and soldiers' dependants from exploitation and unfairness now. Maude kept a watching brief in 'Notes and Comments' (or 'Notes and News', as it became that autumn). At one labour exchange in one week the number of unemployed women shot up from 250 to 900. The rush of patriotic voluntary workers impeded their absorption elsewhere and unemployment among clerks and typists could be alleviated, she suggested, if relief bodies took on fewer volunteers. Women were already being drawn into jobs which had hitherto been done by men, though it appeared that responsible positions were 'jealously guarded from feminine contact'. What they were offered were routine jobs, at the wage of 'a masculine immature clerk'.

On all sides the crisis exposed a deep ambivalence towards women and work. The Commons, debating whether childless widows young enough to work should receive a pension, showed no awareness, it seemed to Maude, 'that the problem went right to the heart of the question of women's position in the world.' If these women were classed as individuals they could be expected to do other work now; if, however, they were classed as dependants, they had a right to be pensioned off. The government shouldn't try to have it both ways: saving money now by calling wives individuals, only to treat them as chattels later, with no rights apart from their husbands. 'If they must work they must also vote!'[13]

But everything she had ever said about the exploitation of the politically helpless was exemplified as England stumbled into war. 'Notes and News' drew attention to the plight of British-born women with alien husbands. Such women had to register, report to the police and confine themselves to a five-mile radius (though no similar restrictions were placed on British-born men with alien wives). A vastly larger but still vulnerable group were the wives and dependants of ordinary soldiers. In the first month of war the 'Notes' protested that soldiers' wives were kept standing for hours, with babies in their arms and little children clinging, waiting to register for payment of allowances. Later on, various attempts were made to supervise the recipients' behaviour. It was proposed to limit drinking hours for women. Police surveillance of soldiers' wives was also introduced in some places. It was unbelievable, wrote Maude in November, that the Army Council should be clamouring for more men and insulting the wives of those they had already.

The soldier has earned his pay, and has allotted some to his wife. She is not to

[13]CC (27 Nov. 1914) Notes & News.

have it if 'unworthy'. This is a new principle. Well, let us all adopt it and get a certificate of good behaviour from the police before we draw our money. At least, those persons who are receiving Government pay should be put under super-vision immediately – Cabinet Ministers, Ambassadors and others. Who knows whether their private conduct would commend itself as 'worthy' to the police?[14]

Common Cause readers who wrote to ask why women should insist on freedom to get drunk had their attention drawn by Maude to the wrongness of restricting one sex and one class on a matter which concerned everybody. Here again, she said, was the double standard so disastrous to morality.[15]

But for those who claimed full humanity for women the early war months were not encouraging. For one thing, women were virtually shut out from what was now humanity's main activity: preparing for battle. 'Not at them,' wrote Maude, 'does Lord Kitchener look fiercely from the front of taxicabs . . . . Their patriotism must find another vent and if people will only forbear to say "You are superfluous" they must be thankful.' Besides, war strongly reinforced the tendency to define women in terms of sex. The *Common Cause* strove to maintain its balance in the face of countless atrocity stories of female purity defiled, women brutally dishonoured by the Hun. Why, asked Maude, among the horrors of war, was the violation of women unique? Men might boast of honourable scars but reference was always to women dishonoured. 'The belief that a woman can be dishonoured by the act of any human being but herself makes every woman a slave,' she said.

> No other crime is treated so. In none is it supposed that the victim of cruelty . . . is himself or herself the 'dishonoured' person. . . . The women of the future must reject a conception of honour so profoundly dishonouring to them as to make them all unfree.

To desecrate the body was indeed a sacrilege against the holiness of life.

> But even the human body may be broken and shattered without touching the spirit; and to say of this worst of all wrongs that it 'defiles a woman in the inmost sanctuary of her being' is to give the body what belongs to the spirit. . . . No man can hurt another except by his own will. . . . Until women realise the truth of this . . . they can in no sense be the captain of their souls.[16]

Elsewhere, speaking of atrocities, she said 'A stand should be made for the human race, not for women only.'

From womanhood defiled to the image of womanhood defiling: one MP claimed there were only two causes of wastage from the army: drink and women. If many men could not understand, wrote Maude, why women

[14]CC (13 Nov. 1914) Notes & News.
[15]CC 1 Jan. 1915, 629.
[16]CC (19 March 1915) 770, 'An Ancient Wrong of Women'.

should resent the word 'woman' being used as another name for vice, 'they must at least learn that women do resent it, and that most bitterly.' But prostitution as a threat to the troops loomed as large now in the public mind as it had ever done in the heyday of the Contagious Diseases Acts. There were even moves to revive those Acts. That there should be any thought of returning to the system discredited by Josephine Butler was peculiarly painful to such as Maude, who yet again insisted that the only protection against venereal disease was chastity; and yet again affirmed that the professional prostitute represented 'in an extreme and final form' the woman exploited by society. It was thus futile to drive her away, imprison her, flog her, or appeal to her patriotism. A prostitute had no patriotism. 'A prostitute is without nationality. . . . What has her country done for her, in heaven's name, that she should know patriotism?' But she was human, and every proposal which assumed otherwise was bound to fail. It was supremely the duty of those who had asserted their own human value, through the women's movement, never to forget that their claim was invalid unless it was made, equally, for every other human being.[17]

Failure to acknowledge human value seemed also to vitiate public response to the problem of young girls hanging round the camps. People talked of appealing to their self-respect. But society had never respected them.

> Let us be honest. As long as girls are taught that to attract men is the first duty of woman, and to attract one sufficiently to persuade him to marry her is 'the vocation of woman'; so long as a woman who fails in this vocation is regarded as a maimed and wasted being who, whatever her work and value, is really 'superfluous' . . . so long will the temptation to hang about those places where men congregate exist.

Women, after all, were hardly regarded as having a human value outside marriage. Yet every human being was of infinite value, whether male or female, married or unmarried. 'Marriage, when it comes, is a great happiness, a sacred duty; but it is not upon marriage that the value of any human soul depends.'[18]

Patriotism was the touchstone now, though – distorting every other value, it seemed. Sexual assaults committed by soldiers were held to merit very light sentences. Suggestions were made that the bastardy laws should be changed 'even if only temporarily', since children (well, boys) were 'badly needed'. In an article entitled 'Morals and Militarism' Maude summed up the argument with heavy irony.

> The awful loss of life caused by the war must somehow be made good. How else shall we fill our factories, our workshops, our mills? Let us have babies anyhow

and hope they may be boys. And if our laws of illegitimacy create any difficulties, let them be drastically amended, *even if only for a time* (the italics are ours). . . . The one thing for which everything else must be sacrificed is a rise in the birth rate.

Of course, it was good that society's attitude to illegitimate children had changed. ('Suffragists have had a large share in this humanising of public opinion.') There were, after all, no 'illegitimate' children – 'no child should bear the stigma of a guilt that is not his' – though there were 'illegitimate' parents, whose offspring resulted from a passing emotion, a moment of loneliness or sudden temptation. 'Let us give such a child the maintenance, the care, the respect that is his right. We can never give him all that belongs to his happier brother.' Conscious of all that could never be given – the two loving parents, the stable home – Maude was sickened by the facile sentiment whipped up now over 'war babies'.

> The old cruelty of public opinion towards the unmarried mother is forgotten, and a new cruelty towards her child creeps in. For it is a real cruelty – based on a real irreverence – to preach that children must be born – anyhow, merely for our convenience, to fill up the cogs of our social and industrial machinery.

It was said that printed slips, urging men 'to forgo no opportunity of paternity' were being widely distributed in England. 'The consequences to the women and to the children are disregarded with a levity which is as cruel as levity always is. We protest with all our strength against this abominable advice.' She added:

> The nations have gone to war. They have . . . jeered at the work of pacifists . . . and . . . given nothing . . . to less frightful methods of deciding international disputes. Now . . . we have what we have worked for – destruction. Let us bear the anguish with what fortitude we may: but let us not consent to the reckless lowering of the moral standard involved in the advice 'forgo no opportunity of paternity'; in the brutal disregard of the rights of the unborn; in the reduction of women to the status of mere breeders of the race.[19]

In April 1915 when Maude wrote this she was no longer editing the *Common Cause*. Hers had been the first of a string of resignations from the National Union's executive committee which split that body from top to bottom.

The fuse was really laid when war broke out. Not that there had never been clashes before, but individual commitment to the cause – combined with the Union's democratic structure and Mrs Fawcett's restraint and prestige – had served to counteract the inevitable tension among strong personalities who drove themselves hard. This was different. When war broke out they had of course voted to suspend campaigning in favour of

[19]CC (30 April 1915) 46.

supporting efforts for peace and working for the relief of suffering. But the hurried resolutions of that shocking moment could not conceal the differences between them as to the relative importance of these aims and especially as to what was meant by the first. 'Not that we are not all in favour of peace,' said Mrs Fawcett, 'every sane human being must be.' To her, though, and to Lady Frances Balfour and others of the old guard on the executive 'The very word "peace" put the Country in the wrong' while there were German soldiers in Belgium.[20] Mrs Fawcett was intensely patriotic – even to the point of jingoism. She had been 'unspeakable' during the Boer War, according to the Quaker Isabella Ford, who debated whether to resign from the Union as early as October 1914.[21] The radical element on the executive (mainly but not wholly the younger members) felt – however deeply involved in relief work – that the very ethos of the women's movement compelled them at least to think about peace.

One could hardly exaggerate the strength of this feeling. Maude got down to the roots of it later in an article, 'War and the Woman's Movement', in which she affirmed the irreconcilability of militarism and feminism. Possibly war had destroyed the illusion that women were innately more pacific than men, she admitted (writing in 1915); but the women's movement, of its very nature, was 'for ever asserting a principle of which war is a perpetual denial'. The women's movement could only make sense as 'an assertion of moral force as the supreme governing force in the world'.

> Women, whatever other claims may be made for them, are not equal to men in their capacity to use force or their willingness to believe in it. For them, therefore, to ask for equal rights with men in a world governed by such force is frivolous. Their claim would not be granted, and if granted would not be valid. But if moral power be the true basis of human relationship, then the Woman's Movement is on a sure foundation and moves to its inevitable triumph.[22]

So in 1914 she asserted with passion that suffragists had to prepare for peace and that if they confined themselves to relief work, 'they no longer deserved to be suffragists'.[23] Just as in the past they had looked for the causes of sweating, prostitution and other social evils, so now they should be thinking of the causes of war and trying to influence public opinion, 'so that when peace came it did not contain the seeds of war'. The same

---

[20]National Union executive minutes (15 April 1915). At an earlier meeting of the executive Mrs Fawcett had pointed out that if Germany won the war 'it would be a great blow to the women's movement and to all representative institutions'.

[21]Wiltsher, *Most Dangerous Women* 63.

[22]'War and the Woman's Movement', in Charles Roden-Buxton, *Towards a Lasting Peace* (1915)

[23]CC (16 Oct. 1914) 499, report of Kingsway Hall meeting. She had taken the same line at the NUWSS executive meeting on 14 October, arguing that if they failed to face the war issue they might indeed avoid 'violent splits', but only at the cost of a disintegration which would be far more harmful to the Union.

conviction moved Catherine Marshall, who was the Union's parliamentary secretary and prominent in this confrontation. 'I feel very deeply,' she told Mrs Fawcett, 'that we are responsible, both as individual women and Suffragists, & as a Union with an organisation which can do effective propaganda, for taking some part in forming public opinion in this grave crisis.'[24] Kathleen also declared that the shaping of public opinion on lines likely to promote a permanent peace was 'the most vital work at this moment' and one, she felt sure, 'entirely in accordance with the principles underlying the suffrage movement'.[25]

The radicals focused on the hope expressed in a recent speech by Asquith himself that Allied victory would lead to the rejection of militarism as the main force in Europe and to the creation of a European partnership 'based on the recognition of equal right . . . established and enforced by a common will'. At its provisional council in November the National Union approved the idea of trying to build up opinion on these lines and the *Common Cause* took up the message: women must ensure that when peacemaking came the government was backed by a force of opinion making for justice, self-control and wisdom. 'This is not treachery, but a sacred trust "to see that the sacrifice shall not be in vain".'

It had been agreed at the provisional council that the *Common Cause* should publish a range of views on the prevention of war and the series was launched with G. Lowes Dickinson's views on arbitration and J. A. Hobson's on disarmament. Evelyn Gunter wrote warmly to the paper, praising this new initiative.

> Let us not fear the reproach of anti-patriotism; it is the future only that is ours. In this matter we must lead, not follow, and we look to the *Common Cause* – for lists of books to guide our study, as well as for a continuance of your valuable articles. We want to hear all sides and to form our own judgement.[26]

But what were becoming serious differences on the Union's executive committee were reflected on the same page, where Mrs Fawcett voiced her opposition to a proposal that the International Women's Suffrage Alliance, unable now to meet in Berlin as planned, should hold a congress in some neutral country. This had the support of the radical element. It would be immensely worthwhile, Maude had argued, for those who believed in the solidarity of women all the world over, to meet in war, as in peace, and to declare in war, as in peace, *La Guerre contre la guerre*.[27] It seemed mad to Mrs Fawcett. They would run the risk of 'outbursts of uncontrollable nationalism'. She would have none of it.

In the event, Mrs Chapman Catt, an American and president of the

[24]Wiltsher, *Most Dangerous Women* 68.
[25]National Union executive minutes (4 March 1915)
[26]CC (8 Jan. 1915) 641.
[27]CC (1 Jan. 1915) Notes & News.

Alliance, decided against it and the radicals planned an independent congress at The Hague. This is how things stood at the beginning of February when delegates assembled in the Kingsway Hall for the National Union's annual council meeting where both sides hoped for endorsement of their views. The council gave a very ambivalent lead. For instance, they approved the Asquith line on the need for international arbitration in future but rejected the idea that the Union should work to build up opinion in support of it. And the public meeting at the end of the council brought no comfort to the radicals, either. Mrs Fawcett made clear from the chair that in her view their national duty was to drive the Germans out of Belgium and France, adding, memorably, that until that was done 'it is akin to treason to talk of peace'. And a final twist came from Marie Vérone – that rousing orator who had once thrilled them with her cry for 'La guerre contre la guerre!'

> Femmes, pacifistes, ayant prêché dans toutes les capitales l'idéal de la paix, devons-nous encore aujourd'hui crier 'à bas la guerre!'? Plus nous avons été pacifistes, plus aujourd'hui nour devons déclarer que la guerre doit aller jusqu'au bout. . . . plus nous sommes pacifistes, plus nous devons aujourd' hui demander l'écrasement non pas de l'Allemagne, mais du militarisme allemand.[28]

The executive met a fortnight later and argued over the council's resolutions. It was far from clear, Kathleen said, whether urging the government to strive to ensure that disputes were settled by arbitration meant active propaganda on the part of the Union or simply sending up resolutions. Then again, the Union was to take 'every means' to further international goodwill. Did 'every means' include sending delegates to the forthcoming women's congress at the Hague? (She, with others, had just come back from the meeting in Holland of the pilot group.) Did it cover propaganda in the *Common Cause*? Here indeed was a stumbling block. Though it passed the resolution in support of Asquith, the council 'had deliberately omitted that part . . . which provided for the building up of public opinion'. Members discussed the significance of this but Maude at least was quite clear about it. At this meeting of February 18 she resigned, saying that if the Union did not wish to work for the building of public opinion it was clear that the Union's journal could not do so. A paper on the present lines might still be valuable. She did not wish to be editor, however, since she had always hoped to be allowed to build up support for the Asquith principles. In fact she thought this task so urgent she would have been ready to give up other work in which she took 'a much more extreme line about peace' in

---

[28]CC (12 Feb. 1915) 711. Women, pacifists, having preached the ideal of peace in all the capitals, should we still shout 'down with war!' today? The more pacifist we have been, the more we must declare today that the war should go on right to the end. . . . the more pacifist we are, the more we must insist now on crushing, not Germany, but German militarism.

order to be able to devote herself to it. But the council was not willing to go even so far.

Maude's resignation was the first of their losses. At the next meeting, on March 4, Kathleen and Catherine Marshall resigned, giving reasons similar to Maude's – that the council's policy prevented them from doing work which they not only regarded as vital but as wholly in line with the women's movement. To lose the 'building up opinion' resolution had obviously been the last straw. In her letter of resignation Kathleen wrote:

> It was the whole attitude of the Council which made me realise that it was not willing to adopt any definite views about the war, much less to undertake any propaganda in support of the principles to which it gave its assent. To my mind this refusal . . . is not only a refusal to do the work which the moment demands, it is also a refusal to recognise one of the fundamental principles of the Suffrage Movement.[29]

So here at a stroke went two leading officers – the Union's secretary and parliamentary secretary. It was a misfortune to be faced, said Mrs Fawcett, 'and faced in a courageous spirit'. But more misfortunes awaited her.

That passions ran high at the committee's next meeting is plain from the long and much-amended minutes. The Union had now been invited to send delegates to the forthcoming women's congress at The Hague – that ineffably foolish and ill-starred project, as Mrs Fawcett saw it. She was ready to admit it was not called a 'peace' congress, but whatever it was it would be unrepresentative since several countries could not be present: including Belgium, 'still in its agony'. Some of the draft resolutions were 'grotesque'; and the whole thing out ot touch with national feeling. In seconding Mrs Fawcett's resolution that they should not send delegates, Lady Frances Balfour said that to participate 'would cast dishonour on our Sons who were fighting at the front'.[30] No argument could prevail against such feeling – certainly not Catherine Marshall's assurance that she did not intend to take part in a stop-the-war or peace-at-any-price campaign; or Kathleen's, that her thoughts were on the postwar settlement, 'which was not at all the same thing as working for peace in the sense intended by Mrs Fawcett'. The vote went firmly against sending delegates, and the meeting turned its thoughts to more everyday topics with whatever concentration it could muster. But at the next meeting on 15 April a further seven members resigned and two more signified their wish to do so.

So, in the spring of 1915, this issue of the freedom to prepare for peace achieved what had never been achieved by the 'Antis' or Mr Asquith's numerous 'betrayals' or any of the disappointments endured: a bitter split in the National Union, the largest women's suffrage organisation. Such an

---

[29]National Union Executive minutes (4 March 1915).
[30]ibid. (18 March 1915).

exodus, Eleanor Rathbone had feared, might well lead to the break-up of the Union and probably the break-up of Mrs Fawcett. 'I don't believe younger people often realise what it means to older people to pull up old roots or try to strike new ones,' she told Catherine Marshall.[31] In fact Mrs Fawcett did not try to strike new ones. Nor did she break up. She was nearing seventy but continued as president of the Union which she had founded in 1897, a stoical exponent of that necessary virtue: the diligence of beavers rebuilding a dam. Inwardly, though, she was deeply hurt, and Kathleen, for one, was never forgiven for things she had said in the heat of this battle.

In April 1915, however, the radicals had no time to look back. The Hague Congress was practically upon them and the interest aroused among internationalist women in Europe and the United States already seemed to justify the hopes of its promoters. Delegates were expected to attend from a wide range of women's societies. At a Caxton Hall meeting at the end of March, Maude (on the British Committee of the congress – Kathleen was chairman) told the audience that at least two societies of German women would be represented; apart from which, 'a considerable number' of individual women were coming from Germany and Austria-Hungary. There would be great problems in French women attending but delegates were expected from Belgium, as well as from Switzerland, Denmark, Italy and, of course, the United States. A hundred were expected from Great Britain and Ireland and 'it was not anticipated that there would be any difficulty about passports'.[32]

With these last words she gave a hostage to fortune. One might almost say that at this point the remarkable story of the Hague Congress took off into the realms of romance, for the *Morning Post* report of the Caxton Hall speech came to the attention of Lady Jersey, and Lady Jersey must be deemed 'an enemy', though one perhaps no longer at the front of Maude's mind. Lady Jersey was a *grande dame*, a political hostess of the old order, although sufficiently abreast of the new to have become vice-president (under Lord Cromer) of the National League for Opposing Woman Suffrage. In that capacity she was of course familiar with the long-drawn-out and well-publicised wrangle which had gone on in 1912 when Maude would not enter into public debate with the League's secretary, Gladys Pott, about the figures she had used in *Votes and Wages*. The 'Antis' had been baulked then but Lady Jersey made it up to them now.

She wrote from the *Villa Luynes* in Cannes to Sir Arthur Nicolson at the Foreign Office, apologising for troubling him. Regarding the account in the *Morning Post*, she knew nothing, she said, about one speaker, 'but I know that Miss Maude Royden is a singularly inaccurate sentimentalist – very

[31]Wiltsher, *Most Dangerous Women* 68.
[32]*Morning Post* (1 Jan. 1915).

eloquent – misrepresents facts about the female labour market – a keen
suffragist – and is, I understand, successful in rousing male feelings.'

> She is exactly the kind of woman who would make a moving address on
> Lyttelton – Carnegie – Simpson – Courtney of Penwith lines, which would (like
> Dr Lyttelton's sermons) be re-produced to our injury in neutral countries. I think
> it is a dangerous idea that 100 English Women of the Suffrage – Peace – Ethical –
> Reconciliation Class should, at this crisis, go and orate at the Hague in company
> with 'a considerable number of German women'.[33]

Lady Jersey was well-accustomed to giving a guiding hand to politicians.
'The one way to stop it.' she went on now, 'would be absolutely to refuse
the Passports.'

> I think (if I may venture to suggest) that whoever gives Passports should find out
> quietly *in advance* who the Women are – but not refuse them absolutely till near
> enough to the time to prevent their making other arrangements! Probably our
> Minister at the Hague could throw some light on the subject. We are supposed to
> be under Martial War [sic] but I suppose these women could not be stopped from
> talking indirect treason if they once got onto Neutral ground. Please forgive my
> troubling you . . . but I commend the matter to your wise consideration.

One can see why Lady Jersey did not need a vote: what she suggested is
exactly what happened. It is true that three Englishwomen got to The
Hague: Kathleen Courtney and Chrystal Macmillan went over there ahead
of all these machinations, while Emmeline Pethick-Lawrence, who had
been in America, arrived with the American delegation. But the rest of the
180 women who wished to go from Britain were prevented from doing so;
Maude among them. She had been deputed, with Lucy Gardner, to represent the Fellowship of Reconciliation and was one of those – twenty-four
in all – who got the necessary Home Office permits, and passports from the
Foreign Office too, but only in time to find that the Admiralty had decided
to close the North Sea to shipping. They waited at Tilbury for over a week,
on the offchance of getting a passage – a sitting target for the *Daily Express*.

> All Tilbury is laughing at the Peacettes, the misguided Englishwomen who,
> baggage in hand, are waiting at Tilbury for a boat to take them to Holland, where
> they are anxious to talk peace with German fraus over the teapot.

Sometimes 'peacettes', sometimes 'cranquettes' – a new vocabulary came
into being. 'Even from the ranks of the super-cranks at the back of the
Liberal benches there rose no champion of the misguided women who have

---

[33]Jersey to Nicolson, (7 April 1915) Public Record Office, FO 372/771. I am grateful to
Anne Wiltsher for drawing my attention to this letter. (Dr Lyttelton, Headmaster of Eton, had
preached in 1915 on 'Love Your Enemies', Andrew Carnegie had endowed peace work,
Canon Simpson thought clergy should not bear arms and Courtney of Penwith had spoken
against the war in the House of Lords in 1914).

been trying to reach The Hague for an international chirrup.'[34]

Many did get there: five from Belgium, forty-three from Germany and Austria-Hungary, thirty from Sweden, Norway and Denmark, forty-seven from the USA, 1,000 from Holland. The American party, including the social pioneer Jane Addams, who was to act as congress president, crossed the Atlantic risking torpedoes only to be checked in the English Channel by naval action and reach The Hague shortly after proceeding began. The Belgians came by permission of the Germans but, contrary to what Mrs Fawcett had feared, there were no violent nationalist outbursts and the congress succeeded in defining principles to form the basis of a lasting peace (some of them foreshadowing President Wilson's). It also proposed continuous mediation by a conference of neutrals to end the conflict; and then and there sent envoys to the European capitals and the USA to press for such a conference. So through the summer of 1915 statesmen in fourteen capitals were visited by these women on extraordinary journeys back and forth across warring Europe. They got good hearings but no results.

Maude, unable to reach The Hague, lost no chance to speak about peace and its relation to the woman's movement. To a quip that suffrage was now forgotten, she answered with unpacific wrath, ' "If I forget thee, O Jerusalem, let my right hand forget her cunning!" ' 'To work for peace was to work for the woman movement, and to work for the woman movement was to work for peace.'[35] At the time she resigned the editorship she had said that, outside the National Union, she was taking 'a much more extreme line about peace' and the previous November she had asked Catherine Marshall to come and hear her 'discourse on the war' to the reconciliation group at the Collegium.

> The Quaker publishers have offered to publish my statement of the case, and I feel that if I accept this offer I am very definitely pledged to an extreme course. I think no one understands quite how much this means to me as you do, and I want you, if possible, to hear what I am thinking of publishing before I finally decide.[36]

A few months later *The Great Adventure* blazoned her position beyond all doubt. It was a call not to take up arms but to lay them down in the cause of peace.

> Whose heart is not stirred, whose breath does not come faster, when soldiers pass us in the street? Look at their faces, and realise how much they are prepared to sacrifice. Everyone of them faces death, and there are things worse than death, and they go gaily to face all these things. Is it not heroic? Well, I tell you that there is a mightier heroism still – the heroism not of the battle but of the cross; the adventure not of war but of peace. For which is the braver man when all is said,

[34]Wiltsher, *Most Dangerous Women* 89, 90.
[35]*Free Church Suffrage Times* (May 1915) 48.
[36]Maude to Catherine Marshall, (18 Nov. 1914) Cumbria Reford Office, Marshall Papers, D/Mar/3/39

the man who believes in armaments or the man who stakes everything on an idea? Who is the great adventurer – he who goes against the enemy with swords and guns, or he who goes with naked hands? Who is the mighty hunter – he who seeks the quarry with stones and slings, or he who, with St Francis, goes to tame a wolf with nothing but the gospel? We peace people have made of peace a dull, drab, sordid, selfish thing. We have made it that ambiguous, dreary thing – 'neutrality'. But Peace is the great adventure, the glorious romance. And only when the world conceives it so, will the world be drawn after it again. 'I, when I am lifted up, will draw all men unto Me.'[37]

The worst sin of all, she had told Gilbert Murray, would be simply to have 'stood aside' and she was far too much of a patriot not to feel a contempt for that. 'To remain spectators only of the agony of Belgium would have been the basest of all betrayals.' Was Christ 'neutral' then, on the Cross? 'War was better than neutrality,' she said, 'if these were the only alternatives.'[38] But they were not. There was 'the great adventure.'

In similar words – addressed also to Christians – she had framed the spiritual claim of women's suffrage: 'To us is offered once more the great adventure.'[39] And at the heart of it is sacrifice – in the case of peace, on a massive scale, for *The Great Adventure* returns to the idea that peace may demand a martyr nation – a thought which chokes the *Daily Express*. ('Peace Crank's Mad Plea! . . . *The Great Adventure* . . . is practically a plea for national suicide . . . Rather than fight the poor Germans, Britain should have disarmed and shared the fate of Belgium.')[40] 'What I proposed in *The Great Adventure* was not that the nation should commit suicide, but that it should risk crucifixion,' said Maude, 'a distinction all Christians will understand.'[41]

'I have read another "war pamphlet" by Maude Royden,' wrote Eva Slawson, a London typist whose diary casts a vivid light on these years. 'I think it very fine, but feel we *must* recognise that all people are not ready to see a nobler vision. Still,' she allowed, 'that must not prevent those who *do* see from striving to realise their ideal, working for and preaching it day by day!' 'Are you not trying to "hurry God"?' wrote friendly Bishop Winnington-Ingram.

> Even God can only get out of each age the morality of which the age is capable. . . . Your 'ideal morality' is not possible yet, but ideas of arbitration etc. are growing and we shall look back from (we hope) Paradise when we are working together there in 1,000,000 years and find it done.[42]

[37]Maude Royden, *The Great Adventure: The Way to Peace* (1915) 7, 12.
[38]ibid. 4.
[39]*Extracts from May Mission Speeches delivered in London by A. Maude Royden* (May 11, 1910) 8.
[40]*Daily Express* (4 Aug. 1915).
[41]*South Wales Daily Post* (8 March 1917).
[42]Eva's diary, 8 April 1915, in Tierl Thompson (ed.), *Dear Girl* (1987) 266; Winnington-Ingram to Maude (28 Jan. 1915) Fawcett 221.

Meanwhile, nations could not take risks like individuals. 'Could we risk the violation of thousands of young girls . . . as . . . in Belgium and France, if the "adventure" had failed?'

But Maude claimed not only the high moral ground but the lower pragmatic ground as well.[43] In the immediate prewar period 'the fact . . . that we were not trusted was crucial.' Arms fever drove each of the belligerents to justify war in self-defence and nothing short of a laying down of arms could have broken the vicious circle. Only thus could England have convinced Germany that she had no aggressive intent.

> In this way only, could we really have saved Belgium. For who, looking at that unhappy country now, will claim that with all our efforts and all our sacrifices we have 'saved' her? . . . Had we disarmed, we should at least have saved Belgium intact, or suffered with her.

She believed that leaving to the first aggressor the appalling moral responsibility of marching on a nonresistant people might in fact have prevented war. 'I must also admit that it might have failed'. But war was not exempt from the risk of failure. 'War also is a great adventure.' It was even possible – God forbid – that they might fail to drive the Germans from Belgium. As to the risk of national destruction – nations were ready to die for freedom.

> Will no nation be found ready to die for peace? Or is peace too small a thing to die for? Truly, if the nations do not desire peace, none will be found to die for it; only do not let us deceive ourselves by pretending that a nation must not dare all for an ideal when only today we pay our homage to the heroism of little Belgium.

As to the hope of making peace through war, was it even likely that Germany, defeated, would turn away from the Prussian ideal?

> It seems to me almost more . . . than one can expect of broken and humiliated nations. It seems . . . far more likely that a defeated country will merely wish it had sacrificed . . . more to a still mightier army or blame its diplomatists.

Maude dismissed now, as often before, the argument for waiting till the world was 'ready'. If war was wrong, then they should say so; even at a moment when every nerve thrilled with the desire 'to be "one with the nation".' And, from her own experience surely, she speaks of the urge to respond to an audience which every speaker feels

> when he knows that with a word . . . he can strike out the laughter or applause which makes electric his touch upon them. Perhaps even as he says it he betrays them; and would, that word left unsaid, have been more true. This thrill of sympathy the peace-maker . . . forgoes.

It is another glimpse of what cost her most. Again and again she comes back

---

[43]The illustrative passages that follow are taken from Royden, *The Great Adventure*.

to the fear – not of abuse, but of being, as she said, cut off 'from the great torrent of my country's suffering'. 'There is something terrible in the standing aside of the absolute pacifist,' she wrote, years later.[44] This is her dread: to be cut off from people. In retrospect it seemed to her almost a miracle, 'considering how terribly strongly we all felt about the war' that she had not lost a single one of her friends, 'deeply as they were divided from me in many cases in opinion'.[45]

The Roydens were positive in war, as ever. Indeed, the soldiers Maude saw marching through Oxford may very probably have got to France thanks to the efforts of her brother Tom, for it was his genius with shipping and resources which embarked the British Expeditionary Force.[46] Her sister Ethel helped Katherine Furse to establish the Women's Royal Naval Service. Daisy's three sons were all in action by the spring of 1915 since Ralph, rejected for military service, managed to join the Friends' Ambulance Unit. 'He was an enthusiast about the war; as utterly convinced as anyone could be of its rightness' Maude recalled. As for his view of pacifism then, 'If you can stop war with spiritual power, do it,' he had told her. 'If you can't, let me do what I can.'[47] And, strangely, it gave her no relief, later, that he seemed to change his mind. By 1918 he had become convinced that war was altogether damnable. and useless. 'I said, "How merciful that you are doing Red Cross work"'. Ralph replied that he had thought so once, but now he wondered whether he shouldn't give it up 'and come home and face the music'. 'I remember the pang of terror that seized me.' For she could not help feeling how much she would prefer even the horrors of war for Ralph than 'the unspeakable anguish of conscientious objection'.[48]

Hudson was never a pacifist. Maude comments that their love did not depend on thinking alike and recalls his pride as chaplain to the Honourable Artillery Company, the regiment in which Bernard enlisted. He liked wearing uniform and preaching to the men. Kathleen was not Maude's sort of pacifist either. More of her life than of Maude's, in fact, was to be given to work for peace; but the form this took was shaped not only by a difference of conviction but a difference of style. 'I don't appeal to your

---

[44]Royden, 'Bid Me Discourse'.

[45]'The Loneliness of the Prince of Peace', preached at the Guildhouse, 10 July 1927. The sermon is a moving account of the isolation of the pacifist.

[46]The younger Thomas Royden was by this time deputy chairman of the Cunard Line. Before war broke out he had been asked by the government to report on the facilities available for transporting an expeditionary force to France and, according to a family memoir, 'it was largely owing to his recommendations that so much was done, particularly on the French side' to facilitate its passage to France and Flanders and maintain the flow of munitions and supplies. He became Assistant Director of Transport, a member of the Shipping Control Committee and the Royal Commmission on Wheat Supplies. He represented the Controller of Shipping at the peace conference, and in 1919 was created a Companion of Honour for his services. See John Royden Rooper, *The Uncompleted Journey* (privately printed 1966).

[47]Maude Royden, 'The failure of the Pacifists', *Survey Graphic*, 30, (Dec. 1941).

[48]'The Loneliness of the Prince of Peace'.

heart but to your head!' she had told them at the Hague congress where she struck one American delegate as excessively cool and detached.[49] While she was an excellent platform speaker ('of course I could never cast a spell like Maude Royden') there was more of the mandarin than the missionary in her. One could hardly imagine Maude, for instance, sitting month after month in Geneva, as Kathleen did through the 1920s, following the stultifying convolutions of the Preparatory Disarmament Commission; nor could one easily imagine Kathleen setting out as Maude did in 1915 to convert England to passive resistance.

The idea of embarking on a peace mission seems to have arisen spontaneously at the Fellowship of Reconciliation's first conference which took place at Swanwick in July. The mood of those present was clearly more confident, not to say exalted, than it had been in December. 'How can one, even in many words, describe "that which passeth understanding"?' ran one account which tried to convey their sense of Pentecost, 'unconquerable faith' and conviction that 'war of every kind, even this awful, colossal struggle' could be ended through spiritual power.[50] The 'great adventure' seemed to lie before them. One of those to whom Maude's book had spoken powerfully was Constance Todd, then in her twenties and ordained soon after in the Congregational Church (the first woman minister ordained in England). She and Claude Coltman, the man she was to marry, were there at Swanwick, where Maude on the platform appealed to young people to follow her. Women who asked her 'What can we do whilst our brothers fight?' were told, 'There is the country! Go! Convert England to Christian pacifism!'[51]

The organisation was simple enough. A large horse-drawn caravan was found, big enough to carry stores and literature and provide sleeping space for the women. After a service of dedication, they set out, Maude in the open caravan, some of the young men and women with her and others cycling or walking alongside. They were from various denominations, a mixture of ministers, clergy, Quakers, theological students, laymen and laywomen. Constance Todd was one of the party, which, it was planned, fresh speakers would join as it passed through their part of the country. They had worked out a route through the Midlands to London and all its details, Maude said later, were conveyed to the public by two newspapers, which, while deploring the thought of violence said that no one could be blamed if it occurred. 'Is the Sermon on the Mount practical politics? We think so,' ran one of their pamphlets. But of course they knew there was risk involved. The recent sinking of the *Lusitania* had produced a wave of

[49]Wiltsher, *Most Dangerous Women* 91.
[50]*Free Church Suffrage Times* (Aug. 1915) 74.
[51]The Rev. Claude and the Rev. Constance Coltman, interviewed 26 Sept. 1967 by Emil Oberholzer.

anti-German riots which in Maude's own city of Liverpool had at length to be checked by troops. London had by now suffered aerial bombardment. And the experience of other members of the Fellowship was ominous. Earlier in July Dr W. E. Orchard, the well-known minister of Kings Weigh House Church, had a very hostile reception in Beaconsfield. Before he could begin his planned address ('How to prevent War') a man got up and said it was indecent to talk about peace when there was no prospect of peace and such a meeting 'at this time' was an outrage on the feelings of the English people. The audience drowned out any response by singing the national anthem and then by whistling a patriotic air to 'a walking stick and umbrella obligato'. Dr Orchard eventually left, amid cheers and the singing of 'Rule Britannia'.[52]

One participant in Maude's expedition later wrote a detailed account.[53] Each day began with prayers round the caravan, reports of the previous night's meetings and discussion of plans for the coming day. They progressed slowly through Derbyshire arousing curiosity but little opposition. Sometimes they came across Christian pacifists who had not heard of the FOR, sometimes lonely 'friends of peace' glad to be reassured and encouraged. Clergy and ministers were usually wary but a few opened churches for meetings and services. The writer, looking back across fifty years, stresses the novelty of pacifism then.

> These were the days long before the PPU, the League of Nations Union and other such bodies of peace propaganda existed, so that the Christian pacifist position was new and strange, Quakerish and Tolstoian. Popular arguments for and against had not been worn threadbare and there was much excited discussion. Keen converts were made, while others scoffed at ideas which seemed utopian, fantastic, unpatriotic and even unscriptural.

At open-air meetings the most vocal opposition came, it seems, from recruiting sergeants, for conscription had not yet come in and of course, the mission hindered voluntary recruiting.

When the caravan reached Mansfield in Nottinghamshire 'rumblings of the coming storm were heard'. This mining town amid Sherwood Forest was not deficient in patriotism, as can be seen from the local paper which reported the Fellowship mission. On the front page are portraits of soldiers – local boys – 'well-known in cricket circles' or 'when not in khaki . . . a postman'; with the message:

> THESE BOYS DIDN'T SHIRK. *THEY WANT HELP !!* Listen for a moment – can't you hear them calling *TO YOU ? BE A MAN* There's a King's uniform waiting for *YOU* – go and put it on *NOW !*

A few pages later comes the account of 'the extraordinary spectacle' the

---

[52] *Bucks Examiner* (9 July 1915).
[53] *Reconciliation* (Feb. 1964) 25–27. Unfortunately the author's name is not given.

previous Sunday 'of a crowd, composed of soldiers and civilians, jeering and scoffing at a young woman whilst praying from the market cross in Westgate'. This was very likely Constance Todd.

> They bore with her for a few minutes while she preached the gospel of reconciliation . . . but when one of her male companions . . . said he believed in the Biblical precept, as applied to the Germans, 'to pray for those who despitefully use you' then there was a general hubbub. . . . 'Will all of you who are not Christians please be quiet while I pray?' she asked. 'Who aint a Christian?' queried several. The young woman, who throughout showed much self-possession, commenced her petition, but there was so much noise that she stopped and said, 'Will you please uncover your heads while I pray? No! roared the crowd. Then she proceeded to pray . . . but could scarcely be heard, for booing and jeering. . . . The scene for a minute or two was a painful one, and several people were shocked . . . and moved away.[54]

The missioners also thought it wise to move on, so they cut short their visit and went to Nottingham where they had a number of successful meetings. They went to Loughborough in Leicestershire, where, it seems, the mayor's sister-in-law, a great admirer of Maude's suffrage work, invited her to stay in her house (though the Mayor himself was in charge of recruiting). By now, runs the account, there were articles appearing in certain London dailies saying they were spies, financed by 'German gold' to frustrate the war effort and that they should be given 'the treatment they deserve'.[55] What this was they discovered at Hinckley.

In the afternoon of their second day there an indoor meeting addressed by Constance Todd and other women missioners ended in disorder, while later that same day two of the men, after a similarly hostile meeting, were attacked in the street by a large crowd and forced to take refuge in a chemist's shop. Two others, returning to Hinckley that evening from a meeting in a neighbouring town, found the place in uproar. One went to investigate and had himself to be rescued by police. The other ran to warn those at the caravan site.

> The only preparation Maude Royden made was for all of us to leave the caravan, where supper was being prepared, and sit in a circle on the ground in silence and prayer, waiting for any attack. Hundreds of people headed by the local recruiting sergeant and a man, half drunk, clanging a big bell, poured down the lane leading to the farmer's field where we were camping.

Most really believed they were spies. It was payday, anyway, and many were drunk. The tents were pillaged and torn down, the caravan tipped

---

[54] *Mansfield Reporter* (23 July 1915).

[55] In an article entitled 'Peace Crank's Mad Plea' the *Daily Express*, (4 Aug. 1915) derided Maude's pamphlet *The Great Adventure* and appealed to readers to send advance particulars of meetings to be held by the Union of Democratic Control, the Stop-the-War Committee, The Fellowship of Reconciliation and the No-Conscription Fellowship.

over and set ablaze. So things went on for two or three hours.

> We remained in their hands and at their mercy . . . saved from physical attack
> that night by our sheer pacifism. Not one of us – there were about a dozen,
> including Ebenezer Cunningham, later Chairman of the Congregational Union of
> England and Wales, and Reginald Sorenson, later a member of Parliament – made
> the slightest resistance or protest . . . and not one of us received a blow. Many
> times some of the crowd would threateningly approach us . . . with raised fists
> and with violent reproaches threaten what they were going to do to us, but they
> always stopped at the last moment. One man seized Maude Royden by the throat,
> but he was the worse for drink and, looking foolish when no one interfered,
> released her. Several of the men in khaki dragged two Church of England young
> curates to the burning caravan, now a big bonfire, to throw them on it, but
> refrained at the edge of the fire.

The shouting and flames attracted more and more people, milling round, jeering, threatening and looting. A mattress which one man tried to make off with was fetched back and pitched on the flames and the crowd broke out into 'Tipperary' as the roof of the caravan fell in. Police were unable to cope with a mob which they reckoned at two to three thousand. It did not lessen till the flames died down. Then one by one the missioners were able to creep away to the police station, and at about three o'clock in the morning were bundled onto the Leicester express – which the Inspector had stopped for the purpose. 'Just as the train was about to leave, the stationmaster . . . poked in his head and called out, "Keep on with it! I share your beliefs." ' And they left 'unexpectedly comforted'.

There is no comfort in Maude's recollection. 'If I must be killed by an enemy, may I be killed at long range!' she said, at a later time, when the Second World War gave point to her words yet could not erase the memory of those terrible faces. To be, at close range, an object of hate – this indeed it was to be cut off from people! Some of those in the crowd at Hinckley had 'husbands, fathers, sweethearts and sons [who] had been mown down in Suvla Bay. They could not hear or see us without hatred, convinced as they were we were betraying the cause sealed with that blood.' They could not reason, or listen; they were almost physically unable to hear. Hinckley, she admitted, shook her judgement on speaking 'in season and out of season' – though whether one was silent from wisdom or cowardice at any given moment was hard to tell. 'I only know that to go on preaching peace to people in such straits . . . seemed intolerable.'[56]

[56]'Bid Me Discourse'.

7

Ecclesiastical Militancy

If . . . you feel the situation is intolerable and . . . the best way of
getting the law mended is to break it, are not these the methods of
the WSPU? . . . It seems to me that it is a sort of ecclesiastical
militancy.

Rev. Francis Eeles to Maude Royden (1917):

'Miss Royden described herself as a pacifist,' ran an account of an interview
with Maude for a Sunday paper in 1917, 'but her views in regard to the war
are, after all, of such a reasonable kind.'[1] *The Great Adventure*, the writer
went on, had been written very soon after war broke out, when its author
was dominated by the idea of 'a tremendous appeal to the conscience of the
nations'. But now she thought war could not have been avoided – or not
without something like a League of Nations to forestall the outbreak of
conflict. 'Miss Royden,' the readers were assured, 'does not belong to the
"Be-kind-to-Germany" school, although she admits that she does not want
to hate Germany.'

> The barbarities of the Hun – so strongly accentuated since those early days of the
> war when she wrote her book – she has no desire to minimise; but her admission
> of a distaste for hatred of Huns is based on the Christian theory that we should
> love our enemies.

Allowing for the writer's obvious desire to play down the 'peace-crank'
angle, it does seem that Maude, while she may have continued to believe
that war was always wrong, did not continue to insist upon it. A few
months later when she was invited to preach regularly at the City Temple
she felt bound to explain that she was a pacifist 'in a sense more extreme
than that to which you . . . as a church have committed yourselves'.
Nonetheless,

> I am more and more convinced that the word 'pacifist' should not be claimed only
> by those who hold my position, but belongs to all those who hope and work for a

---

[1] *Illustrated Sunday Herald* (18 March 1917).

time when we shall find some other way of settling international differences than war.[2]

Casting the net as wide as this takes the term 'pacifist' a long way away from the apparently simple idea of someone totally opposed to war. Knowing as we do that twenty years later Maude was one of a number of people who found they could not hold to their pacifist creed, faced with the abomination of Hitler, it is tempting to read such things as portents.

Constance Coltman, in retrospect, thought that Maude had been shaken by the incident at Hinckley where preaching peace had created war; also that Hudson had urged upon her the need for prudence after that debacle.[3] In the months that followed, personal experience brought fresh pain to standing apart. Just after Hinckley Ralph came home to have shrapnel removed from his face. Hudson and Effie's much-loved Bernard was killed at the beginning of 1917. 'Even among so many young lives, this one stands out to me,' wrote A. L. Smith from Balliol, recalling a summer's day at South Luffenham years before when Bernard had been 'a most engaging companion to me'. As he had to Maude – the most simple and cheerful of those among whom she had found herself: 'small Bernard Shaw', who played ping-pong with her and had immediately reminded her of Ralph.

Effie bore her terrible loss without words, and also, it seems without the comfort of 'a sure and certain hope' of reunion. Bernard had been even more necessary to her than only sons usually were to mothers, in Maude's view, because her range was so limited. She was intensely proud of him – and of his courage in taking a commission in response to appeals put out at a time when the future of young officers was measured in weeks. He was killed in weeks. At the time of his death, another young friend of Maude's, Gerald Booth (of whom we know little but his name), wrote to her on his final leave.

> It amuses me . . . to think that I am going out to fight. How the Fates must laugh at us when we who before the War had the views we used to talk about and now they twiddle us round their fingers and make us do all sorts of things we should never have thought possible. Personally, I am quite reconciled to killing as many Germans . . . as I come across but I must admit I don't like to hear of the deaths of German children . . . brought on by food substitutes and yet I don't see how we can raise the Blockade.

> Dear old Maude, [the letter ends] I should have liked to have seen you again before I went out.

---

[2]Maude to Executive Committee, City Temple (1 July 1917) Fawcett 222. Martin Ceadel, *Pacifism in Britain 1914–1945*, (1980) restricts the word 'pacifist' to the 'no war' position and uses 'pacificist' for those who, in Maude's words, 'hope and work' for peace. As he shows, the interwar pacifist scene was complex and confused.

[3]The Rev. Claude and the Rev. Constance Coltman, Oberholzer interview.

'I cannot tell you how much I owe to you. I wonder if you ever realised what a tremendous influence you have had on my life. I have sort of worshipped you all my life and I cannot tell you how much I admire you for sticking to your guns over the War, though of course I did not agree with you or I shoudn't be a Captain now.[4]

For Maude, since Hinckley, sticking to her guns had meant working for the Women's International League. This was launched in the autumn of 1915 as the British section of the peace committee which had been established in Holland to carry on the work of the Hague Congress. Like all the other sections – and groups were formed in most European countries, and the USA – the League was to work for 'permanent peace' and promote the cause of internationalism. Helena Swanwick was elected chairman, Kathleen, Maude and Margaret Ashton vice chairmen, Catherine Marshall, hon. secretary. In the manner of the National Union the League was organised through local branches and the tone, if not the size, of its ha'penny news sheet is reminiscent of the *Common Cause*. In a violently hostile climate any kind of peacemaking needed courage. 'Live Dangerously' was the WIL motto. And though former militants who became members thought it did not live dangerously enough, it attracted attention from the Home Office (always on the lookout for anti-war speakers) and derision from the gutter Press. 'How can we educate people as to the spirit and purpose of our League?' wrote Emmeline Pethick-Lawrence, despairing. 'It is almost impossible to obtain halls or to hold public meetings.'[5] Yet hundreds were held – many broken up by hooligan violence as frightening as Maude's experience at Hinckley but of a more deliberate and organised kind. An Anti-German League had come into being whose main object was to rouse the mob.

Despite the problems, members of the WIL tried to keep up with their contacts abroad. It was no longer possible to talk to 'the enemy' but their monthly news sheet had 'International Notes' and they knew that other women were working for peace, even in Germany. The scraps that came through showed that such women were as worried as themselves about the war's effect on the minds of children and the growth of militarism in schools. This was something which preoccupied Maude; she spoke about it on various platforms and ran a successful WIL conference on the theme of national bias in the teaching of history.

Kathleen's work for the WIL was interrupted at the end of the year when she left England to work with refugees for the Friends' War Victims Relief Committee. Letters came from her in Alexandria, then from a hospital ship in Greece, then from Bastia in Corsica where she was in charge of a relief

---

[4]Gerald Booth to Maude Royden (n.d., but from internal evidence just after Christmas 1916) Fawcett 222.
[5]*WIL News Sheet* (June 1916).

camp for Serbs and evidently finding the French *Croix Rouge* ('Really, these women!') most incompetent by the standards of the National Union.[6] Maude herself took a nursing course at a maternity hospital that autumn. Dr Annie McCall's hospital in Clapham seems to have attracted a number of women who wanted to prepare themselves for relief work through a training in midwifery.[7] Whether or not she had this in view, Maude left Clapham awed by her experience of the courage of women in childbirth. Here, she said, was the answer to those who felt their feminism 'oozing away' in the all-pervading atmosphere of war. Let them go and work in a maternity hospital.

> There they will see, to match the heroism and the sacrifice of the soldier, an equal heroism, an equal sacrifice, but without Victoria Crosses. . . . There they will see the war which women suffer to bring life into the world.[8]

For an audience which had gathered to hear her speak with Margaret Bondfield, Catherine Marshall and others on 'The Women's Case Against Conscription', it was no doubt a sharp reminder that the old causes of women went on: that the case against conscription did not extinguish the case against prostitution, for instance. In 1916 she wrote a foreword to *Downward Paths* ('An inquiry into the causes which contribute to the making of the prostitute') and a pamphlet, *Notification – And Then?* which countered the arguments of those who favoured compulsory notification of venereal disease and summary police powers against suspected women in the old Contagious Diseases Acts style.

In 1916 though, in pacifist terms, the issues were conscription and negotiated peace. The Military Service Act was passed in February – 'the gravest infringement of the rights of conscience' the WIL said, faced like other peace groups with the question how far to go in backing those rights. The No-Conscription Fellowship went to the limit: that is, rejected military service and any form of civil alternative. Whether or not it approved the hard line, the WIL was supportive enough to lend its secretary, Catherine Marshall, to help to make the NCF mor efficient. And so it happened that within a few months, 'the ablest woman organiser in the land' peeled away from the WIL.

Maude regretted the loss very much. For one thing, for all her regard for conscience, she did not herself approve the law-breaking aspect of NCF activities, and wrote to Marshall,

> I have for it much more respect, yet rathér the same *kind* of respect, that I had for

[6]See Fawcett KDC/C1/1–4 for Kathleen's letters home.

[7]Charis Frankenburg, *Not Old, Madam, Vintage* (1975) 78–86 describes how she went to Dr McCall's when the Friends War Victims Relief Committee advised her to get midwifery training in preparation for work with young babies. 'One student was outstanding, Maude Royden.'

[8]*The Coming Day* (Jan. 1916) 3.

the best kind of Militant. I think it wrong, though not nearly so wrong, in much the same kind of way. The more I see, both of Militants and political Pacifists, the more I realise that their mistakes are only possible to very fine people. But I still think them mistakes.

She had a high regard for Marshall, whom she once described as the statesman of the women's movement – 'a statesman who was also something of a prophet' – and the letter goes on in terms which imply the sad loss of a kindred soul.

> Yours was the most constructive, the most fruitful, the most essentially pacific mind that I have ever met. It made you, to me, seem a greater mind than either Nellie [Swanwick] or Kathleen. Your leaving us was a greater loss to constructive Pacifism than either of the others would have been. Even now I feel a certain confidence that you would understand what I want the WIL to be, better than Nellie does, because your mind is made that way.[9]

Whatever Maude wanted the WIL to be she had not been able to convince Nellie Swanwick and told Marshall she had come up against a temperament which could be called 'critical, or analytical or destructive, according to taste!' Marshall got similar complaints of Maude from Swanwick, who wrote in October 1917,

> You've heard Maude has definitely refused to stand again? She is an extraordinarily unfair and intolerant person. Nothing she has ever done or proposed has been criticised and turned down but she has some vague scunner at me and apparently can't live in the same room as me. I'm sorry, for the sake of the WIL. I wish she would not so grotesquely misrepresent my opinions. I suppose officially 'religious' people are quite hopelessly antagonistic to rationalist minds like mine.

And this, taken with a later reference to liking Maude 'much better as a speaker than as a preacher' gives a good enough clue to their relationship.[10] Maude's irritation with Nellie Swanwick may even have tended to intensify the feeling she seems to have had at about this time that she was spending herself on too many causes. Apart from conscientious objectors and peace negotiations and the prospect now, if Asquith revised the electoral register, of being poised again to press the claims of women – there were things of her own which came to boiling point that summer: she was in the forefront of a struggle to make some claims for women in the Church of England.

Maude never dated the beginning of this struggle – which became, in effect, the struggle of her life – with the precision she applied to suffrage. Nothing

---

[9]Maude Royden to Catherine Marshall (10 Aug. 1916) (Marshall Papers, Cumbria Record Office).
[10]Marshall Papers, D/MAR/4/79 (11 Oct. 1917); Swanwick, *I Have Been Young*, 185.

equivalent to reading Lecky caused scales suddenly to fall from her eyes. Though there must have been times at South Luffenham when they talked about the ministry of women, all we have is Hudson's memory of his sermons being 'riddled with hot shot' over lunch and comments being made on his reading of the lesson. 'I would have given worlds.' he reports her saying, 'to have ejected you from the lectern and read that magnificent lesson myself, *properly*,'[11] But there is no hint that they discussed the fact that as a woman, she could not have done so. On one occasion, as Maude remembered, Hudson had organised a mission week and asked her to speak at the last service.

> For this purpose the congregation had to be marshalled in procession and marched off to the schoolroom where it sat in acute discomfort, crowded, asphyxiated, and in children's desk-seats, to hear me explain 'Why I am a Christian.'[12]

She may, she fancied, have wondered dimly why such a trek should be necessary, but, with the prospect of the ordeal ahead, remembered only 'feeling quite sick'.

The question of women speaking or preaching had hardly been raised then in the Church of England but there was debate about the role they should play in the new arrangements for church government – on which the general view was: none. Whether Maude noticed such things or not, while she was at Oxford and much engrossed in confession and the Cowley Fathers, the Church of England had been taking its first steps to involve laymen in decision-making – steps well-marked by a determination to keep lay-women out of it. Thus, when the bishops in 1897 encouraged the formation of parochial church councils they ruled that, while both sexes were entitled to vote, only men could stand for election. Women lost even this modest franchise a few years later because it was held to give them influence indirectly on the Church's more important national body, the Representative Church Council.

Not everyone was happy about this. Mrs Louise Creighton, widely respected by the church hierarchy on her own account and as widow of a former bishop of London, thought the exclusion 'must tend to alienate thinking women from parish work'.[13] Bishop Gore called it 'a great act of injustice' while Edward Talbot urged his fellow bishops to pay more respect to 'the fundamental principle of the equality before God of male and female'. Following such pressure, in 1905, women got back their parochial vote, but not on an equal footing with men. Men could vote for parochial church councils simply as churchmen; while women were required, additionally, to own or occupy property – on the lines of the municipal franchise. At Gore's insistence, in 1911 the Representative Church Council

[11]Shaw, 'Maude Royden 1901–1920'.
[12]TFC, 16.
[13]Brian Heeney *The Women's Movement in the Church of England 1850–1930* (1988) 99.

agreed to set up a committee to review the question. Three years later it reported in favour of an equal franchise at parish level – and of letting women serve on parish councils. These proposals met fierce opposition on the Representative Church Council itself but were passed at length in 1914, though the bar against women on higher councils remained till the Enabling Act of 1919 wiped out such distinctions.

There is some irony in laying all this alongside the view which Maude held more passionately than anyone else of her generation: that the women's movement stemmed from Christianity; *was* Christianity, a working-out of the Christian ideal in their own day, 'the most profoundly moral movement . . . since the foundation of the Christian Church.' From which it followed that the forces against it could 'only be conquered by faith and prayer' since they were not based on reasoned opposition, but on prejudice and moral baseness. And against these there was no weapon but 'the faith that removes mountains'. Given the fact that the biggest mountains were to be found in Anglican territory and that Christianity took tangible shape in Maude's life through the Anglican Church there was no way to avoid collision.

The church council question touched on the problem. Behind it lay the great mass that rested on *Genesis* (woman was made 'after man, out of man and for man' as one Victorian bishop said) and on St Paul's advice to the Corinthians ('Let your women keep silence in the churches'). Nowhere was the Victorian ideal of 'separate spheres' more deeply entrenched or sheltered womanhood more warmly extolled than in the average Anglican pulpit. St Paul was often cited in the discussion over whether God meant women to sit on parish councils and it goes without saying that the suffrage campaigns, particularly the outbreaks of violence from those the *Church Times* called 'unsexed foes of womanhood', strengthened opinion on the negative side. Where was Maude looking for 'faith and prayer' to back her 'profoundly moral movement'?

In its broad sense, the women's movement drew most support among Anglican clergy from Anglo-Catholic Christian Socialists – 'Gore's crowd' as an opponent called them.[14] Bishop Gore had founded the Christian Social Union back in the eighties to apply Christian principles to contemporary social problems and, among others, his 'crowd' included Henry Scott Holland, Edward Talbot – who had sponsored the 'women's Church Congress at Southampton[15] – and the much younger William Temple (later on archbishop of Canterbury) who, like Gore, had given an address at the

---

[14]Hensley Henson, Dean of Durham; see his *Retrospect of an Unimportant Life* (1942) 208. For the speeches of Gore and others at the Queen's Hall meeting in 1912, see *The Religious Aspect of the Women's Movement*.

[15]Encouraged by the success of the congress Bishop Talbot appealed to the militants for 'a truce of God' and to their opponents for recognition of the 'reality, depth and strength' of women's aspirations. Nothing came of it.

Queen's Hall meeting in 1912 on 'The Religious Aspects of the Women's Movement'. The bishop of London, Winnington-Ingram, was also sympathetic. He was one who had pressed the claims of laywomen to a voice on Church councils, and in 1914 gave his backing to the last of the women's suffrage bills, which Lord Selborne introduced in the Lords.

It would, of course, be very misleading to present such people as typical Anglicans – if such a category could be defined. The *Church Times,* that model of High Church rigidity, when it came to comment on the Queen's Hall view of 'The Religious Aspect of the Women's Movement' said it was unclear what the movement was.

> There are, as there have always been, women who have lived in accordance with the highest standard of duty, who have brought up their children in the fear of God and obedience to the lawful authority. They joined no Movement, for there was none to join; it was enough to walk in the paths of virtue.[16]

If the women's movement would enable women to do all this even better, all well and good. But it did not seem that this was its aim. And if it had a religious aspect, this had been obscured by agitation for the franchise.

It would also be highly misleading to imply that every Anglican supporting the movement understood it in the same sense as Maude. Winnington-Ingram certainly did not, as she discovered later to her cost. Gore and Talbot were attached, she found, to that especially Christian paradox which can reconcile spiritual equality with temporal subordination. Temple, who called himself 'a very keen suffragist' nonetheless could not see the vote as a subject where the Christian conscience was, or ought to be 'plainly on one side'. He therefore 'sincerely regretted the existence of a Church League for Women's Suffrage' and would not allow it to use his church.[17] In fact this League, which sought to draw out 'the deep religious significance of the women's movement', came the closest to what Maude stood for.

It had been founded in 1909 by the Rev. Claude Hinscliff with the formal aims.

> to secure for women the Parliamentary Vote as it is or may be granted to men; to use the power thus obtained to establish equality of rights and opportunities between the sexes, and to promote the social and industrial well-being of the community.[18]

Hinscliff was hon. secretary and Maude the first chairman. A great stroke of luck, as she recalled later, was finding a bishop who was willing to be president. Edward Hicks, Bishop of Lincoln, consented.

---

[16]*Church Times* (21 June 1912) 851.
[17]Temple to Miss Corben, Church League for Women's Suffrage (henceforth CLWS), (18 Jan. 1915) Fawcett Autograph Collection, 'Women in the Church'.
[18]*Church Militant* (March 1918) 31.

I doubt if there was another Bishop on the bench who would have done so, though there were some who sympathised. They felt . . . that they ought not to commit themselves officially to a highly controversial movement.[19]

A difficulty which she could understand – 'without ceasing to wish that the representatives of so revolutionary a religion as that of Jesus Christ might have overcome it'. Hicks was a champion of social causes: committed especially to the temperance movement, the cause of peace, and the claims of those whom he once described as 'the unenfranchised, the unrepresented, the unemployed, the unprivileged'. He perceived – more than any man she knew, said Maude – the bitter sense of *waste* from which suffragists suffered.

The only methods employed by the League, as it insisted time and again, were prayer and education. It had to insist, for there was always Miss Gladys Pott of the anti-suffragists ready to point out that there were some militants among its members, 'The name of the "Church" has been usurped . . . by a faction,' complained Dr Ryle, Dean of Westminster, 'and is being exploited by fanatics.'[20] The Church, it was said, was the Church of the nation and ought to stand above politics. The League's response was that politics nowadays touched every aspect of human life. 'If, as we believe, the spiritual equality of the sexes is an indisputable principle of the gospel; and if, as we further believe, that principle should find expression in our public life . . . we are . . . bound to pray for God's blessing upon it.' Such was certainly the earnest belief of Bishop Maud of Kensington who declared at one meeting,

> In spite of the assertion that there ought not to be a Church League of Women's Suffrage, I am here to take the chair tonight because I believe that the Church cannot in honour decline to take her place in any great movement for the raising of the life of the community.[21]

This was the view too of Canon Scott Holland, and of Hudson Shaw, who belonged to the League, and of Evelyn Gunter, reported in its journal as having read 'a valuable and suggestive paper on the Ideals of the Church League for Women's Suffrage' in Oxford in the spring of 1912.

'Prayer is our weapon.' For Maude among others, this simply enlarged the devotional practice which was an integral part of life. Through the League she formed a Fellowship of Prayer 'to unite in intercession for the women's movement those who believe that prayer is work and that all work should be done in the spirit of prayer.'[22] The League announced monthly its schemes of intercession along with the rest of its suffrage

---

[19] J. H. Fowler (ed.), *Life and Letters of Edward Lee Hicks* (1922) 217–19.
[20] Brian Harrison, *Separate Spheres*, (1978) 184.
[21] CLWS (Jan. 1914) 6.
[22] CC (9 April 1914) 19. A discipline of prayer was part of Maude's life. Later, in her house in Hampstead, she was able to set one room apart as an oratory.

programme (a national week of prayer for Bishop Talbot's idea of a 'truce of God' between government and militants; thanksgiving for the success of the suffrage pilgrimage). Prayer was a weapon, but the CLWS did not mean to use it in confrontation – in the style of those militants, for instance, who would call out in the middle of a service 'O God, save all the women who are being tortured for conscience sake!'; or of those who boycotted nonsuffragist clergy with the aim of 'breaking down [their] apathetic indifference . . . towards the Women's Movement and . . . causing them to *think*'.[23]

The League's activities, apart from prayer, were those of every other suffrage society: publishing pamphlets, organising meetings and educating members – through its journal – on developments important to women. Naturally, in 1914 it protested against the Representative Church Council's refusal to consider women's participation in the councils of the Church above parish level. In 1915 it began to campaign. A petition to the Church Council was drafted, urging that such an exclusion infringed that spiritual equality of the sexes which was fundamental to the Christian faith; and that in practical terms it barred women from discussion in fields where they were often the real experts. Maude was the principal speaker at a meeting which was held to launch the petition. Evidently she did not mince words.

> They were always told when they tried to discover the real objection men had to [the] women's claim, there were 'fundamental reasons' against it. They were tired of being told that; they wanted to know what those fundamental reasons were.[24]

Women's work in the mission field, for instance, provided an 'unassailable' argument for their right to an equal voice with men on church councils and missionary boards. It was not enough to offer them consultative positions; or to say, as one ecclesiastic had said, that they should be regarded with sympathy and encouraged to work for the Church. They did not want that kind of encouragement. 'The Church was losing many from the ranks of her workers through failure to realise the . . . nature of their claim.' By way of illustration she gave instances of women who, if they went to church, left before the sermon 'and . . . felt something like despair because the Church spoke with no clear voice on matters of vital importance'. The speech ended with an expression of her views which immediately became notorious. 'Speaking only for herself and not for the League,' she said she thought that nothing but equality 'not only on governing bodies but in the priesthood' would satisfy women in the long run.

There may well have been those among her audience who thought this admission very ill-timed. They were there, after all, to approve a petition to the main Church Council to change its mind and admit women to serve on such bodies; and that Council had been shocked, the previous year, by the

[23]CLWS (Dec. 1912) 133.
[24]*Challenge* (19 March 1915).

revelations of one lay member concerning a women's 'plot' for ordination. The disclosure had been dramatic. Mr H. W. Hill, in the course of speaking on the question of women and church councils, described how some ladies had received a letter asking if they favoured holding a conference to discuss the question of ordaining women. They had also been invited to complete a questionnaire indicating the range of their views, and the answers had been summarised and circulated.[25] Mr Hill – who must have got his information from a lady who had not been pleased to be approached – then quoted from a few of the answers in favour: selectively, of course. But had he given the whole text, it is doubtful whether its judicious tone would have done anything to mitigate the shock that women could even consider such a question. 'For any sane person,' declared the *Church Times,* 'the thing is so absolutely grotesque that he must refuse to discuss it.'

> The monstrous regiment of women in politics would be bad enough but the monstrous regiment of priestesses would be a thousandfold worse. We are not inclined, however, to treat the proposed Conference as a sane scheme; we regard it as of a piece with that epidemic of hysteria which has manifested itself in the violence of feminine militants. It will pass with time.

But – with an eye, no doubt, on Talbot – 'in these days of sentimental bishops and eccentric deans we seem to be without any security against the most extreme revolutionary changes.'[26] However, as one writer noted in the *Challenge,* though 'henpecked and sentimental bishops' had not been prevented by the disclosure from voting in favour of women on church councils, 'laymen, happily, are not so sentimental'.

No name had been mentioned by Mr Hill but in fact the letter he spoke of originated with Ursula Roberts, the wife of the Rev. W. C. Roberts of St George's, Bloomsbury. She and her husband were ardent suffragists and belonged to the Church League; they were also pacifists and he was active in the Fellowship of Reconciliation. Maude, whom she knew through suffrage work, was one of the first Mrs Roberts had written to in 1913 when she looked for means of approaching the question of women's ordination. The suffrage pilgrimage was then in full swing, 'leaving me no sense or coherency for *anything!*' Maude admitted. But she expressed deep interest. She also advised going 'exceedingly slowly'. 'Experience has shown me – what no doubt it has proved even more abudantly to you! – that there is no subject which puts people in such a fever and alarm as this one. The vote is

---

[25]*Guardian* (18 July 1914). Mrs Roberts approached about 150 people and got favourable replies from thirty or forty. Those who objected did so on grounds which ensuing decades were to make familiar: that there was no woman among the apostles, that the Church of England could not act without regard to the Eastern Orthodox and Roman Churches; and that, for many reasons, 'the time was not ripe'.
[26]*Church Times* (24 July 1914).

nothing to it!' In her view, therefore, they would need to undertake a great deal of study before forming a society for action. They ought, for instance, to find out more about the old order of deaconesses. 'I . . . will gladly help if I can. I am horribly busy, but I think it very important. Only I would rather we studied first, and those who, like yourself, probably know a great deal already, must be patient with us.'[27] As to reading a paper, she wrote 'No – too ignorant' on this part of the questionnaire. And in 1914, when definite plans for a conference were under way, she argued that her views were too extreme for a paper. 'I think the clergy should be celibate, and I go cheerfully as far as women Bishops and Archbishops and Popes.'[28] However, the final circular stated that Miss Maude Royden, Dr Jane Walker and Miss Elizabeth Sturge had agreed to read papers.

In the event, no papers were read for the conference was postponed when war broke out. But it was not forgotten. The League's petition that women be allowed to serve on church councils provoked intense argument in 1915 and was linked with this other, more sinister threat – proof of which was the 'plot' revelation and Maude's allusion at the Church League meeting to equality on councils and in the priesthood. She was soon dubbed 'High Priestess' of the 'movement' and those who read their *Daily Express* were caused to realise 'that this same lady has seceded from the National Union of Women's Suffrage Societies because they will not follow her lead in proposing a premature . . . and . . . dishonourable peace conference.' Other writers, avoiding personalities, concentrated on the right now urged 'to disregard the plainest of Apostolic teaching'. 'Women should be silent,' wrote one who signed himself 'A Lover of St Paulos' in the *Challenge*.

> No doubt a woman's voice must be heard in these 'modernist' days. . . . But all this is unofficial. . . . The really pleasant and devout communicant does not speak where she has any single man (brother, husband or father) to be her spokesman.

But was it really a question of 'rights'? asked another (who signed himself 'An Old Proctor'). Were they talking about 'rights' (as in the case of suffrage) or about 'divinely appointed function'?

> What is God's Will and Purpose with regard to the different. . . . functions of men and women respectively . . .? Will those who support this revolutionary proposal [i.e. women on church councils] maintain that there should be no difference?

Where would such people draw the line?

God had not actually drawn a line, was one response; and those who did so were 'opposing a source of inspiration and light, opposing the development of a Divine gift, thereby hindering the growth of their own spirituality'. To which An Old Proctor's reply is revealing:

---

[27]Maude to Ursula Roberts (24 July 1913) Fawcett, 'Women in the Church'.
[28]ibid. (8 March 1914).

Does it seem to be God's Will that women should rule the world, as their mere numbers might make it possible for them to do, if they are to be admitted to the governing departments of the corporate Body on an equality with men?[29]

The controversy ran on. The Church League's petition proved to be rather a damp squib for it seemed that women's participation was not even to be on the agenda for the Church Council in 1915. Early in 1916, however, the question was revived through the National Mission.

Its full title sounds strange today. The National Mission of Repentance and Hope was a bid for spiritual revival: a demonstration that, they might, God willing, find a phoenix in the ashes of war. For war had forced upon the Church of England – the Established Church – a new awareness of its role as the church of the nation. The crisis offered a fresh beginning, or so it seemed in 1914. Church services were packed that autumn, inspiring hope of spiritual change, as if people had been shocked out of selfishness. There was a great desire to build on this. And a great need to respond to the charge – intensified as time went on and the papers filled with lists of the dead – that the Church had somehow failed the nation.

'The past blindness of the privileged classes' was one of the things which Gore, for instance, thought germane to a mission of repentance; and hopes arose of a future nation less divided through experience of war. 'The furnace is doing its work,' said Randall Davidson, Archbishop of Canterbury, in the sermon with which he launched the Mission in October 1916. For the first time they could think and pray 'as a compacted . . . a unanimous people'. Response to the call of 'King and Country' could take shape in 'a kindred readiness to respond to the call of God, the call to make something new of England's life.'

Months had been spent in preparation, hundreds of pamphlets and sermons written, outlines for study circles drawn up, special hymn books and litanies prepared; and of course, the Anglican hierarchy from archbishops to parish priests – and numbers of the laity – had been drawn in to organise a venture for which there was no precedent. William Temple was a key figure (at this stage rector of St James' Piccadilly – 'suffragist rector', one paper said) and early on he proposed the names of several women to serve on the Council which was to direct the whole affair. Maude was one of them – and very much pleased, though she also had some misgivings.

'I am very much honoured by your invitation,' she wrote to Davidson, 'and . . . feel very reluctant to do anything but accept it at once and gratefully. . . . But I am so anxious about the course that the Mission is going to take that I should be exceedingly glad if I might see you before I join the Council.' Her doubts, it seems, concerned the need for the Church

[29]*Challenge* (14 May, 17 April 1915).

of England itself to repent before it looked for repentance in others. Davidson seems to have reassured her – up to a point – for a few days later she agreed to served on the Council.

> I feel I understand better what it is hoped to effect than before I saw your Grace and I hope you will not feel that I have been – and perhaps still am – a little uncertain as to what would have been the ideally best way to begin.[30]

In the event, the beginning was marred by an unexpected and unseemly row over the role to be assigned to women. The organisation of the Mission depended on recruiting large numbers of 'archbishops' messengers'. Hundreds of people, clergy and lay, were needed to speak in all the parishes and raise the nation's spiritual consciousness. It had been assumed that some would be women. Certainly Louise Creighton assumed it when Archbishop Davidson consulted her.[31] But Davidson was a cautious man, disinclined to go to excess and by this time supremely experienced in recognising the tendency in others. Possibly in consequence of meeting Maude he began to feel anxious about the implications of allowing women to 'speak' in church. In June he wrote to Winnington-Ingram.

> I share what I think is your view on the difficult question of these women's gatherings in Church. I have been talking it over here. . . . There are country churches in which little gatherings of women and girls take place where one of them in the Nave of the Church leads a few others in Intercession. To say that this is wrong seems to me impossible.

On the other hand,

> Some would say that it will lead to actual Addresses to a multitude of people in Church by a woman, and that Miss Maud [sic] Royden, whom you mention, is exactly the sort of person who might gather a congregation and address them, and thus introduce quite a different character into such gatherings!

He was inclined to risk it, 'or at all events, to abstain from forbidding it,' impressing on such women the need to be cautious and avoid publicity. He concluded, 'I see the difficulty of all this when we are dealing with excellent and enthusiatic people of Miss Royden's temperament. But that is the kind of advice I have given to the ladies who have consulted me.'[32]

It soon became clear that something more would be needed. The Mission Council approved a report accepting that the 'aims and ideals' of the women's movement were 'in harmony with the teaching of Christ and His Church as to the equality of men and women in the sight of God'. The

---

[30]Maude to Davidson (11 and 17 March 1916) Lambeth, Davidson Papers 360; for her doubts, see her article 'The Church and Women Preachers', *Church Family Newspaper* (11 Oct. 1918).

[31]Creighton to Davidson (4 Aug. 1915) Lambeth, Davidson Papers 359.

[32]Archbishop Davidson to Bishop of London (3 June 1916) Davidson Papers, 360/146.

report urged that women should serve on church councils 'in relation both to the National Mission and also to the permanent work of the Church'; 'which I thought rather going beyond our Province', wrote Gore to Temple a few days later. 'I think the resolutions on the women's movement went beyond what could wisely be said.' One of them, which had been proposed by Maude, urged the bishops to give definite directions 'as to the best ways of using the services and receiving the message of women speakers, whether in Church or elsewhere'.[33]

So it was up to the bishops. So far as his diocese of London went, Winnington-Ingram stated at once that he would allow women to speak in church only where there was no other suitable place; only, of course, for the period of the Mission; only to audiences of women and girls, and only from the aisle in front of the chancel steps (not from the lectern or the pulpit). 'They were apparently to speak from soap boxes or from a perch on the reredos,' Rebecca West wrote of these 'insulting conditions' which, she said, the Bishop was handing out 'as one pokes buns on the end of umbrellas into a cage at the Zoo' to keep things quiet while the Mission went on. But insults worse than this were to follow with the intervention of Athelstan Riley, of the deeply conservative English Church Union; the kind of layman who, as West said, seemed to think the Church of England was his back garden. 'Since he has asked for it, let us repeat that name, "Athelstan Riley",' she wrote with scorn.

> and note how much less meaning it holds for those interested in religion than the names of St Clare, St Catherine of Siena, St Theresa, or to choose one example from modern times, Mrs. Creighton. One does not doubt that Mr Riley has done what he could, but it shows that the Creator has imposed natural limitations upon Mr Riley from which he has freed many women.[34]

Athelstan Riley, who chanced to be absent from the Mission Council's meeting in June, wrote in July to the two archbishops, retracing the dangerous steps that had been taken.

> That women should speak in the Church is in direct conflict with Holy Scripture, with the express injunctions of St Paul . . . and with the common order of the Catholic Church. If this innovation is to be imported into the methods of the National Mission, disaster must inevitably follow.[35]

Were the faithful to sit in their parish churches and listen to women 'in Dioceses unfortunate enough to have a Bishop under feminist control'? He

[33]National Mission Bulletin no. 5: Lambeth, G 2860–1–25. Gore to Temple (12 July 1916) Davidson Papers 360/212.
[34]Rebecca West, article in the *Star*, quoted *Christian Commonwealth*, (23 Aug, 1916).
[35]*Guardian* (20 July 1916). Athelstan Riley was a vice-president of the English Church Union which represented the ultra-conservative Catholic element in the Church of England. For his views on the roles of the sexes see 'Male and Female Created He Them' *Nineteenth Century* (Oct. 1916).

then turned to 'a graver matter': the feminist conspiracy to capture the priesthood. At the very moment, he said, when the suffragettes had been burning churches, 'a section of them were secretly preparing for an attack on the ministry of the Church'. The plot had been revealed to the Representative Church Council in 1914 but nothing was done. He now sent the Archbishop documentary evidence (Mrs Roberts' inquiry and her summary of answers, which he had actually had printed as a pamphlet) pointing out that 'in this enterprise, Miss Maude Royden was deeply implicated.'

The letter closed with a wringing of hands over women who were 'snatching at empty shadows'.

> They will not stoop to copy the Mother of God, who by her obedience and her humility co-operated with her Maker in His scheme for the salvation of mankind, and who by her earthly self-effacement has set an example to all women while the world shall last. . . . They refuse to be bound by the Divine Laws . . . and do not scruple to lay sacrilegious hands upon the sacred Ark of God. What can we do to enlighten them?

The Archbishop's response was courteous, though he concluded by expressing the view that Riley's apprehensions were not well-founded. He began, though, to think of getting round the problem by making only clergy Archbishops' Messengers. The Archbishop of York saw difficulties here. For one thing, some people had already been invited to fulfil this special role. 'I fear the whole thing has been rather sadly bungled and there are bound to be some heart burnings.'[36] Mrs Creighton also advised that it would be seen as a breach of faith now to limit Messengers to the clergy. She and Davidson roughed out a list – a very safe list of eleven women (Maude not among them) who might be chosen and the Archbishop of York approved it, reiterating his own opinion that there was something essentially 'unreal' in having women Messengers at all. 'But we must accept things as they are.'[37]

Riley was furious with Randall Davidson, whose letter convinced him

> that the Women's Movement in the National Mission has reached a point . . . beyond Your Grace's control. . . . It is intolerable that women like Miss Maud Royden, engaged in a conspiracy to capture the priesthood step by step, should be on the council of the National Mission, and taking a leading part in its deliberations.[38]

The clergy and laity must act, he said, if the bishops would not. He got a chilly reply. But if Davidson did not see Athelstan Riley as the saviour of the Church there were plenty who did. From July to September 1916 the church press buzzed with the controversy. It was evident, said the Dean of

---

[36]York to Canterbury (22 July 1916) Davidson Papers, 360/252.
[37]ibid. (28 July 1916) 360/265.
[38]Quoted, 'Women and the Priesthood', *Yorkshire Post* (11 Aug. 1916).

Canterbury, that the danger Mr Riley apprehended was real, for the Mission Council had approved the resolution about women on church councils 'on the motion of a lady whose action conspicuously illustrates the consequences of giving women this representation. Lord Hugh Cecil, a strong opponent of women on church councils, expressed to Davidson his 'earnest hope' that they would not be allowed to speak in church for the National Mission.[39] A clergyman in the London diocese, far from being calmed by his bishop's directions, announced that he would take no part in the Mission 'unless the proposal that women should be allowed to speak in church be entirely withdrawn'. Another wrote in fury of the 'sexual hysteria' which prompted women to make such claims.[40]

As to the nature of these claims, there was confusion. The only point of fact was that the Mission Council had by implication approved women speaking 'in church or elsewhere' for the National Mission since it called on the bishops to give suitable directions. Some of the critics confined themselves to this, but many assumed – or professed to assume – that the real issue was ordination and reacted, as Rebecca West said of Riley, with the frenzy of a savage warrior who sees a woman touch his spear and believes that she will infect it with her weakness. The other great fear was that the Mission would suffer if this wrangle over women went on. 'Nothing must be allowed to harm the Mission; the Devil is no doubt working for some way of doing it, and he must not be allowed to succeed', wrote Winnington-Ingram in the midst of the storm.[41] The Bishop of Chelmsford, who had also been willing at least to poke buns through the bars of cages, was also inclined to put the blame on the Devil.

> Yet what is to be done? The natural man would say 'Resist the unfair agitation, largely begotten of ignorance and prejudice.' But such a spirit would surely wreck the mission. . . . I have therefore decided that during the mission I shall not sanction any woman telling her sisters of the Saviour's love in any church in the diocese of Chelmsford.[42]

Winnington-Ingram made the same decision.

So women in the end, ran one letter to the *Challenge*, had suffered the fate they were accustomed to. 'They have been the first to be thrown overboard to lighten the ship.' And it was hoped they would not struggle too much but patiently scrape the barnacles off the sides of the vessel until it was in dock and had fulfilled its purpose.[43] The modernist Canon Streeter of

---

[39]Henry Wace, Dean of Canterbury 'The Mission and a single Eye', Davidson papers 360/263; Cecil to Davidson, (Aug. 1916) Davidson Papers 360.

[40]'Women and the Priesthood', *Yorkshire Post* (11 Aug. 1916); 'Women Messengers in Church', *Church Family Newspaper* (Aug. 1916).

[41]*Challenge* (18 Aug. 1916).

[42]*Times* (21 Aug. 1916).

[43]Letter from Edith Catlin, *Challenge* (1 Sept. 1916).

Hereford made some sharp comments, naturally incensed not only by the injustice to women (he was one of those interested in ordination) but by what he saw as proof that the Church was ruled by its ultra-conservatives. 'A Church which trembles . . . at the frown of Mr Athelstan Riley . . . will neither command nor deserve respect.'[44]

The women of the 'ordination' group published a dignified statement in August to say that the purpose of the resolution on women speaking had never been to exploit the Mission for feminist ends. With regard to women who felt called to the priesthood, they knew that

> it may be very many years before the Church . . . is prepared to ordain them, or their children or children's children. But it is their desire to seek, by . . . corporate prayer and corporate study, the guidance of the Holy Spirit, both for themselves . . . and for the Church as a body, with regard to this very serious question.[45]

'What a ridiculous storm in a teacup it has been!' Maude wrote now to Ursula Roberts. In fact, until the Bishop of London decided to withdraw his original directions – restrictive as they were – she had been optimistic. 'The women's "message" is to be heard and it is to be delivered by women.' One or two voices might be raised against them but 'the tide has turned, and a great movement now is surging through our beloved Church.'[46] Her later disappointment makes itself felt in the tone of a pamphlet she wrote that autumn entitled *Women and the Church of England*. Here she takes a hard, sad look at the facts: which were, not only that women were barred from the priesthood for what were referred to as 'fundamental reasons' but that they were barred, as matter of course, from virtually every office in church.

> Deacons, choristers, churchwardens, acolytes, servers and thurifers, even the takers-up of the collection, are almost exclusively men. If at any time not one male person can be found to collect, the priest does it himself, or, after a long and anxious pause, some woman, more unsexed than the rest, steps forward to perform this office. In one church I am told, it was the custom for collectors to take the collection up to the sanctuary rails, till the war compelled women to take the place of men, when they were directed to wait at the chancel steps. In another it was proposed to elect a woman churchwarden, when the Vicar vehemently protested on the ground that this would be a 'slur on the parish'. In another, the impossibility of getting any male youth to ring the sanctus-bell induced a lady to offer her services. After anxious thought the priest accepted her offer 'because the rope hung down behind a curtain, so no one would see her'.[47]

'Are there, then, "untouchables" in the religion of Christ after all?' For to

[44]*Times* (1 Sept. 1916).
[45]*Guardian* (17 Aug. 1916).
[46]Maude to Roberts (27 Aug. 1916); CLWS (Aug. 1916).
[47]*Women and the Church of England* (1916) 8–9. Stanley Unwin told her George Allen & Unwin would be 'glad to be identified' with this pamphlet's publication.

be told, as women were, that they could not do this or that because 'the church is a consecrated place' was an insult – 'perhaps the most comprehensive that could be offered to a human being'.

At the time they reversed their decision to allow women to speak in church the Bishops of London and Chelmsford had promised that the whole question would be looked at properly once the National Mission was over. Maude now pinned her hopes upon that. She had many other preoccupations – speaking a good deal for the WIL, working with Eleanor Rathbone and others on the 'endowment of motherhood' question, and writing and speaking on 'the social problem', in the light of the recently published report of the Royal Commission on Venereal Diseases. The campaign to get women on Church councils went on but attempts were made now to distance all that from the alarming idea of ordination, which had in fact alienated some members of the Church League for Women's Suffrage.[48] Maude did not cease to urge that the Church should look squarely at what it meant when a priest, unrebuked, might keep women away from the altar or when all the men in a congregation received communion before the women. Such things really seemed to imply a fixed belief that women were inferior. 'What is the truth? We . . . have a right to hear.'[49] But she expected an episcopal pronouncement on the subject of women speaking, and had no thought of jumping the gun by speaking for Hudson in St Botolph's, for instance (though according to a poll he took at one weekday service the great majority of his congregation of city men were quite ready to approve).

'I . . . regretted from the bottom of my heart,' he said later 'that the Bishop of London and other bishops took back their permission for women to speak.' His audience was a CLWS conference on the role of laywomen in the Church of England. Maude was one of the principal speakers.[50] 'She preached her first sermon in my parish in Rutlandshire fourteen years ago,' Hudson told them, no doubt remembering the trek they had made then from church to schoolroom in South Luffenham. Maude too may have remembered that when she commented on the bishops' ruling and asked the conference,

> Do you think if Christ had seen . . . a congregation slowly gathering itself together . . . with prayer-books, hymn-books, and umbrellas, and walking across to the schoolroom to listen to a sermon preached by a woman . . . He would have recognised . . . any great principle?

[48] A letter to the *Guardian* (15 Feb. 1917), signed 'Watchman' states 'The Church League for Women's Suffrage is now committed to women-preachers and women in Holy Orders. . . . This has led to several important Churchwomen leaving an organisation which has been captured for so outrageous an attack upon the Church.'
[49] CLWS (Jan. 1917).
[50] The speeches are reported in the CLWS pamphlet *The Laywoman in the Church of England.* (1917)

She moved on to a larger question: the Church's relation to the women's movement. 'It is the tragedy of the Church that she is so anxious to see what is safe that she loses her leadership in what is right.' It was not because women had been accepted elsewhere that it was now safe for the Church to consider them. A great movement of the spirit like the women's movement 'should first be tried by the Church to see whether it is of God or not'. That they wanted to turn the world upside down 'should have been claim on the . . . Church of Christ rather than an accusation against us.' How much the Church had lost by always playing for safety. 'In that safety what death!' she said.

> What opportunities we have lost – in the rise of democracy, in the advance of science, in bettering the condition of the people, in the coming of feminism – one chance after another we have thrown away.

'The Church is like a mighty river *almost* run dry,' someone had said to her. Outside its channel the great movements of the time poured into swamps or cut new channels to the sea.

Soon after this she herself cut a new channel. Despite the earlier promise of the bishops, nothing had happened since the National Mission to suggest that the question of women speaking had arrived on any Anglican agenda. Therefore, in March 1917, when she was formally invited to preach at that great Nonconformist church, the City Temple, after some turmoil she decided to accept. 'I ought to explain,' she wrote to one enquirer, 'that I have spoken in Nonconformist churches for many years. Indeed I have spoken in Labour Churches, Socialist Churches, Brotherhood Churches and Ethical Churches.'[51] Most notably, perhaps, she had preached in the Ethical Church in Bayswater in 1913 to mark the end of the suffrage pilgrimage. But the City Temple was a very different thing. – a 'real' church, even in Anglican eyes, and to Nonconformists, a kind of St Paul's. Built on the grand scale, its opening in the seventies had been attended by the Lord Mayor in state; its 'great white pulpit' was the gift of the City, and had seen some notable ministers. That a woman should now be asked to preach there was in sharp contrast, to say the least, to the Church of England's restrictive ruling over women and the National Mission.

The opportunity arose, in fact, because the City Temple was between ministers. A well-known man, Dr R. J. Campbell, had departed in 1915; there had been delay over choosing his successor and the one who was eventually chosen – an American, Dr Joseph Fort Newton – was unable to take up his post before the summer of 1917. In the meantime it fell to Albert Dawson, hon. secretary of the City Temple and editor of the *Christian Commonwealth*, to 'supply' the pulpit. When one preacher fell ill, Dawson asked Maude to take his place for the morning and evening of 18 March.

---

[51] Maude to Miss A.M. Procter, Headmistress Surbiton High School (20 March 1917) Fawcett 222.

Even in this Congregational Church, and in 1917, the year Constance Coltman became the first woman Congregational minister, to invite a woman to preach was bold. Catherine Booth, 'Mother of the Salvation Army' had preached there in 1888; and the great Dr Parker, minister then, was known to have favoured the ministry of women, saying he would like 'some good motherly woman' to preside at the sacramental table.[52] Whether or not Maude met this prescription, Dawson, an active suffragist, had been struck by hearing her speak on the religious aspect of the women's movement.

There was another side to all this, however. If some Church people were deeply offended by the idea that a woman should preach, some (not the same ones, necessarily) were deeply offended that *any* Anglican should preach in a Nonconformist church. In professing, as she now did, that here was a chance to advance not only the women's cause but the cause of 'reunion', Maude was well ahead of her generation. Hudson certainly did all he could to forge links with fellow Christians. And another rare priest, her friend Harold Anson (later to become Master of the Temple), wrote now, 'I hope it is like Peter and Cornelius: the opening of a new stage of reunion . . . *Deus custodiet introitum et exituum tuum.*'[53] But to most clergy in 1917 – decades before that gradual rapprochement between the Church of England and the 'separated' churches which began after the Second World War – an Anglican who worshipped in a Nonconformist church was stepping outside that Catholic tradition of which, for all the trauma of the Reformation, the Church of England remained a part.

The fact that no less a man than Hensley Henson, Dean of Durham, in the cause of reunion, had himself agreed to preach at the City Temple, had already made a stir in High Church circles and upset Maude's old friend Scott Holland, who wrote beseeching her to think again. ('You know how I care for you; and how deeply I value what you have to do for us.')[54] Hensley Henson, on the other hand – keen on reunion but anti feminist – was peeved to find himself taking a pulpit that would only just have been vacated by Maude. He wrote in his journal:

> I am considerably annoyed to notice in the *Times* the announcement that Miss Maude Royden is to conduct the services in the 'City Temple' on March 18th, the Sunday next preceding that on which I have promised to preach there. Surely 'an enemy hath done this' in order to bring ridicule upon me. Happily the Bishops have entangled themselves so hopelessly with that shameless Feminist that they cannot decently do more than chuckle furtively![55]

[52]*Christian Commonwealth* (14 March 1917) 293.
[53]Harold Anson to Maude (8 March 1917) Fawcett 222. *God guard your coming in and your going out.* The apostle Peter when he met Cornelius perceived that the gift of the Holy Ghost was bestowed on Gentiles as well as Jews.
[54]Scott Holland to Maude (10 March 1917) Fawcett 222.
[55]Henson's Journals, no. 20: 16 (7 March 1917) Durham, Dean and Chapter Library. I am grateful to Keith Francis for drawing my attention to this.

In the little group of those (High Anglicans, mostly) who backed Maude's campaign for women in the Church, opinion was divided as to whether her preaching in a nonconformist pulpit at the City Temple would actually advance the cause or not. 'You are right, most right,' wrote Edith Picton-Tubervill, one of the coterie Ursula Roberts had gathered together in 1914.

> I rejoice so greatly when people just *do* things and here you are leading the way and making it easier for others to follow, and that my friend is one of the finest things a man or woman can do. . . . On the 18th I shall be at the City Temple and many angels will surround you.[56]

But Dr Jane Walker, another of the group (who had earlier written to Ursula Roberts 'it does not do to let people think we are fanatical and we want to prove to them that we are really Catholic') evidently wrote so anxiously to Maude that she replied with a three-page letter, listing her reasons and giving vent to the frustration which had built up inside her since the National Mission fiasco:

> (1) Feminism is a part of Christianity. Therefore for any organised body of Christians to make a move in this direction is good. . . .
> (2) The Church of England has refused to make a move. She was asked to let women speak in church during the Mission, and refused: she was asked to appoint . . . a commission on the Women's Movement after the Mission, and refused . . . As for the promise to raise the question of women speaking in church again. This has been shelved by a committee on *research*.

'The official C of E is not going to lead, it will only follow,' was the sad conclusion. 'Let someone therefore give it a lead.'

> My doing so will not prejudice but help the case of other women. The church will regard me with horror and say what a lot of harm I am doing; but in course of time it will begin to consider the possibility of asking more religious and modest women to speak in its sacred places. That is the way the official mind works. I shall be condemned but you will be exonerated and both you and I will rejoice. . . Now forgive me if I am wrong for the sake of the fact that I believe I am right and am truly not acting heedlessly.[57]

'I don't think that any of us should offer to preach or read Lessons merely as a protest,' wrote Zöe Fairfield, Secretary of the Student Christian Movement, to Francis Eeles, the ecclesiologist, who interested himself in the women's case. But Maude, she felt, was not doing that.

---

[56]Edith Picton-Turbervill to Maude (8 March 1917) Fawcett 222.
[57]Jane Walker to Ursula Roberts (21 Aug. 1916) Fawcett 'Women in the Church'; Maude to Jane Walker (13 March 1917) Church House Archives, CWMC/FCE/2/1. Maude received warmly supportive letters from Greenfield Women's Guild, Bradford, and Hinckley Women's Adult School.

It is quite clear, I think, and not a mere figure of speech, that Miss Royden is a woman with a real spiritual message, in fact a prophetess, and she cannot refuse such opportunities as come to her to deliver this message. The cure is for the Church of England to provide her with the opportunity.[58]

Eeles was very upset, however, and had written Maude a long letter begging her to step back before too late.

I fear you have taken a most disastrous step by consenting to preach in the City Temple. It will make endless difficulties for all of us who are trying to do what we can to improve the position of women. . . . It plays directly into the hands of our opponents who . . . will now have some grounds for saying – however unjustly – that the leaders of the women's movement in the church are infected with a spirit of schism, and that the movement is essentially destructive. I cannot tell you how disappointed I am.[59]

No one knew more about schism than Eeles, for he was a specialist in early Church history; secretary, in fact, of that research committee which the Archbishop had recently set up to report on women's role in the Church historically – the committee whose existence, Maude told Jane Walker, 'makes any forward movement impossible'. Eeles did not like to be called a feminist but his suffragist wife and his researches had given him some sympathy with the Anglican women's case. 'To say that women are incapable of receiving holy orders is to make a very dangerous assertion,' he had written at the time of the National Mission, in the course of a scholarly piece on 'The Ecclesiastical Ministrations of Women'. But Eeles did not pull his punches now. 'You are too valuable to the Church to waste your influence by prejudicing your position in this way. . . . I fear Mr Riley will rejoice exceedingly!' If she was acting out of a sense that the situation was intolerable, he said, and that the best way of getting the law mended was to break it, 'are not these the methods of the WSPU, only slightly modified as far as physical force is concerned? It seems to me that it is a kind of ecclesiastical militancy.'

Maude answered that she was deeply distressed to know he felt she was acting wrongly, though she believed he was mistaken. However, if she were forced to choose,

between working for the improvement of women's position in the Church of England and working for its improvement in the whole nation, and especially among Christian people, I cannot hesitate to choose the latter.[60]

She made no comment on the charge of ecclesiastical militancy.

---

[58]Zoë Fairfield to Francis Eeles (23 March 1917) Church House Archives CWMC/FCE/2/1
[59]Eeles to Maude (10 March 1917) Fawcett 222.
[60]Maude to Eeles (14 March 1917) Church House Archives CWMC/FCE/2/1.

8

The City Temple

As England was at that time a world of women, and they were entering on a life new, strange and dangerous, with a freedom they had not known before, it seemed to me that if a woman of genius could be found the problem would be solved.

Dr Joseph Fort Newton (1928).

'Fancy Maude Royden at the City Temple!' wrote old Miss Wordsworth of Lady Margaret Hall. 'However, one can't call it preaching in a *church*. I daresay she was very good . . . in a sort of way, and of course the novelty went for a good deal. I don't think she is quite as wise as she doubtless is well-meaning!'[1]

Long queues that had to be controlled by police had formed in Holborn Viaduct that Sunday (18 March 1917) to hear Maude preach in the morning and evening. Many people came out of curiosity, suggested the *Daily Mirror's* reporter, who spotted some of the unlucky ones from the morning queue being turned away. Some perhaps were readers of the *Daily Express* which had done its patriotic duty in giving notice of the occasion under the heading 'Woman Crank's Sermon'. 'Miss Royden, it will be recalled, is the authoress of the notorious book, *The Great Adventure: The Way to Peace*. . . . Will she . . . preach on her favourite text "Britain should have committed national suicide rather than help our allies to fight the Germans"? ' 'It will be interesting to know how the City Temple will welcome Miss Royden,' said the *Daily Sketch* at the end of an article which began by quoting a letter from a soldier's widow protesting that Maude's presence would be 'keenly resented' by members of the congregation whose husbands or sons had given their lives for their country. This kind of thing, though it did not in fact result in any antipacifist disturbance, gave the seventy-two-year-old Lady Royden 'horrible nightmares of your being mobbed', as she wrote to Maude, 'and the people making a row and not hearing you'. However, she had been reassured.

[1]Elizabeth Wordsworth (19 March 1917) LMH archives.

Your dear letter has just come a 1000,1000 thanks for it. You will never know the *enormous* relief to me I feel I can never thank God enough, the impression the papers gave me has caused the greatest suffering, but I don't mind the least bit, now it all looks so different. I am sure you will be helped to say great and hopeful things.[2]

As the crowd trooped into the City Temple eyes would naturally turn to the pulpit. While in an Anglo-Catholic church the High Altar would dominate the scene, here it was the pulpit: a work on its own, its marble facings and colossal size proclaiming the generous wealth of the City, the great prestige of old Dr Parker and, of course, the importance of the preaching of the Word. In this pulpit the preacher could be seen from all over the church, including the gallery; so on this occasion, no matter where they sat, people could at once resolve the vital question: what would a woman preacher wear?

'She was very simply attired,' in one account, 'wearing a black cassock, relieved by a white net collar, and a small hat suggestive of a biretta but of a less pronounced shape.'[3] The *Globe's* reporter, working on his feature article ('A Portia in the Pulpit') saw a simple black dress with white lace collar, 'above which was a young and sensitive oval countenance with a crown of abundant black hair, disregarding, so far as masculine eyes could discern, the Pauline injunction that women should be covered'.[4] He sketched in a good deal of background as well: the choir of 'strikingly presentable ladies' in mortar boards and blue academic robes over plain white garments ('a very seemly vesture'); the male singers in the row behind, similarly dressed, who yet in his eyes, 'looked like a chorus of members of a hunt'; the minister in charge of the service, with his white hair, black gown and linen stock, who might have stepped from an engraving by Hogarth.

In his account, until her turn came, Maude 'sat modestly in the background'. According to her own, she had not slept the night before. It was in fact only the second time she had ever worshipped in a Nonconformist church, and the first occasion dated from childhood when the Roydens had taken some of their children to hear a Presbyterian preacher in Liverpool, a project undertaken, as she recalled, only after consultation with the vicar and still 'in some degree of trepidation'.[5] The view before her now,

[2]Lady Royden to Maude (16 March 1917) Fawcett 222.
[3]*Christian Commonwealth* (21 March 1917). The black cassock and biretta-style cap (shown in the portrait by René de l'Hôpital) were to be her usual preaching costume, though she sometimes also wore a surplice; and after receiving honorary doctorates (Glasgow and Liverpool) in the 1930s, she sometimes wore a doctoral gown (as in Philip de Laszlo's portrait). She was interested in clothes and had the small cap designed to be soft and easy to fold in the pocket. While she could not take seriously St Paul's injunction that women cover their heads in church she did not think it worth fighting about.
[4]*Globe* (26 March 1917).
[5]Royden, 'Bid Me Discourse'.

stretching row after row to the gallery at the back nicknamed 'the Rockies' (like the Rocky Mountains it went on for ever) was perhaps more reminiscent of the Albert Hall than of any church with which she was familiar. However, she appeared entirely composed. Somewhere out there was Hudson, in khaki. She had been asked if he approved of her action and had quoted him: 'You are entirely right and I am *glad* you are going to the City Temple.'[6] Her sister Daisy was out there too, and Tom, and other members of the family. 'My heart was beating hard for you,' wrote Daisy later. But 'the moment I saw you, all that went. . . . I saw by your face that *you* were in God's care and keeping and all nervousness left me.'[7]

The theme of her sermon, 'The Laws of Life', was probably a letdown to the *Daily Express* which certainly did not trouble to report it, though the *Sketch* ran a few lines under the heading 'Girl Preacher in Parker's Pulpit'. The *Manchester Guardian* correspondent observed that she held the unflagging attention of her listeners who were plainly impressed 'by the quiet force and the matter of her sermon'. 'How quiet and attentive they were,' wrote a friend, 'there was a deal of sympathy with and admiration for your ardour and courage.'[8] Several accounts stressed the charm of her voice while one noted that her 'evident ability to meet the great demand made upon her won all hearts and disarmed criticism'.[9]

So much for Dr Johnson.[10] At least till the next time. For the novelty angle could not be dismissed and stood, she felt always, to distract from the message. 'I like this phrase – "delivering, or giving a message",' was her comment later on, as an experienced preacher.

> No abuse of it by those who have no message to give . . . can spoil its intrinsic truth. Every time I hear it it is brought home to me that the preacher has nothing of his own to say . . . He is the bearer of a message. I have fallen below this standard, God knows – I do not know how often – but the standard is set before me in that word.[11]

She did not fall below it on this occasion. The verbatim reports (she used only 'slight notes') show that her words were well-ordered and lucid; eloquent, framed to the message within. Yet verbatim reports are a kind of husk, and the kernel, the message, begins to die as soon as the last word has been uttered and the magic spell with the audience broken. *Cor ad cor*

---

[6]Maude to Jane Walker (13 March 1917).

[7]Daisy Rooper to Maude (19 March 1917) Fawcett 222.

[8]Mary Thresher to Maude (19 March 1917) Fawcett 222.

[9]*Christian Commonwealth* (21 March 1917). Lord Fenner Brockway, who was sub-editor of the *Christian Commonwealth* at this time, recalled to the author the calm precision with which Maude spoke.

[10]'Sir, a woman's preaching is like a dog's walking on his hinder legs. It is not done well; but you are surprised to find it done at all.' (James Boswell, *Life of Samuel Johnson*.)

[11]Royden, 'Bid Me Discourse.' For verbatim reports of her sermons on 18 March see supplements to the *Christian Commonwealth* (11 and 25 April, 1917).

loquitur, Newman said. Heart speaks to heart, and her message that day to an audience racked in the third year of war – readers of the *Daily Express* or not, believers or not, bereaved or not – was broadly her own belief in goodness. She did not say, 'good will triumph over evil' but when they listened to her they felt it, and came out into Holborn Viaduct to face whatever they had to face.

Her plea in the morning ('The Laws of Life') is a plea to repose in spiritual law the confidence given to scientific law – the law of gravity, for instance. Both kinds of law proceed from God; and the God of an invariable gravity cannot be the God of a variable love. 'Looking back now,' she wrote in 1925, 'it still seems to me that if I had only to preach one sermon it would be that one.' (And in fact by then it formed the theme of her most widely-known address, 'Can We Set The World In Order?') In the evening she spoke about prophets.

> We are looking for a prophet today. Helpless before the agony of the world, which of us is not looking around for a leader and for a prophet? . . . . We hope, with hearts that are almost sick with hope deferred, for the great spiritual revival which should come to a nation that has been bought at a price . . . and we look in vain for a leader.

But did it matter if they could not find one?

> I believe that revival will come again from . . . ordinary men and women like ourselves. Wherever there is a humble heart and a confident expectation, there we may receive a message. For, if you come to think of it, it is among such people that Christianity is working, even today.

They had experience in their own homes of 'the great spiritual law of love' and must generalise it to change the world. 'Let us make the experiment and be done with it!'

> Let us clear out of the way this incubus of an unpractical religion that tears at our hearts and will not let us go. . . . If Christianity is a mistake, let us find it out and put it away. . . . But I believe it is not a mistake. I am certian, though I fumble so uncertainly at the great solution, that it *is* a solution and that there is no other solution. . . . I believe that those who take Christ for their Master . . . will find that the man whom they follow is God.

Some of those who listened were less struck by what she said, Maude decided, than by the fact that the City Temple was still standing after she had said it; 'that the ceiling did not crack and the walls did not totter . . . it was nothing to make a fuss about.'[12] Among those who came into the vestry to congratulate her were the singer Clara Butt, from that moment one of her supporters; and the radical Bishop of Lincoln, Dr Hicks, to whom she admitted having felt awkward pronouncing the blessing (which

[12]*The Christian Work* (16 Aug. 1924) 179.

she did at the evening service) knowing that an Anglican bishop was there. 'It was the best blessing I have had since my mother died,' he told her.[13] In the next few days she was overwhelmed with the messages. First, a telegram from her mother ('So thankful of splendid report from Tom') followed by two letters in quick succession. 'I have often felt that words failed one when wanting to express very deep feeling,' wrote Lady Royden, 'and they seem to do so today when I would like to tell you of the deep joy welling up in my heart for the great service you have done your country.'

> I am altogether unworthy of so much honour and am now chastising myself for mis-trusting My Child, it all came through that horrid notice in the papers 'More Peace Talk' and then Miss Maude Royden will preach on Peace in the City Temple on the 18th, those wicked few words have punished me terribly but never mind. . . . I am longing for a verbal report I wonder if any papers will publish it, surely yes – it is rather hard I could not have been there, it is so different to hear it delivered and your appearance left nothing to be desired, so what a libellous representation was that in the *Mirror*.[14]

Maude sent her press cuttings, which pleased her.

> But nothing has helped me like your own Brothers and Sisters reports, I am more thankful. . . than words can say they managed to hear you; and I am thankful, my darling Maude if anything I could do was of the smallest use – I hesitated so much about writing but feel with you it was really for the best, Oh! I have had so many direct answers to prayers I ought indeed to be a believer and think I am but I know if I were faithful enough I would not get into the panics I do.[15]

'Darling – though it is late,' wrote Daisy, 'and I have been writing 3 sheets full to Mother.'

> I just felt I *must* write and thank you for all you did and said yesterday – and for all that you are . . . I cannot tell you one scrap of all I *feel* about it. . . . Mrs Fishbourne said when we got outside 'If she were not a woman, she would be Archbishop of Canterbury'!![16]

'You would be amused,' wrote Harold Anson, from his parish of Birch near Manchester, where she had stayed, 'to see how the people here quite regard it as a triumph for Birch. One of the mothers was handing round your picture from the *Sketch* and saying "Ain't she loovely?" I am glad too that dear old E. Lincoln was there.'[17] An admirer of Maude's from suffrage

---

[13]Royden, 'Bid Me Discourse'. Because the form of service was new to Maude it had been arranged that a Congregationalist minister should conduct it in the morning; but she took the evening service herself and so pronounced the blessing.

[14]Lady Royden to Maude (19 March 1917) Fawcett 222.

[15]ibid. (23 March 1917) Fawcett 222.

[16]Daisy Rooper to Maude (19 March 1917) Fawcett 222.

[17]Harold Anson, to Maude (22 March 1917) Fawcett 222. E. Lincoln = Edward Hicks, Bishop of Lincoln.

days had been specially moved by the evening service, where 'one felt at the end of the sermon that the whole congregation, as one soul, was thrilled by the power of your message'.

> You will not remember me but we often met . . . when you attended committees at the N. U. offices, and often lunched at the office. You will smile if I tell you that I usually contrived to make errands to Miss Crookenden's room at lunchtime on those days! . . . You know, do you not, that there is an ever-increasing number of young women, enthusiastic and full of hope, 'ready for anything', who are willing to follow Maude Royden wherever she may lead, if and when she needs?[18]

As to her preaching from a Nonconformist pulpit, another woman wrote, 'I am a Churchwoman, but I do not believe you could have allowed an opportunity like last Sunday's to go by. How one longs for the Church to become less blind and realise the need for women in all the Offices!' She added a postscript: 'People you have never seen pray for you in your work. I know that I am one.' Another wished 'the Arch, and the whole bench of bishops' could have been there to hear Maude preach. She nonetheless went on to admit, 'The service itself did not appeal to me', adding very reasonably 'but naturally it would not and one has to remember "many men many minds" '.[19]

There were those, though, who, could not take this view; and who, looking to Maude as a leader, were disquieted and puzzled by her action. 'Dear Miss Royden,' wrote one such, Zoë Procter, 'It is no use apologising for bothering you – because we always do it nevertheless – and as so many of us look to you for leading and help (they *do* need it and need it *from you*) I hope you will accept the position and forgive us.'

> There were, of course, crowds of us – Suffragists – there today – but I speak only for Churchwomen, and we would value greatly a word of explanation from you as to your position and attitude toward the Church in preaching and taking the service at the City Temple.[20]

They wanted to understand, not criticise. It was just that since Maude herself had asked them to be patient with the slowness of the bishops it was hard for them ('as Catholics – if we must have labels') to understand why she had done what she did. 'We feel intensely the stupidity and blindness which prevents you and others from speaking in Church, but what can we do? We, at heart, cannot leave her for that or any other reason.' And, in a postscript: 'You will say there is no need for us to go to the City Temple –

---

[18]Margaret Hardy to Maude (21 March 1917) Fawcett 222.
[19]Dorothea Brock to Maude (22 March 1917); Marion Rowles to Maude (19 March 1917) Fawcett 222.
[20]Zoë Procter to Maude (18 March 1917) Fawcett 222.

and I don't think I ought to go again – but still, we need the message.' The
same point was made by the Headmistress of Surbiton High School, Miss
A. M. Procter. It had come as a blow to find Maude at the City Temple, she
said. 'Some of us want to know if it means that you think the Church of
England must be given up as far as Women Preachers and Women Priests
are concerned?' 'I felt how hampered you were in some ways – the
Sacramental side had in one sense to be ignored.'

> I want to understand your motive and your point. Is it tactics? There are so many
> women growing up ready to leave the Church because they find a spirit there so
> contrary to what they believe is God's spirit that I feel I must know where we
> stand. I write because I care so tremendously for the cause.

'You write with such a kindly interest that I count on your wishing to
understand my position,' came Maude's reply. And she explained to Miss
Procter that it had been her rule to speak wherever she was asked, 'if I feel
that I have something to say, and that they are willing to hear it. . . . I have
no sense whatever of wrongness in joining in the worship of my fellow
Christians of other Churches.' To which she added, 'I wonder whether this
will shock you?' (thinking perhaps of a typist she employed whose High
Church soul revolted greatly at having to inscribe such sentiments). There
had been nothing in the service, she said, which didn't come out of the
Prayer Book or the Bible, 'except my own prayer, and my own sermon,
neither of which, I trust, were heretical'. She made no comment on having
been obliged to 'ignore' the sacramental side of worship but it is likely the
remark struck home, for in all the years that followed and the countless
times she conducted services in Nonconformist churches, this was something she never got used to. Though she denied having thought about
'tactics' she ended,

> The Church will never believe that women have a religious message until some of
> them get, and take, the opportunity to prove that they have. My taking it in a
> Nonconformist church will ultimately lead, I believe, to other women being
> given it in the Church of England.[21]

Of the various criticisms which came from her own 'side', probably the
one she found most wounding was contained in a letter to *The Challenge*
written by her old friend the Bishop of Winchester. Edward Talbot had not
moved far, ecumenically speaking, since the turn of the century when – at
that time Bishop of Southwark – he had felt obliged to refuse an invitation
to attend the centenary celebrations of the Baptist Sunday Schools in his
diocese, fearing to countenance 'the breach of unity which is so colossal an
evil'. That breach of unity he addressed now, hinting that her 'preaching' at

---

[21] A. M. Procter to Maude (18 March 1917); Maude to Miss Procter (20 March 1917) Fawcett
222.

the City Temple had been a kind of opportunism. For she had had other chances to speak,

> as . . . those who heard her address 2000 men at the Church Congress will not easily forget. She thinks they should be larger, less restricted, more recognised as a ministry. But is it the part of loyalty to anticipate the judgment which her Church should quietly, slowly and deliberately make, and *for the purpose in question* turn from her own Church to another communion?[22]

Maude's answer shows that this criticism stung.

> I have not 'turned from my own Church'. . . . . I shall never turn from her, I trust. But neither shall I refuse to say what I have to say on that great body of truth which the Church of England holds in common with the Free Churches, within their buildings should they wish me to do so.

Would it make things right if she asked the City Temple to put the word 'preaching' in inverted commas or to announce her as 'giving an address'?

> I am not speaking flippantly. I honestly wish to understand this distinction. I am entitled, I understand, to 'address audiences' of Free Churchmen. . . . Only I must not call it a 'sermon'. Very well, I will not call it a sermon. I do not feel the matter is important.

She urged that the whole question of women preaching in the Church of England be considered 'on its merits'. The Bishop's letter had treated it

> in a manner so personal to myself as to make me almost despair of a right solution. It is not a question of 'opportunities' I have been given. Let me be ruled out altogether. And let us think of those other women, many of them quite young, still at the universities, perhaps, full of enthusiasm and hope, with keen minds and trained intelligence. Some of them, I know, desire to serve the Church, and surely the Church needs such women? But, if they are to be met with the persistent assumption that their wish is a merely personal wish for 'opportunities', can they be expected to persist? Shall we not in the end loss them, as we have lost the intellectuals through our unwillingness to recognise the truths of science, and the Labour movement through our dread of democracy?[23]

Though *she* might wait, 'the great movements of our time will not wait while the Church "quietly, slowly and deliberately" makes up her mind to accept what all the world has accepted already.'

Maude's sense of 'great movements' could not but be enhanced by the cataclysmic events of that March. A fortnight after her pulpit debut she was with Lansbury in the Albert Hall facing thousands of excited people who

---

[22]*Challenge* (22 April 1917). And see Adrian Hastings, *A History of English Christianity 1920–1985* (1986) 86. The Church of England and the Free Churches did not draw appreciably closer together until after the Second World War.
[23]*Challenge* (4 March 1917).

were there to applaud the Russian Revolution. Clara Butt sang the Russian national anthem, a message was read from G. B. Shaw and many greetings sent to 'the Democrats of Russia' who, in one step, Maude said in her speech, 'had passed from bondage into freedom'.

> While we are still consulting with one another . . . whether this or that barrier should be put up between this or that part of the people and the expression of their will . . . we may yet send a message to those brave and gallant spirits who dare the great deeds of the world in one stride . . . Tonight we know that everything is possible.[24]

But not in the Church. 'The National Mission has come and gone leaving hardly a ripple on the surface of the water,' was her comment in *The Hour and the Church*, which she published the following year – noting that none of the committees of enquiry appointed in its wake had terms of reference relating to the role of women in the Church. And though there was also what she jokingly called a half – or quarter-committee set up (the one that Eeles was secretary of) to research their position in past ages, this was confined to its historical theme and had no power to make recommendations.[25] In April 1917 Ursula Roberts's long-postponed gathering on women's ordination took place in the form of a 'Quiet Day and Conference' held at St Saviour's, Pimlico. Maude gave the addresses, stressing that they had to avoid any element of self-seeking, and papers were read on aspects of the priesthood. The purpose of the meeting, as its title suggests, was prayer and education; no action was discussed.[26]

In May Maude preached again at the City Temple; then at the Kings Weigh House Congregational Church, where Dr Orchard was minister. There was a particular interest in this, for Orchard was assisted at the Celebration by Constance Todd and Claude Coltman – soon to be ordained and married. Maude was present later at their ordination and found the service both moving and significant of changed attitudes to women in the church. Her own way forward was less clear than Miss Todd's, though. Hudson had suggested she preach at St Botolph's, but while she was ready to preach to Nonconformists she was not yet ready to consider preaching in an Anglican church in defiance of the bishop. 'I have been offered a pulpit in London and have, up till now, refused it,' she said. 'I do not know, of course, what the future may bring.'[27]

It was a time of domestic change. In her memoir *A Threefold Cord*,

[24]*Herald* (7 April 1917). Like many others she was soon disillusioned with the Bolshevik Revolution.

[25]The committee had only one woman member, Alice Gardner of Bristol. The rest were clergy. Maude had been unhappy when it was set up, Zoë Fairfield wrote to Eeles on 23 March 1917, 'thinking it might be used as a block to any immediate reform.'

[26]Report, Fawcett 'Women in the Church'.

[27]Maude to Miss A. M. Procter (20 March 1917).

Maude describes how an aged aunt came to be added to the Shaw household and Hudson and Effie moved to Hampstead. There was no room for her and she went to live in Poplar. Why? 'Because I like it,' she told a journalist. It made little difference to her contact with the Shaws ('I was constantly with them . . . and we took our holidays together') but in other ways there was a major change – for here at length was realised the youthful dream of two friends setting up house together. When they were young and Kathleen had proposed it, Maude had been adamant that she could not accept. 'I am not a prophet,' she insisted then – by some irony using the word which was sometimes used to describe her now – 'that my friends should sacrifice themselves for me.'[28] Now she accepted. But not from Kathleen. She set up house with Evelyn Gunter.

'I wouldn't think it wrong in some cases,' she had said. And certainly Evelyn's case was different from Kathleen's. For all her good sense and proven ability, brilliance had never been claimed for her; nor ambition, at least in the sense in which Maude felt it and claimed it for Kathleen. 'I wish there were a *good* word for ambition,' she had told Kathleen long ago. 'I mean that I always feel you ought to be leading, and have the capacity for it, and therefore must *need* to do it, as one does *need* to exercise a gift.' At the time of the move to Poplar, Kathleen was involved again with the vote, as one of the leaders of the National Council for Adult Suffrage: lobbying for women in regard to the measure of electoral reform which was currently being discussed.

As for Evelyn – since 1897 she had been the perfect second-in-command at the Oxford University Extension Delegacy; the organiser, virtually single-handed, of countless lecture circuits and Summer Meetings. The work had been intensely interesting, she said now, in her letter of resignation, 'and I cannot tell you how much I value the opportunities, the experience and the friendships which it has brought me.' But she made clear, however courteously, that Extension's failure to come to terms with its organisational and financial problems (such as had defeated Hudson Shaw) had been a factor in her decision. For Evelyn to give up what had clearly developed into a post of some authority to go and help with Maude's correspondence and write 'secretary' under her name (as she did in the early days) was not promotion. There can be no doubt, though, that she identified with everything Maude had undertaken. She was a suffragist, and active member of the Church League for Women's Suffrage. She was a committed churchwoman, and had been one of those circularised by Ursula Roberts in 1913 on the subject of women's ordination. With her usual candour, caution and diffidence, Evelyn had replied then, 'I am in favour of the admission of women to the priesthood' adding, though, that she thought their first need

[28]TFC 46; Maude to KC (2 Nov. 1901) LMH archives. Kathleen later set up house with Dr Hilda Clark whom she got to know when they were engaged in relief work in Vienna.

was to undertake study on the subject – it was too soon to form a pressure group ('Please believe that I speak very tentatively for I have no foundation of scholarship').[29]

She went to Poplar at a critical time, for by the summer of 1917 the Church Committee of the City Temple, having heard Maude preach on several occasions, had decided that the 'many-sided ministry' appropriate to their church should 'have in it elements that only a woman can supply', and offered her a post as 'pulpit assistant'; in effect, created it for her. The incoming minister, Dr Fort Newton, had accepted his appointment on the understanding that there would be some reduction of a work load which had practically killed his predecessor. 'He wants me,' as Maude put it to a friend, 'but if not me, then somebody else';[30] which rather understates the conviction of this very forceful American – still in his thirties and himself the choice of the innovative party at the City Temple – that she was uniquely suited to the job.

In retrospect he stressed that the war had not only given him the opportunity to appoint 'a woman of genius' but had created the conditions which made the appointment of a woman most fitting. At the practical level it was hard to find ministers. And war had turned women's lives upside down. They were engaged in all manner of work which they had never done before; they were about to be enfranchised. A woman of particular vision was needed 'to interpret the new life of woman'.[31] 'It will be an honour and a joy to have you as a fellow worker,' he wrote to Maude. But at first she refused, committed, as she said, to 'the forward movement' in the church of England. Dawson, hon. secretary to the City Temple, now wrote pressing her to reconsider.

> How profoundly disappointed we are . . . it is impossible to express. We had set our hearts on the arrangements proposed . . . it seemed . . . the natural sequel to tendencies in which we see the working of the spirit of God.

'It is apparent from your letters,' he went on, 'that you appreciate the greatness of the opportunity. I am not sure that you realise that *you are the only person that can turn it to account.*' He pointed out that there were many who could work for the forward movement in the Church of England.

> There is only one woman known to us who can do the special kind of work that is crying out to be done. The urgency of the need and your unique fitness to meet it seem to constitute an irresistible call. By responding to it you would be enabled to serve causes which . . . far transcend the bounds of any branch of the Christian Church. . . . Not only so . . . you would indirectly but powerfully promote those ends on which your heart is set.

[29]Evelyn Gunter to Ursula Roberts (6 Sept. 1913) Fawcett 'Women in the Church'.
[30]City Temple Committee to Maude (26 June 1917); Maude to C. H. S. Matthews and Tissington Tatlow (19 June 1917) Fawcett 222.
[31]Joseph Fort Newton, 'Maude Royden', *The Century Magazine*, MS (March 1928).

Dawson understood the forces of resistance.

> I hope I am not going too far if I say that . . . if you allowed yourself to be guided
> by your own intuition, without taking counsel with flesh and blood (. . . least of
> all ecclesiastical flesh and blood) . . . you would say Yes to our invitation.[32]

He gained at least her promise to rethink. He may or may not have been
fully aware of the current state of preparation of that 'forward movement'
which she had referred to, and which was soon to break upon the public as
the movement for 'Life and Liberty'. Here was a dilemma. The previous
year the cry had been that to let women 'preach' would ruin the prospects of
the National Mission. Now it was urged that if Maude accepted the post
offered at the City Temple it would blight the prospects of 'Life and
Liberty'.

'Life and Liberty' arose in part out of the failure of the National Mission.
While hopes of 'free-ing' the Established Church through a measure of
self-government went back to the nineties, it was the sense of spiritual
bankruptcy exposed by war and the National Mission that had created this
ginger group. Its logic was simple: 'before the Church could hope to catch
the ear of the nation, it must set its own house in order'. 'It is a scandal that
the right to appoint a man to the cure of souls should be bought and sold,'
ran one pamphlet. 'It is a scandal that there should be no place for women in
the councils of the Church.'[33] But in order to tackle such scandals the
Church must be freed from the cumbersome necessity of waiting for
Parliament to act; free in some measure to govern itself.

The moving spirit was Dick Sheppard, the young vicar of St Martin-in-
the-Fields who had returned from the horrors of Mons to fling its doors
wide open to the people. 'The church is open all night for soldiers', ran the
notice beneath the red light. By 1917 St Martin's was everything – an air
raid shelter, 'a little Sorbonne' for its programme of speakers, a refuge for
derelicts and the lonely, and a place where the services drew such crowds
his own parishioners could hardly get in. It was Sheppard who impressed
on William Temple that the Church of England must move now; and it was
in reference to Sheppard and his friends that Temple said to Archbishop
Davidson (who deplored any such move in wartime) 'the War and the
Mission have brought them to boiling-point. It is a psychological necessity
that they should explode. To ask them to wait six months may be right, but
is requiring . . . a miracle'.[34]

[32]Albert Dawson to Maude (7 June 1917) fawcett 222.
[33]Carolyn Scott, *Dick Sheppard (1977) 93*. For an account of 'Life and Liberty', see F.
Iremonger *William Temple*, (1948) 220–40.
[34]K. A. Thompson, *Bureaucracy and Church Reform* (1970) 159.

Maude was one of this combustible group and soon felt for the charismatic Sheppard a love, she said, 'just this side of idolatry'. She was immensely cheered, as she told him, to find herself part of a movement for reform. 'Having discovered that there really is one whole person willing to go ahead, besides myself, I immediately feel that we are an army. If you and I, why not others? Thousands of others? Now I feel full of hope.'[35]

The others included well-known names. The first signatory of the letter to the *Times* which started things off was Louise Creighton; and the other lay signatories were A. L. Smith of Balliol and Albert Mansbridge of the WEA. 'Amid the ruins of the old world,' it began, 'the new world is already being born.'

> But as soon as we consider the changes that are needed to make the Church a living force in the nation, we find ourselves hampered at every turn by an antiquated machinery which we are powerless to change except by a series of Acts of Parliament. . . . If the Church is to have new life . . . it must have liberty.[36]

To test support, a public meeting was planned.

Meanwhile, the City Temple's Committee awaited Maude's response to their invitation; and the advice of her clergy friends was not encouraging, as Dawson had feared. Even those who could swallow the idea of her preaching there felt strongly opposed to her accepting an official position, as one of them explained. To which Maude answered that she thought 'reunion' was the urgent question.

> If we Christians don't come together . . . the Churches, including of course our own . . . will find themselves in the position of the Jewish race – destined by God to give Christ to the world, but capable only of crucifying Him. I think a great number of people realise this, but are inarticulate . . . and give up hope.

'*It seems to me* that I see the way along which we should go,' she ventured 'and I have a certain facility of expression, by which I could . . . be a voice to the people who see . . . and probably see much more clearly than I, but . . . have not got a voice or have not got a platform.'[37]

At the time of writing (19 June) she was still in process of taking counsel with 'ecclesiastical flesh and blood' – including the very significant part of it represented by William Temple, whom, if her first thought had really been tactics, she would have consulted at the start. For if Dick Sheppard was the inspiration of Life and Liberty, Temple was its pilot; the only man who could bring it to harbour. Son of an archbishop, outstandingly able and still

---

[35]Maude to Dick Sheppard (11 May 1917) Sheppard Papers (Leuceforth SP)

[36]*Times* (20 June 1917). The letter was signed by Louise Creighton, A. A. David, Headmaster of Rugby, Albert Mansbridge of the WEA, J. B. Seaton, Principal of Cuddesdon Theological College, A. L. Smith, Master of Balliol, William Temple, A. P. Charles and Dick Sheppard (Hon. Secs.)

[37]Maude to C. H. S. Matthews and Tissington Tatlow (19 June 1917) Fawcett 222.

in his thirties, his path back to Lambeth seemed preordained. But he was too much the statesman for Maude, as she confessed to Ursula Roberts.

I don't (privately) think very much of Mr Temple's opinion on anything . . . progressive. He is a dear, but he is the sort of dear that will inevitably be a bishop, and probably an archbishop, quite soon. He is incurably 'safe', has sown all his ecclesiastical wild oats, and isn't going to sow any more![38]

Temple had a statesman's feeling for priorities. 'Personally I want . . . to see women ordained,' he had told Roberts in 1913,

but still more do I want to see both real advance towards the reunion of Christendom, and the general emancipation of women. To win admission to the priesthood now would put back the former and to moot it would put back the latter.[39]

Priorities change. And the reunion of Christendom (arguably to be nudged forward a little by Maude's going to the City Temple, as she had finally decided to do) took second place to Life and Liberty now. 'I confess I very much hope you will really succeed in keeping out of the papers the statement of what you are doing at the City Temple until after July 16th,' he wrote, thinking of the public meeting ahead.

I am sure you will see that it is really important . . . I am perfectly prepared to defend your action . . . on the ground that the scope offered is sufficient to make some constructive work possible, whereas when you went for one occasion only it did not seem to me that the amount of good you could do was sufficient to balance the incidental damage through terrifying people etc. Of course I shall support you . . . along these lines, and you will not think it absurd if I say that the less I have to do this the better I shall be pleased. You will not, I imagine, be in any way quoting our names, at any rate unless persecution arises in an acute form.[40]

Meeting the Bishop of London at a luncheon around the time the news did break Fort Newton found him wondering if Maude wore a hat to preach in and reflected that, in the Bishop's shoes, he would be concerned not so much with the hat as with 'what she is doing with the brains under her hat'.[41] Canon Scott Holland was one of those puzzled by conflicting statements as to Maude's new role.

It makes me sheerly miserable to be in any way against you. . . . I am asking only for your consideration of the cause of Life and Liberty and how it must affect that. We have got to win a crowd of people who would be thrown helplessly back by what was put in the Papers. . . . If we are out to reform the Church from within,

[38]Maude to Ursula Roberts (27 Aug. 1916) Fawcett 'Women in the Church'.
[39]Temple to Roberts (27 March 1913) Fawcett, 'Women in the Church'.
[40]Temple to Maude (4 July, 1917) Fawcett 222.
[41]J. Fort Newton, *Preaching in London: A Diary of Anglo-American Friendship* (1922) 59.

our own loyalty to her must be obvious and untarnished. We could not afford a
discussion on that. . . . Nor did I look forward to meeting incessantly a challenge
in which I should have . . . to throw you over! I love you too much to enjoy the
prospect.[42]

'As it is,' he concluded with relief, 'the notice in the Paper was wrong. You
are only giving addresses.' Her reply evidently reassured him that she was
not taking an official position at the City Temple as pastor or minister and
she wrote to the *Challenge* in similar terms.

So 'Life and Liberty' was launched, and brilliantly. The Queen's Hall was
packed and Temple opened with a speech which even Hensley Henson,
Dean of Durham ('the fly in every ointment')[43] could not fault. Maude's
speech, seconding the resolution that the archbishops be asked to ascertain
'whether and on what terms Parliament is prepared to give freedom to the
Church . . . to manage its own life', he described as 'confused, incoherent,
and when intelligible, irrelevant'. 'An anarchic feminist . . . now claiming
the priesthood' was unlikely, he thought, to commend the movement to
most Anglicans. But the Nonconformist paper *The Christian World* felt the
bid for Liberty gained from the fact that 'Miss Royden at once proclaims
herself a "lover" of Anglicanism and is apparently ready to act as Dr Fort
Newton's assistant at the City Temple'. With what it called 'a certain
careful passionateness' she denied that Christianity was always conservative. It had started as revolutionary and 'we must not be afraid of the word'.
She appealed to those who had worked for freedom in the labour movement and the women's movement to devote themselves to 'an even greater
cause'. The resolution was carried, with cheers. Of the 2,000 present, three
quarters were women, and the rest 'youngish parsons', according to
Henson, who was proud to have been the only dissentient. The meeting,
after all, was 'Gore's crowd', as he explained to Archbishop Davidson, and
he did not look for a 'virile' church policy from 'the academic, the feminist,
the socialist, the clericalist'.[44]

Meanwhile the Life and Liberty people let no grass grow under their feet.
In August an approach was made to the Archbishop who received their
deputation courteously and assured them that he, too, wished to go forward with what he called 'all reasonable speed'. They saw, though, that
Davidson's understanding of what this meant was different from their own
since he was unwilling to take further steps until the Representative Church
Council had met. This was perhaps the first intimation to radical members
such as Maude of the kind of thing they were up against. The second came a
month or two later when her own position was called in question and she

---

[42]Scott Holland to Maude (26 July (no year)) Fawcett 222.
[43]Hastings, *A History of English Christianity* 176. And see *Challenge* (20 July 1917).
[44]Henson's Journals 21: 83, 108 (references kindly supplied by Keith Francis); and see
Henson, *Retrospect of an Unimportant Life* (1942) 207–8.

was forced to resign her place on the council of Life and Liberty. Once again the problem was the City Temple and how she interpreted her role there.

At the successful launching meeting Maude had begun her speech by declaring that they were all there, first and foremost, as lovers of the Church of England. She had also made her allegiance clear when she wrote to accept the City Temple's offer.

> I should like very briefly to explain to you . . . I am an Anglican and my Church is very dear to me. I hope and believe that when the re-union of Christendom becomes an accomplished fact (which God grant) she will have something to give as well as to receive. I have no desire to leave her; I have an active desire to serve her. But I am convinced that the best service that one can do at this time to one's Church as well as to the cause of Christianity is to work for re-union; and that co-operation between the Churches (such as your invitation would make poss-ible) is the first step in this direction.[45]

On 17 September she preached for the first time in her new role of pulpit assistant, and it was announced that the following Sunday she would conduct a brief christening service. Next Sunday came and four children were baptised. Almost at once she received a letter from the Reverend J B Seaton, a leading figure in Life and Liberty and – more important – Principal of Cuddesdon, the theological college near Oxford where the Life and Liberty council was due to meet in a day or two, telling her that her presence in the college would not now be acceptable. 'Mr Seaton forbids me to go to Cuddesdon!' she wrote on 29 September to Sheppard.

> Rather an arbitrary use of power, I think. After all, until the Council casts me out, I have as good a right to forbid him, as he to forbid me, but for the accidental circumstance of our meeting in his house. . . . I had no *idea* that it was such a hideous crime to baptise four infants who *in no case* would have come to an Anglican priest. . . .Yours, feeling rather like a pelican in the wilderness.[46]

'Oh *think* how I should contaminate the little white sheep at Cuddesdon,' she added, 'by "darkening its doors" for three days!!' To the *Challenge* she wrote more soberly, 'utterly amazed' at all the fuss.

> When the mother of one of [the children] first approached me, explaining that she wished her child baptised at the City Temple, that she was obliged to leave London almost immediately, and that she wished me to conduct the service, it literally never entered my head to refuse. . . . Baptism by the laity is as old as the Church.

It might be said, of course, that lay baptism was only permitted where a priest could not be had. But in this case the question of priest did not arise. The parents were not Anglicans, would not have sought one. 'And if not a

---

[45]Maude to Executive Committee of City Temple (1 July 1917) Fawcett 222.
[46]Maude to Sheppard (29 Sept. 1917) SP.

priest, why not a layman? Or a woman? Why not I?'[47]

As for Seaton, Maude had insisted on her right to attend the Council, pointing out that if she were prevented this would invalidate its proceedings. The Principal of Cuddesdon then said she could come, if she did not actually sleep in the college. ('This seemed odd,' wrote Maude, much later. 'Was it held that my malign presence became more powerful in the darkness . . . or what?') 'Miss Royden was presumably to be driven backwards and forwards between an Oxford lodging-house and Cuddesdon each day, perhaps in a closed cab – wrote Freddie Iremonger, Temple's friend and eventual biographer, who was also a member of the Council, and angry with Seaton, as many of them were, he said. He himself, 'the angriest man in the room', was landed with the awkward task of going to Poplar to convey the decision to Maude. He found her giving a baby its bottle.

> With a grace which the messenger will always remember, she agreed to come down to Cuddesdon and meet the Council. Temple asked her to put her point of view to the meeting, which she did with dignity and courtesy, expressing at the same time her willingness to resign her membership of the Council if this was their desire. The Principal again made his offer, throwing out a hint that he might be prepared to think differently if Miss Royden had no intention of repeating her offence. Miss Royden was unwilling to concede the point and again asked leave to resign her place. . . . A taxi was ordered; the tainted lady returned to Poplar; and the incident was closed.[48]

But it 'left an extremely unpleasant taste'. A distinguished modern church historian suggests that the taste was not unpleasant enough; pointing out that Temple 'had just one woman upon his 'Liberty' committee yet was willing to lose her because neither he nor his committee of stalwart radicals was prepared to . . . stand up to the Principal of Cuddesdon.'[49] The boldest stand, in fact, seems to have been made by the general secretary of the Student Christian Movement, Canon Tissington Tatlow, who wrote to the *Challenge* deploring the outcome and the secrecy surrounding it.

> I can easily find out exactly what has happened by reference to Miss Royden, as I have the privilege of counting her as one of my friends, but I prefer to ask you to tell us publicly why so valuable a person . . . is to be lost to the Life and Libery Movement. Is it because she has offended ecclesiastically by having baptised in a Nonconformist place of worship? I thought her action unwise, and told her so at

---

[47]*Challenge* (5 Oct. 1917). At South Luffenham Maude had been called to a sickly new baby while Shaw was away and wired for a clergyman to come and baptise it, explaining to the parents that in case of need anybody could christen a baby. 'I'm not at all sure that they believed me!' she told Kathleen.

[48]Iremonger, *William Temple* 236–7. The baby was probably the handicapped child of Maude's friends, the sculptor Alec Miller and his wife, which she took into her household for a time to help them.

[49]Hastings, *A History of English Christianity* 44–5.

once, but it was not a more unwise action than is indulged in from day to day by clergy who remain unreproved.

'I cannot think of anyone in the Church of England – bishop, priest, lay-man or lay-woman,' he went on, 'who has an influence among young people equal to Miss Royden's.' It was due, he said, to a combination of courage, vision, and devotion to our Lord. 'People who dislike her, and there are plenty, will say that young people are attracted by her because they are inclined to like lawless people.' He did not think the young admired lawlessness.

> What they are attracted by is great moral and spiritual qualities. Let there be no mistake about it; in so far as Miss Royden has a following today, she has got that following because she is a woman of high courage, because she has the gift of insight, and because she is deeply religious. Some of us frankly admit that she is a very poor ecclesiastic, but we forgive her for this defect and bear with it, because she has got qualities we long to see in our official leaders and too often miss in them.[50]

This must have been heartening reading for Maude, who was certainly upset by the incident. 'I am far sorrier than I could trust myself to say – for fear of disgracefully bursting into tears – that I shan't be able to help you in this movement,' she told Sheppard. 'I do hope – I don't know what to hope. And I know God will guide you however perplexing things are so perhaps I needn't help Him! Good-bye, AMR.' She added a postscript: 'I *don't* really believe much in a Billy-Temple movement, although he is a dear. Why do they treat him as if he were God?'[51]

The great achievement of the 'Billy-Temple movement' was the Enabling Act of 1919, which gave the Church delegated legislative power, to be exercised through a national assembly. 'Our first objective is won,' said Temple. And it had been hard enough to win. As to any others – as to what he had meant by the passionate words with which he launched the movement ('The day is come that burns like fire!') that was some time ago; and two hard years of compromise and politics had changed the balance between radicals and moderates in 'Life and Liberty'. Anomalies once listed as scandals remained – though, through Temple's determination, women could serve on the new assembly and on all lesser Church councils at last. Otherwise, Iremonger recorded later, power in the Church remained where it was; and the dominant voice in the new assembly was the voice of the administrator, not the prophet. Maude had passed judgement long before that. 'When Life and Liberty chose wise, able, prudent Temple instead of you, it lost its soul,' she wrote to Dick Sheppard.[52]

---

[50]*Challenge* (19 Oct. 1917).
[51]Maude to Dick Sheppard (n.d.) SP. AMR = Agnes Maude Royden
[52]ibid. (17 Oct. 1917) SP.

Shut out from that movement, she committed herself almost entirely to the City Temple until 1920. When she had agreed to act as pulpit assistant in the summer of 1917 it had been for the period up to Christmas in the first place; but Albert Dawson was soon making signs of their tremendous anxiety to keep her. If there really were, as somebody said, people who would sooner be seen in hell than in the City Temple when she was preaching, they did not surface. 'Your acceptance of the Church's invitation has been more than justified,' he wrote in November, calling it one of the most fruitful things that had happened in the City Temple's long history.

> The size of congregations when you preach and the expressions of appreciation that we are continually hearing constitute the 'call' to you and the endorsement of the step you were courageous enough to take. I should not like to have to confess to you how some of us would feel if for any reason you were unable to 'go on'.

Just before Christmas he referred again to 'the great work' she had been doing. 'It has prospered more than we ever dared to hope'. Indeed she had become so much part of the church that they could not imagine it without her, 'and should be more concerned than I can tell you if we had to face such a contingency'.[53]

For all that Maude had been at pains to emphasise the limits of the work she was undertaking, especially in Anglican circles ('I am not a member of the City Temple Church. I have not been ordained or "set apart" as a minister, pastor, or official of any kind; nor is it possible that I should be, seeing I am not a Congregationalist'),[54] the modest title 'pulpit assistant' does not begin to convey what she did. In addition to taking one Sunday service and sometimes the Thursday service as well, the authorities had asked her at the beginning to 'set apart an hour or two a week to see callers, particularly young women' in need of advice. So began her 'clinic', as Fort Newton called it, and her extended pastoral role as 'guide, confidant and friend to hundreds of women, and . . . confessor to not a few'.[55] By the time of his formal 'recognition' as minister at the beginning of 1918 they were obviously working very well together. He had taken a great risk, Maude said in her tribute, 'and I do not think he has ever ceased having postcards referring him to the First Epistle to the Corinthians'. When he first approved her appointment, 'I thought he would go scouting round the church to see how many places he could forbid me to stand in, and that perhaps he might ask the congregation to retire to the crypt before I began – for this is a consecrated building – or suggest that all male persons should go out before I began to speak.'[56]

---

[53] Albert Dawson to Maude (28 Nov. and 20 Dec. 1917) Fawcett 222.
[54] Letter to the *Challenge* (5 Oct. 1917).
[55] J. Fort Newton. 'Maude Royden', in *The Century Magazine* (March 1928).
[56] *Christian Commonwealth* (23 Jan. 1918) 210.

In fact, his courage in appointing a woman was paralleled by the generosity which enabled Fort Newton to work with one whose pacifist views he did not share – still more, to accept a female colleague who stood much higher than he did as a preacher. She was left free to develop her own style and soon introduced an 'after-meeting' where she was able to leave the pulpit and sit on a level with the congregation for a discussion of questions raised. That she so evidently loved a challenge was no doubt part of that appeal to the young which Tatlow and many others stressed and which finds proof in such diverse sources as the newspaper cutting of Maude in her preaching dress found on a battlefield in 1918, and Vera Brittain's account much later of her effect upon Winifred Holtby, who as a twenty-year-old in London went one Sunday to the City Temple. 'The famous preacher's reputation was now so high that Winifred went apprehensively, fearing disappointment'; but she came away uplifted by a 'gracious tolerance' which awoke echoes of her own conviction, formed as a schoolgirl in the Scarborough shelling, that there could be no way to genuine peace through reprisals and Hun-hating.[57]

It was easier for Maude not to hate the Hun than it was for her not to hate the British government when it set up brothels in France – *Maisons Tolérées* – where women were kept, under medical inspection, for the use of soldiers. She launched her protest with a passionate sermon. 'I have never seen such flaming wrath of outraged womanhood against the degradation of her sex!' wrote Fort Newton.

> Denouncing the Government as a procurer, she said, 'To any woman who believes the sacrifice to be necessary, I would say that she ought herself to volunteer! The men who urge regulated prostitution on grounds of national necessity, ought to invite their wives and daughters to fill the places left vacant by the women who are worn out! I use words that sear my heart, but as a woman in a Christian pulpit I cannot be silent in the presence of such an infamy!'[58]

In a sermon marking the passage of the Bill which would at last enfranchise women, she recalled having come into suffrage when she learned the truth about prostitution.

In January 1918 votes for women became a reality and the National Union marked the event with a celebration in the Queen's Hall presided over by Mrs Fawcett. Lord Lytton, Arthur Henderson and Sir John Simon had been invited to represent supporters in the three political parties and Maude, who thanked them on behalf of the women, 'spoke with all the seriousness and all the wit that Suffrage audiences have learned to expect from her'. 'Miss Royden was . . . splendid, as she always is,' was the

---

[57] Vera Brittain, *Testament of Friendship* (1940) 65.
[58] Fort Newton, 'Maude Royden'. The campaign against *maisons tolerées* was pressed by the Church League for Women's Suffrage and also, notably, by Dr T. G. Fry, Dean of Lincoln. In the end the government backed down.

verdict of one participant.[59] And her speech was splendidly followed by Sir Hubert Parry's setting of Blake's *Jerusalem*, composed for the occasion and sung for the first time by the Bach Choir, the composer conducting. 'That was a good hymn!' Maude told him later. And he replied, 'That was a better speech!' No request to speak ever pleased her more. 'Even at this distance,' she said in old age, 'I feel again the emotion which seized me when this invitation came.' She had been touched that Mrs Fawcett ('the most warlike of us all') had chosen her, a pacifist, for this honour; and on the occasion she was lifted up by the greatness of the cause, the sense of sisterhood.[60] A few weeks earlier in the City Temple she had also risen superbly to that theme, bending the words of *Ecclesiastes* to pay tribute to the first pioneers: 'Let us now praise famous women and our mothers who have borne us; for these are our spiritual mothers and all that we have today we have from their hands.' The fight for the vote was only one battle in a great campaign against the world's suffering. They must forget its bitterness and disappointments.

> But let us for ever remember what links us to all the struggling causes of freedom. Some of you who have stood at street corners to plead with men for what seemed to you the barest justice, *do not forget* what it is like to be a beggar. . . .You who remember when the fight went against you, *do not forget* what it is like to meet great odds.

Some of them, she said, had learnt for the first time what it was like to meet insult and indifference. 'All this is nothing, my sisters, tonight, but *do not forget* what the world is like to those who have neither position nor wealth.' If they forgot, then the fight had been in vain 'though every woman in the country had a vote'.[61]

Her feeling that personal suffering could create 'a sense of compassion for all humanity' found expression, too, when she preached on bereavement – that terrible, unseen amputation which marked so many now in every gathering. Even that might be turned to account. But she did not seek to minimise the pain. Death when it came in the course of nature after a long and active life (as indeed it had come to her father in the summer of 1917) – 'there is no sting in such a death'. But the death of the young. . . . She spoke of the longing to see them again, to hear their voices.

Her sister Daisy's youngest son, Trevor, had been killed a few months before. And a few months later, Ralph was killed. Probably no death until

---

[59]*Common Cause* (22 March 1918) 661; and see letter, unsigned, to Catherine Marshall (March 1918) Marshall Papers.

[60]'Bid Me Discourse'. Maude says that though the NU Committee was not unanimous in choosing her to speak, Mrs Fawcett herself wished it. If so, her friendliness was in contrast with her enduring hostility to Kathleen, whom she refused to meet in 1916 because of 'wounding' remarks at the time of the split.

[61]'Thanksgiving and Consecration; *Christian Commonwealth* (13 Feb. 1918)

Hudson's in old age was so terrible to Maude as this. His loss at twenty-four, ran the *Common Cause* obituary, had 'deprived the Feminist Movement of one of the most brilliant and devoted of its younger supporters'. In a brief memoir Maude tried to capture the promise, courage and spirituality of her beloved fellow 'freak'. 'I never met any human being who had such a genius for friendship.' Theirs had been crowned in 1917 by the appearance of *The Making of Women* (to which they both contributed essays) edited by Ralph's college friend, Victor Gollancz.[62]

These 'Oxford Essays in Feminism' published when the women's vote was virtually assured, look ahead to the endowment of motherhood and other aspects of the 'new' feminism characteristic of the postwar years. Yet Maude was still very much concerned with the 'old'. 'What of the Church?' wrote Zoë Fairfield, in November 1918. 'We are assured that there is movement – perhaps there is, but it is nothing in comparison with the movement everywhere else.'[63] The committees which followed up the National Mission had now reported, some even recommending that women should participate more. But no report had come from the research committee specifically concerned with their historical role, and without that, it seemed nothing could be done. This at least was the Bishop of London's response whenever he was asked if a woman might preach; and the more impetuous of those concerned found it increasingly hard to bear. Hudson especially (who, according to Maude, was not in favour of women priests, or even deacons) was passionately keen that women be allowed to 'prophesy', and by the end of 1917 had evidently run out of patience, saying it was useless to wait for committees, and most reluctantly deferring to the view of other members of their little group (which included Tissington Tatlow) that they send a deputation to the Archbishop before taking more precipitate action.

Meanwhile, Maude sometimes read the lessons in St Botolph's; on the first occasion, with trembling lips, Hudson noted – made angry at the thought that such a thing as that, for such as she, should have been a matter for trembling. She feared there would be some interruption or protest. However, there was none. 'As a matter of fact,' wrote Edith Picton-Turbervill in her memoirs, 'when Maude Royden stood by the lectern and read, it did not seem in the least extraordinary; the only difference being that the lessons were better read than usual.' And if Maude trembled, Hudson did not.

The rector began his sermon that evening with these words: 'Today for the first time in this historic church you have heard a woman's voice proclaiming the glad

---

[62]'Ralph Bonfoy Rooper: A memoir by A. Maude Royden' (n.d.) Fawcett Box 379, 23. *The Making of Women* came out in September 1917. Maude contributed 'Modern Love' and 'The Future of the Woman's Movement'; Ralph Rooper 'Women Enfranchised'.
[63]*Challenge* (1 Nov. 1918).

tidings of Christ's gospel. Some of you may have objected to the innovation. If so, I think you should call yourself Jews and not Christians.[64]

He would have gone further and asked her to preach, but she, through most of 1918, held that they must wait for the Bishop's permission. On that front, things were not going well. In response to their proposal to send a deputation, Archbishop Davidson requested notice of the points they wished to discuss and that was the last they heard of it. In May Maude declined an invitation to preach from the Reverend W. C. Roberts (whose wife Ursula had taken the lead in forming the group concerned with women's ordination). But it is noteworthy that her refusal was not based on the lack of episcopal authority.

> I could not speak on Sunday evening as I preach every Sunday in the month, except one, at the City Temple evening service. I could manage perhaps some Sunday afternoons or a week-day, but I promised Mr Hudson Shaw . . . that I would preach first in his church. He was very anxious indeed to proceed with a course of addresses by me earlier in the year, and rather distressed when I refused, in order to give Mr Tatlow time to go on with his deputation to the Archbishop. This delay was against Mr Shaw's judgement and I feel that I ought to consult him now as to what he wants to do. Unfortunately he has been ill and is not yet really well, but I will see him as soon as I possibly can and then write to you.

'Do you think it would be better to have someone else at St George's, Bloomsbury?' she added. 'I am not the only pebble on the beach and I hate to seem as if I were!'[65]

The Bishop of London, Winnington-Ingram, had assured the reformers in 1917 that the report of the research committee would be out by January the following year. But months had passed with no sign of it. And was it, in fact, worth waiting for? Maude was not alone in doubting its relevance. 'I cannot think,' wrote one of the committee, Dr W. H. Frere of Mirfield, to Eeles, 'that a great deal of the medieval discussions is really to the point, or that the papers on the curiosities of the Middle Ages, interesting as they may be . . . are of any importance.' He was clearly disappointed at the way things had gone.

> The first and main question to my thinking is the question of the admission of women to the priesthood and the episcopate. This is hardly discussed at all. In fact we have never really tackled the question . . . nor have those who are pressing for such a change ever been asked . . . to argue the point; and until this is done I don't think we shall get far.

As to the matter of women preaching, 'This also is hardly dealt with at all . . . nor have we had an opportunity of hearing the claim put forward by

[64]Edith Picton-Turbervill, *Life is Good* (1939) 132–3.
[65]Maude to Rev. W. C. Roberts (3 May 1918) Fawcett 222.

the women for such facilities.' He thought they had never got over the drawback of having only one woman on the committee 'and being out of touch with the greater part of the organised women's work as well as the aspirations of the younger women'.[66]

For Hudson and Maude, breaking point evidently came in September. On the nineteenth she gave an address at the Thursday midday service at St Botolph's on 'The League of Nations and Christianity'. 'For the first and only time since I have been Rector,' Shaw told the Bishop, 'the Church was packed from end to end, both galleries included, scores of people standing. The address was worthy of the great cause pleaded.'[67] She took as her text St Matthew's line which describes the onlookers at the crucifixion: 'Sitting down they watched Him there.'

> Can we really do nothing but sit down and watch the crucifixion of the youth of the world! . . . Must we face the returning soldiers after all with empty hands and bankrupt hearts? Must we admit that, after all, their friends have died and they have suffered in vain?

People said you couldn't change human nature. But science taught, not that it couldn't be changed, 'but that we *must* change it, if it is to survive'. This was the lesson of evolution. 'The fighting instinct in us,' she said, 'has brought us to the cross-roads of civilisation.'

> Humanity must change or it will commit suicide. We can go on developing the means of destruction, or we can re-organise the world for peace: 'See I have set before you this day, life and good and death and evil. Therefore choose life that both thou and thy seed may live.'[68]

Two days later, Shaw received a letter from the Bishop of London:

> I see that I begged you in my last letter *not* to go on with this question of women preachers until the Church has decided after the production of this long-delayed report. I am *pressing* the Committee to get the report out but meanwhile I hear you have already invited women to speak. Of course I can't ask you to withdraw any invitations you have given and there is not the same objection to these *lectures* on Thursday, but I do ask you on no account to arrange anything for the Sundays and not to start another course for Thursdays without consulting me.

Shaw spread his answer over four sheets. It was too late, he said, to withdraw the invitation to Maude to preach the next Sunday evening as this had already been announced, but he assured the Bishop that her address would be separated by an organ recital from the service proper, which he

---

[66]Frere to Eeles (11 Nov. 1918) Eeles Papers, Church House Archives. Dr Frere was head of the Community of the Resurrection, Mirfield.
[67]Shaw to Winnington-Ingram (23 Sept. 1918) Fawcett 221.
[68]'Substance, address at St Botolph's Bishopsgate, Sept. 19, 1918', handwritten summary by Maude, Fawcett 221.

would take himself. It would be suicidal, though, to lose her services, 'and those of many other splendid women to whom God has entrusted the gift of prophesying'. He described the packed church, the eloquent address. 'In 10 minutes Miss Royden had done more for the League of Nations than all the rest of us have been able to do in weeks.' He could not help adding, 'It positively hurts me to remember what good she might have done if she had been allowed, as you wished, in the National Mission.' The bulk of his letter is a cry of despair over the failure of the Church to give a lead or even recognise the challenge of the times.

> The present position in the Church we both love is grave and . . . dangerous beyond expression. We are suffering from a lack of bold, courageous leadership, more especially, if I [may] say so without disrespect, on the part of the Archbishop of Canterbury. We are missing glorious opportunities day by day. We have lost Labour! We are rapidly losing our *best* thoughtful educated Women. Before long, we may now hope, our millions of soldiers . . . will return, to find the Church of England unchanged . . . our shameful divisions unhealed, the great Church, like Nero fiddling while Rome is burning.[69]

Thirty years ago, as a curate at Horsham, he had written to Michael Sadler, 'Whether I shall retain my Orders in this respectability-ridden, comfortable, damnable Establishment is more than I can say.' Now he said, 'It is simply awful, and it has made me, in my 60th year, a rebel.'

> Authority refuses to lead. Then mere privates in the ranks must do what they can. . . . If God gives me life and health I intend to follow the dictates of my conscience and the guidance of the best men in the Church in these directions until I am stopped by force.

Shaw made clear that he did not think the Bishop was to blame for the maddening delay and signed himself 'Yours always affectionately'; adding, in brackets, 'whatever betide'.

It seems, though, as if both he and Maude badly misjudged their support in this quarter. Winnington-Ingram, as bishops went, certainly felt for the underdog ('the idol of the East End' when Bishop of Stepney) and supported women's suffrage (Maude drafted the speech he delivered in the Lords on Lord Selborne's Bill). He was a strong social purity campaigner ('no one did more to secure the passage of the Criminal Law Amendment Act' she had noted in 1913). But on the question of women preaching he had already backed down under pressure and was to present, as A. G. Gardiner said, 'a somewhat forlorn figure of amiable futility' in his handling of the matter now. He was not a strong man, like Temple, nor an inspired one like Dick Sheppard. His outstanding gift of responding to people was inclined to tempt him into overresponse (as with his tub-thumping patriotic

[69]Winnington-Ingram to Shaw (21 Sept. 1918); Shaw to Winnington-Ingram, (23 Sept. 1918) Fawcett 221.

sermons) and perhaps this is why the prime minister, Asquith, called him 'an intensely silly Bishop'.[70]

He was certainly a very sentimental one, from whose full heart emotion had flowed in Maude's direction as they worked together to do the best for Lord Selborne's Bill. 'Nothing has helped me more than your saying . . . "Father, be as good as we think you are",' he wrote in the spring of 1914, 'for surely nothing is more inspiring than the *trust* of the good and the pure. I will . . . pray to live up to your ideal of me.' He became concerned that she was overworking. 'I thought you looking *worn out* when I saw you.' Would she not like to spend a day or two at Fulham and lie out in the lovely garden? 'Miss Hughes will "chaperone" you,' he went on, 'but fancy you and me needing a chaperone!'[71]

In February 1919 when the Upper House of Convocation debated the subject of women preaching, Winnington-Ingram's contribution was certainly not what might have been expected of a man who favoured the women's claim, and one moreover with a kind of time bomb ticking away in Bishopsgate. He praised the gifts of women as speakers and acknowledged the resentment 'among the best women' at the restriction of their role. Yet he did not support the motion that suitable women be allowed to speak in consecrated buildings at services and meetings other than the regular Church services; proposing instead (and his plan was adopted) the setting up of a joint commitee of the two Houses of Convocation to agree the principles on which the bishops might be disposed to 'approve' such women.[72]

Maude reacted to this latest twist with a satirical article on bishops. ('It would be wrong to say officials never move. The earth moves round the sun: officials accompany it. The earth revolves on its axis: officials revolve too.')[73] That this was not her only response became clear when she accepted Shaw's invitation to give the addresses in the Three Hours Service to be held in St Botolph's on Good Friday. Canonically, this was no more momentous than her giving an address on any other weekday – or, as some said, than a female teacher taking a Sunday School class in church, for such activities were equally outside the statutory requirements of the Church of England. Despite all that, the Three Hours' meditation on the words Christ spoke from the Cross had gained a special place in the Christian year and seemed to many people especially holy.

'The rector knows he is disobeying my express wishes', – so Winnington-Ingram was reported in the press. On Maundy Thursday he acted with

[70]Hastings, *A History of English Christianity* 45.
[71]Winnington-Ingram to Maude (Whitsunday 1914); (20 April 1914); (23 July 1914) Fawcett 221.
[72]Chronicle of Convocation 1919, 82–114. The Bishop went out of his way to insist that 'this was no wreckling or delaying Amendment'.
[73]*Star* (17 March 1919).

The Bishop of London (Dr. Winnington-Ingram) as Mrs. Partington trying to keep the tide back with a broom.

Plate 5 Cartoon by Effie Shaw published in *A Threefold Cord. Reproduced by permission of Mrs Helen Blackstone.* (Photograph: British Library)

decision. 'Dear Shaw, I absolutely *forbid* you on your honour and your oath of canonical obedience to me to allow Miss Maude Royden to take the Three Hours' Service in your church tomorrow.'[74] To write thus was certainly distasteful to him and he tried to soften it the following day – Good Friday evening, when the danger was past. (Shaw had responded by closing the church, putting up a notice of the prohibition and inviting worshippers to gather instead in the adjacent Parish Room). 'I was sorry to have to write such a letter but one has to hurt those you love sometimes for their good. It was much better in the schoolroom, and of course there was no objection to that.' In fact it had been dreadful, in physical terms. One account spoke of the Three Hours' devotion taking place in a crowded room where kneeling was almost impossible 'and many stood the whole

[74]Winnington-Ingram to Shaw (Maundy Thursday 1919) Fawcett 221.

long time on the grass near the open windows or outside the door.' Another writer had seen young soldiers hanging on to the windowsill, 'spellbound in that uncomfortable position, one of them 'remaining to the very end'.[75] 'I have written an affectionate letter to Miss Royden,' the Bishop rounded off his letter to Shaw. 'May you have a Happy Easter and get well as soon as you can.'[76]

Shaw's response is a curious mixture of gratitude and intransigeance. On the one hand he felt strong ties of personal affection for Winnington-Ingram and was indeed helped to have a happier Easter because of the Bishop's desire to 'make it up'. But on essentials he did not budge. He rehearsed once more the long delays (nearly three years now) since the Church set out to consider its verdict on women 'speaking'. He quoted those reports of the Archbishop's committees from which he felt he drew moral authority, and pointed out that the research committee had still not published its own report.

'As regards Good Friday, I have been totally unable to understand that there is any difference *legally* between addresses given on Thursdays and addresses on that most sacred of days. Both are non-liturgical, non-statutory and there is no Church law which can be appealed to forbidding them.[77]

The same view was taken by 'high authorities on ecclesiastical law' consulted by the *Manchester Guardian*, who thought the Bishop had exceeded his powers; as did Francis Eeles, whose scholarly piece signed discreetly 'X' in the *Westminster Gazette*, concluded that 'much more questionable things' went on in the London diocese.[78] Against this was the powerful if irrational feeling (certainly experienced by Winnington-Ingram) that because 'the Three Hours' was 'especially sacred' it was especially unseemly that a woman should take it. To Shaw the implications of this were painful. 'Religiously,' he said, 'I am quite sure of this, that no addresses on the Seven Words more reverent, more spiritual, more sound in the Faith, more illuminating and more helpful were given last Good Friday anywhere in the land than Miss Royden's.' A petition was sent to the Bishop declaring that there was something seriously wrong

when an Evangelist so plainly called of God . . . is . . . harassed and impeded by those who, it seems to us . . . should be her chiefest upholders and strengtheners. . . . Some of us have tried to be patient, but after the scandal of Good Friday, we feel . . . the time for silent acquiescence is past.[79]

---

[75]'Petition to the Bishop', *Christian Commonwealth* (23 April 1919) 351; Margaretta Byrde in *The Churchman* (21 Aug. 1920).
[76]Winnington-Ingram to Shaw (Good Friday 1919) Fawcett 221.
[77]Shaw to Winnington-Ingram (22 April 1919) Fawcett 221.
[78]A letter from Maude to Eeles of 6 May 1919, FCE/C/IV/17/Royden, Church House Archives implies that Eeles was the author of 'Women as Ministers', *Westminster Gazette* (2 May 1919).
[79]*Christian Commonwealth* (23 April 1919) 351.

To the opposition, though, the incident revealed a vein of destructive Protestantism. 'Miss Royden is a mystic,' ran one letter to the *Times* 'and has a deep veneration for the saints. She has also a strong grip on Catholic sacramentalism, but she fails entirely to understand what the Catholic Church is.' It was notable, he said, that she had treated the laws of the State with a respect she had never shown the laws of the Church.

> To her it seems an imperative thing that she and other gifted women should be allowed to deliver their message to the Church and to effect this she is willing to force the Church of England into a position which may gravely imperil its Catholic claims. Such has been invariably the attitude of the schismatic and the heretic.[80]

He recommended to her St Theresa, who had been obedient to the Church. Yet she, of all the saints, would surely have entered into the anguish behind Maude's cry: 'I suppose we are going to take risks some day. Mayn't it perhaps be time now?'[81]

---

[80]*Times* (6 June 1919). The argument that the Anglican Church cannot change the role of women 'unilaterally' since it is part of the wider Catholic Church is still a familiar one today.
[81]Maude to Tatlow and C. H. S. Matthews (19 June 1917) Fawcett 222.

9

A Parting of the Ways

[The Church] received me into her bosom. But what has she ever
done for me? She never gave me work to do for her nor training to
do it if I found it for myself.

Florence Nightingale (1852).

In an article published in the *Evening Standard* on Maundy Thursday 1921
Shaw traced the events which had led him once more to ask Maude to
preach at the Three Hours' Service – this time in St Botolph's itself;
concluding, 'I have invited Miss Royden . . . because of all human beings
known to me, cleric or lay, men or women, she possesses in pre-eminent
degree the necessary gifts of reverence, sincerity, eloquence, spiritual insight, and devotion.' This he was ready to proclaim from the rooftops. 'It
fell to me seventeen years ago,' he said on one occasion, at the City Temple,
'to be of some help . . . in her religious life, and since then I have come to
know what some of you are coming to know, that here is a chosen spirit, a
woman of large and brilliant intellect, I think a genuine religious genius.'[1]
Years before, as they left the Queen's Hall where she had captured
attention with her speech on the religious aspect of the women's movement, he told her 'it would have been a crime for me to marry you. You
don't belong to any man; you belong to the world.' There may have been a
kind of consolation in that. At any rate, he spoke with pride of his role,
delighted she should call herself his pupil, though he insisted that it was not
so. 'Neither I nor any human being . . . has inspired you. You have been
your own teacher . . . *I have only loved you.*'[2]

But it was not simply for love of Maude that Hudson took his stand now
on women and the Church. While his whole life was bound up with her and
he had learned his feminism from her and thought that nothing was too
great for her, all this fed into the dissatisfaction he had felt with the Church
from his curate days. He had never been able to come to terms with what
seemed to him the failure of the Church of his heart, in so many respects, to

---

[1]*Evening Standard* (24 March 1921) 5; *Christian Commonwealth* (9 Oct. 1918).
[2]TFC 39, 77.

follow Christ; and a transformation of the role of women became yet another of his longed-for reforms. He had women in the choir at St Botolph's and Maude's first Thursday address in the church had been followed by a series of addresses by women. Indeed they almost entirely supplied Shaw's Thursday preachers in 1919 – an impressive demonstration of his claim to have provided 'a sort of safety valve' through these months of delay. 'Large numbers of women,' he told Winnington-Ingram, 'have been induced to hold on *in hope*.'[13]

Maude drew the biggest congregations. 'I remember you speaking there,' one woman wrote later, 'and how my heart swelled with pride at the sight of the packed congregation of city men. To me, steeped in the teaching of St Paul, this had a special significance.'[4] After Maude, the best-known was Edith Picton-Turbervill, another of Ursula Roberts' little group. In the aftermath of the National Mission she and the modernist Canon Streeter had made the case for women preaching in a book called *Woman and the Church*. Miss Picton-Turbervill spoke often at St Botolph's, heard by 'interested congregations of apparently superior intelligence and seriousness'; and in the summer of 1919 preached at North Somercotes in Lincolnshire, at the invitation of the vicar and with the approval of Bishop Hicks.

But on the wider front, no change. At last, in the autumn of 1919, appeared the report on the ministry of women compiled by the Archbishop's research committee, that great work which for more than two years had been billed as the key to decision-making. Fifteen collotype illustrations of medieval nuns adorned its pages. Knotty points were tackled: did the nuns of Las Huelgas wear mitres and carry croziers in choir? Did those of Roncerai adopt the surplice before or after the canonesses? Maude naturally had some fun with this, but it in no way advanced the question which, by 1920, had been virtually shelved till after the forthcoming Lambeth Conference. This conference (of bishops assembled at Lambeth from the Anglican Communion worldwide) was due to meet at the beginning of July. So, like the parcel in the party game – but one which nobody wanted to open – the vexed question of the ministry of women was bundled onto its agenda.

If there was virtually no change at the top, the mood of the suppliants was changing. Indignation that Maude had been obliged to preach in a crowded parish room on Good Friday had found vent in a petition to the Bishop

---

[3]Shaw to Winnington-Ingram (22 April 1919) Fawcett 221. Other women preachers at St Botolph's included Edith Picton-Turbervill, Zoë Fairfield, Lucy Re-Bartlett, Phoebe Walters, Mary Morshead, Fanny Street, Cicely Ellis, Ellen C. Higgins, and Beatrice Picton-Turbervill.
[4]Mrs Ruth Pusey to Maude (8 Jan. 1948) Fawcett 221, 3/3.

which gathered over 1,000 signatures. Some of her supporters would have gone much further. Miriam Homersham 'late of St Hugh's College, Oxford', suggested in a letter to the *Common Cause* that in view of the Church's attitude to women, as evinced in the recent prohibition, the time had come for a new 'Protestant' movement.

> I would suggest that all the Church of England members of Miss Royden's various congregations, and all those who desire to see qualified women who have the vocation given an official position in the Church, should join the City Temple – as I did some months ago. An individual more or less makes no difference to the Established Church, but an exodus of several hundred – or thousand – at a time might make some slight impression. We should lose something for ourselves . . . but we might gain the inestimable treasure of women priests and preachers . . . for those who come after us.[5]

She also suggested that the ministry of women should be added to the programme of the National Union (the National Union of Societies for Equal Citizenship: NUSEC, as it now called itself). And Maude approved. To her, as she said, the assumption that women were spiritually inferior was more fundamental than the assumption that they were politically inferior to men. She did not favour secession, however. 'For myself I believe that it is right to stay, so long as there is any hope whatever of reform.' She thought there was hope; and that its realisation depended on their willingness 'to endure a good deal for it,' and on their power to believe in it.[6]

But if she found Miriam Homersham extreme, Maude's own concept of spiritual equality – extending to the priesthood – was too extreme for many of those who had laboured long to improve the position of women in the Church. Mrs Creighton, for instance, opposed ordination. The Central Committee of Women's Church Work (chaired by the Archbishop of Canterbury's wife and with Mrs Creighton as vice-chairman) favoured women being allowed to preach – under regulation – but not women priests. The well-known modernist, Canon Streeter, who had been linked with the Roberts group, felt, by the time he wrote *Woman and the Church* in 1917 that the priesthood question 'should be indefinitely postponed'. While not convinced that objections to it 'depend on principles of absolute validity' he thought such a serious break with tradition should not be made until most Church people were convinced that it was desirable; and 'no one can pretend. . .this is at present the case.'[7]

The priesthood question aroused conflict too in the Church League for Women's Suffrage, a body which, as some pointed out, was much better suited than the National Union to campaign on the issue of women and the

[5]*Common Cause* (25 April 1919) 17.
[6]ibid. (2 May 1919) 26.
[7]B. H. Streeter and E. Picton-Turbervill, *Woman and the Church* (1917) 100.

ministry. In 1918 when the vote was won the League, like other suffrage societies, had been forced to think hard about its future. Like the National Union it changed its name, and was now the League of the Church Militant. But militant for what? Some members thought it should extend its fight for equality in the Church right up to the priesthood. Others regarded this with abhorrence. The question was debated in 1918 at a meeting which reaffirmed the League's commitment to secure unrestricted opportunity for women in the life of Church and State, and which also declared that it could see no reason, apart from 'the witness of Catholic usage', why women should not become priests. 'For my own part I am sorry that the Church League (of which I have been a member since its inception) should handle the matter at all,' wrote one woman who found the idea very disturbing. Another said that if the women's movement were ever actually to 'carry' the altar, 'that altar from that day will be no more than the table of a freak sect, another wound added to the body of Christ'. Maude naturally took a different view. 'The CLWS ought to be *really* "militant" ought it not' she wrote to Miss Corben, 'if it takes such a terrific title? It seems strange to me, who fought against militancy years ago, when it took the form of physical violence, to have to urge on the League now to a more energetic spiritual warfare!'[8]

The real split came at a council meeting on 30 April 1919, a week or so after Maude had been prohibited from taking the Three Hours' Service in St Botolph's. This, though it did not touch on the priesthood, could hardly have failed to raise the temperature in what was described as a 'stormy conclave [at which] the League decided to burn its boats'.[9] After passionate discussion the majority voted in favour of challenging 'the custom of the Church of confining the priesthood to men' – a decision seen as 'one of extreme gravity' – not least since it was followed by a crop of resignations. Brave Bishop Hicks resigned the presidency. ('I cannot quite abandon the belief that he would have come, had he lived, to this also,' wrote Maude, at his death in 1919). Claude Hinscliff, who had started the League, resigned (though he in fact came back later). Apart from such sad and significant cases the sudden loss of members meant a loss of funds big enough to threaten the League with extinction. At this point it seemed most likely that it would not be in existence long enough to fight for women priests or anything else. But somehow it managed to turn the corner. By July there were prayers of thanksgiving 'for the interest awakened in the public mind on the question of women and the priesthood. . .for new members joining the League [and] for the financial support that has been given'.

The League opened its campaign with a public debate which filled, and

[8]*Church Militant* (June 1918) 67 and (Aug. 1918) 87; Maude to Miss Corben, (23 Jan. 1919) Fawcett Autograph Collection. 'Women in the Church'.
[9]*Churchman* (21 Aug. 1920) article by Margaretta Byrde.

more than filled, Church House, Westminster. The motion, that 'There are Fundamental Principles which Forbid the Admission of Women to the Priesthood' was proposed by the Reverend J. A. V. Magee and opposed by Maude. Magee, like Athelstan Riley, was a stalwart of the ultraconservative English Church Union, a body which now played a part reminiscent of the Anti-suffrage League in the franchise struggle. Indeed, there was much in this fight to recall the 'Pros' and 'Antis' of earlier days, with opposing bodies, opposing journals, meetings, and petitions, and now and again opposition formalised in public debate. These debates did not always turn out well, as the Church League found on the present occasion. Some of the audience were undoubtedly drawn by an article ('The Obstacle of Sex') which Magee had just written for the *Evening Standard*, setting out the seamy side of the question. Readers were asked to imagine talk in the smoking room on a Saturday night:

> 'I say old chap there's an awfully pretty girl going to preach tomorrow at St Simon's. I'm there, don't you know!' Right ho! And I'm jolly well going to hear Mrs B. on Sunday night at St Jude's on divorce. *She* ought to know all about it. What?'

Fifty years ago, he went on, fair maidens worked slippers for the curate and fervour and flirtation were often combined. 'Although those days have passed away, human nature remains the same. . . . In all seriousness we suggest that a woman priesthood is morally inexpedient.'[10]

In the debate Magee again suggested that one reason behind the judgement of the Church 'and behind the will of Almighty God' against women priests was the risk of impropriety.

> I cannot forget – who indeed can? . . . that already the sex question has too much invaded the Church of God. Already that peculiar combination of faith and flirtation which the French call *folle de sacristie* is too much with us. I ask you, are you going . . . to increase the risk?

To those who cried 'Shame!' Magee replied, 'The shame of it does not rest with us. We cannot help it; we are made as we are and life is as God has settled it' – an attitude hardly less shocking to many.

Folle de sacristie had thus to be disposed of and Maude disposed of it: acknowledged it existed.

> I also know that there are many women who are so filled with loathing at the thought of that attitude . . . that they sometimes will not go to a man priest for help. . . . I know from my own personal experience that they often . . . go without the kind of guidance that they need most, because of this. To ordain women to the priesthood would make it much easier for such people to get help,

[10]*Evening Standard* (28 March 1919).

without laying themselves open to a charge which is hateful to them. When we come down to fundamental reasons —[11]

But fundamental reasons stood no chance in an atmosphere where feelings ran high and provoked outbursts of partisan clapping. The *Common Cause* thought the mood had been unsuited to 'the serious discussion of so grave a subject' – and blamed Magee; while another critic said the debate brought out 'the peculiar animosity' which lingered on in regard to the changed position of women'. 'What some men really think of women comes out too unpleasantly at times.'

Ursula Roberts' clergyman husband did something to restore them to fundamentals by his own account of having progressed from an initial strong resistance to the idea of women priests. He now admitted accepting the principle. But said, 'I can remember for a long time . . . dodging it. It is so clean against tradition and history.' And therefore inexpedient, he thought, at the present. But to regard it as 'eternally impossible' was another thing and he could not do that, for he had come into contact with women who showed every sign of having a vocation.

> There are women – and I am not at the moment thinking of women who know Miss Royden or have been influenced by her – who believe themselves called to the . . . office of the priesthood with as much reality as any man . . . desiring to say Mass, desiring to exercise the cure of souls . . . with all the humility, sincerity and ardour that I have ever come across in any man.

Meeting them, it was impossible to say, 'What you desire is profane and blasphemous.'[12]

The League of the Church Militant pressed on with its campaign, with an eye to the coming Lambeth Conference. In October 1919 the Church Congress was made the focus of a drive for signatures to a petition to be sent to the bishops. The Congress itself discussed the ministry of women, with Canon Streeter taking the lead and Magee heard among the opposition, while the League sponsored a separate meeting addressed by Maude on 'Women and the Priesthood'. They went all out to mount a strong campaign and revive the spirit of suffrage days.

> This is not the time for apathy. If we really feel that we are called of God to this work there must be no hesitation, no shyness, no holding back, no sitting on the fence. Everyone's help is needed at this critical juncture. . . . Wear the familiar badge – the Cross in the Circle – to show what you stand for. It is the same badge that we wore in the old days . . . [and] a tremendous link just now when we have to face such strong opposition.[13]

[11] LCM leaflet, *Women and the Priesthood: A Verbatim Report of the Principal Speeches at the Debate in the Church House, Westminster, June 6th, 1919.*
[12] Verbatim Report. Ursula Roberts, interviewed 13 Sept. 1967 by Emil Oberholzér, said she thought her husband's career had suffered because of his association with the women's ordination issue.
[13] *Church Militant* (March 1920) 19.

They got symphathetic backing from the National Union. Its renamed journal, the *Woman's Leader* (formerly the *Common Cause*) published their petition and appealed for signatures, while in March the League organised a public meeting in collaboration with the National Union, whose president, Eleanor Rathbone, took the chair while Maude and Edith Picton-Turbervill spoke. 'The summer of 1920 finds the League . . . acutely conscious of its call to pioneer work,' declared the *Church Militant* confidently. Continuous intercession in St Martin-in-the-Fields was planned for the day when the Lambeth Conference was going to discuss the ministry of women while on the day the bishops assembled a procession was arranged to march 'wet or fine' from Mr Roberts' church of St George's Bloomsbury to hold a meeting in Trafalgar Square.

Maude gave the address before they set out. 'It is always rather a difficult thing, and spiritually a dangerous thing, to be a pioneer,' she told them.

> It is always right to establish a right but it is always difficult and dangerous to claim a right, and this great principle [spiritual equality] must be established through individuals and must be in one sense the claiming of a right, even if it is only the right to serve.

When women asked to be allowed to read Lessons, to officiate at the altar, or preach, they were claiming that God could speak through them.

> And it is a tremendous claim; and just when you desire most, and need most, to forget yourself . . . at that time it becomes most difficult, because all the world is listening, criticising and blaming . . . I say to you that when you stand up to preach, every weakness, every cowardice, every fault and every sin strive to get between you and the things you are to say, so that your prayer can only be that God will not *let* you stand between the thing you have to say and the people to whom it is to be said.

She urged them to enter into the feelings of those who found it difficult to contemplate change. 'Let us realise the greatness of that tradition from which some find it so hard to go forward.' But,

> Let there be in our hearts a great conviction, for assuredly we are right. Let there be no possibility of hanging back, or of not claiming what we believe to be right; but let there be no bitterness, no resentment, no lack of understanding, no hurrying to defend ourselves. It does not matter what is said of any one of us.[14]

The crucifer then led them out of the church and under a blue sky the procession formed, with the banners of St Teresa, Joan of Arc, St Catherine of Siena and more; the band in red coats, the clergy surpliced, Hudson there with the choir of St Botolph's. 'Very effective the women looked,' wrote one observer, 'as they started off to the strains of "Onward Christian Soldiers".'

---

[14]Maude Royden, *The Spirit of the Pioneer: Address given at St George's, Bloomsbury, July 3 1920* (LCM pamphlet).

Miss Maude Royden in a black silk cassock, and the choir in purple cassocks; bearers of the Fellowship Service banner in bright blue gowns, others holding aloft staves and lilies of leaves, and a large company in the varied garb of everyday clothes bringing up the rear.

Another was reminded of the Middle Ages when colourful religious processions were common. 'It came almost as a shock to see how fitting it all was, the banners, the music, the beflowered poles and the bright splashes of colour made by ecclesiastical robes or scarlet or blue uniform.' The streets were thronged with Saturday crowds. Hats were raised and heads were bowed as the processional cross came in view. A child said 'Is it the Boy Scouts?' 'No dearie, it's THE CHURCH,' the mother answered, unaware of the irony. They placed a cross of evergreens at Nurse Cavell's monument and moved on towards Nelson's Column where the young Dr Letitia Fairfield duly proposed that women be admitted to all the lay ministries of the Church and Hudson seconded the resolution. 'I am not thinking about women's rights . . . I am thinking of the benefits . . . to the Church,' he said; adding – shrewdly as it soon appeared – that even if the bishops said 'yes' at Lambeth they would not be much further on.[15]

The bishops said 'yes'. And the League of the Church Militant openly and humbly gave thanks to God for the Lambeth Conference of 1920. The Church had undervalued the gifts of women, the bishops stated in a report which urged that the ancient female diaconate should be restored and also that laywomen should have the same opportunities as laymen to speak in consecrated buildings. Not everything they said pleased Maude and the League; for though their theology favoured the presumption that the evangelistic charge of the Gospels was delivered to women as well as to men and they reaffirmed belief in spiritual equality, they also accepted that, as things were, 'man has a priority, and in the last resort authority belongs to him.' Their support for deaconesses was expressed in terms which made clear that this was the only order which they regarded as open to women (i.e. they did not look to the priesthood) and even then it appeared that the deaconess would not be on a par with the male deacon. For all that, as the League admitted, 'the position in the Ministry accorded to women marks a tremendous advance on anything the present generation has known.'

It was certainly too much for the *Church Times*. Whatever limits the bishops had set,

> who can believe that, even if they think they have banged, barred and bolted the door against a female priesthood, those bolts will hold? This is a truth written in vivid letters on the pages of history. After the Girondins, the Committee of Public Safety; after Kerensky, Lenin; after the Bishops of the Lambeth Conference, who?[16]

[15]*Church Family Newspaper* (9 July 1920); *Church Militant* (Aug. 1920) 61.
[16]*Church Times* (3 Sept. 1920) 219.

The answer of course was Convocation.

For Lambeth was merely a deliberative body whose resolutions took effect only insofar as they were endorsed in the various parts of the Anglican Communion. Whatever the bishops might say at Lambeth, convocation would finally decide. Yet there is no doubt – and the League recalled it, bitterly let down by that decision when it came – that they had been led to pin a great deal on Lambeth – 'repeatedly asked to wait' for Lambeth, as they put it to Winnington-Ingram, unable to conceal their disappointment at his own part in the decision-making. It was indeed more ironic than they knew that the very bishop who had said to Maude as she faced 2,000 men at Southampton, 'God will be with you every moment of the time' should be the one to devise the check which Convocation placed now on women speaking: they would preach 'normally to women and children'.

'I do wonder what that means,' wrote Maude, in a mocking little piece for the *Daily News*.

> So far as I have noticed, all preachers preach normally to women and children; at least, it is only the abnormal ones in whose congregations men are to be found in any considerable numbers. Still, it might happen that some of the women-preachers were the very ones in whose congregations this abnormality occurred! What will happen then?.

Would they see such notices as 'Abnormal Sermon by Miss Cecily Ellis', or perhaps 'Sermon by Miss Maude Royden to Women, Children and Abnormal Men'? The Bishops had thought long and hard about the wording.

> On Feb. 22 the Bishop of London moved that women should preach 'primarily' to their own sex'. Women were quite pleased, thinking it meant they would all sit in the front seats. But the Bishops were not satisfied.
>
> On Feb. 23, in the morning, it was suggested that we should preach 'normally for women, girls, and children'. This did not please. On Feb. 23, in the afternoon, it was moved that the sermons of women are 'intended normally for congregations of women and children'.[17]

Effie, who had Maude's sharp eye for the ridiculous, drew a cartoon on this particular theme, and another of Bishop Winnington-Ingram as Mrs Partington trying to sweep back the tide. Hudson, though, did not share their capacity to allow humour to alleviate pain. 'I have not often passed a sadder week,' he wrote to Winnington-Ingram now, 'studying closely the extraordinary and as I am forced to think, entirely disastrous discussions and resolutions of the Bishops on Women's Ministrations.'

> You cannot imagine how you have startled and deeply shocked those of us who have hitherto looked upon you as our one courageous reforming leader in this matter. . . . We asked for bread, equal privileges in Church for laywomen as for

[17]*Daily News* (5 March 1921).

laymen. You yourself over and over again promised us bread, and now you offer this stone.

He detected the conspiratorial hand of the English Church Union (villains of the piece ever since the National Mission fiasco).

> I cannot speak for others but for myself I say frankly that I will not submit to this tyranny of a society which is planning to defeat the *whole* splendid scheme – especially as regards Reunion – of the Lambeth Conference, and is always threatening to secede if it does not get its way. I have again to seem a rebel, sadly and all unwilling. My answer to the ECU is just this: that henceforward, if the Convocation resolution is the final word of the Bishops, I intend, within the limits of the law, without touching statutory services or infringing any rights of parishioners, to make *every* opportunity I can in St Botolph's Church for qualified women to preach Christianity to *mixed* congregations from lectern or pulpit . . . in order to keep open for Women a door of hope for a better future.

He added that he had asked Miss Picton-Turbervill to take the midday services in Holy Week and Maude to conduct the Three Hours' on Good Friday.

> I know you must disapprove and I am very sorry, but there is nothing else now to be done. I cannot complain if you publicly censure me, though I shall break no law of the Church. A fundamental and sacred principle is at stake, for which even if I stand alone amongst your clergy I am constrained to contend and suffer the consequences.
>
> My dear, dear Bishop, it looks to me like a parting of the ways, and it hurts badly. I do not think in all my life I have given to any man the strong personal affection that I bear to you. Nothing can ever change it. I beg you to believe that I would not act contrary to your wishes if I did not believe surely that the Church, as Lambeth declared, has been unjust and ungenerous to women in the past, and now threatens to destroy the hopes it had created and bring upon us needless, shocking disaster.
>
> Yours always affectionately in real sorrow.[18]

'Dear old Friend,' the Bishop replied,

> I am sorry you feel so very badly over the resolutions of last week, but the wise Archbishop . . . thought it was as far as the public opinion of the Church would go now. . . . I shall take no notice of what you propose to do, except to ask one thing as a personal favour – that you take the *Three Hours* yourself and not ask even Miss Royden to do it. It was not merely "spikes" and the ECU but moderate men . . . who came to see me and they are convinced that we are erecting an insuperable obstacle to Reunion with both East and West by rash action over Women and they hold their views as passionately as you do. I have tried and am trying to prevent a break up of the old ship.[19]

[18]Shaw to Winnington-Ingram (28 Feb. 1921) Fawcett 221.
[19]Winnington-Ingram to Shaw (1 March 1921) Fawcett 221. Reunion was topical for the moment since the Lambeth Conference had appealed to the churches to seek means of drawing closer together.

According to the account which Maude wrote later, Hudson then went to see the bishop and they discussed the Three Hours' Service, Winnington-Ingram admitting that the rector had the legal right to invite her to preach since the service was non-statutory, but saying he thought no woman should take it because it was *especially sacred*.

> 'Hudson broke loose. He came to me raging and asked if I would agree to defy the Bishop and hold the service in St Botolph's Church. Truth to tell, I was much outraged as he. Had I been refused on the score of my personal unfitness I would, God knows, have felt the reasonableness of the objection. But to be refused because I was a woman was what I could not consent to, and surely all women would have felt joy, as I did, in Hudson's indignant rejection of such a command. But was he not bound to obey his Bishop? 'Only,' said Hudson firmly, 'in his godly admonitions and godly judgements: this is not godly – not at all.'[20]

'If Miss Maude Royden takes the Three Hours' on Good Friday,' the Bishop wrote to the English Church Union, 'it is not only without my sanction but against my expressed wish conveyed in writing both to the rector . . . and Miss Royden herself.' The ECU's secretary wrote back admiring 'the firm position which your lordship takes up'. He also drew up a memorial to be signed by churchwomen all over the country protesting against the ministry of women. The drama heightened as Good Friday drew near. Enthusiastic defenders of the faith offered the Bishop not only moral, but 'if need be, financial support . . . to bring these ecclesiastical Bolshevists to book'.[21] Hudson let fly in the *Evening Standard* against 'distracted ECU reactionaries' who had used the threat of secession to defeat the Lambeth proposals – which he called the churchwoman's Magna Charta. As for those who supported the women, 'We are only a little army . . . and our chieftains have fled from the field.' 'The Bishop of London . . . after fighting gallantly for the cause from 1916 to 1921, has to all appearances deserted to the enemy.' There was no question of surrender, however. He enlarged on Maude's supreme fitness to occupy the pulpit at St Botolph's next day.

> Two years ago . . . she had to deliver her message in a small, hot, overcrowded parish room amid undevotional surroundings, while hundreds of people were turned away and the church remained empty. I will not, if I can help it, endure such a scandal again. All arguments used . . . against women preachers . . . on the mere ground of sex seem to me simply monstrous. In Carlyle's rough phrase, they are enough to make, not the angels, but the very jackasses weep.[22]

A congregation of over nine hundred attended the Three Hours' Service on Good Friday. Long before it started 'men, women, children, and even clergymen arrived from all parts of London and the doors had to be closed, so large was the crowd.' Hudson began by drawing their attention to the

[20] TFC 61. Hudson is quoting the words of the service for the ordination of a priest.
[21] *Church Times* (18 March 1921) 263; (24 March 1921) 292.
[22] *Evening Standard* (24 March 1921) 5.

Brawling Act of 1860, saying that if anyone wanted to protest they should do so at once and depart. No one did so. Maude (who was surpliced) spoke on the last seven words of Christ 'in soft, low but emphatic tones,' according to the *Daily Graphic* report, which summed it all up as 'the most wonderful thing that happened in London yesterday'. Later she admitted to '*unutterable* relief' that the service had proceeded without disturbance, in spite of 'some silly threatening letters'.[23]

'I am sorry Maude Royden defied the Bishop,' wrote eighty-year-old Miss Wordsworth tartly. 'Even if it was defensible on legal grounds it was not behaving like a lady.' Hudson had a heavier cross to bear. As long ago as 1919 he had described himself to the Bishop as 'a marked and discredited priest in your diocese'. Now he was howled down by fellow clergy at the London diocesan conference when he rose to second a resolution in support of the Lambeth proposals. Winnington-Ingram was in the chair. 'Did this priest refuse to obey your lordship's direction last Good Friday?' someone called out. To shouts of derision Hudson maintained that he was not a rebel; had in fact given way two years before when the Bishop inhibited the service in church; this time there had been no inhibition. Those who opposed the ministry of women were in danger of quenching the Spirit, he urged, amid much heckling. His main antagonist rose to an ovation to express the view that the ministry issue had really begun 'with women chaining themselves to railings, breaking windows and putting a bomb under the Bishops's seat in St Paul's.' An amendment that it was 'inexpedient and contrary to the interests of the Church that women should . . . minister in consecrated buildings' was carried by almost two to one; while the Bishop himself gave the *coup de grâce* by saying in his presidential address that he thought the vast majority of women 'were against other women haranguing them in church'.[24]

He may well have been right. An ECU petition designed for women who were against the ministry of women picked up 54,000 signatures without the slightest difficulty. No doubt, as someone on the other side suggested, thousands of women in medieval France could have been found to sign a petition against Joan of Arc wearing male attire. No doubt, also, this one did well because it highlighted the priesthood threat. But the fact that this could be done was a present Maude made to the opposition. She, above all, had given the issue the kind of standing it lacked in the days of Athelstan Riley's 'feminist plot'. The ECU now ventured to say that 'It regards Miss Royden as a person . . . promoting a mischievous agitation which but for her would never have arisen', and resolved to set up its own committee to investigate her activities. 'Have they *no* sense of humour?' asked Miss Corben, secretary of the Church League in a note to Evelyn

[23]Maude to Miss Corben (28 March 1921) Fawcett 'Women in the Church'.
[24]*Church Times* (27 May, 1921) 73.

Gunter. 'Darling Effie,' wrote Maude from Sorrento, where she was beginning her summer holiday,

> Fancy creating a committee to enquire into me!!! And *such* a committee! Hanbury-Tracey is the fellow who practically said he would refuse me Communion; and when Miss Procter asked him if that was what he meant he hesitated and said he would refer it to the Bishop. The Bish . . . looked amiable and said nothing.[25]

'Miss Royden's following is not a band of hardly-won disciples,' declared the *Church Militant* 'but a company of enthusiasts who find in her the leader they have long desired, the eloquent mouthpiece of aspirations and convictions which have long filled their hearts.'[26]

It is evocative of suffrage days – the single purpose, the inspiring leader, all uncommon in these postwar years when feminism shrinks and is hard to define. Now it is the case for spiritual equality which provokes the old antiphonal debates where the same objections demand the same answers. And Maude, who had been expert before, was expert now at this kind of thing: using theology to trump theology; history against history; Christ above St Paul; the Holy Spirit in their own generation alongside the Spirit in Apostolic times. With those who point to a difference of function between men and women she will agree – and challenge them to prove it is a difference of function relevant to spiritual life. To those assured that spiritual equality does not mean equality in Church she will say, tell us plainly what it does mean, then. To those who fear that the ministry of women will blight any hope of Reunion, she answers: you have to go for right principles first; you cannot bind the Churches with a rope of sand. Fortunate in having the kind of temperament which allows her to be courteous under stress, she will meet the opposition on high ground or low. Only, at the end, when the chips are down and everything said that can be said about the evangelistic charge in the Gospels, and St Paul, and what the Orthodox think, she nails the question for what it is: antiwoman, a matter of sex. The Church of England, she has to admit, is 'the last ditch of the anti-feminist',[27] and any disturbance of the mud at the bottom produces a most unpleasant smell.

'In the course of our fight for political freedom,' she wrote much later, 'I never came across quite such a quality of slime and "yellowness".'[28] For it was said – and not only by Magee and other leaders of the ECU – that the ministrations of women would introduce into the pure, impartial, sexless character of public worship a most disturbing erotic quality. How could a

---

[25] Maude to Effie (27 Aug. 1921), Fawcett 222, 5/2. The committee was to consist of Magee, Athelstan Riley, the Rev. P. H. Leary, Hanbury-Tracey and Mr Hill (who had 'leaked' Ursula Roberts' questionnaire on ordination).

[26] *Church Militant*, (Sept. 1921).

[27] Royden *The Church and Woman*, 150.

[28] *Christianity and Crisis* (10 Dec. 1951) 167.

priest be expected to process behind 'a pretty red-haired girl acolyte'? How could he offer the great Oblation with women near him in the sanctuary? The real case against the ministry of women lay here, then, in 'something that was better not described in an audience of both sexes'. Women had certain 'psychical characteristics' allied to their 'physical characteristics' which might well have influenced St Paul when he laid down his prohibitions. 'The subject before them was a sex question.'

Maude did not doubt it. Religious feelings and sexual feelings were obviously intertwined. But with regard to men and women in the sanctuary, 'I have yet to hear even the most grimy-minded politician complain that, if he must stand side by side with a woman on a platform there will be "real danger . . . of distraction and . . . scandal".'[29] There were, of course, unfortunates (of both sexes) who were abnormally engrossed with sex, but instead of adapting the world to them they should be directed to . . . a psychoanalyst. As to the 'sexlessness' of public worship, 'Why do not men realise there may be a hardship to women in having men only in the pulpit?' Many women were averse to confessing intimate sins to a male priest.[30]

There were murkier depths in this last ditch, though. She devotes a chapter in *The Church and Woman* to the influence of taboo. For what was the exclusion of women from the sanctuary, their prohibition (in the Roman Church) from washing the communion linen, the embargo on their speaking in *consecrated* buildings or at a *specially sacred* service but the survival of that primitive concept – powerful still if less freely acknowledged – of woman as ceremonially unclean? 'It is this belief that stands today between women and the establishment of their equality with men in the Church . . . and it is this belief alone.'[31] A few years earlier, amid her satisfaction with the Lambeth proposals she had noted with regret

> that not even a beginning has been made in breaking down the peculiarly loathsome superstitions which bar the sanctuary to women. It is true that many people neither understand this prohibition nor are aware of its existence. It remains a fact that it crystallises a prejudice indescribably insulting to womanhood, and one which, when a young woman first hears of it, fills her with a very deep (and honourable) sense of resentment.[32]

[29] *The Challenge* (10 Sept. 1920) 271.

[30] LCM leaflet, *The Lambeth Conference and the Ministrations of Women* (1920) 5. Maude signed a memorandum to the Conference from the Interdenominational Society for the Ministry of Women which argued the need for women confessors.

[31] Royden, *The Church and Woman*, 207–11; *Church Militant* (April 1921) 30. It says something for the force of this idea of uncleanness that, as late as 1960, the then incumbent of North Somercotes in Lincolnshire, commenting on the recent obituary of Edith Picton-Turbervill who had preached there, said 'a friend of mine suggested I should sprinkle the pulpit with holy water!!' (Information from Canon P. C. Hawker)

[32] Royden 'The Lambeth Conference on "The Position of Women"' *Guardian* (20 Aug. 1920).

For it was an exclusion based not on some alleged inferiority of physical, mental – even spiritual power (there were very many female saints) but on the nature of womanhood itself; and – which sickened her most of all – on the functions of maternity. Along with a conventional reverence for motherhood, not to say devotion to the Mother of Christ, went 'heathenish ideas . . . of ceremonial uncleanness' attached to menstruation, conception and childbirth. 'Is motherhood in any way less spiritual, more animal than fatherhood?' Dr Letitia Fairfield had asked, when the Lambeth Conference invited her comments on medical aspects of the ministry of women.[33] Wartime service in France had shown her the extraordinary persistence of taboo. She recalled, for instance, a sugar refinery from which women were entirely excluded in case they chanced to be 'in such a state that the sugar would turn black in their presence'. Like Maude, she urged the need for a pronouncement 'that ceremonial uncleanliness is no Christian doctrine'. But in this respect it seemed that bishops were little in advance of sugar refiners. Many years later Maude recalled the comments of a man who came to tell her that her sermon had converted him to the ministry of women.

> I thanked him, but he seemed reluctant to go. At last he burst out with an anxious question – 'You wouldn't think it right for a *married* woman to preach, would you?' With some surprise I asked him why not? He looked as though something very unpleasant had touched him and said in deep disgust, 'Not a *married* woman – a woman who had *had children*.'[34]

Behind such twisted views of humanity she saw the Church's ambivalence on sex. If women had had more to do with theology could the doctrine of the Virgin Birth have arisen? 'Can we believe in the Virgin Birth?' had been the theme of one of her sermons at the City Temple in 1919.

> One cannot resist an uneasy suspicion that it arose in the minds of men out of a sense that there is something fundamentally base about sex, that for God to be born of the ordinary love of an ordinary man and woman . . . was impossible, because the human desire of men and women for each other is ignoble, is even base.

This belief, reflected in the Jewish mother's purification after childbirth, implicit in the Roman Catholic ceremony – even in the Anglican 'churching' of women – Maude rejected utterly. In 1924, preaching to mark the City Temple's jubilee, she called the idea of uncleanness in woman and in sex 'our last worst enemy . . . which must be defeated if the relations

---

[33] *Church Militant* (May 1921) 37–8.
[34] *Christianity and Crisis* (10 Dec. 1951) 168. Maude goes on to relate how a married woman Congregational minister she knew (Vera Kenmure) received filthy letters from 'respectable' members of her congregation when it was known she was going to have a child.

between men and women are to be as sane, as wholesome, as sweet . . . as
God surely meant them to be.'

> It is, people of the City Temple, because you stood against that, because there is in
> you no element of taboos and superstitions and ritual uncleanness . . . that the
> passionate gratitude, not of one woman but of all women, must ultimately be
> yours.

As to what would be gained from the ministry of women,

> Is there not something here for this century? The idea that God is a Mother as well
> as a Father; that there is in the Divine something that is symbolised by mother-
> hood?

Because of the publicity and momentum of the struggle which began with
the National Mission and came to a head in 1921 when she took the Three
Hours' Service in St Botolph's it is easy to overlook the demands of
Maude's ordinary working life. Most of her time was taken up with her
duties at the City Temple but she preached frequently elsewhere. Anglican
pulpits were closed to her, except for St Botolph's, but many invitations
came from Nonconformist churches in the London area. She also preached
in Liverpool, Manchester, Glasgow and a range of provincial towns. She
was much in demand to speak in colleges. 'You have done us immense
service in the Student Movement,' wrote Tissington Tatlow of the SCM, 'I
think you yourself must surely have been gratified by the reception you
have had.' He thought speaking to students especially worthwhile because
what was said, 'if it touches them the way you are able to touch them,
affects their lives in a permanent way'.[35] The pressures on her were becoming as great as at the height of the suffrage campaign. One paper comments
romantically, 'Of frail physique, Miss Royden is endowed with intense
nervous power which enables her to conduct missions, preach, lead social
movements and write numerous books without tiring.' Hardly. She
worked with economy, it is true and preached her sermons from the
slightest notes. She could take more than an average load of pamphlet
writing and chapter drafting, and much more of that peculiar strain which
comes from pouring out the spirit to others. But not without tiring. She
suffered from migraine and at times was utterly exhausted. Thus the *Daily
News*, in what is almost a bulletin a few days after the Three Hours' Service,
says 'Miss Maude Royden . . . is resting in the country'. 'We all want her to
take a thorough rest,' declared the *Church Militant* anxiously, 'but, alas for
the contradiction, we also want her help in many ways – either for lectures,
sermons, meetings, for personal advice . . . attending committees.' In her
world she had become unique.

[35]Tissington Tatlow to Maude (26 Feb. 1918) Fawcett 222.

But she was not only in the world of the Church. In these postwar years both she and Kathleen were convinced 'new feminists' of the Rathbone school; believing that, now the vote was won, it was time to give up 'the boring business of measuring everything that women want or that is offered them, by men's standard'.[36] It was Kathleen indeed who hit off the old style as 'me too' feminism: should they go on like a little girl running behind her brother and shouting 'me too!' or turn their attention more these days to what *women* needed? The main goal and symbol of the new feminists was 'the endowment of motherhood'. The idea went back to prewar days but its promotion now (and achievement at last as 'family allowances' in 1945) was the work of Eleanor Rathbone who in 1919 succeeded Mrs Fawcett as president of the National Union. Maude and Kathleen had served on the committee which she set up in 1917 to formulate an endowment plan and one of Maude's essays in *The Making of Woman* that same year concerns endowment. They were thus in sympathy with the general direction which the National Union was to take through her leadership. Nonetheless, like others, when the vote was won they seem to have gone through a period of uncertainty as to where their main efforts should lie.

Kathleen went to Austria when the war ended and worked with the Friends' Relief Mission in Vienna. Before that she had evidently thought of Russia, for Maude wrote in January 1918,

> Russia is surely a *pis aller* for a person of your ability. I don't feel that you have a *right* to do merely charitable and administrative work, when you have the capacity to create the thought of the future. I know it is hard and dangerous and so on, but it isn't nearly so hard and so thankless as constructive thinking is.

Moulding the future had to be done through some kind of organisation. Kathleen had weighed them all and found them wanting: the WIL, the Labour Party, the ILP, the Adult Suffrage Council, the NUWW and the National Union.

> Your verdict on each has been that they are not worth it. Well, they are *going* to 'reconstruct' whether you help them or not. You should either make an organisation on more hopeful lines, or make one of them *be* more hopeful.'

This vigorous logic she had applied to herself, though not, it seems, without moments of doubt.

> Dearest, What I was really thinking when you were urging me to accept nomination to the NU was simply that it was too late. For some time after the war began, I dissipated my energies among several 'causes', and I then decided that this was no use: I must make *one* the first claim. The two that I cared most about were feminism and religion (in the more definite sense of the word). I was inclined to choose feminism, and with a view to this, saw both Nellie Swanwick and you.

[36]'The Old and the New Feminism', Eleanor Rathbone's presidential address to the National Union for Equal Citizenship, 1925.

Her inability to meet me half way, and your decision not to take the Hon. Secretaryship of the WIL decided me. I cannot now unmake a decision which has brought me very many and great responsibilities. It is no longer *possible* for me to make feminism my first claim.

'Sometimes' she added 'I wish it were. I could make a much more "effective" job out of the National Union, I believe, than I ever shall out of the City Temple or the Church of England.'[37]

But the die was cast, though she never regarded the claims of religion as exclusive of others. 'Her activities seem almost limitless. How can she rest with so many calls upon her?' asked the *Church Militant* fruitlessly. There were also new calls on her private life. In 1918 she adopted a baby and the next year the expanded household – Maude, Evelyn, the baby and the baby's nurse – moved from Poplar to Rosslyn Hill, Hampstead.

To talk of adoption is strictly misleading since the Adoption of Children Act was not passed until 1926. But in all but the narrow legal sense she acquired a daughter in 1918, not long before her own forty-second birthday. Helen was one of those 'war babies' on whose account Maude had taken up the cudgels more than once in the *Common Cause*. Her mother died a few days after her birth; her father, who was said to be an officer, was probably killed before that, even. Born prematurely, 'a pathetic little specimen . . . looking almost as if it could not live', Helen remained in the nursing home for about six months before she came to Maude.[38] Nowadays the context and ethos of adoption has changed so greatly it is hard to think back to a much more casual state of the law, to the teeming 'war babies' of the Great War era, or further, to those Victorian widows helped, as Hudson's mother had been, by a relative's taking a child off their hands. It was not unheard of for a woman of means, even though single, to adopt a child. Indeed, other leaders of the women's movement – including Christabel Pankhurst – had done so.[39] And Maude, though not rich by Royden standards, was able with her income from the family trust, plus what she earned by writing and speaking (and Evelyn's contribution) to maintain the household and pay a cook, a nanny for Helen, a secretary and (for a time at least) a *chauffeuse* in conduroy breeches.[40]

But she had to think carefully now about the future. 'I have just been talking to Tom about my infant,' she told her sister Mary in 1921.

[37]Maude to KC (16 Jan. 1918) Fawcett KDC/H1/1–8.
[38]Legal documents relating to the adoption (lent by Helen Blackstone); Maude Royden, *Women at the World's Crossroads* (1923) 55.
[39]Emmeline Pankhurst adopted four war babies (girls), one of whom was brought up by her daughter Christabel. Elizabeth Blackwell and Frances Power Cobbe, among earlier feminists, adopted daughters; as did Maude's contemporary, Elizabeth Robins.
[40]In true Victorian fashion, Sir Thomas Royden, who died a millionaire in 1917, left virtually nothing outright to his womenfolk. The capital Maude had from the family trust was due to return to the trust when she died, so she knew she would have very little to leave Helen.

Plate 6 Maude with Helen, 1918. *Reproduced by permission of Mrs Helen Blackstone.*

'I have insured my life for her, but I can't insure enough at my age, to do more than keep her from starving. So I must save for her education and hope to live long enough to do it! But if I *don't*, he has promised to see she doesn't actually perish. Two friends of mine – George and Margery Chettle – have promised to look after her too, but not financially. I have made them her guardians . . . partly because they are themselves poor and Helen will be with people who expect to earn their own living and take it for granted. But if anything should happen to upset this arrangement . . . would you see that she came to no harm?'[41]

'I hardly know what to ask,' she went on, 'for I know you would have adopted a child yourself if you had felt justified in doing so.' Why Mary did not feel justified is not clear but it may have been because, since the death of their father, she was Lady Royden's companion at Frankby; or else that she felt some hesitation about bringing an outsider into the family. Maude herself was not free from this. In the years before her legal adoption Helen was known as Helen Derwent – the surname, faintly reminiscent of the Lakes, having simply been invented by Maude, who did not wish her to be known by her own name but yet did not choose then to make her a Royden. Helen's surname was changed to Royden at her legal adoption in 1927 when Maude told her mother and the family at large that 'it would be very great happiness to me . . . if she were allowed to take my name', pointing out that this was not so serious as it would have been in the case of a boy. ('A boy would probably marry and start a new line of Roydens who in fact were not Roydens at all.') Lady Royden's comments do not survive – she was in her eighties and much preoccupied with Christmas arrangements at the time of asking ('whether you would like Helen to sleep in the North Room or if you would like her to sleep with you in the Lilac Room and dress in the North Room'). Tom Royden said he would hate to say no to any wish of Maude's and it seemed quite reasonable. Her sister, Evelyn Royden, wrote that it would be a very *great* joy, and Ernest, 'good luck to the little lady.'[42]

Why did she decide to adopt a baby? The young apostle of the ILP, Caroline Martyn, once confessed, 'I think it would be dreadful to be *quite sure* one could never have a little child of one's very own.' She had passing thoughts about adoption. 'I want to bring up a little girl from babyhood; I want to cultivate a little mind, to watch an intelligence expand, a pure soul grow into holiness.' This is not Maude.

I would like to have had children. There are few women, I believe, who would not, though certainly there are some. But there are many women whose wish for children is not only a wish but a passion. These give a greater love to the children . . . than to their husbands, however dear. . . . On the other hand, there

[41]Maude to Mary Royden (8 July 1921) lent by Helen Blackstone.
[42]Letters lent by Helen Blackstone.

are women whose love for their husbands is greater than for their children . . . I
should, I believe, always have loved my husband best.[43]

People were ready to bestow upon Maude all the attributes of an idealised
motherhood. What they sensed was her gift of compassion and they did not
know how else to express it. Iremonger cherished his little vignette of
arriving in Poplar as the wretched messenger from the Life and Liberty
Council to find her giving a baby its bottle. 'Women love her,' wrote one
admirer,

> for she is the very incarnation of womanliness, with a face which recalls some of
> the madonnas of the old masters, not strictly beautiful but bringing to those who
> look at it satisfaction to their ideals of motherhood. . . . There is . . . a quite
> feminine audacity about her attacks on conventionalities, but withal a tender
> consideration for the conventional which is only less admirable than her concern
> for the young. For the cause of the young, Miss Royden is a champion, a true
> mother. And you feel that she draws more than half her inspiration for reform
> from that womanly passion.[44]

'I do wonder what that means,' Maude might have said. Or she might have
been flattered. She had, as we know, an intense admiration for motherhood, for the heroism she had seen in childbirth and in the burdened lives of
working women. Nothing, not even social purity, roused her to more
passion than the wrongs of children: society's hypocrisy over war babies, its
cruelty towards the illegitimate. There were no illegitimate children, only
illegitimate parents, she said. All that the State could do for them would
never make up for what they lacked – a stable family, with two parents. But
the State must try, they must all try, for the children's sake and as some
small part of the debt they owed to the fighting men. 'We accept as a sacred
trust the children and the beloved of those dead.' So she took Helen. And in
1920 she took in Friedrich Wolfe as well, an Austrian famine victim, four
years old.

Famine hit Europe in 1918 on a scale reminiscent of the Thirty Years'
War, exacerbated by the British blockade against which Maude and other
members of the Women's International League protested. In 1919, with
Norman Angell, GP Gooch and Ramsay Macdonald, she signed an appeal to
the British government not to cut off food supplies to German children.
Her one disagreement at the City Temple seems to have been when Dr Fort
Newton, as an American, thought it unfitting that his church should
petition against the blockade. Maude was a member of the Fight the Famine
Council which at one time considered sending her to appeal for support in
the USA, though nothing came of it. Kathleen, who started in 1920

[43]Lena Wallis, *Life and Letters of Caroline Martyn* (1898) 78, 84; TFC 32.
[44]Margaretta Byrde in *The Churchman* 21 Aug. 1920).

working with the Friends' Relief in Vienna, was in the very heart of the battle to save many thousands of children like 'Freddie'.

'There is in my home a little Austrian boy,' said Maude in a sermon in 1921.

> When he landed in this country a year ago he was four years old and he had never walked. He was so ricketty that he could not walk . . . That little boy's face was like a little old man's. He had that terrible, anxious, harassed look that is pitiful on any human face, but is heartrending on a child's. He was only two years old when the war ended. He was not born when the war began. His fathers, you will say, made the war. Yes, perhaps. But we made the peace, and it was the war and the peace together that made Freddie look like that.[45]

She was preaching on the theme that a preacher is sometimes bound to deal with political questions. Freddie now had enough to eat, and could be loved. But his brother in Vienna was almost an idiot through lack of food and care. '*And that is a political question.* Am I to be silent when the world treats children like that?'

A year or two later Maude published this sermon (with 'Christ and the Unemployed', 'The Cry of Russia' and others) in *Political Christianity*. By no means all her sermons were political: most were not, perhaps, except in the sense that they reflected a view of life in which politics, religion and morality were one. She could not hear Freddie say the Lord's Prayer without wondering whether, when he could understand it he would still be able to say it. 'All the world has trespassed against that child.' She could not glimpse working men outside the windows of a luxurious London store – men who were on strike for £3 a week – without wondering that they did not hurl a stone through the glass. The government's policy on brothels in France, its treatment of pacifists in prison, its attitude to the discharged soldier or now-expendable munitions worker – everything suggestive of official contempt for human personality in ordinary people she laid at some time before a congregation. She had been asked to preach on purity in a demobilisation camp where there were 15,000 men. 'They could not demobilise the whole lot at once, and so they were kept there, month after month, going through drill and wasting their time; and because they were not going to be soldiers it was *not worth while training them.*'

> It was not worth the country's while to train them because they were human beings . . . And they had the effrontery to ask me to go down and preach purity to these men! . . . I said I would rather go and preach to the War Office.[46]

Nothing shocked her more than the reversal of attitudes, after the war, towards working people. 'We took men for whom their country had done

---

[45]*Church Militant* Supplement (July 1921).
[46]*Church Militant* (Jan. 1921) 5.

nothing, took them out of the slums of our great cities . . . and sent them into the hell of war.' Of such, perhaps, was the Unknown Soldier. But 'there are soldiers more unknown than he. . . . On Wednesday I watched a march of the unemployed going through the streets of London – the unknown soldiers in their civilian clothes, buried much deeper . . . than that man in the Abbey.' In an imaginary labour exchange Christ confronted the unemployed. 'He would have thought it a cheap thing to say "There is work for you to do if you choose to do it."' It was not enough to tell discharged soldiers 'You can go and mend roads'; nor to say to women suddenly turned off the assembly line, 'Mistresses are shrieking for domestic servants'.[47]

Yet the overriding political question, the overriding moral question was peace. As the treaty-making continued at Versailles it became clear that, though worn with war, 'we *will* not have the things that belong to peace. . . . We know that if you injure one nation, the others suffer. But we will not accept it. . . . Do you think it belongs to peace to starve a generation of children in Austria?' she asked in 1921.

> Or to force from Germany what Germany cannot pay? I am not arguing now whether there is not much excuse, much justice, if you like. . . . All I want to say is that you cannot get peace out of war, any more than you can get grapes from thistles.

The Germans in retreat had left Belgium and France 'colourless, fruitless, harvestless, unpopulated'.

> And today, in the Terms of Peace, we ask from Germany, whose children perish for lack of milk, 140,000 milch cows for those they took. Who shall dare to say it is unjust? . . . We can indeed do to Germany as she has done in the face of the sun to all those whom she had the power to . . . destroy, and yet if we do it, how are we to save the world from this endless cycle of injustice and wrong?[48]

She preached many times on the League of Nations, and in the summer of 1920 at a conference of the International Women's Suffrage Alliance made the enduring foundations of peace the theme of a sermon delivered from the pulpit Calvin had once occupied in Geneva. No woman had preached in the cathedral before – much less sat in the great man's chair. And the verdict: 'Elle a la voix de cathédrale . . . Ce sermon aura donné à tous l'impression la plus favorable du ministère féminin,' the *Journal de Genève* recorded. 'Tout, en effet, y respirait la simplicité, la modestie, et un profond sérieux moral. Il laissera parmi nous le durable souvenir d'une

---

[47]'The Unknown Soldier', sermon preached in Kensington Town Hall, *Church Militant* (December 1920) 93–4; 'Christ and the Unemployed', sermon preached in Kensington Town Hall, *Church Militant* (Jan. 1921) 5.

[48]*Church Militant* Supplement (April 1921); 'Justice: Human and Divine', sermon preached in the City Temple (25 May 1919) *The City Temple Pulpit*, no. 11.

date historique.'[49] The internationalist, Margery Corbett Ashby wrote to her husband,

> Miss Royden looked very dignified and what the French call 'recueilli' – I don't know our word – shut up in herself communing with God. Her prayers were splendid. She read the parable of the Prodigal Son and preached quite well. I was a little disappointed but the Swiss lady next me murmured 'magnifique' and shook me warmly by the hand to express her emotion.

Kathleen took up her pen that night and wrote four pages to Lady Royden.

> I know you will like to have news of this great day for Maude. She is too tired to write herself and besides could not tell you what a wonderful sermon she preached . . . The Cathedral was crowded . . . Of course Maude was nervous but she did not show it, and everyone was struck with the dignity of her presence.

It had taken great skill to manage the acoustics; the secret was to speak straight at a pillar and Maude did this wonderfully and everyone could hear. 'She made, I think, a really profound impression. There were people there of all creeds and of no creed and all were deeply moved. I wish you could have been there to be proud of her.'[50]

Yet the Geneva occasion, though striking, was not the most notable event of that year. In March 1920 she resigned her post as pulpit assistant at the City Temple, though in fact the decision to do so had been made some months earlier when Dr Fort Newton left for a pastorate in New York. Though she agreed to carry on for a time to ease the problems of the interregnum, Maude had always seen her own post as temporary and judged the moment had come to depart. It was at this juncture that Percy Dearmer, a friend since her early days in London when he was vicar of St Mary's, Primrose Hill, came up with the amazing suggestion that she start what he called a place of her own, and the two of them founded the Fellowship Guild.[51]

Percy Dearmer has his own reputation. 'Copious author on artistic, theological and liturgical subjects' reads one brief entry, 'unconventional editor of hymn books and the like.' The musical and religious taste of untold schoolchildren between the wars was moulded by Dearmer's *Songs of Praise*. Like other of her friends among the Anglican clergy he had rare talent, but not the kind of talent that would ever make him a bishop. Harold Anson, Dick Sheppard, Dearmer – they are mavericks, however distinguished. Dearmer as a young man had worked for years in the Chris-

---

[49] *Journal de Genève* (7 June 1920). 'This sermon will have given everyone the most favourable impression of the ministry of women. Everything about it breathed simplicity, modesty and a deeply earnest morality. It will leave with us a lasting memory of an historic date.'

[50] Corbett Ashby Papers, MCA 13, Fawcett; Kathleen to Lady Royden (6 June 1920) Fawcett 222, 5/2.

[51] The account which follows is based on Nan Dearmer, *Life of Percy Dearmer* (1940).

tian Social Union with Gore and Scott Holland. His idea of socialism – and of worship – was linked with his feelings for art and beauty. He had transformed St Mary's, removing the clutter and covering its red brick nave with whitewash to throw into prominence the reredos and altar. With help from Cecil Sharp and Ralph Vaughan Williams, he began to build a new musical tradition and St Mary's, Primrose Hill, when Maude first knew it evidently make the kind of impact on her which All Saints, Cheltenham had made in her schooldays or the Cowley Fathers' when she went to Oxford. 'This liturgy, this ritual, these surroundings were to me a spiritual home.'

After wartime service and other work abroad Dearmer came back to England in 1919 and a Chair in Ecclesiastical Art was created for him at King's College, London. But he had no church and missed this deeply. His suggestion that Maude seek a place of her own was accompanied, therefore, by an offer to help. On Easter Sunday 1920 they held the first of the Fellowship Services in Kensington Town Hall while the following year their move to the Guildhouse (a converted chapel in Eccleston Square) gave the venture a permanent home.

'I will not start a new Church,' Maude had told Kathleen when she was trying to persuade her friend to build on structures that already existed. And she and Dearmer made it very clear now that they were not going to start a new Church. 'People are still starting new Churches,' he wrote, 'thus losing their influence with the great mass of Christendom, and adding to the . . . weakness of the Church Universal.' The experiment they had embarked on was new 'because it springs from the Church of England, and remains within the Church of England'. And since, for all that, some people were puzzled, they spelled it out in another statement, after the move to Eccleston Square: 'The Guildhouse exists to show that it is possible to have a religious centre – a meeting house, in fact – without forming a new Church or a new religion, or any kind of schism or separation.'[52]

They even hoped the Church might encourage the experiment.

> The Church of England. . . . is at present appealing to that minority of English people who go to church on Sunday. . . . She ought to appeal to the public at large, by means of addresses and informal gatherings. . . . Very probably there should be a centre of this sort in every district of our great cities.[53]

But no schism. At the City Temple Maude reminded those who thought she was leaving to go back to 'her own' Church, 'I have never left my own Church'; and spoke of the beauty of Anglican worship and those great phrases which in the Communion lifted one into the presence of God. She could not think of cutting herself off from that.

[52]Percy Dearmer, 'The Fellowship Service at Kensington', in *The Venturer* (June 1920). He gave as examples of new Churches, the Christian Scientists and the Spiritualists; see also *Church Militant* (March 1922) 19.

[53]Nan Dearmer, *Percy Dearmer*. 245.

As free lances, though, they hoped to create 'a more vivid sense' of Christian fellowship; to involve the laity – even to draw in sympathetic Nonconformists as an earnest of their hopes for reunion. They meant to develop the ministry of women (Dearmer, a suffragist, had also formed part of the group which was interested in women and the priesthood). Naturally they hoped to bring into worship 'all that is lovely in music and the other arts'. Especially music – which at one time had been 'the peculiar gift of the English Church'. The organist and composer Martin Shaw took charge of music for the Fellowship Guild. Like Dearmer, Shaw had a creditable record of supporting women's suffrage and expunging weak hymns. He was organist now at St Martin-in-the-Fields but made time to seize this new opportunity.

Three diverse and exceptional talents, then, combined to form the Guild. And the venture was backed by a numerous advisory council, including such confidence-building names as Mrs Creighton and Mrs Fawcett, William Temple among the clergy, and Maude's brother, Sir Thomas Royden, among those of acumen and wealth.[54] 'We had a splendid press,' she recalled. Indeed the *Church Militant* welcomed her departure from the City Temple, for all its generosity in having given her a pulpit in the first place.

> We do not believe Miss Royden can do her best work unless she is held to be a devout and loyal member of the Church of England. Such a reputation cannot be permanently enjoyed by anyone who is holding a position which is at least popularly regarded as that of assistant minister at a Nonconformist place of worship.[55]

With her greatly strengthened belief in reunion, Maude would probably have qualified this. But she could not have denied that for her, at that moment, the Guild seemed to open a way ahead. Though the Church of England could not use her vocation it does not seem to have entered her head that that vocation should be repressed. The Spirit bloweth where it listeth, she said once, and even the ECU could not prevent it sometimes descending upon a woman.

> We speak too much as though the Church gave the vocation. It does not. The vocation . . . is given by God. The Church cannot give you a message to deliver . . . create in your heart the passion for souls. These are the gifts of the Holy Spirit. . . . It is for the Church to recognise them.

And again, 'If the vocation is a real one, no ecclesiastical order can prevent its fulfilment.'[56]

[54]Names that were more to be expected included Bishop Maud of Kensington, Harold Anson, Clara Butt, Kathleen Courtney, Margaret Bondfield, George Lansbury, Dick Sheppard, Edith Picton-Turbervill, Tissington Tatlow, Dr Jane Walker and Hudson Shaw.
[55]*Church Militant* (February 1920) 13.
[56]LCM leaflet *The Lambeth Conference and the Ministrations of Women*, 7; Royden, *The Church and Woman*, 161.

As to the approach which she now proposed, the *Church Militant*, surprisingly perhaps, expressed some caution about the new centre, finding it rather too experimental.

That Miss Royden will succeed in bringing together large congregations and proving spiritually helpful . . . we entertain small doubt. . . . Miss Royden will succeed, but her success will be the index of the power of her personality, not of the value of the methods she employs.[57]

[57] *Church Militant* (February 1920) 13.

10

Can We Set the World in Order?

It is a religion of hope, this belief that we have the power to put things right.

Maude Royden, (1924).

The Fellowship services in Kensington Town Hall were from the first a very great success. But with up to 1,000 in the congregation, well-dressed women sitting in the aisles and the London County Council ever alert for infringement of its fire regulations, the need for a more suitable home was plain. At one time a disused Catholic church seemed a possibility but the Bishop of London offered it to Russian refugees. 'One cannot help feeling that the Bishop has been to some extent influenced by the opposition of a small but active body in the Church to the development of the Ministry of women,' Maude told a *Daily News* reporter – while the liberal *Challenge* (whose editor, Charles Raven favoured women priests) accused the Bishop of taking steps to prevent her exercising her vocation. At this time he also turned down a request that Mrs St Clair Stobart be allowed to preach and as Mrs Stobart was very well-known (she had run the English Field Hospital in Serbia) the case aroused interest. A few months later he approved certain churches being used as halls, the chancel carefully curtained off. But such expedients meant nothing to Maude for a building had been found for the Fellowship Guild. The Congregationalists offered to hand over their large church in Eccleston Square, '4 minutes from Victoria Station' and this, on conversion, became the Guildhouse.

Maude was dismayed by its ugliness but Dearmer was absolutely delighted.

> He pointed out that it was . . . honest and well-built, no sham Gothic, no shoddy work. The painting and 'decoration', we agreed, was hideous. He applied his favourite remedy – whitewash – and. . . . gave us, on this background of white, brilliant colours. The great lanterns, the pulpit cushions, the stewards' blue cassocks.

It amused her when these splashes of colour were ascribed to 'the woman's touch'. Not everyone liked it. 'I did. It was the first time that anyone had seriously proposed to me that a church should be a joyful place – and look it.' Reporters found almost every seat taken.

> The building is an old-fashioned London chapel, with long pews and shadowing galleries. It has been newly re-decorated and its walls are dazzlingly clean. Plants in brass jars stand on the window-ledges. . . . A red book of 'Cansons', compiled by Dr Dearmer and Mr Martin Shaw, was handed to everybody. The church flashed with scarlet when all these books were opened.[1]

On that first Sunday evening, in June 1921, Maude addressed the vast congregation not only on the Fellowship Guild's ideals but on its need now for cups and saucers, scrubbing brushes, soap – and money. 'We want roughly a thousand pounds.'[2] In a moment it seems that she had half that sum, with 'I'll give £1! and 'I'll give £5!' A clever bit of begging, said the *British Weekly*, whose reporter was impressed on the whole, though irritated by Maude's habit of blaming the Church for not defending the poor. In general, though, the press was sympathetic to what one paper called 'Miss Royden's Fresh Start'.

Bonds had been formed in that year in Kensington and most of those present were already familiar with the evening service Dearmer had fashioned. 'It seemed to me then, and still seems, quite perfect,' Maude recorded in later years. It was very largely the Anglican Evensong, but there were Free Church elements there; and at its heart a Quaker silence ('a *real* silence of two or three minutes,' as she described it, 'not a gasp'). Speaking was encouraged, though, during the collection. ('You will know . . . how lonely people can be in London'); and after the service they discussed the sermon, following her practice at the City Temple. 'For everyone here has an experience of God, and I am not the only person, nor is Dr Dearmer, who has something to say that may help the others.' She spoke of the music, and their Master of Music, Martin Shaw, composer of beautiful hymns. There was a quartette to lead the singing, but the *real* choir would be the congregation and Shaw was eager for people to come and rehearse the settings with him in advance. All this posited something rather different from the average, passive church congregation.

The Guildhouse building had great potential, with rooms that could be used for all manner of things, and not only on Sundays but during the week. The Fellowship had already established a branch of the League of Nations Union. There would be room for a library now, for study circles, a dramatic society, a children's rally, a music club. People said, 'What has this to do with religion?' 'But if you are going to cut religion out of any part of

---

[1] Nan Dearmer, *Percy Dearmer* 242–3; *British Weekly* (16 June 1921).
[2] Her sermon 'The Future of the Fellowship' (June 5 1921) from which the following extracts are taken, was printed in the *Church Militant* Supplement, (July 1921).

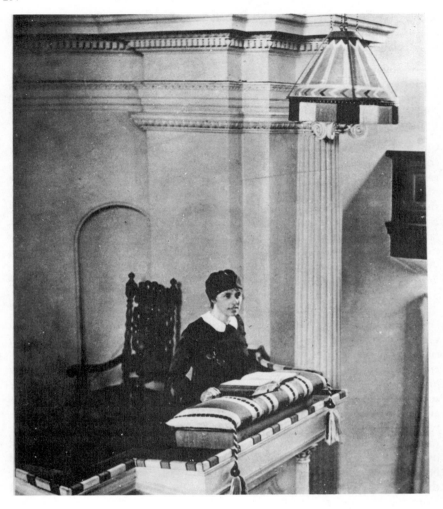

Plate 7   Maude in the Guildhouse pulpit, *Sketch*, 10 August 1922.

your life,' said Maude, 'you might as well do the thing properly and cut it out of *all* your life, because if it is not everywhere it is nowhere.' And Dearmer, who felt this to the roots of his being, especially in the aesthetic sense, gave it particular expression at the Guildhouse in the programme which he called 'Five Quarters'.

There were certainly those for whom 'Five Quarters' was the main attraction in Eccleston Square, as there were those who came to the

Guildhouse mainly to hear Maude preach in the evening. For an hour and a quarter every Sunday afternoon Dearmer provided what was partly music – partly a service – partly a lecture or poetry reading, the whole combined by his gifts as a teacher of idiosyncratic distinction and skill. Later, after he had left the Guildhouse, 'Five Quarters' continued in a different form, with a lecture courses on particular themes. To glance through the programmes for the 1920s is to be reminded, first of all, that Maude (and her friends on the advisory council) could attract a battery of well-known names. Thus, a course on art brought in Lilian Baylis, Percy Scholes, James Agate, Will Rothenstein and others; that on 'Ideals in Commerce and Industry' – Lady Rhondda, Sir Thomas Royden, Professor Soddy, Sir Josiah Stamp; on 'The Press and the Service of Ideals' speakers of the calibre of Henry Nevinson, Norman Angell and TP O'Connor.[3]

There was a lot of emphasis on ideals. 'We take for our principle the pursuit of "the good, the beautiful and the true"', the Guild declared at an early stage.

> For, believing that the Guildhouse platform is one of wide and ever-widening influence, and that here idealists will find good means of furthering the ideals that move them in their different forms of service, we seek to make the Guildhouse a clearing-house of thought and, increasingly a centre whence shall be generated that moral energy and intellectual enthusiasm that will in the end remake the life of the people.[4]

Thus, the very first course, in 1924, was entitled 'Ideals in Politics'; and the speakers, who included Margaret Bondfield, Oliver Stanley, LS Amery and Mrs Wintringham MP, were asked to focus on the ideology underlying the measures they proposed rather than on the measures themselves. 'We had in consequence illuminating speeches of a constructive kind,' runs the comment, 'embodying just that spirit of tolerant enthusiasm for the respective parties' ideals which we had sought to find and to foster.'[5] They took care to choose speakers from all three parties. In the same spirit, the course, 'World Beliefs' brought in representatives of Hinduism, Buddhism and the Bahai's, as well as both liberal and orthodox Jews and the East End mission priest, Father Andrew. Maude had no patience with the man who protested that this kind of thing gave the impression that other religions were as good as Christianity. 'I want to combat the idea . . . that we cannot desire to understand . . . the central truth of the other great faiths . . . without in some way reflecting on our own. Christianity is not a religion that forces us to declare that every other religion is false.'[6]

The emphasis then was on tolerance, enlightenment, enlarged awareness

---

[3]Programmes for 'Five Quarters' addresses, Fawcett 219.
[4]'Five Quarters' (printed on back of Art course programme 1925).
[5]*Five Quarters at the Guildhouse*, pamphlet (1925).
[6]'Christ and the Other Great Teachers', Guildhouse sermon (16 Jan. 1927).

of current trends. A very favourite theme with Maude was the impact of science on religion and society – here presented in forms as varied as 'The Wider Meaning of Relativity' (Haldane) and 'The Sound Film' (Alfred Hitchcock). One course offered a stand to reformers: Margery Fry on prison reform, Julian Huxley (birth control), Eleanor Rathbone (family endowment) Lord Buckmaster (divorce) and so on. 'The World I Want' was the catch-all title of another, in 1932, which recruited such diverse talent as the feminist Cicely Hamilton and the fascist Oswald Mosley. Given Maude's devotion to ideals of beauty (and Dearmer's aesthetic criteria at the start) it is not surprising to find GK Chesterton talking about 'Beauty in the Commonplace', Osbert Sitwell on modern poetry – and indeed a whole course called 'The Beauty of Speech' where Peggy Ashcroft read modern poets, Laurence Housman devotional poetry, Maude read Tennyson, Dearmer the Old Testament, and Gilbert Murray Euripides.

Most of the courses were very popular and an attendance of 500 was common. But 'Five Quarters' was not the only means by which the Guildhouse influence grew. Every inch of the building in Eccleston Square with its two halls and smaller rooms seems to have been used to the limit and 'the place was like a hive of bees' in the style of the famous Whitefields Tabernacle. Monday was assigned to the Women Citizens, the Boy Scouts and the Guildhouse Lawyer. The Guildhouse Players rehearsed on Tuesday, which was also the day for the play centre and the junior branch of the League of Nations Union. The Guides met on Wednesdays, while every Thursday there was a service of intercession. Fridays were free of regular meetings but the Guild of Girl Citizens met on Saturday. On Sunday 'Five Quarters' began at 3.30 and there was time for a cup of tea before the evening service at half past six (though anyone who sang in the choir was expected earlier by Martin Shaw).

In addition to the regular programme there were many incidental activities: some Guildhouse people took poor children to play in the parks on Saturday afternoons, and there was a Saturday ramblers' club. There were frequent recitals and bazaars and other functions to raise money. For apart from its own renovation fund the Guildhouse always had some need in view: whether it was the Christmas tea and garments and presents for Bermondsey children, or the substantial 'unemployed supper', or donations to the South Wales miners or the new Stratford Memorial Theatre or – and a great deal was given here – Dr Schweitzer's hospital at Lambarene. 'It is really from the poor that we get all our support at the Guildhouse,' Maude wrote to Schweitzer, 'and how I do love and value it.'[7]

'I think it would be difficult to read the New Testament . . . and not

---

[7]Maude to Albert Schweitzer (13 May 1927) Archives Centrales Albert Schweitzer, Gunsbach, Austria. Not-so-poor benefactors of the Guildhouse included Clara Butt, who gave two recitals in its honour, and Sybil Thorndike who gave poetry readings.

feel . . . that our Lord did really like the working people best,' she said; appealing, in 1924, for understanding of the aims of Labour, which was now for the first time in office but not 'in the ordinary sense' in power. 'I was brought up in "high Tory" circles, and if I am now in the Labour Party it is because I have been convinced that its ideals, its programme and its policy most clearly express the spirit of Christ.'[8] She went on to try and describe those ideals and to counteract the impression that Labour aimed to make everyone alike. Two years earlier she had been invited to stand as Labour candidate for Wirral Division. ('With your local associations in the constituency there would be every prospect of a very successful contest.')[9] Maude said she was not contemplating parliamentary work, and declined that and subsequent offers. For all her admitted sympathy with Labour, she continued to perceive the high ground in moral rather than political terms. 'Christianity at a General Election', preached in the autumn of 1922, is certainly 'political' in the sense that it turns on such bitter questions as reparations and unemployment. But these are related not so much to the failings of politicians as to the failings of humanity at large. 'Those who will the end must will the means.' If we ask politicians for the kingdom of heaven we must be willing to pay for it. If we want peace we must relinquish revenge; if we want to reduce unemployment we must be willing to help former enemies to regain their purchasing power. At the election of 1918 'we electors asked the government to make Germany pay, and yet expected to be prosperous ourselves.' To talk of wanting such general blessings as peace and prosperity was sentimental, 'because we will not realise or pay the price.'

Maude spoke passionately of this failure as it affected the lives of children. 'To stunt or deprive them is the meanest form of economy.' And her congregation was left in no doubt that a mean form of economy indeed inspired the Geddes cuts of 1922.

> It is something more than book-learning that we take away from children if we adopt the economies proposed. For see what they are. One of the first is that children should not be admitted to the schools till they are six . . . In bad districts today children are admitted at three, but the Committee on Economy affirms that 'no appreciable difference in their attainments or knowledge' has been observed.

This might well be true. Perhaps they did not read or sew any better. 'They cannot explain to you the action of the tides any better. . . . But there is a difference in their souls!' cried Maude. 'I wish some mother or some teacher had been on this Committee.' They would have understood that the street was the main alternative to school. What other choice had a mother got?

[8]'Labour in Office', *Church Militant* Supplement (June 1924).
[9]Secretary, Wirral Divisional Labour Party to Maude (24 Feb. 1922). And see Maude's note that she received four invitations to stand for Parliament: Wirral (Labour once and Liberal once) Newcastle-on-Tyne and Birmingham. Fawcett 222/5/2.

What does a child of three do all day long? It picks up everything you put down and puts it in another place! And then it swallows something and turns on the gas fire. Those of you who are rich would be worn to a shred if you had your children around you *all* day. But the working woman is expected to manage.[10]

As to the need for economy cuts, 'There is always money to kill with. It is when you ask for the lives of little children that you are told there is not enough.'

The case of the miners spoke still more plainly of this failure to 'realise or pay the price'. In the conflict-ridden years before the General Strike Maude had contact with mining communities through the preaching crusades she conducted in South Wales, the Rhondda, Newcastle and Durham, and would return to Eccleston Square burning with the sense of what she had seen: of work leaving the old coalfields, of miners – encouraged in the postwar boom to buy their cottages, unemployed; and of the danger. That extra hour which the owners meant to add to the miner's day was surely different from an hour in an office! 'If we are going to ask that man to stay another hour in the mine, let us not ask it as we might ask a clerk . . . or even a shop assistant in a shop. . . . Ask it rather as we might say to the soldiers in the trenches, "Stay there another hour!"'[11]

In 1926 the miners' lockout led straight into the General Strike. Baldwin's text was 'A challenge to Parliament'; Maude took as her text 'Sirs, ye are brethren.' It was said that the miners must be taught a lesson. 'Is it about our enemies we are speaking? . . . These are the men whose sons and brothers have shed their blood and left their bones where your sons and brothers and husbands left theirs.'

> Miners are not a race apart . . . whom a beneficent Providence has created black so that the coal does not show on them, broad-shouldered so that they shall hew without fatigue, short-legged . . . so that they can walk through the galleries . . . Providence has not created for us a special class of people . . . for work in the mines. . . . They are people exactly like you and me.

When the General Strike ended a few days later she feared the easy reaction of relief. 'Let us not cry Peace where there is no peace.' And in the bitter months while the miners held out she arraigned the 'indecent joy' with which the number of those going back was trumpeted every day in the press. Yet most shocking of society's failures 'to realise' came in 1927 with the Trade Disputes Act, which Maude marked down as a savage piece of class legislation. Labour would one day return to office. And when that

---

[10]'Education: Our Responsibilities', *Church Militant* Supplement (March 1922). After the collapse of the postwar boom an economy committee under Sir Eric Geddes promoted drastic cuts in public spending.

[11]*The Strike – And After*, pamphlet (1926). Maude took the same theme in 'Is there a Christian solution of the industrial conflict?' (sermon, St Martin-in-the-Fields, 30 April 1927) and 'Christ and industrial disputes' *The Miner* (2 July 1926).

time came, if a bill was drafted 'as one-sided, as class-conscious, as the Bill before us now, will you remember that it was not Labour that started this vicious game?'[12]

Though she had resigned in 1919 from the Fellowship of Reconciliation, on the grounds that she was 'largely out of sympathy with its outlook and methods of working', reconciliation sums up her approach, whether to industrial conflict at home or to issues of international peace. 'I believe in President Wilson, a League of Nations and the Brotherhood of Man' was her joking suggestion for a new 'creed'. And, like Kathleen, she affirmed that creed up and down England in the 1920s. A hymn expressing the League's ideals (composed by Martin Shaw) was dedicated to her[13] and the Guildhouse branch of the League of Nations Union was one of the largest and most active in the country. Naturally, Maude shared the disappointment of Kathleen and other internationalists who found the League had come into being tied to 'a disastrous treaty of peace' – more, in fact, as a club for winners than a true internationalist body. Yet she also seems to experience that rededication of women for peace which was so apparent at the postwar congress of the Women's International League. 'We dedicate our lives to Peace!' they cried.[14] Kathleen was among those present in Zurich and whether or not she was caught up, like Helena Swanwick, in that very emotive moment, it sums up the direction of her life from then on. Despite the discontent with organisations she had expressed a few years back, in 1923 she succeeded Swanwick as chairman of the WIL in Britain and was soon an important figure in the influential League of Nations Union.

Speaking on 'Women and the League of Nations' in 1920, Maude began:

> I am not fond of sweeping generalisations about the sexes. Yet it may be true that the male represents the 'katabolic' and the female the 'anabolic' elements in the race; the male, the destructive; and the female, the constructive or conservative. If it be true, then this coming age must be the 'woman's age' in some more real sense than the rather sentimental idea of old-fashioned 'womanliness'.[15]

She took the same line in a series of addresses given in Arkansas in 1922 and published as *Women at the World's Crossroads*. The League, she said, whatever its faults, did at least aim to abolish war and should have full backing – especially from women.

In 1923 she was back in America on a lecture tour which took her 9,000 miles. Hudson's son, Arnold, who made the arrangements, may or may not have been strictly honest in stating on the publicity leaflet that he had been unable to accept more than a tenth of the engagements offered, but what he

---

[12]'The Trade Unions' Bill', Guildhouse sermon (22 May 1927).
[13]Shaw set to music a poem by John Addington Symonds, 'These things shall be'. The author remembers being made to learn it at a girls' grammar school in the 1930s.
[14]Wiltsher, *Most Dangerous Women* 211.
[15]'Women and the League of Nations', *The Englishwoman* (Feb. 1920).

did accept involved 75 speeches in 57 cities on 65 days: preaching in St George's Church, New York, and in the cathedrals of Portland, Boston and Detroit (where the service was broadcast to an estimated 100,000 in addition to the 2,000 present); speaking in opera houses, high schools, town halls; at Bryn Mawr, Vassar, Wisconsin University, Iowa State and Mount Holyoke College; to groups of business and professional women, lecture leagues and the YWCA. Maude did not really like Arnold Shaw and perhaps she did not like his publicity, which billed her as a 'World Famous Woman Preacher' and included a 'Brief Sketch of a Romantic Career' as well as quoting from a book which described her as 'at once a true woman and a great man'. However, she was always thrilled by New York and exhilarated by skyscrapers; and before embarking on what she found very gruelling journeys in Pullman cars, had a day or two's comfort with the Rockefellers and tried to define for the American press her attitude to the Church of England, England's attitude to war and peace and to the USA, and her purpose in coming.

'I want to understand the American point of view and the spirit in which she is facing the future.' In England she had put it another way: that she hoped to convey to the United States the British view of Europe's situation. Either way, it boiled down to a plea that America should not ditch Europe. In a mood of growing disgust with the Old World the United States had not ratified the Peace nor joined what was seen as a 'League of Victors'. In England a revisionist movement had started as soon as the Versailles Treaty was signed. Lord Robert Cecil, promoter of the League, Gilbert Murray and the League of Nations Union, the Labour Party, the various peace groups and the WIL – however they might differ – all pressed for admitting Germany to membership and modifying demands for reparations. Maude had not been able to attend the Women's Conference for a New Peace held in December 1922 but she had been briefed on the conference view that the problems of getting Europe back on its feet were inherent in the Treaty of Versailles and was to convey to Washington their plan for a world congress to make a new peace. In fact, by the time she docked in New York the situation had become more serious, since, as Maude learned during the crossing, France had sent troops into the Ruhr.

In fact, the Washington visit was a flop. By the time she arrived there, in March, Congress had risen and the President had left. She spoke to Hughes, the Secretary of State, and Hoover, Secretary of Commercial Affairs, suggesting that since the United States had repudiated the Versailles Treaty it would not be too hard now to press for revision. America, she said, through the ties of friendship would be well placed to influence France, the country most likely to oppose such change. But they told her America could not act. The government could not risk a rebuff and the matter must be left to public opinion.[16]

[16]*WIL News Sheet* (June 1923).

Her most popular address throughout this tour was 'Can We Set The World In Order?' and it is one which shows very plainly her characteristic weaknesses and strength. The title (implying the answer yes) immediately reflects her optimism. For nothing is more typical of Maude than this: that she can look into the pit without fear – or at least without that fear 'which conceives it possible that Evil in the end may be triumphant over Good'.[17] 'Can We Set The World In Order?' stands at the chasm, as she had once stood at the quarry's edge, and looks down into it and does not blink. In stressful America it was a winner. 'We can't afford to miss it, John,' runs the caption in one small-town newspaper cartoon where Mr and Mrs Public together contemplate a heavily-bandaged and disordered World.[18]

Maude picks up the theme of spiritual law and spiritual power which had formed the basis of her first sermon at the City Temple – taking a rather romantic view of scientific values and the natural world to make the contrast between natural laws (such as gravity) which we respect, and spiritual laws, which we evade and break (such as 'that the principle of creation is love and the principle of destruction is hate').[19] A logician could pick plenty of holes in this, for she never defines such terms as 'law'. But what she contemplates, with every reason, is a world on the way to destroy itself. 'It is as reasonable for us to sit down now to create a new world by hating half the nations . . . as it would be for us to seek to rebuild the ruins of . . . Ypres with high explosives.' And what she pleads for is spiritual renewal – starting always with the individual – which shall generate the spiritual power sufficient to raise not one man, as Christ did, 'but all civilisation from its grave'. Her strength is here, in the moral plea. In that hall in North Carolina, Mr and Mrs Public do not ask themselves whether in the whole of human history individual regeneration has ever produced the sort of chain reaction Maude seems to envisage. They feel it is possible because she says so. As they listen they sense through her a kind of reality in spiritual power; for, as the *Toronto Globe* put it, she speaks 'with the spirit of a Jeanne d'Arc'.

Maude came home in the spring of 1923 and gave an account of her Washington mission to the WIL; and of the skyscrapers, perhaps, to Helen, for according to one American report, her eyes 'sparkled with the light of deep maternal love' when she was asked about her plans for the 'little one now in her home in England'.[20] Helen was five now and Freddie seven, neither yet old enough to ponder the fact that they lived in a rather unusual household. 'A child should have a father and a mother and a home,' Maude had stated. And there was no father: though there was an 'uncle' whom they saw sometimes – Hudson, who was Helen's godfather and known to

[17] *May Mission Speeches* (1910) p. 2.
[18] *Sunday Citizen*, Asheville, North Carolina, (11 March 19230) (see p. 222 below).
[19] *Can We Set The World In Order? LCM pamphlet, II 14.*
[20] *Evening News* Newark (NJ) (12 Jan. 1923).

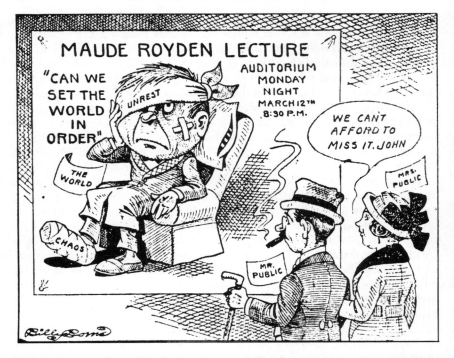

Plate 8 Cartoon from *The Sunday Citizen*, Asheville, North Carolina. *Reproduced by permission of* The Asheville Citizen-Times.

the children as Uncle Bill. 'I loved to see Hudson with children,' Maude wrote, looking back to South Luffenham days and some rollicking children's parties.[21] He was a rollicking kind of uncle, photographed at St Botolph's fête with three year old Helen tucked under his arm and famous, his god-daughter recalls, for a trick of slitting his throat with a carving knife.

There were two 'mothers' at Rosslyn Hill. Maude took the view that adoptive mothers should not claim to be what they were not, and Helen did not call her Mother but Minkie, a name the child invented as she started to speak. Evelyn was Aunt. 'Aunt brought me up.'[22] Unquestionably it was Evelyn who showed the tenderness and ready affection which Maude pronounced in a dozen different articles to be the birthright of every child. The children she had charge of saw little of her, except at meal times; no more, perhaps, than she as a child had seen of her father – 'the man who

[21]TFC 37.
[22]Helen Blackstone, to the author.

came to cut the beef'. Indeed, if she had been their father the pattern would have been conventional enough. She was 'the Breadwinner', often out, or absent for a time on necessary business. 'I have a little girl at home whose custom it is, when I am starting out for the day, to race my little Ford car down the street,' she tells them at the Guildhouse; and goes on to demonstrate the touching nature of childlike trust, which indeed she found very moving. For Helen was not allowed to race down the street without a grown-up, and on this occasion, lacking such support, had hailed a totally unknown gentleman in silk hat, kid gloves and patent leather shoes, crying '*There* is someone who will run with me!' 'I have never forgotten it,' said Maude; though she noted, many years later, 'How easy it is to be sentimental about children while in actual life one finds them a nuisance.'[23]

Often, of course, she worked at home, but the children did not go into her study, unless they were taken up to say goodnight. Did Freddie really remember correctly that she never gave them goodnight kisses? Naturally the children compared her with Evelyn. They had certainly not read those bits in her writing where Maude says love requires physical expression.

> How dear to us are the bodies of those we love! . . . Should not we think it a strange kind of love which never wanted . . . even to touch the body of a friend or a lover? . . . It would be a cruel kind of love which, in the presence of the loved one, should never desire any physical expression. I am speaking now [not] only of the love of sex . . . there is a physical side to every kind of love.[24]

Whether or not she gave goodnight kisses (Helen says she did) both children remembered authority applied in a reasonable way. Maude was not too hard on Freddie when he played with matches, willing to let Helen keep white mice, and thought of conjurers for birthday parties. But the Rosslyn Hill regime of separate spheres was in marked contrast to that of the Dearmers. Rather eccentrically, Percy Dearmer took his children with him into lecture halls – and even, sometimes, onto public platforms.

It was undoubtedly a blow to Maude that he left the Guildhouse in 1924. She understood very well what she owed him. 'For an Anglican priest to become a minister in such a place' she wrote after his death, 'and to accept as his colleague so damaging a person (from the Anglican point of view) as myself, meant an indifference to his own prospects . . . and an absence of personal ambition which . . . I always felt was hardly understood.'[25] Pressure of literary and other work was given as the reason in the Fellowship Guild Notes, but a prominent Guildsman reflected later, 'Dearmer *was* somebody, and the Guildhouse was not large enough for two somebodies!'

---

[23]'Resist Not Evil', *Church Militant* Supplement (15 June 1926).
[24]'Christ's teaching about the body', City Temple sermon (9 June 1918). Fr Martin Wolfe OSB (Freddie) discussed his recollections with Emil Oberholzer (23 Oct. 1969).
[25]Nan Dearmer, *Percy Dearmer*, 244.

While another friend – Martin Shaw's wife – surmised that though he and Maude worked well together (and he was her confessor) 'there was a sort of barrier, possibly born of rivalry' between them.[26] That the Guildhouse was able to sustain his loss reflects the strength it had achieved by now. There was a sympathetic rallying to Maude, upon whom, as was formally acknowledged, extra responsibility would fall. At a special Guild meeting it was announced that Hudson Shaw, Dick Sheppard and Harold Anson were among the clergy who had offered help. A board was set up to reorganise 'Five Quarters' and a resolution passed expressing gratitude to Maude 'for her magnificent leadership', and assuring her of vigorous support in developing the work 'so happily established'.[27] From now on the Eccleston Guildhouse became essentially a one-woman show.

At the time she started the Fellowship Guild Maude had been impatient of the suggestion that it would succeed through her personality rather than through the methods she employed, for she was naturally attached to her methods. The give-and-take of the after-meeting expressed the spirit she wanted to encourage. 'We are in ourselves an experiment in . . . democratic government,' she claimed.[28] And this was true, in the formal sense. Policy was made by the executive committee. In practice though, as one of its members, the Hon. Humphrey Pakington, recalled, she took for granted that on things that mattered the executive committee could endorse her line. As for 'her people' ('she would clasp her hands on that cushion in front of the pulpit and say "My people, I am persuaded . . ." in that wonderful voice of hers') with most of them there was nothing to temper the magnetism of her personality. 'I beg you not to *worship* me!' Maude said once, exasperated, to a devotee.[29] But many did so. Martin Shaw's wife recalled an occasion when she mentioned that her favourite colour was red and at the service the following Sunday everybody wore something red.

She was the focus of even more devotion in the Little Company ('Little Company of Christ') which she formed in 1919 to follow a rule of prayer and meditation. (A little modest guild for personal religion, one writer called it, 'the lady chapel of her cathedral services to mankind').[30] Its numbers were small and it started by meeting in the room in her house that she used as an oratory. Martin Shaw's wife declined to join, feeling there was 'too much Maude' about it. Maude herself saw the danger of this but never arrived at a satisfactory way of handling the problem of her own charisma. Did she try to? She liked admiration. All the way from her early letters to the devotional jottings of old age she recognises her own vanity

[26]Lord Hampton (Humphrey Pakington) interviewed 21 Oct. 1968 by Emil Oberholzer; Mrs Martin Shaw interviewed 19 Aug. 1969 by Emil Oberholzer.
[27]*Fellowship Guild Notes* (April 1924).
[28]Maude Royden, *Story of the Guild* (June 1929) p.6.
[29]Florence Hill, to author.
[30]*Painted Windows* by A Gentleman With A Duster (1922), 113.

and the need to keep it in check.[31] So far as can be judged by the text of her sermons and the reactions of many who heard her, she never let it corrupt her preaching. Far from any hint of playing to the gallery, what most commentators seek to describe is the inner stillness from which she spoke – the quality so well caught by Margery Corbett Ashby when she employed the French word *recueilli* after hearing her preach in Geneva: 'shut up in herself, communing with God'. When she was communing with people, however, Maude was not always proof against impatience at the dependence her style of leadership almost inevitably encouraged.

What kind of people came to the Guildhouse? An early visitor found many young people, 'visibly rejoicing in defying St Paul's injunction "that a woman should not be uncovered in Church"'.[32] The impression is that by the 1930s the audience was older; and probably poorer. Maude often spoke of 'her people' as poor. 'I never had a rich congregation,' she said; and a member admitted, 'The Guildhousites are not rich, most of them earn their daily bread by hard work, but there is nothing too great for them to do or to give to their much-loved Sunday home.[33] The American writer, Frances Parkinson Keyes, found the Guildhouse in 1928 'crowded with a heterogenous gathering, most of its members shabbily or at least plainly dressed'. While another American eight years later was shocked to find 'The saddest and most depressing lot of human beings I had ever seen.'

> They were all dressed much alike, in the cheapest of calico prints and ginghams. One thing did distinguish them. There were no odors. Such a crowd in America would have smelled to heaven. But these were clean, decent, respectable poor. They were washed until their very faces shone with the soap.'

And when Maude spoke, those faces were transformed. 'I declare to you I saw they all had become beautiful!'[34]

It is clear, though, from other sources that there must have been a number of people present who could not be described as poor in this sense. Though not rich, they were independent women – schoolteachers and minor civil servants; secretaries – like Daisy Dobson, who became Maude's own secretary in 1924. 'Our congregation comes from all parts of London,' she said once; and the literature stressed that the Guildhouse was close to Victoria Station. If there were no women in evening dress such as had been forced to sit in the aisles when the Fellowship started in Kensington Town Hall, there were certainly middle-class people who travelled some distance

[31]In the *Guildhouse Fellowship* (Nov. 1942) Maude writes that she agreed to lead the Little Company 'much against my will'. Lord Soper (who worked with her on peace campaigns) asked by the author if he thought she was vain, answered promptly 'She fought against it!'
[32]'The Woman's Point of View', *Derby Daily Express* (24 April 1922).
[33]TFC 78; *Woman's Leader* (3 Dec. 1926) 325.
[34]*Good Housekeeping* (Jan. 1928) 31; L. O. Bricker, 'Maude Royden', *Christian Century* (24 June 1936).

to Eccleston Square. The wife of an academic, Betty Tucker, remembers how, before she married (and she chose, in fact, to be married by Maude) she used to travel in from her work in Hendon, always arriving rather late. An elderly cousin of hers, who was blind, got a friend to bring her to the Guildhouse from Norwood. One does not suppose that the Hon. Humphrey Pakington, president of the Architectural Association, who became the Guild's secretary, lived next door; nor Douglas Sladen, the well-known author (another who chose to be married by Maude) nor such as Mrs Philip de Laszlo, wife of the society portrait painter, or the headmistress of the Channing School. The Pakingtons are a good example of sophisticated people who came to the Guildhouse because they found it more congenial in every way than their local church. They came for the preaching, the fine music, the building itself (as reformed by Dearmer, more to their taste than 'revival gothic') and the excellent programme of 'Five Quarters'.[35]

There were always more women at the Guildhouse than men, especially after Dearmer left – though whether the disparity was more marked than in churches generally is hard to say. In society at large the preponderance of women had been conspicuous all Maude's life. 'Women form seven eighths of the audience here,' she had said of a prewar Summer Meeting, 'and are in that startling majority which is so noticeable everywhere nowadays, except on race courses and at music halls.'[36] The war had done nothing to redress the balance. Preaching in October 1927 on 'The Ministry of Women' she said to her flock,

> You say sometimes . . . how wonderful it is and how splendid that men come to the Guildhouse. Do you realise how deeply I resent it? My brothers, you will not doubt that I welcome you here with all my heart; neither, I am certain, will you resent it if I say that I welcome you not more than others. It is as great a privilege and honour to minister to a woman as a man.

'How dare you think . . . [it] a depressing sight to see a church filled with women?' she once demanded, of a group of Australian clergy. 'Has a woman no soul, gentlemen?'[37] In 1932, of some 330 members on the overseas roll of the Fellowship Guild only about 12 per cent were men.

The Guild's great days were the later twenties. Activities expanded, funds increased and every difficulty found its solution. Faced with a need to raise £2,000 for building work when the lease was renewed, Hudson, who in every parish he went to had conjured money out of the air, proposed that each member (1,000, roughly) should raise £1 and give it to Maude on her fiftieth birthday (November 1926). A £1,000 was raised in six weeks.

[35]Scattered impressions of the Guildhouse congregation from letters to Maude, Fawcett 221, 222; author's interview with Mrs Betty Tucker, 30 Aug. 1985; Oberholzer interview with Lord Hampton.
[36]CC (12 Aug. 1909) 229–30.
[37]Guildhouse sermon (30 Oct. 1927); Sydney Sun, (31 May 1928) report of address to Australian clergy.

'It was a wonderful time for us both.' Hudson was happy and absorbed at St Botolph's. Though subject always to bouts of depression he was a remarkable teacher still. She speaks of his staggering absorption of knowledge. 'He fell on a subject and tore the heart out of it.'[38] From time to time he preached at the Guildhouse, brilliant and fizzing at the after-meeting, by all accounts, in Extension style – 'walking up and down the aisle, answering all sorts of questions from what seemed an inexhaustible fund of knowledge' until she came and bore him away, to the amusement of her congregation. 'To see you and Dr Hudson Shaw at the after-meetings,' one woman wrote, 'we always felt what depths of feeling and understanding there was between you'.[39] So the public face of shared commitment formed a part of the 'wonderful time' in which the Guildhouse vied with St Botolph's in supporting causes that were dear to both. One was the mission at Lambarene. (The Guildhouse 'adopted' Dr Schweitzer, raising funds for a mental ward and for a well and he spoke his thanks from Maude's pulpit in 1927). Another and different thing was the League.

Hudson was a League of nations man and the League of Nations Union had an active branch in Bishopsgate as in Eccleston Square. For all its setbacks, peace campaigning – with its purpose, hard work and carnival moments – exhilarated Maude, as suffrage had done. In 1921 she participated in the first peace pilgrimage, from Southend to London. The Women's Peace Pilgrimage of 1926 was very much bigger and aimed specifically to urge the Government to agree to settle all international disputes by arbitration and to take the lead at the Disarmament Conference which had been proposed by the League of Nations. Converging on London from all over the country, 8,000 women poured into Hyde Park where eighty speakers were to address them.

> With each procession came a forest of . . . banners bearing such inscriptions of peace as 'The World is a family, not a barracks', 'War is Hell' . . . and at the head of each rode a woman on horseback wearing a long blue mantle with the dove of peace handpainted on it in silver. . . . Every pilgrim had a blue armlet. . . . The women of the Guildhouse wore their blue cassocks with white collars, and with the League of Nations Union and their brilliant national banners there was a picturesque group in deep orange.[40]

Kathleen had addressed the Manchester contingent as it set out on the journey south, telling them 'Law can be substituted for war as law has been substituted for duelling.' Maude walked for three days with those from South Wales and was then too exhausted to speak in Hyde Park. Millicent Fawcett took her place. But she recovered in time to form part of the

---

[38]TFC 54.
[39]Maude from Betty Johnstone (11 Jan 1948); Kitty Tappenden (31 Jan. 1948) Fawcett 221, 3/3.
[40]*Observer* (20 June 1926).

pilgrims' deputation to the Foreign Secretary, impressing upon him that the Government could count on solid support for arbitration, to judge by the response the pilgrims had met with at hundreds of meetings along their way.

To this picture of purpose and activity there was, as usual, a darker side. Though in her memoir she is vague about dates it is against such lively scenes that Maude notes their 'one cloud' – Effie unhappy. Effie is a shadowy figure in London. She had been sorry, according to Maude, to leave the anonymity of Bedford Square for the neighbourly Garden Suburb. One friend recalled her at a parish party. 'She had a black velvet coat on, I remember, which enhanced her "otherworldly" look. She stayed quite a while and smiled at the people but did not speak to them.' Another remembered on one occasion having commented on Effie to Maude, 'as I was struck by the strange things she said. You laughed it off and I never suspected that at times she was mentally deranged.' But in spite of her unbalanced state, said another, Effie in fact 'possessed a great sanity, even beyond that of . . . so-called sane people'.[41] And her drawings poke fun at them all. Yet, Maude says, she fell prey again to terrors. Their house in Hampstead was further from St Botolph's than the flat in Bedford Square had been. 'Hudson disappeared into the City in the morning and was away till evening fell . . . Effie suffered paroxysms of terror and rang him up continually, begging him to come back', even, sometimes, during a service. 'The strain on Hudson was very great.'

Bernard's death hung over them both still, 'the one great catastrophe of our married life', Hudson called it. Effie found no words for it, though in several letters to friends she expressed what she could not utter. The letters were not sent, nor meant to be; they came to light at last with her own death, thirty years after the tragedy. 'I have not forgotten . . . it is . . . *his* death–day!' Hudson had written on the eighth anniversary, from Switzerland where he had been sent for a rest. 'We seem to have a secret compact not to speak of Bernard together and . . . I respect what I guess is your instinct.' Though it probably was not his. 'Sometimes I feel as though I *could* not endure it . . . as if thought about that young life with its harsh cutting off would drive one out of one's mind. All . . . so apparently sacrifice in vain.'[42]

His own depression was sometimes disabling. He could not preach. Appointments were cancelled. Neighbours who got to know the Shaws in Hampstead were quite clear, as they told Maude later, that 'there was something lacking in his life'.

He needed love and companionship which . . . his wife was unable to return.

---

[41]Maude from Margaret Tuck (20 Dec. 1947); Edith Picton-Turbervill (3 Jan. 1948); Warwick James (26 Nov. 1947) Fawcett 221, 3/3.
[42]TFC 63.

Through this tragedy he suffered from repression and became introspective and subject to those fits of depression of which we were all aware. Had his love been reciprocated he would have lived a full life and . . . risen to great eminence.[43]

To all this was added his relationship with Maude which, she admits, was not free from stress. They quarrelled sometimes, hurting each other. In one of her best-known books at this time, *Sex and Common Sense* she contrasts the tension of sexual feeling in men and women. Passion in a man is often violent, 'like a storm at sea', she says, but yet more liable to leave him in peace at other times. The strain on a woman is less dramatic, much less violent and more persistent, 'something like that silent, uninterrupted thrust of an arch against a wall. There is no sign of stress.'[44] The image fits well with the glimpses she gives of herself and Hudson in *A Threefold Cord*. As they return from riding on Dartmoor and the lights come on in the cottage windows, it is he who says, 'Every peasant in the land can have tonight what I must never have'; he who finds it intolerable sometimes that she can sit in a room with him and work.

> For many years we had a standing engagement to read theology together on Saturday mornings, in his study at St Botolph's Clergy-house. . . . I was always more than content to be in the same room with Hudson, he with his work, I with mine: but in certain moods this exasperated him. 'Why are we wasting our time?' he would ask. 'What is the sense of our sitting in the same room in silence?'[45]

'I almost felt the restraint you practised was in itself a pleasure and certainly a stimulus – to you if not to Hudson,' a friend said later.[46]

Against this picture is the other one: the pleasure they had, the gaiety; 'entrancing days in boats' on the Cherwell, bowling through the woods in her little car, picnics, talking talking and talking; theatres.

> Hudson's ideas of a 'bat' were always on a large scale. We would go to the theatre – a matinée because 'it would tire me to go in the evening'. After the show it always seemed to him a pity to go home, so we dined somewhere. After dinner it was still a pity to go home so we went to another show. This is my idea of a 'bat', too.

When they could not see each other they wrote letters. Or even when they could. She got into the habit of giving him a little note on parting.

> I had *such* a struggle not to read it at once, in the booking-office, almost while your car was still audible. But I *did* wait until I had a quiet corner to myself. I read it again before dinner, during dinner, after dinner, and I don't know how many times before I reached Paddington.

[43]Maude from Michael Campbell-Gordon (19 Feb 1948) Fawcett 221, 3/3.
[44]*Sex and Common Sense* (1921 edn) 117.
[45]TFC 123, 79.
[46]Warwick James to Maude (26 Nov. 1947).

Sometimes, she writes, they tried to imagine what their lives would have been if they had never met. 'We could not imagine it. We could as well imagine how we could have lived if we had not lived. At the heart of all we did and were was this passion.'[47]

When people came to know of it at length, through the book, some of them felt they at last understood the secret of Maude's own understanding. 'How it illuminates the Guildhouse years!' 'I used to come often and sit in the gallery. . . . I came because I sensed you understood "life" . . . it seemed to me you spoke out of deep experience.'[48] However that might be, there is an obvious link with the whole corpus of her teaching on sex, whether in sermons at the City Temple, at the Guildhouse, in *Sex and Common Sense* or in the many popular articles in which she was asked to express her views on modern marriage and the modern girl.

Sex and Common Sense came out in 1921 – three years after *Married Love* had 'crashed into English society like a bombshell', in the words of its author, Marie Stopes. Maude had reviewed it for the *Common Cause*, welcoming it as a first attempt to throw scientific light on the human problems men and women encountered in marriage, and pleased by its challenge to the old assumption 'that desire is all on the side of the man', with a consequent indifference to the needs of the woman. Though she does not say so she must have approved of the book's explicit anatomical detail since she felt every bit as strongly as Stopes about the disastrous results of ignorance. For those who had recently sustained the shock of words like 'penis' and 'vagina', however, *Sex and Common Sense* was very mild. 'I do thank you for taking this subject and speaking so courageously and frankly about it,' wrote one reader. But Maude, unlike Marie, was never told to think of publishing in French. And her own book is mainly concerned with women who have no place in the other, since they have no prospect of married love.

The 'surplus woman' problem which oppressed the Victorians had been made worse by the Great War. There were, Maude said in her opening chapter, now two million more women than men. She thought most women would like to marry (a view for which she was criticised later by the more radical Cicely Hamilton, author of *Marriage as a Trade*)[49] and stressed the anguish that many must feel who would be unable to do so. 'I affirm this, and with insistence, that the normal – the average – woman sacrifices a great deal if she accepts life-long celibacy.' 'Remember,' she had said once

---

[47]TFC 89, 75–6, 74.

[48]E. Watts to Evelyn Gunter (14 Dec. 1947), 'Agatha' to Maude (22 Dec. 1947) Fawcett 221, 3/3.

[49]*Time and Tide* (14 Oct. 1927) 901.

at the City Temple to the men in her congregation, 'remember that a woman told you that it is not always easy for women to control the passions of which the world has denied even the existence in their nature.' There might be no outward sign of stress. But was not Italy covered with the ruins of churches where the silent thrust of the dome had at last caused the walls to crumble?[50]

There is no crumbling in *Married Love*. Stopes was not writing for single women and her flowery, mildly inflammatory effusions about the transports of the marriage bed may even have added to the pain of those who feared they would never know 'the apex of rapture'. Maude's book is written with a different purpose and her style is infinitely more austere, but clearly she too believes in rapture – as many women were coming to do, under the influence of Havelock Ellis, Edward Carpenter and the new sexology. Sex, she says, is not a grimy secret but 'the secret of existence . . . of the meaning of life . . . like the sense of music to the musician, of beauty to the artist, of insight to the poet'.

> A woman who has no sex instincts will speak and think of men as though because they have, there is something low and animal in their nature . . . It is as impossible for such women to understand life as for those who are tone deaf to play the violin, and those who are colour blind to paint a picture. It is not a sin not to have an ear for music or an eye for colour, but it is a lack.[51]

Like Stopes, then, she attributes almost mystical significance to sexual union in true marriage. And in her case the mystical element is religious as well as romantic. Sex is a sacrament. Nonetheless, she passionately rejects the 'un-Christlike belief that women miss their object in life if they are not wives and mothers'. Society's view of old maids makes her 'see red'. 'Perhaps this is because I am an old maid myself'.[52]

Once again, in these postwar years, with popular concern at the breakdown of morals largely focused on single women, she pits herself against the double standard. If they said to women who had lost their mates,

> 'We now invite you in the interests of morality to accept as your lot perpetual virginity', it is not difficult to imagine their reply: 'What is this morality in whose interests you ask such a huge sacrifice?' . . . 'Is the whole community willing to pay it, or is it exacted from us alone?'[53]

You could not set women on a level with men and expect them to accept a different standard of morals.

---

[50] *Sex and Common Sense* (1921 edn.; henceforth SCS) 10; 'The Sex Problem Today', City Temple sermon (16 June 1918); SCS 117.

[51] SCS 32; 'The Future', City Temple sermon (30 June 1918).

[52] SCS 29; 'An Open Letter from Miss Maude Royden to Miss Cicely Hamilton', *Time and Tide* (21 Oct. 1927).

[53] SCS 12.

'It seems to me that the average young woman is adopting the moral standards which have hitherto been those of the average man,' Bertrand Russell had written to her in 1917,

> and the main effect so far is to make almost all sex relations rather frivolous. Perhaps this is an unavoidable result of freedom. If so, I value freedom enough to be willing that the price should be paid. But I do think the price is a heavy one.[54]

In Maude's mind, though, there was the heavier price of the abominable double standard. 'The casual connection of a man and a woman who like each other' was to her 'more human, less utterly diabolical, than the brutal buying and selling of a woman's body'. 'I am prepared, in spite of all protests' she writes in *Sex and Common Sense*, 'to affirm that it is not a step backward but forward; that promiscuity is not as vile as prostitution – prostitution which has been accepted, which has been *defended* by Christian people!'[55]

Still, it was not for this that the vote had been won. And, however conscious of the claims of women, she would not exalt them above all other. She could not, for instance, accept the view that a woman deprived of her mate by war had an inherent right to motherhood. ('Is it really motherhood that sets her right before the right of the child she would create?' 'A child should have a father and a mother and a home.')[56]

Nor did she see a female lover as supplying the place of a husband. Maude's attitude to homosexuality altered somewhat over the years. Charis Frankenburg, who worked with her in 1915 at the maternity hospital in Clapham, remembered how a warning from Maude had rescued her from 'a predatory Lesbian' and Maude herself, in the 1940s, was to recall the feeling of repulsion' which homosexual love had once aroused in her. By that time, though, she felt her reaction had been due to 'a rather conventional morality'.[57] She is broadly conventional in *Sex and Common Sense* but her attitude there is very different from the violent revulsion expressed by Stopes. Maude's predominant response is compassion. 'If the homosexual is still the most misunderstood, maltreated and suffering of our race, it is due to our ignorance and brutal contempt. How many have even tried to understand?'[58] In 1929 she was to condemn the banning of *The Well of Loneliness*. 'I wish publicly to state that I honour the woman who wrote it, alike for her courage and her understanding.' Radclyffe Hall wrote later to say how much this support had meant to her 'during the past months of government persecution'.

---

[54]Bertrand Russell to Maude (5 Oct. 1917) Fawcett 222, 5/1 'Letters kept for Autobiography'.
[55]'The Sex Problem Today' City Temple sermon (16 June 1918); SCS 17.
[56]'The Future', City Temple sermon (30 June 1918); SCS 61.
[57]Frankenburg, *Not old, madam, vintage!* 83; *Sex and Commonsense* (1947 revised edn), 110.
[58]SCS 145.

I wrote the book in order to help a very much misunderstood and therefore unfortunate section of society, and to feel that a leader of thought like yourself had extended to me your understanding was, and still is, a source of strength and encouragement.[59]

But although Maude acknowledges with feeling the plight of the congenital invert, suffering from what seems to her a dislocation between body and spirit comparable with that produced by physical disability, the most that she offers is acceptance of suffering and the chance to transcend it (as she did her lameness?) She admits that society's view of homosexuals has made this struggle impossibly hard. But in her eyes (at least in the 1920s) inverted love disqualifies itself, as true love, by being inverted. The sex instinct is essentially creative. 'To use it in a relationship which must for ever be barren is "unnatural" and in the deepest sense immoral.'[60]

The hunger of single women for love and their hunger for children she understood well. But 'do not think that marriage is the one . . . panacea.' Maternal feelings could be sublimated. 'There are more children in the world already than there is mother-love to care for them, and that hunger of yours should find expression . . . in the love of all who are . . . helpless and oppressed.'[61] Whatever the hunger, she deplores self-pity.

I think there is something really pitiful, at any rate . . . among younger people, in simply resenting the fact that society has not made a place for you. You have now the power to make a place for yourself. . . . Any woman who has physical strength can earn her own living. I have heard people say, 'I would rather go and be a housemaid than do such and such a thing!' Well, why not be a housemaid? You will then be acclaimed . . . for everybody desires housemaids, and if your family does not like you to be a housemaid, well, they can make a better arrangement, can't they?[62]

This may have raised a smile; but her purpose really was to raise a sense of adventure – 'the great adventure' of feminists, pacifists – and now, if need be, of old maids. 'You are not called upon to slip through the world between good and evil, never very good and never very bad, not expecting much of yourselves, with no great adventure and no great pain.'[63] She spoke of St Francis sublimating sex-love in a greater love of the world; of Christ, who must have suffered sexual frustation. She threw down the gauntlet to single women. 'It is not easy, but it is possible. It is possible and it is glorious!'[64]

[59]'The Well of Loneliness' *Guildhouse Monthly* (April 1929); Hall to Maude with congratulations on her CH (1930). Fawcett 221.
[60]SCS 143
[61]'The Future.'
[62]'Unmarried People', Guildhouse sermon (31 July 1927).
[63]'The Future.'
[64]SCS 39.

If they could have marched out then with banners, as in the prewar suffrage days! But this was postwar. Could it even be said that the women's movement loved them as much as it used to – given its growing preoccupation with matters relevant to wives and mothers? Maude (though she was to preach her last sermon at the Guildhouse with a thought for the single – 'of all the people I have tried to serve . . . it is you whom I have most carried in my heart'[65]) had her share of this preoccupation. Her early interest in the endowment of motherhood had found expression in one of the essays she contributed to *The Making of Women*. The other (which she said Ralph liked so much she nearly told him what it owed to himself)[66] concerned the changes in marriage relations which might be expected in the postwar world. It is a highly optimistic piece: full of faith in the young and a warm conviction that greater knowledge and honesty will make for a better start in sex relations (nothing made her angrier – apart from prostitution – than the ignorance in which many middle-class girls were deliberately kept until their wedding night). Apart from all this, though, she sees a need to change some fundamental attitudes in men, and singles out the 'wish for mastery' which Bertrand Russell in a recent book had presented as essentially male.[67] It is not exclusively so, says Maude. Life itself is the exercise of power – and it has always been hard for those who are dominant to feel their own lives can be preserved 'or be in any honourable sense worth preserving if they must forgo this "natural leadership"'. But men must change. In marriage, she says, the desire for mastery has led to horrors. Men must stop thinking that this desire 'is noble or essentially virile, or that it is an invasion of their own life not to be allowed to invade the lives of others.'

This, in effect, evokes the principles against the use of women by men which underlay the fight against the double standard. And since Maude was deeply committed to that, her explicit challenge to male sexuality within marriage itself is not surprising. It is radical, nonetheless. In an area where some would think change unlikely she expects great change – indeed, demands it. Woman, alone of all creatures, she says, is claimed at all times, regardless of her wishes; man has gone 'far beyond the desires of the "natural" animal, and it is certain that he must retrace his steps'. Yet on another page of 'Modern Love' she hesitates over the more soluble problem of married women who want careers. 'For most of us it must be a choice.'[68] The claims of children weigh with her against a more radical solution here. One of the objections she expressed later to Dora Russell's views on free love concerned the 'stable home and two parents' which she was convinced

---

[65]'Old, young – and the missing generation', Guildhouse sermon (15 Nov. 1936) in *Guildhouse Monthly* (Dec. 1936).
[66]Royden, 'Ralph Bonfoy Rooper: A Memoir', Fawcett 379, 23.
[67]*Making of Women* (1917) 58.
[68]ibid., 55.

that children needed, where Russell thought they were nurtured best in the generous sunlight of a great passion.

Dora Russell gave a paper on marriage for 'Five Quarters' in 1927 and her views raked the Guildhouse like machine gun fire. With clarity and verve she put it to them that the usual view of marriage was 'wrong from top to bottom'; that sexual experience was highly advisable both for men and women before they got married and that sexual relationships outside marriage could promote a tolerant, unstrained atmosphere in which both parents and children throve. 'Sex . . . can release you tremendously and make you into a joyous and generous human being, instead of a separate tight little entity going on one little orbit like the billiard balls in the eighteenth-century materialist universe.'[69] Some members, according to the *Guildhouse Monthly*, objected strongly to Russell's views and thought she should not have been asked to expound them. However, to exclude such discussion at the Guildhouse would, it argued, give the impression 'that the "religious" will not hear because they know they cannot answer the case for "free love".'

In fact Maude had tackled 'companionate marriage' in a recent sermon – claiming, of course, that it could not be a 'trial' for the real thing. And there was plainly an unbridgeable gap between her view of sexual relations as appropriate only to marriage, and to sanctify a spiritual harmony already existing between the couple, and Dora Russell's view of them as more or less free-standing. But on some matters their views are compatible. Maude, for all her faith in marriage as a sacrament, does not see it as indissoluble. Her contribution to the debate then going on about change in the divorce law comes close to the idea of 'irretrievable breakdown' which defines the position today. For she thought it entirely unchristian to pretend that a marriage was real when it was not; and begged the Church to consider the spirit and not just the letter of Christ's teaching.[70]

She parts again from her Church's view on the subject of birth control, strongly supporting the efforts of Russell and other women throughout the twenties to make contraceptive advice more available.[71] The desperate predicament of working-class mothers had been highlighted in 1917 in *Maternity*, a collection of letters published by the Women's Co-operative Guild; and a means of reaching such mothers was presented by the introduction the following year of maternity and child welfare centres. But did the government wish to reach them?

The controversy raged in the early twenties. Maude admitted to a per-

---

[69]Dora Russell, 'Marriage', Guildhouse address (30 oct. 1927) in *Guildhouse Monthly* (Feb. 1928).

[70]*Time and Tide* (27 Jan. 1922) 27.

[71]The Lambeth Conference of 1908 condemned contraceptives utterly. In 1930 it accepted their use where conception would injure the mother's health but not for social or economic reasons.

sonal ideal which had little bearing on the problem at hand. 'I still believe,' she wrote in 1922 in the first issue of *The New Generation*, 'that the ideal relation between men and women in marriage is one in which sexual connection only takes place when a child is desired.' She speaks later of knowing married couples, 'married lovers' who 'realise that dream'.

> They are able to live together without strain, and without alienation consummate their marriage only when they desire a child. In such marriages it has seemed to me that I perceive a grace and beauty, an austerity indeed, and yet a romance which we do not often associate with a very long married life.[72]

But not for a moment does she suggest that this is an answer to the current problem. Let idealists preach their ideal 'but in the name of humanity not seek to impose it'. She herself had often advised contraceptives.

> I know a woman who at the time I met her, had borne eight dead (syphilitic) babies and was about to bear a ninth. . . . In each confinement she suffered unspeakably. . . . Will anyone suggest that it was her duty to go back to her husband and conceive other children until such time as I or somebody else succeeded in convincing him that he ought to cease entirely from marital relations with his wife?[73]

It was just such cases that Dora Russell and those who accompanied her in 1924 on a deputation to the Minister of Health in the new Labour government brought to his notice. Unluckily for them, Mr Wheatley was a Catholic and did not see his way to instructing doctors at the centres to advise contraceptives. Maude preached a passionate sermon of protest, citing from the deputation's report its scarifying figures of maternal mortality (four times higher than the death rate in mining – which was men's most dangerous trade). In this context she made short work of what was said about the sanctity of life.

Her election to the National Church Assembly – that 'parliament' of the Church of England which met for the first time in 1920 following on the Enabling Act – gave her a voice on other aspects of the situation of wives and mothers. She was watchful, when they discussed the Divorce Bill, that nothing they put forward should impede the proposal to equalise grounds between husband and wife. And in 1923 she threw herself into the fight for revision of the marriage service.

This figured, of course, as part of a revision of the 1662 Book of Common Prayer, a formidable and contentious business and one which had been in the air for some time. As long ago as 1913, when Maude was still editing the *Common Cause*, she had noted with approval a draft revision, published with a foreword by Bishop Gore, where 'all that offends modern

---

[72]'The Ethics of Birth Control', *Church Militant* Supplement (6 June 1924).
[73]*New Generation* (Jan. 1922).

opinion' had been expunged from the marriage service. She thought there was a good deal that needed expunging ('the implication of subordination of women throughout is extraordinarily strong') but the chief thing was the bride's promise to 'obey'. Now, ten years later, in the House of Laity, she proposed (with Mrs Creighton seconding) that this objectionable vow should go. Her motion was defeated. For Lord Hugh Cecil the vow expressed ('and never more necessarily than now') the Church's acceptance of St Paul's teaching about the relation of the sexes, though he insisted that subordination need not imply inferiority. Athelstan Riley thought religion would crumble if Pauline authority were set aside. There was nothing derogatory in obedience, he said; Christians had always gloried in it.

The press spoke up for ordinary people. Ordinary women loved to obey (and sent letters to the *Daily News* signed 'Concord', 'Untrammelled', and 'A Happy Obedient Wife'. 'It is jolly nice to obey a husband such as mine,' one wrote). But ordinary husbands did not really expect it. Therefore, 'Why should Miss Royden worry?' 'I have an infinite respect for Miss Maude Royden,' wrote the editor of a women's page,

> She looks well, speaks well, is sincere to the point of being burnt up by her intensity, deeply religious, anxious to leave the world a better place than she found it. But – there is usually a 'but' in the case of these good women who set out to reform the world – I think she is inclined to run after the shadow when she might be attending to the substance. Why, for example, should she worry so much about that little word 'obey' . . . She is not a married woman.[74]

'The House of Laity has made the mistake of admitting unmarried women to its councils,' wrote 'Grandfather' in the *Daily Express*. 'A Modern Young Man' agreed with 'Grandfather' and was giving modern women 'a very wide berth'. 'In the nature of the case the man must be the head,' wrote 'Old Fashioned' in the *Northern Echo*. 'They are one in heart, but she is the weaker vessel, and gladly submits to her lord in all things that are reasonable and good.' In fact the wife's vow was unconditional (differing, as Maude said, from the qualified obedience pledged to a bishop when a priest was ordained) and did not appear in the Catholic rite. But to ordinary people in 1923 the wedding of the King's niece was much more telling. To judge by appearances, Princess Maud was 'supremely ready to promise to obey'. 'She listened as if entirely in agreement while the minister prayed that "this woman may be loving and amiable, faithful and obedient to her husband".' And the Princess's attitude was surely that of the normal bride, 'notwithstanding the efforts of Miss Maude Royden and . . . others of her kind to make them feel fierce against "the inequality of the marriage vows"'.[75]

[74] *Glasgow Bulletin* (12 July 1923).
[75] *Scots Pictorial* (24 Nov. 1923).

Maude certainly felt fierce. When she spoke of obedience as 'especially inappropriate to the relations of the sexes', what she had in mind was no abstract principle but the fact that 'many working women do really believe that, having promised to obey their husbands, their bodies cease to be their own.'[76] The writer of one of the letters in *Maternity* declares 'No animal will submit to this: why should the woman?' and answers bleakly, 'Why, simply because of the Marriage Laws of the woman belonging to the man, to have and to own [sic].' Others affirm: 'We must let the men know we are human beings'; 'I often think women are worse off than beasts; 'fathers ought to control their bodies'.[77] Similar admissions, made to Maude by women who 'begged her to be their spokesman' convinced her that 'squalid and sordid misery' was caused by the popular conception of 'obey', in the context of the marriage service.[78]

For what was this context? What impression was given by placing last among the 'causes' for which marriage was ordained the one which came closest to the Christian ideal ('for . . . mutual society, help and comfort')? The first cause was stated to be procreation; then, remarkable as it might seem, marriage was said to be ordained as a relief for persons who 'have not the gift of continency'. Such people, she said, were hardly fit to marry. In fact, the teaching contained in this paragraph had made some marriages a perfect hell.[79]

Although her amendment came to nothing, the fight went on; and later that year support for Maude's efforts came from NUSEC, whose president, Eleanor Rathbone, insisted – against some criticisn – that this was a topic with which the Union shóuld concern itself. At a demonstration organised by NUSEC in November, Maude ('who had to wait some time before the applause which greeted her subsided') set out the case all over again; and resolutions calling on the Church Assembly to recommend revision of the service were passed. The League of the Church Militant led the campaign and Maude spoke on it during the Church Congress which was held in Oxford in 1924. Though the service in its final revision did not incorporate all she had hoped for, she thought it showed an extraordinary advance: the changes in the causes for which marriage was ordained, and the omission of the vow to obey 'lifts the whole service to a higher plane'.[80]

By this time, though, her own role had changed. By January 1924 she had resigned from the Church Assembly and later that year she gave up the

---

[76]'Miss Royden as Marriage Service Critic', *Evening News* (2 Oct. 1924).

[77]Margaret Llewelyn Davies (ed.), *Maternity: Letters from Working Women (1915)* (1978) 28, 68, 48, 65.

[78]*Church Family Newspaper* (15 Nov. 1923); see also *Manchester Guardian* (13 Nov. 1923).

[79]*Church Militant* (15 Oct. 1924) 156.

[80]*Westminster Gazette* (9 Feb. 1927). In 1928 the revised Prayer Book was rejected by the House of Commons. It was neither authorised nor withdrawn and in the late 1980s there are still brides who choose to 'obey'.

presidency of the League of the Church Militant. As to the Assembly, the *Manchester Guardian* wrote that her retirement would be much regretted, 'especially by those who consider that a woman with progressive views and a talent for expressing them . . . was needed as a tonic to . . . ecclesiastical sedateness'.[81] She had not been prominent in the debates but had always carried weight and had 'well represented the women of the Church'. Maude did not think so. Her own view was that she was 'so much out of touch with the main body of opinion as to be almost useless as a member, and that her advocacy of certain reforms damage[d] their prospects of sympathetic hearing'.[82] There may have been a touch, too, of the disenchantment of those who had once dreamed of 'Life and Liberty' but found the reality extremely dull.

Giving up the presidency of the League was different, though prompted, it seems, by a similar feeling that someone of more 'orthodox' views than herself 'would be a more useful . . . pioneer' on 'our great question'. She remained a member. And while there was a certain symbolic loss (for virtually nothing was said by anyone, friend or foe now, on women in the Church without a reference to Maude Royden) the League remained a vigorous body, driven by that passion for a single cause which most of the other women's organisations had lost, perforce, when the vote was won.

What did it achieve, though, in the course of a decade which had opened with 'the dawn of a new era'? (For so the Lambeth Conference report was rated in the calendar of Church feminists – linked with Maude's 'historic appearance' at the Good Friday service in 1921). In the summer of 1922, under such headings as 'At the Ebb' and 'As You Were' the *Church Militant* noted that very little had been done so far. As regards women being allowed to preach, discussion in the Canterbury Convocation was bogged down for weeks on the word 'normally'. As regards deaconesses, this was not now seen as a holy order comparable to the male diaconate. 'Indeed, the Deaconess narrowly escaped having her baptismal ministrations limited to women,' wrote the League's chairman – conjuring up visions of girl and boy babies having to be sorted out at the font.

Maude herself may have felt less buoyant for, according to one newspaper report, on the eve of her departure to speak in America in 1922 she expressed the opinion that the British women's movement had 'gone to pieces'. It may have been tiredness that prompted the remark for she admitted later to a sense of relief in escaping, if only for a week or two, from the stresses of postwar England, including the moral and economic problems connected with the large preponderance of women. Alongside class bitterness there now existed 'a disastrous sex antagonism' she said,

---

[81] *Manchester Guardian* (5 Jan. 1924).

[82] *Church Militant* (Jan. 1924) 12. Maude did not just mean reforms concerning women. Her democratic and ecumenical tendencies put her at variance with the majority.

arising though widespread unemployment: with men trying to shut women out of jobs, and women desperately needing to get them.[83]

The Church debate was not carried on in a vacuum. The League of the Church Militant might protest that it saw the priesthood as a vocation, not as a prize; but given the resistance to anything that looked like women pushing, such an assurance did not cut much ice. And so after Lambeth came disappointment, as Maude admitted in her president's message to the League in 1924; though here, at least, she was determined to hope.

> I believe we shall begin increasingly to see how great, in spite of all, was its effect. The Authorities are beginning to act. Women are being licensed to preach in churches. (In America I was told that my invitations to preach in cathedrals were the direct result of the Lambeth Report).

Yet only the previous year she had said, 'It is hard to go on serving a Church in which women are treated with such extraordinary discourtesy'.[84]

The way they were treated was liable to vary from one province, diocese and parish to another. The licence to preach at nonstatutory services (for there was no question of women preaching at matins, evensong or Holy Communion) was subject, in the province of Canterbury, to the 'normally to women and children' rule; there was no such rule in the province of York. Within each province, the bishops of the dioceses were to lay down conditions for licensing women. But even one concerned, like Temple of Manchester, to raise the status of women in the Church, saw their preaching as a rather exceptional occurrence, while those who were hostile did everything they could to discourage clergy from inviting women. When the rector of Ayot St Lawrence in Hertfordshire wanted to invite Maude in 1922 the Bishop of St Albans tried to dissuade him.[85] In individual churches there was much variety in the reception of a female preacher. 'Some clergy invite her to sit on the front pew and speak from the middle of the nave, some provide a special reading desk, and others boldly ask her to use the pulpit,' ran an account in the *Daily Telegraph*. Maude recalled once being permitted to preach only on condition she did not use the pulpit, did not call her address a sermon or wear a surplice – conditions so insulting, in the eyes of the vicar, that he discarded his surplice too.[86]

A strong supporter of the women's cause, Canon Guy Rogers, looked forward to the time when in the light of the 'broad statesmanship' of Lambeth such pettifogging restrictions would go. But it was not happening. Mrs Marston Acres, chairman of the League of the Church Militant,

---

[83]Maude Royden, 'As I see Your America', *Our World* (Sept. 1922) 54–9.

[84]*Church Militant* (Jan. 1924); *Daily News* (4 May 1923) 69.

[85]Bishop of St Albans to Armar Corry de Candole, Rector of Ayot St Lawrence (19 July 1922) Oberholzer papers.

[86]*Daily Telegraph* (5 Jan. 1924). Royden 'Bid Me Discourse'.

admitted, looking back on 1924, that 'surveying the progress of women in the religious world would be a distressing experience if one had expected the Millenium.'[87] She picked out the good things – among them, the fact that such a public figure as Dean Inge of St Paul's had spoken out in favour of women priests 'and the skies have not fallen!'; that Lady Barrett had preached in Bristol Cathedral before the bishop and other dignitaries; that it was now possible to find women acting as servers, choristers, churchwardens and sidesmen. But the limited nature of these last innovations is clear from Mrs St Clair Stobart's account of being made a sidesman in her Church in Hampstead. That she had been given 'the very humble service of handing the bag round' was supposed, she said, to be a marvellous concession; but among some fifty churchwardens and sidesmen 'your humble servant is the only female!'[88]

The League was delighted in 1925 to gain the open support of NUSEC and the National Council of Women. That such a broad body as the NCW should back the idea of women priests provided an answer to those who said that except for a few feminists women themselves did not want the spiritual ministrations of women. 'Shall we not now prepare for a still greater advance? Largely owing to Miss Royden's great spiritual work, public opinion is slowly changing.'[89] The English Church Union did not change. No safeguard or licence could allay its fears of women in the pulpit and in 1926 it raised strong objections to Maude's being asked to preach in Liverpool Cathedral, pointing out that 'the authorities must have known that she herself desired to be a priest and that she represented a body of people who were desirous of seeing women priests'.[90]

Of course they knew. To such as Charles Raven, not long appointed Canon of Liverpool, the vivid recollection of her preaching there remained through life to feed his conviction that women ought to be admitted to the priesthood. In old age he recalled the occasion: Maude speaking in her native city and the cathedral crowded out by 'a critical and inquisitive congregation'.

> Few of us facing such an occasion could have avoided some signs of self-consciousness or of self-display. She was wholly transparent, people who had come . . . prepared to scoff, saw God and were themselves transfigured.[91]

Raven was a don who had been in the trenches; a naturalist, historian and theologian; a man who came out of the horrors of war looking, as he said, for 'a new Pentecost' and seeking vigorously to tease out new issues:

---

[87]E. Louie Acres, 'Women and the Church' *Woman's Leader* (2 Jan. 1925).
[88]'Ministry of Women', *Church Family Newspaper* (10 March 1922).
[89]LCM leaflet *Thanksgiving* (n.d. probably 1925).
[90]*Church Militant* (Jan. 1927) 9.
[91]Untitled article by Charles Raven reprinted in *Women in the Church* (Society for the Ministry of Women in the Church, n.d. probably 1967–70) Fawcett pamphlets 262.14.

Christianity and war; religion and science; the new relationship between the sexes. In the matter of women priests, he found, like Ursula Roberts' husband, that for him the decisive factor was contact with women of great spirituality. Maude was one.[92] He belonged to the League and had written before on the ministry of women. But in 1928 he nailed his colours to the mast with a book *Women and Holy Orders*. 'If Canon Raven wants to be a bishop,' wrote Dean Inge in the *Evening Standard*, 'he has done a rather courageous thing.' Which was true. He did want to be a bishop, and never became one, though in 1932 he was made Regius Professor of Divinity at Cambridge. 'I am not a feminist,' he wrote in the preface (a disclaimer unlikely to impress his critics: 'an ardent feminist' said Hensley Henson) 'and I have no desire to be a revolutionary. But for some years the conviction has grown on me that the admission of women to Holy Orders . . . is inherent in the teaching of Jesus.'[93]

To Raven it seemed entirely fitting that women should take a sacramental role. How could the Church spend years debating the need of the sick for the reserved sacrament and dismiss 'the vastly greater spiritual change' represented by the Women's Movement?' But to Hensley Henson, Bishop of Durham, Raven's book was an abomination. 'The world wants desperately not female priests and bishops but Christian wives and mothers!' he roared. 'What is the most menacing evil of our time? Is it not precisely the repudiation of wifely and motherly function by women?' The existence of 'a multitude of single women' now 'casting about for alternatives' to marriage, should not blind people to the real problem:

> This repudiation of natural function, dictated by the perverted notion of sexual equality, and made possible by misapplications of science, implies the disintegration of the female, and the withdrawal from society of the principal discipline under which citizenship is . . . ordained to develop.[94]

The perverted notion of sexual equality was reflected, of course, that very year in the act which finally gave women the vote on the same terms as men, at twenty one. But this welcome conclusion to a long struggle led to the disbandment of the League of the Church Militant. 'The original work of the League is over,' declared their journal; though it hastened to explain,

> This does not mean that the question of the Ordination of Women has been achieved, *nor that it has been given up as hopeless*, but simply that a Society founded

---

[92]He also singles out the Quaker, Lucy Gardner, the poet and mystic, Evelyn Underhill, and Beatrice Hankey, who founded the community of Blue Pilgrims at Sevenoaks.

[93]F. W. Dillistone, *Charles Raven* (1975) 261. To a clergyman who asked how women could be priests 'when God is masculine', Raven once said 'That is so extraordinarily heretical that I can hardly believe a priest of the Church could give utterance to it. . . . Yours is a good Mohammedan doctrine, but bad Christianity.'

[94]Hensley Henson, 'Most Menacing Evil Of Our Time'. *Newcastle Evening Chronicle* (24 March 1928).

for one purpose, and that a political one, may not perhaps be the best possible means of influencing a non-political Church. [95]

Another article in the same issue sums up achievements since 1918 (when the League toook on the ordination commitment) and while affirming that, in terms of argument, 'the opposition has been beaten off the field', has to admit that in all that time 'no steps have been taken by the Church in the direction of our desire'.

There were many reflections of this sad fact. In 1922 a profile of Maude in the *Westminster Gazette* had opened boldly,

Maude Royden's name is safe among the pioneers. She has broken through one of the thorniest and most rigid of barriers: that which, ever since Protestantism existed as an ecclesiastical establishment, closed the priesthood against women. She has, it is true, not yet won her formal admission to the hierarchy; she may, in her own person, never achieve that ultimate, symbolic stage . . . but for all that the barrier is down. The rest is only a matter of time. The woman bishop belongs to the near future. [96]

In 1928, when the writer Sinclair Lewis was trying to make arrangements to be married in London (it seems, by Maude) he wrote to his fiancée, Dorothy Thompson, explaining that Maude was out of the country. 'In any case, it is doubtful if she could help. She proves not to be a nonconformist but Church of England with a position which, for all her fame, seems technically only that of a lay preacher.'[97]

[95] *Church Militant* (Oct. 1928) 49.
[96] Xanthippe, 'Women of Today and Tomorrow' *Westminster Gazette* (4 March 1922).
[97] Vincent Sheean, *Dorothy and Red* (1963) 90.

11

Another Way of Life

One simply can't go on *waiting* for a vocation which does not
come . . . and one must work while it is day.

Maude Royden (1936).

'The tidal wave that has swept away the secular inequalities of the sexes
breaks against the spiritual rock in vain,' wrote A. G. Gardiner in his essay
on Maude in *Certain People of Importance*. Obviously, she comes within his
purview as a protagonist of women in the Church, one who has fought
'valiantly, incessantly' for them, issuing 'the most formal and sustained
challenge' against their exclusion that has yet been made. He describes that
challenge as 'implicit even more than explicit'.

> It is expressed in her life and character more than in her actions and words. If it
> can be said of any that they are born to the priestly function, that they have
> received the commission to minister to the spiritual needs of men from a source
> more authentic than any ecclesiastical ordinance, it may be said of Miss Royden.

But 'she is not without importance as a personal influence apart from that'.
And 'it is not on the ground of sex that she exercises that influence'.
Though her field is religious rather than political, in his view it has a much
wider impact. 'She represents as effectually as anyone the conscience and
moral sense of the community.'[1]

Maude, on the other hand, had frequent misgivings about whether she
was effectual at all. Writing in 1923 to Dick Sheppard (in answer, it seems,
to some question raised about involvement in peace campaigning) she
debates the claims of 'pulpit' and 'platform' in a way which reflects more
uncertainty than her followers might have suspected. The letter opens with
a list of reasons against her giving up preaching crusades. 'I love them.'
'What is called "religious" work . . . has gradually absorbed me more and
more and I think I have been growing – very slowly – into some crude kind

[1] A. G. Gardiner, *Certain People of Importance*, 235–42. Xanthippe (*Westminster Gazette* 4 March
1922) also sees Maude as a 'representative figure' because she stands, 'in a sense in which it is true
of hardly any other public character . . . for that . . . human sympathy . . . which is outraged by
the sufferings of the helpless.'

of spiritual life by being forced to deal with fundamentals.' Also, 'I have been able to get a few doors open to women of the younger generation and I don't want to leave them in the lurch.' On the other hand she also likes political work; and 'it is the psychological moment for peace'. Perhaps she is leading younger women into a blind alley. 'Perhaps the Churches aren't worth serving and won't last much longer without some vast upheaval which will change everything.'[2]

Like Sheppard she hoped for a vast upheaval. 'It may be . . . that in the course of . . . the next few years we shall see organised religion transformed,' she told them at the Guildhouse in 1927.[3] It was a year which pointed to change. Hudson had preached there a few months earlier on the New Prayer Book, affirming joyously if unprophetically, 'I do not think Parliament will dare throw it out.' Dr Barnes, the modernist Bishop of Birmingham, was raising a new theological storm, and – what mattered intensely to Maude – Dick Sheppard, her beloved friend and mentor, came out that year with a book which expressed everything she felt about the Church of England.

'I have felt at times that I could throw bombs,' she once admitted in another context. This is the kind of bomb she could have thrown. *The Impatience of a Parson* calls for a Church which shall reflect the values of Christ. Sheppard, who made all England his parish with his broadcast sermons from St Martin-in-the-Fields, asks the Church to abandon privilege, reject competitive values and war, embrace other sects; and as Maude said often, try to make Christianity work. '*You* honestly inspired the book by your teaching,' he wrote to her as the counterfire of the Establishment burst upon him.

> You were *the only one* whose blessing I longed for and I think if you had been compelled to criticise it would have broken me. . . . all the time I was writing . . . I kept on saying to myself 'would Maude agree' and . . . when the book came out I looked through my pile of letters to see if *you* had written and then trembled when I saw your envelope.[4]

His book was dismissed by many reviewers. But Maude wrote, passionately supportive, '*You* reach "the common people"; they can't' – keen for him to know how ordinary people stopped to read the extracts which Hudson Shaw had put up on the board outside St Botolph's.

> That article in the *Times* makes me see red. My only consolation is that it is *exactly* what the *Times* would have written about S. Francis of Assisi, so really it is a great tribute. Indeed it is just what the *Times* would have said about our Lord.[5]

[2]Maude to Dick Sheppard, (26 Oct. 1923) SP.
[3]'The Ministry of Women', Guildhouse sermon (30 Oct. 1927) *Guildhouse Monthly* (Feb. 1929).
[4]Dick Sheppard to Maude, (18 Oct. 1927) Fawcett 220, 2/2.
[5]Maude to Dick Sheppard (15 Oct. 1927) SP

She preached on his book. 'Mr Sheppard demands that the Church shall exemplify the teaching of Christ. . . . He is asking for reality. So now do we women.' In a sermon which presents exploitation by class, colour and sex as one ('[it] is all part of the same world order') she declares

> If I speak tonight about a thing that is very near my own heart – the ministry of women – it is not because . . . I once wished to be ordained, but because I am more and more convinced that the ministry of women in the Church is essential.[6]

Did the Royden-watchers of the English Church Union pounce upon this? At what point anyway had she ceased to wish to fulfil her vocation? Her lack of priesthood was always present – if not at the Guildhouse, then in the society which she had founded especially for prayer. Whenever they of the Little Company wished to arrange a few days' retreat there was the need to look for a priest willing to come in and celebrate the Eucharist. 'It seems . . . quite extraordinarily artificial,' she said,

> that at such times, we, who are joined together with a very deep and real fellowship, should have to scour the country for some priest, who knows nothing whatever about our society . . . and does not in the least wish to be fetched . . . to minister to us in the early morning, when after all, in a very real sense, I am myself their priest.[7]

And if some wished to confess, 'It seems . . . natural . . . that, if they have confidence in me, and if it is through me that God has brought them to repentence, they should desire to make their confession to me and receive absolution.' Which could not be done. And among people who sought her advice in the ordinary way, some wished to confess, and for them too a priest must be found. Such a case had arisen in 1919 when a woman she had sent on to Dick Sheppard could not bring herself to talk to a man about her sin (which was evidently masturbation) and he could not bring himself to press her. 'Does not this show how badly women in Orders are needed?' she had written to him, saying that she saw his problem.

> But I also sympathise a good deal with her. She probably finds it quite impossible to tell you in detail what she has been doing . . . What are we to do when the Church won't let me help and it is very difficult for you to do so?[8]

Even the Guildhouse, for all it offered, could not offer a solution to this. She was indeed minister in Eccleston Square. The Guildhouse people were

---

[6]'The Ministry of Women.'

[7]'Women and Priesthood'; memorandum submitted by the Anglican Group for Bringing the Subject of the Admission of Women to the Priesthood before the Next Lambeth Conference' (1930) Lambeth Palace Archives, LC 168, 32.

[8](17 May 1919) SP: In a letter to a woman who wanted her to act as her confessor (11 Nov. 1947, Fawcett 223) Maude says she told Sheppard that she never attempted to give absolution. 'Dick asked what I did say and I said "I give them the assurance of God's forgiveness." He could not help laughing and said 'What's the difference?'

proud to be hers. Some recalled that she had baptised their children ('Noel is twelve now and is doing well at the County School. We often tell him of you'). Some she married, though this could not be done without the presence of a registrar.[9] Yet even here, she felt, looking back, that her work had been flawed by her lack of priesthood. Her model of a parish priest was Sheppard – his study door open day and night. 'I desire that we should make of this Guildhouse . . . what Mr Sheppard desires that all churches should be.'[10] And in the eyes of her flock she did so. But not in her own eyes. 'If a parson has a church he must make it the first . . . claim on . . . all that he is.' Looking back she felt she had failed on that; and explained, 'the fact that my vocation was narrowed by the refusal to me of the priesthood turned me . . . more and more to the work of the preacher.'[11] Preaching often took her away from the Guildhouse: on preaching crusades outside London (eight in 1927 alone); on visits abroad (she went three times to America) and in 1928 on a world tour.

'Her people' did not see it like that. Maude's fiftieth birthday in 1926 was made an occasion for great rejoicing. 'Shakespeare said, 'A Star Danced When She Was Born' runs the lettering on the hand-painted birthday card, 'and so say all of us: Margaret Ashton, Nancy Astor, Margaret Bondfield, Clara Butt, Millicent Garrett Fawcett, Sybil Thorndike, Margaret Wintringham et omnes.'[12] There were over a thousand omnes present. Two years later, at another occasion of equal warmth, though tinged with sadness, the Guildhouse people said goodbye as Maude and her secretary, Daisy Dobson, left to begin their world tour. Albert Dawson, Secretary of the Guild (who in his days at the City Temple had persuaded Maude to take the pulpit there), spoke 'of the blessings of her ministry among us, of our good wishes for a happy and successful tour, of our resolve to keep the flag flying during her absence and of the joy with which we shall look for a safe and *punctual* return'.[13]

With a natural pride that their beloved minister should carry her gifts to the world at large it was accepted that 1928 would 'undoubtedly be a testing time'. 'We shall miss tremendously the magnetic personality of our Leader. We know that no one can fill her place.' Nonetheless, the Guildhouse was in good heart, financially and otherwise. Maude's departure at the end of December closed a typically busy month which had begun with a great

[9]She agreed to marry people at their special request. The first were the author Douglas Sladen, and Dorothea Duthie who became his second wife. In his autobiography *My Long Life* Sladen alludes to the marriage solemnised 'under a cedar tree in Richmond' on 31 July 1920. Maude married Betty and Archie Tucker in the Guildhouse in 1931, in the presence, Betty remembers, of 'a rather cross registrar'. In due course they asked her to christen their children.

[10]'Dick Sheppard's Book' Guildhouse sermon (16 Oct. 1927) *Guildhouse Monthly* (Nov. 1927) 301.

[11]Royden, *If I Had My Time Again*, 155.

[12]Fawcett 225.

[13]*Guildhouse Monthly* (Jan. 1928) 23.

crusade in support of the disarmament campaign and there were many plans
for the year ahead. The programme for 'Five Quarters' was to be 'the best
yet'. Dearmer, Anson, Hudson Shaw, Raven and Sheppard, among
Anglican clergy, with Margaret Bondfield and Herbert Gray among Nonconformists, were to stand in as preachers. The *Guildhouse Monthly* was to
play its part in keeping Maude before her congregation. The very first issue
after she had gone carried a long article by Albert Dawson, 'A. Maude
Royden and her work'. Her letters from abroad appeared every month and
many of her sermons were reprinted.

Maude travelled westwards, starting off with three months' speaking in
the USA, the proceeds of which were to help to pay for the journey on to
New Zealand, Australia, Japan, China, Ceylon and India. She had great
success in America, despite some initial loss of engagements when the
Methodist Women's Home Missionary Society learned that she smoked.
'I . . . was headlined as "The Smoking, Flirting, Tippling Evangelist".' To
confuse matters, her name appeared beneath the picture of a variety artiste
('a charming girl in little more than a string of beads and smoking a
cigarette'). The editor made his apologies.

> I said that if the young lady was hoping to win fame with a photograph of me in a
> cassock I felt that any apology should be addressed to her. For myself, I could not
> but think that if anyone really believed her picture to be a photograph of me, I
> should have a record audience.[14]

And the tour went on, despite the fact that in Topeka, Kansas, prayer
meetings were held to prevent her coming.

Apart from this it was the usual story: packed halls and churches. (Detroit
was not saved by the Women Missionaries for a group of ministers,
including Reinold Niebuhr took a large hall for Maude). At Ann Arbor she
preached to 5,000 students at a service which they had organised themselves
and afterwards some of them came to see her and they discussed co-edu-
cation. She preached in the chapel at Stanford University and in an episcopal church in Sacramento and in Christ Church Cathedral, St Louis. 'Miss
Royden looks splendid,' wrote Daisy Dobson reassuringly to Eccleston
Square.

> Speaking almost every day and sometimes twice a day [she] has only had one bad
> headache, in spite of which she was able to deliver a striking lecture to . . . 3,000
> people. This is really wonderful – for it is no light strain to be constantly
> travelling and speaking making fresh 'contacts' – to use an overworked American
> word!

There was nothing Maude enjoyed more than fresh contacts and she was in
her element now: sorry to miss having tea with President Coolidge,
learning the valeta from Henry Ford, dining with the Bishop of California,

[14]Typescript, 'American Adventure', Oberholzer Papers.

watching the 'shooting' in the Hollywood studio of Cecil B. De Mille 'who offered to let us see a great building burnt down but alas! we could not stay.'[15]

They arrived in New Zealand on 7 May, sailing in to a great reception by the Prime Minister, the Bishop of Wellington and the Mayor; then proceeding to the South Island and another round of civic receptions. 'The news that for the first time a woman was to preach in New Zealand's finest Anglican cathedral [at Christchurch] had been . . . spread by notices . . . articles and . . . broadcasting,' wrote Miss Chave Collisson to the Guildhouse.[16] As secretary of the British Commonwealth League which had sponsored this part of the tour she was responsible for all arrangements and writes how they suddenly became aware on the night journey from Dunedin to Christchurch that the train was full of parties of women travelling many miles for the great occasion. 'Knowing as I did the weight of domestic work carried by these New Zealand women, I felt that here was tribute indeed.' She describes the densely packed cathedral, from which so many were turned away, and Maude hidden by the vast crowd with people murmuring 'Where is she?' until the moment when she stepped into the pulpit and 'there fell a hush so intense, almost it seemed as if the Spirit of the Lord were descended upon us'. After the sermon 'I struggled to the vestry to try and bring Miss Royden through the crowd. I saw two lame women in chairs and . . . Miss Royden came out and spoke to them.' After that, 'The huge and silently respectful crowd watched her pass through a lane formed by a mass of humanity to a waiting car.'

Later, Miss Collisson paused to reflect on an occasion which had deeply moved her.

> What impressed me was the absolute sense of fitness and of solemn decorum which attended the entry of a woman into the pulpit. . . . It seemed . . . as if that small figure in black belonged in that pulpit in a way indescribably fitting. There was a complete restfulness about the detachment of the preacher. . . . The scene was dramatic, but with the drama of a really great event.

The *Sydney Daily Guardian* was impressed, but differently, when Maude reached Australia a few weeks later. Those who had fixed ideas about suffragettes were in for a surprise, it told its readers.

> After half-an-hour's conversation with this famous woman, who in her tempestuous time has annoyed constables, clergymen, the . . . anti-Cigarette and Gum-chewing League of Dumgufflepottsberg (Mass.) and even the good Bishop of London, one ascertained that she has never . . . struck a policeman with a length of railway iron or put a bomb in a Prime Minister's pocket. Her hair is not cut in an Eton crop, she does not wear baggy tweeds . . . or talk in a booming voice.[17]

[15]*Guildhouse Monthly* (April 1928) 123; (June 1928) 186.
[16]ibid. (Sept. 1928) 265.
[17]Quoted *Guildhouse Monthly* (Sept. 1928) 266.

In fact, 'You could talk with her for some time without realising that she was the really famous Maude Royden.' She had indeed 'that accommodating charm which few carry off so well as the English,' but did not talk in 'a soft boudoir manner'. Rather, with the ferocious conviction 'that made one conscious immediately of a highly complex and indomitable personality'.

Apart, perhaps, from the visit to Brisbane, where the reception was rather cool (owing, in Miss Collisson's view, to the Roman Catholic influence there) the Australian response was overwhelming; and signalled by amazing razzmatazz. She might have been a film star. On the station in Melbourne,

> crowds of people showered flowers upon me and a crowd of photographers photographed me, ordering me to smile, to talk, to walk forward, to walk backwards (these were cinema photographers) and as I went to my car they galloped beside me still turning the handles of their detestable machines.[18]

Thus 'her people' in Eccleston Square followed Maude's progress in monthly letters which were vivid, amusing and full of incident: shared the alarm of their beloved leader in a tiny aeroplane caught in a sandstorm; the glory of her preaching in Adelaide Cathedral (the first woman ever to do so) the novelty of her answering by radio questions telephoned in from the bush. And at length, in spirit, took ship from Australia and arrived with her in Japan.

Maude did very little speaking here, though she preached in the Anglican church in Tokyo. In China, by contrast, where she arrived as the Kuomintang established itself, she was very conscious of political upheaval and eager to discuss the role of Christians in politics.[19] Still more profound, she felt, were the social changes. 'What has been spread over generations and even centuries with us is taking place in a decade', she said. Thus, in regard to the relations of the sexes, China had everything from old style concubines to young foreign-educated men and women who had sat at the feet of the Bertrand Russells. She talked to Chinese men and to Chinese women about Christian marriage and arranged marriage, about birth control and sex education and the status of husband and wife in the home. The League of Nations vied with sex in attracting large audiences and floods of questions. She had to speak through interpreters, of course, but these were among her best meetings in China.

In India she had no public meetings. Her aim was to call on Mahatma Gandhi, then at Wardha in the Central Provinces. She had met Gandhi before, in Poplar. Now it was a little like meeting a saint. For had not he given proof to the world of that great truth she had herself proclaimed from

[18]ibid. (Sept. 1928) 263.
[19]ibid. (Dec. 1928) 359.

her suffrage days to *The Great Adventure*, and in every speech for the League of Nations – the ultimate superiority of moral over physical force? It is clear from Maude's own account that she approached the house with awe. The atmosphere was conducive to that – the moonlit night, the reverent disciples – and it may explain what seems to have been her own unusual diffidence in speaking. 'I would rather the Mahatma had talked to me of God,' she said later,' but my Western shyness overcame me in the presence of so many strangers, and we talked politics instead.'[20] 'Politics' meant the British out of India. And though she thoroughly identified with that there is perhaps just a hint of disappointment in her finding Gandhi disinclined to envisage any special role for the British in the future development of his country. Critic of her own as she often was, Maude regarded the transformation of colonies into self-governing Dominions as one of Britain's gifts to the world. But Gandhi said, 'It is time we got rid of this superstition about the political genius of the British. We are not at all convinced that it has produced anything of value.' 'I persisted,' writes Maude, 'explaining that I did not claim it was the greatest gift of all . . . and that we *ought* to be able to help each other internationally.' 'That is true,' said Gandhi, 'but not by force. . . . Even if you had *all* the political genius and we had *none*, yet yours would be no more to us if you force it on us. . . . You are too arrogant.' She asked him then, 'You think our arrogance poisons all our gifts?' And he said, 'Yes.'

In January 1929 some 500 of her Guildhouse people plus various reporters greeted Maude as she arrived back at Victoria Station. The *Daily News* described her bouquet and the excitement of her cairn terrier, while the *Observer* reported her views on the claims of Anglo-American friendship and the need to convince Australians that the dole was not encouraging pauperism. 'Asked what the chief effect of her tour would be on her future work at Eccleston Square Miss Royden said, "It is too early yet to say: I shall first have to talk things over with the people there."'[21]

The people there felt some satisfaction in contemplating their stewardship. 'All our regular work has been maintained; all our activities have been in full operation . . . our finances are in a healthy condition.' Now it was possible to admit the anxiety they had felt when Maude went away. 'Some of us could not but view with apprehension the prospect of carrying on the work of the Guild for twelve months without Miss Royden.'[22] Though they had always felt that she was with them in spirit.

The Fellowship opened its arms to her again at a service of thanksgiving and welcome in February. Dearmer had written a welcome song which was set to music by Martin Shaw and many hearts were overflowing. As she

[20]'Interview with Gandhi 14.12.28, 8p.m.' Handwritten memo. Fawcett 219.
[21]*Observer* (13 Jan. 1929).
[22]*Guildhouse Monthly* (Jan. 1929) 3.

had already hinted to the press, Maude had new ideas to discuss and at the quarterly meeting in March she laid before the Guild several proposals to extend its work on the international side. First, would they sanction her taking leave in a few years' time to go abroad again? Would they be willing to sponsor travel, where appropriate, by other Guild people? And would they help people from abroad to come to England? To every question the answer was, yes. If there were those whose spirits sank at her talk of going away again, it is not reflected in the loyal comment 'Miss Royden cannot help making big demands and the Guild cannot help doing its best to respond worthily'.[23]

Maude had returned to England at a time when the decennial Lambeth Conference (due in the summer of 1930) offered a fresh chance to press the claims of women. The League of the Church Militant had left the field, affirming that as a political body, it was not best placed to influence a non-political Church, and Maude became president of its successor, the Society for the Ministry of Women. This was an interdenominational group, with Raven its best-known Anglican member and Constance Coltman and the Rev. Herbert Gray among the Nonconformists. More than half its members in fact were Anglican and the Society sent a memorandum, 'Women and the Priesthood', to the Archbishop for consideration when the Conference met.

An Anglican Group made a similar submission – with an appendix on 'Frustrated Vocation' (to which Maude contributed) compiled from the letters of women who had felt a call to the priesthood. These were presented anonymously. 'When a woman feels the call, to whom shall she turn?' the editors ask. It seems likely that some had turned to no one till they wrote these letters. They are very varied. Among one writer's most vivid experiences is 'the ardent and overpowering longing, when preparing the altar for Celebrations, to be a man, just to be able to celebrate the Divine Mysteries'. A clergyman's wife, who seems to have found 'a life-work otherwise than in the priesthood' still feels strongly impelled towards it. Another woman tells how she had to contend with a terrible sense of bitterness until she decided that, wherever she worshipped, she would 'make an Act of Faith that one day a woman priest would stand and minister at the particular altar'. A young Cambridge graduate who had wanted to be a priest 'ever since I can remember' was finding it hard to make herself want any other career. An older woman wrote, 'My own strength is on the wane, but I would gladly seek ordination tomorrow, were it possible.'[24]

The style and allusions of the passage Maude wrote leave no doubt as to its authorship. 'So far as I know there are not many women who feel the

[23]ibid. (April 1929) 109.
[24]"Women and Priesthood', 46–55. See note 7 above.

vocation to the priesthood, and those who do, and who come to me for advice, invariably insist on their desire being kept as a very sacred secret.' It is hard for a woman to admit that she feels "called". There is no authority to test her vocation. Everything hangs on personal judgement and 'the sense of being presumptuous is very difficult to overcome'. In her own case, for many years

> the . . . apparently final impossibility of a woman taking any part at all in the ministry of the Church made it really impossible for such a sense of vocation to arise. I think this inhibition is not sufficiently seriously considered, or its completeness realised, when people speak of the lack of desire among women themselves to be ordained.

Even after becoming a preacher, 'it was some time before I realised how near the office of the priest lay to that of the preacher, and how artificial it must often seem that they should be divided.' She went on to describe the problems encountered by 'a little society' [the Little Company of Christ] over a priest for retreats; ending, 'I fear also to seem very presumptous; but I must sum all up by saying that the relation between myself and these others seems to me to be increasingly that of priest and flock.'[25]

The absence of Maude's name among the sixty signatories of the Anglican submission to the Lambeth Conference would seem extraordinary but for the fact that she was very ill in 1930.The year had actually begun with a fanfare: she was made a Companion of Honour. 'CH! CH! CH!' wrote Hudson, 'nothing in my life, save One thing, will ever have given me one-half the joy.' Letters and telegrams pursued her to Cornwall, where she had gone for a few days' rest. 'I should like to add DBE and Oxford MA and one or two other little things of that kind – but then I shouldn't be satisfied!' wrote Effie. Lloyd George wired his congratulations. 'Glory hallelujah much love,' wired Daisy. 'My dear Missus, What a surprise,' wrote Ethel Lamacroft, Maude's housekeeper. She said she thought she had offended Evelyn by saying when she heard the news, 'Poor little Missus!' 'I was thinking of all the fuss there would be and all the Letters you would get. It's very exciting.' 'Good for Ramsy McDonald and the Labour Government!' wrote another humble supporter. 'Vive Ramsay!' said a French one. 'The snob in me did faintly hanker after a title for you,' wrote Maude's friend, Dr Sybil Pratt, 'but as Evelyn says, it doesn't seem quite suitable for a parson.' Constance Coltman, the Congregational minister, rejoiced that not only Maude herself but 'that for which we stand' should receive recognition. Another friend wrote,

> What it makes one long for is that you should be recognised and ordained by the Church as well as the State, though I rather doubt if that will ever be. But I am sure

[25]ibid. 50–52.

the Ordination of Women will come *some time* – and then the authorities will look back and wonder how they could have been so blind![26]

In fact, Maude was almost at the point of not caring. A few weeks later, at the end of January, she suffered a serious nervous collapse. In the next issue of the *Guildhouse Monthly* members read that she had seen two specialists, Lady Barrett and Lord Moynihan; and while neither found anything organically wrong both recommended prolonged rest. 'For the present, it is particularly asked that friends will refrain from writing to Miss Royden. It is hard to refrain, but we must – for her sake.'[27] 'Maude–' wrote Dick Sheppard, 'I can't bear your being ill and long for you to be well quite dreadfully.

For God's sake
For God's sake } don't answer[28]
For God's sake

The work of the Guildhouse was disrupted again. She had to be away for another year. 'A year is a long time, but we rejoice in the comforting assurances of the specialists' reports, and we must all do our best to justify the trust that Miss Royden puts in us as Guild members.' The household in Rosslyn Hill was also disrupted. Helen, who was twelve, took this philosophically, as one of the enormous number of things over which she had no control, like the world tour, and Freddie's departure. Freddie had never been a permanency and at the age of eight or nine he was fostered by another family. Maude did not lose touch with him, however, and in later life he remembered visits and the pleasure of discussion with her.[29]

In Helen's view, there was too much discussion in the household at Rosslyn Hill.[30] It is true that she was often alone. Whenever the adults were out at meetings the house was empty between her nursery and Ethel in the basement far below. Then it was quiet. (One of Evelyn's sisters, who had probably not come for discussion, many years later recalled her glimpse of 'the cheerful child . . . by herself in the garden . . . practising on extremely short stilts').[31] But when everyone was in, it was a restless place: Daisy clacketing away on her typewriter; bells from the study ('once for Daisy, twice for Aunt and three times for Ethel, I think'); and always people coming and going. If they were famous, like Dr Schweitzer or Ramsay Macdonald, it meant more discussion, certainly carried on through lunch.

---

[26]Hudson's comment, TFC 76; other comments, folder of congratulations on CH, Fawcett 221.

[27]*Guildhouse Monthly* (Feb. 1930) 27.

[28]Card (n.d.) in Fawcett 220.

[29]Father Martin Wolfe (Freddie) Oberholzer interview.

[30]Unless otherwise stated the impressions that follow are based on the author's conversations with Helen Blackstone, 1984–7.

[31]Lilian Gunter to Helen (5 Aug. 1956) Fawcett 223.

Plate 9 Evelyn Gunter in middle age. *Reproduced by permission of Mrs Helen Blackstone.*

For in deference to Maude's fancy for a democratic household they all ate together in the huge kitchen, and even Ethel was supposed to pay attention, though her mind was on dishing up the next course. Helen learned to let it all wash over her, except on Mondays. On Monday nights the house was invaded by the Little Company – 'a great *surge* of people, moving chairs about'. Almost every room – including her nursery – was requisitioned for their devotions and ('the crowning thing') down in the kitchen, which was her other place of favourite resort – Ethel was kept busy making cocoa for them. One or two later recalled the occasion when Helen, driven beyond endurance, shouted 'This house is full of praying women!'[32] She herself recalls the contrasting quietness of Effie's household in Golders Green. Effie sat in the darkest corner, smiling sweetly and stroking her cats. 'She didn't come and go.' And as for discussion, she very rarely opened her mouth.

Helen's feeling about praying women did not check her devotion to Aunt. Evelyn was a member of the Little Company and believed very much in prayer. At the Guildhouse it was she who organised the Thursday services of intercession. This did not count against her. In Helen's young judgement, Evelyn was a far better Christian than Maude. Not soft, she says; you never felt that. She had her own core of determination vis-à-vis Maude (and Helen, too) but she was a person who would never *confront*. Self-effacing, kind, sweet-tempered, she was, her protégée recalls with love, 'the only one who'd ever turn the other cheek'. There was scope for that in Rosslyn Hill where the household that revolved round Maude threw up constant jealousies and tensions. They were all overworked: Evelyn, who ran it, clinging still to old fashioned standards ('a colonel's daughter'); Ethel called upon to feed the five thousand – if it happened to be that sort of day; Daisy typing against the clock. 'It was a funny sort of set-up altogether'. And one in which she learnt more of Christianity from Aunt than from anyone, Helen insists. She was not clever and did not learn it from that impatience with the un–clever of which she always felt conscious in Maude. 'We never hit it off. She had so much ability and I had so very little.'

Naturally Maude thought it was every child's due to be regarded as an individual. But it is true that even in children intellect and originality (such as had delighted her in Ralph) always exercised a strong attraction. That, and responsiveness to what she valued. This did not mean that she required conformity. If Helen grew up among praying women she was never forced into that mould. Maude was not a bigot. But she looked for response. It was second nature, a reflex almost, and in general, part of her appeal: that she could not speak to another human being – from the pulpit, at the breakfast table, or from the platform of the Albert Hall – without trying to build a bridge between them. What if it turned out that no bridge could be built?

[32]Florence Hill to author.

That had always been difficult for her. In her settlement days she had felt cast down when she imagined that the girls did not like her. One of the unbearable things in the war had been the sense of separation from people. To feel a sense of separation from Helen did not bring out the best in Maude. 'Perhaps I shouldn't have adopted a child,' she once said, 'galloping round the world as I do.'[33] Yet it may even have crossed her mind that to Helen her galloping hardly mattered. If it had been Aunt who had made a world tour. . . .

In 1930, when Maude was ill, the difference to Helen, who was now a boarder, was that she came back from school to Torquay, where they were for a time, instead of Rosslyn Hill. Maude picked up again gradually. But that summer brought disappointment. The Lambeth Conference squashed any hope of advance over the ministry of women. 'The times in which we live are new', it was admitted, but the bishops did not feel this called for a departure from the universal custom of the Catholic Church. 'We cannot encourage in any way those who press for the Priesthood of Women.'[34] Of course, the usual bouquets were presented. 'The Church has no more valuable asset than its women workers . . . at home and abroad.' But the means whereby the bishops proposed to make good the current shortage of priests was, in fact, to ordain as 'auxiliary clergy' men engaged in secular professions. To Maude it was the last straw; 'a backward step'. Well enough to write to the *Guildhouse Monthly*, she pointed out that men would be ordained without vocation, 'while women who believe that they have a vocation are not even to have their claim considered, nor – if already ordained deaconesses – to be allowed to administer the chalice'. The *Guildhouse Monthly* appealed for members to join the Society for the Ministry of Women. 'To those of us . . . who have been blessed by the gracious and truly priestly ministry of Miss Royden, the report of the Bishops seems . . . unreal. Miss Royden is an unanswerable fact.'[35]

Maude appeared in the pulpit again in January 1931. They had struggled valiantly in Eccleston Square but the effect of her long absence was obvious in the balance sheets. 'The funds in hand are getting painfully low', the treasurer reported. Whatever they did, attendance dropped when Maude was not there (collections taken in 1930 were a third of what they had been in 1927) and incidental expenses rose – mainly through the need to pay visiting preachers. 'I have been away from the Guildhouse more or less continuously for three years,' she admitted; for although nominally back at work after the end of her world tour, she had been off sick at various times, even before she broke down completely. 'I am now back at work and we all

[33] ibid.
[34] *Lambeth Conference 1930: Encyclical Letter from the Bishops with the Resolutions and Reports*

[35] *Guildhouse Monthly* (Sept. 1930) 207, 208.

believe that the Guildhouse will gather itself together again.' Reluctantly, she accepted the need to appeal for help with running expenses, a thing she had never considered before, having always felt that 'financial soundness was a proof of the reality of the work being done'.[36]

By that summer the balancing of books obsessed not only the Guildhouse but the nation. The terrifying impact of the Depression was felt in Europe with collapsing banks and in Britain with a run on the pound and the formation of a National government. Panic and recrimination prevailed on the domestic and the international scene. Maude's sermons struck an apocalyptic note but her remedy was what it had always been: love instead of hate; a transformation, beginning always with the individual.

Gandhi came to London for the Round Table conference and spoke at the Guildhouse afterwards. Police were needed to control the crowds. At the end, he chanted prayers with his followers, '7 o'clock being his hour of prayer'. Then, at his wish, the meeting closed with the singing of his favourite Christian hymn (which, it chanced, was 'Lead, Kindly Light' – a specimen of weak Victorian psalmody which Martin Shaw was obliged to put up with). 'I was deeply impressed with Gandhi last night,' Maude wrote to Sheppard on 24 September. 'There was a huge crowd. All the police came . . . and listened to "Voluntary Poverty and Non-Resistance".'[37] The context was changing rapidly, though. The very day before Gandhi spoke, China had appealed to the League of Nations against Japanese aggression in Manchuria and Maude's note to Sheppard refers obliquely to possible action by the two of them and the Presbyterian, Herbert Gray. A few months later, at the end of January – amid the deepening Manchurian crisis – she planned the meeting from which emerged their dramatic proposal for a Peace Army.

'The idea of preventing war by interposing, unarmed, between the combatants has been in the minds of many people for many years,' she told the Guildhouse later. 'I remember, after the Great War broke out and we began to look over past records, we found many traces of this idea.'[38] In *The Great Adventure* she had spoken of peace lovers flinging themselves in front of troop trains. There had not been many troop trains in the past ten years but the whole concept of passive resistance had been transformed through the influence of Gandhi and Maude was evidently thinking about it before the Manchurian war broke out. In March 1930 an Australian wrote to her, 'thrilled by your idea . . . of enlisting a Peace Army of people willing to die for Peace'.

It has been so difficult to answer the question one is always asked here. What

---

[36]ibid. (July–August 1931) 166.
[37]Gandhi, 'Voluntary Poverty,' *Guildhouse Monthly* (Oct. 1931) 208–15.; Maude to Sheppard (24 Sept. 1931) SP.
[38]'The Peace Army', Guildhouse sermon (28 Feb. 1932).

would you do if a Japanese Army came to take Australia – just let them overrun it? . . . Are you thinking of having a recruiting centre at the Guildhouse? If so, will you enter my name?[39]

When the Japanese seized Mukden in 1931 Maude did begin to enrol at the Guildhouse, though not yet for positive intervention. Just before Christmas she conducted a service of consecration 'for a small band of people . . . who had formed a group to study constructive ways of peacemaking and "to seek to establish the way of Christ as the basis of civilisation".'[40] But the Peace Army took public shape following discussion with Sheppard and Gray in February 1932. The three of them retired to a cottage in Kent which belonged to Hudson, and a day or two later made known to the press, 'we can no longer believe that the cold wisdom of this world is equal to the task of maintaining peace'. They had therefore offered themselves to the League as volunteers for a Peace Army which should stand unarmed between the combatants.

The plan's 'embarrassing ingenuousness' attracts comment from a modern historian. To think war might be checked in the streets of Shanghai because soldiers would not shoot the defenceless (or that their shooting would raise such an outcry as in itself might stop the war) ranks as 'the most sanguine pacifist initiative of the entire twentieth century'.[41] Certainly such faith in the public conscience predates (just) the emergence of Hitler, but even Maude's loyal secretary Daisy Dobson dismissed it as nonsense, looking back. At the time it was not entirely dismissed. 'It would be very far from my thought "to dismiss such an offer as fantastic"', wrote Sir Eric Drummond, the League's secretary general (and whether or not he meant it, this courteous assurance was much quoted by the volunteers).[42] It is true that the pacifist *Reconciliation* called it 'impractical and slightly theatrical'. The Friends' Peace Committee also thought it impractical (though nonresistance had been discussed among the Quakers in 1914). But the *Manchester Guardian* thought it 'well worth considering'. 'Is it really . . . more fantastic than the actual fact of war? . . . That a pacifist army, once . . . in position, would . . . embarrass the . . . belligerents is not to be denied.'[43]

The *News Chronicle* made a front page splash of this STARTLING STOP-THE-WAR OFFER, with photographs of the three volunteers and, in the next issue, an interview with Maude, who said that the early response was

[39]Letter from a woman at Ulverston Infant Welfare Centre, Melbourne, (4 March 1930) Fawcett 222, 5/2.
[40]*Guildhouse Monthly* (Dec. 1932) 287 (re. Christmas 1931).
[41]Martin Ceadel, *Pacifism in Britain 1914–1945* (1980), 93, 154.
[42]Eric Drummond to Maude (1 March 1932) qouted in pamphlet *The Peace Army: Being a letter to the Secretary-General of the League of Nations and his reply.*
[43]*Manchester Guardian* (27 Feb. 1932).

encouraging. The *Chronicle* reported that the first to enrol for the 'human wall of pacifists' had been an ex-Guardsman. Three days after enrolment began she reported 320 recruits, 'quite a number of ex-soldiers' and 'parents whose sons were killed in the war'. (She was determined the young should not go, and rejected Sybil Thorndike's daughters, who applied secretly to enrol, on the grounds that they were under twenty-one.)[44] Despite the obvious practical difficulties, the *Chronicle* was sure that 'the moral effect of mobilising a considerable number of volunteers ready to sacrifice their lives for peace would be of great value.' There were signs that Japanese policy was changing under the pressure of world opinion 'and this . . . would be an added weight in the scale'.[45]

It is not difficult to understand the immense appeal of the idea to Maude, whose loathing of violence from her suffrage days had always been joined to a desire for action. They had always known, she said, that it would be a race between the makers of peace and the makers of war.

> None of us perhaps realised how close a race it would be; how neck and neck indeed those forces were; so that, at the very moment when the Disarmament Conference at last meets in Geneva, war is actually in progress between two members of the League.

This is the heart of things: the future of the League. 'It is necessary, in my opinion that we should save the League of Nations for it is the only really constructive thing that exists in the world for organising peace.' It must not fail. But how could it succeed? In a sermon at the Guildhouse she outlined the paradox: the Covenant provided for the use of sanctions, *the last of which could be war*, she explained. Because of that, nobody dare use sanctions. 'This is the real difficulty of the situation.' But if, instead of calling for the soldiers of war the League should call for the soldiers of peace . . . .[46]

The soldiers of peace were never called for. And in fact no action by the government was needed to forestall their 'Christians-to-the-lions' behaviour since the foreign secretary was able to announce within a few weeks that hostilities had ceased, and so 'the conditions which inspired the gallant and humanitarian offer of Miss Royden and her co-signatories will not again arise'. The soldiers of peace did not just melt away, though. In May Maude was planning a meeting at the docks to protest against the sending of arms to Japan. In June she was involved in a protest at Hendon against the use of aircraft in warfare. The following year she was one of those shocked by the British defence of 'police bombing'. 'You know . . . how deep has always been my admiration for your single-minded courage,' she told the prime minister.

---

[44]Dame Sybil Thorndike, interviewed 23 June 1966 by Emil Oberholzer.
[45]*News Chronicle* (26, 27, 29 Feb. 1932).
[46]*The Peace Army*

It is only because I count on your knowing this that I dare now to write to you and *implore* you rather to resign from the Government than allow our country to withstand alone – in a dreadful isolation – the wish of the rest of the world to have nothing to do with aerial warfare.

Nor could she follow the government line on the need to conciliate Japan. 'I hope you are not forgetting what I have said to you more than once,' Macdonald had reproved her earlier that year.

It is no good closing our eyes to the fact that the Chinese Government is very largely responsible for the present situation . . . and I think it was a great misfortune that resolutions, passed here by people moved by the most sincere and praiseworthy motives, encouraged it in its attitudes.[47]

She tried unsuccessfully to gain his assurance that the Peace Army would be used in any future emergency.

One must suppose that Hudson, at least, was relieved that Maude would not be courting death in Shanghai. He was getting old. He was seventy-three now and always up and down in health and spirits. 'Ever since I met you in 1928 I have been fighting deadly diseases,' he confided to Albert Schweitzer. He had a bad heart and had terrified Maude by writing to her, when she was in Australia to say that he had been advised to stop work within a year, and might then expect to last for another three. 'Fortunately, I had already had a cable telling me to ignore the letter as Hudson was feeling very well and didn't believe a word the specialist said!'[48] In 1933, though, she was worried enough to beg his old colleague, Sir Michael Sadler, to write and rouse him from a bad depression. Sadler wrote at once – a long nostalgic letter, beginning, 'The announcement of the Summer Meeting makes me think of old days and wish that you lived in Oxford so that we could . . . talk about the tremendous things that are happening East and West and in the middle.' 'I hope,' he said, 'you will not forget how much strength you have given to others . . . You have been one of the great leaders of my generation and we thank Heaven for you.' As for the present, 'It is like living through the French Revolution.'[49]

Hudson gave up work in 1935 and Sadler wrote another consoling letter, full of praise for what he had done, 'by counsel, inspiration and warning, by words from the pulpit and in confidential talk'; hoping he might bring

---

[47]Maude to Ramsay Macdonald (7 June 1933); Macdonald to Maude (20 Feb. 1933) PRO 30/ 69/1443/2, 1189–90, 1187–8. I am grateful to Brian Harrison for drawing my attention to these letters.
[48]Hudson Shaw to Albert Schweitzer (30 Nov. 1934) Schweitzer Archives; TFC 91.
[49]Sir Michael Sadler to Hudson Shaw (10 July 1933) Fawcett 222.

himself to write a book 'which may guide . . . and help us in these tor-
menting times'. Shaw's influence, he said, would be like radium 'animating
for years and years the individuals and institutions which have come within
the range of your love and compassion'. A student from the old Extension
days – one who still kept his photograph and Sadler's in her gallery of
'guardian saints' – wrote to cheer him with recollections of 'the first (Yes,
the very first) Summer Meeting'. 'No one can express the pleasure that
wonderful gathering gave and no one can estimate the influence for good
that it began for hundreds of us.' So he must never doubt the value of his
labours. 'Mine is only a tiny bit of chance testimony to the inspiration of
your teaching. You may be quite sure I am only one of thousands
who . . . would express their gratitude if they knew how.'[50]

When she came to write *A Threefold Cord* Maude dwelt lovingly on such
tributes and on Hudson's own punchy, affectionate letter of farewell to the
people of St Botolph's. Characteristically, he also set forth in the same issue
of the parish magazine what amounted to a modernist credo ('What the
Rector of this Church has tried to teach, 1912–1935') a kind of last testament
of 'Richard Meynell'.[51] The crisis of retirement itself, says Maude, he came
to terms with surprisingly well, helped by the fact that he and Effie moved
to live in exquisite surroundings – the fourteenth-century cottage in Kent
that Maude had told Sheppard was 'a little paradise' when she was arrang-
ing the Peace Army retreat. By a miracle, the house next door to this
paradise became available and Maude and Evelyn moved from Hampstead.

Effie adapted well to the change, 'though at first she had the strange
recurrences of terror which it was so tragic to watch' and they sometimes
had to have a mental nurse. At her best, new acquaintants found her happy
with her cats, 'a good silent companion', but rarely to be tempted out of
doors.[52] Hudson, for all the spells of depression 'when it seemed to him that
he had achieved nothing' still retained enormous vitality. Though there was
small chance of the book Sadler hoped for (in his long and hectic life
Hudson had seldom even written a letter) he still read widely, still loved
controversy, still took the guts out of everything new in the way of biblical
criticism; and added a new obsession – his garden, which overhung the
open Kentish Weald. 'It was the fact that he would plan . . . his flower-bed
for the next five or ten years,' said Maude, 'that cheered me when he had, a
moment ago, threatened me with his immediate demise if I persisted in
leaving home for a few days.'[53]

She often left home for longer than that. Though after her year of

---

[50]ibid. (21 May 1935); Katherine Green to Hudson Shaw (31 May 1935) Fawcett 222.
[51]Along with rejection of the traditionalists' Hell in the style Mrs Humphry Ward had once
noted, he marked his support now for The New Prayer Book, The League of Nations, The
Rights of Animals and The Ministry of Women. Fawcett 222.
[52]TFC 82; Lady Daukes and others, interviewed 25 April 1967 by Emil Oberholzer.
[53]TFC 92.

nervous breakdown she had given up preaching crusades, her work was 'in full tide' as he approached retirement. And there were a host of other claims on her. To throw herself into other interests 'and even other human relationships' had seemed natural and sensible, says Maude. In fact she was almost smothered in relationships – the one-to-one-ness of each exposed in the opening words of a thousand letters: Maude dear, Darling Maude, My darling AM, Dearest and Onely Maude (Martin Shaw), Darling David (Dr Sybil Pratt), Very dear one, Maude – dear Friend, Beloved Maude, My Darling Minnie, Dearest Bess. And then, the strangers: 'Dear Madam, I thought perhaps you would not reply . . . . ' 'Miss Maude Royden – I often hear you say that people . . . at the Guildhhouse write to you, but I am not clear whether you answer personally . . . . If you do answer . . . your task must be endless . . . yet you have never asked us not to write.'[54] She always answered, though the briefest response – multiplied – was potentially a mountain. But when she says 'I sometimes gave Hudson grounds for feeling that I gave to others what he felt belonged to him,' she is thinking of closer relationships.[55]

He may well have grudged her involvement with Dick Sheppard and Herbert Gray. Hudson himself was a Sheppard fan. Who was not, one way or another?

St John Ervine called him a good man. Max Beerbohm called him an enchanter. Shaw called him an actor: 'What an actor!' His parishioners said, 'He knew Jesus, preached Jesus, and made him real. He loved us – and we loved him.'

'He called himself a failure,' the list runs on, 'but it was in his nature to dramatise.'[56]

To those who loved Sheppard, and especially perhaps to those like Maude who saw in him the brightest, most Christlike hope for a Church of which in many ways they were despairing, his terrible struggle for health was agony. He was asthmatic. 'Please *please* take care of yourself,' she had written, back in 1917, 'I suppose there is no really indispensable person, but to the merely human eye you seem very indispensable and very precious.' 'To know that you bring joy wherever you go . . . must make up – partly – for all you suffer,' she wrote later. 'Please let it, if you can.' And another time, 'I do so wish I could give you all the strength I have. What lots of us would quite willingly die to give you health!'[57] Always conscious of the strain on him of 'all our terrible clamorous demands', she often wrote rather than pressing to see him but could not help exploding with pleasure when

[54]Doris Child to Maude (n.d.) Fawcett 222, 5/2. She explains that she has lost all interest in life. 'I'm quite sure I'm not a Christian although I've been baptised and confirmed. You are the only person I can even bear to hear talk about God because you do it so naturally.'
[55]TFC 78.
[56]Scott, *Dick Sheppard* 13.
[57]Maude to Dick Sheppard (12 June 1917); (5 May 1925); (27 March 1928) SP.

he offered to preach at the Guildhouse during her absence in 1928.

Oh Dick!!

(I have to take a large sheet to express my joy)

Let no one say that virtue goes always without reward.

> The Guildhouse Committee asked for you . . . and I flatly refused to ask you. How *could* I trouble you with our affairs when you are going through hell with your own? I daren't even write and tell you I was sorry. And now you have offerred to come.

'The C of E won't let you go,' she says in the same letter, 'whatever you do. Not quite such fools as that. But if you should ever want a job (!) please come and take the Guildhouse and I will be your charwoman or whatever you think a woman ought to be! I would rather be a door-keeper in the house of Dick Sheppard than dwell in Lambeth Palace.'[58]

After his sudden death in 1937 his friend and secretary wrote to Maude, 'There are very few friends whom Dick loved as he loved you. I shouldn't think there are ten people in the world he'd always be glad to see at any time.' Another letter speaks of her power to comfort. 'He never got any *comfort* from any single other person, though you probably won't believe it.'[59] In February 1933, after hearing what was almost her first broadcast sermon, he himself had written

> I do thank you for last night. It was the perfect Christian sermon as well as a perfect work of art. I was lying in bed panting and feeling so hopeless when you began to speak. Later I slept quite well and now I've got my courage back. Why Why Why can't others put Christianity across like that?

Maude's few surviving letters from Herbert Gray strike an entirely different note. Gray was a Presbyterian minister who had worked for the SCM. Like Sheppard he had been a good friend to the Guildhouse; he was also a leading member of the Society for the Ministry of Women. But the other area he shared with Maude (apart from pacifism) was concern for a saner, more open attitude to sex. His best-known book, *Men, Women and God: A Discussion of Sex Questions from the Christian Point of View* sold hugely when it came out in 1923. Later he founded the Marriage Guidance Council. The style of his letters to Maude suggests that he knew the story of herself and Hudson.

> 'That's a wonderful portrait . . . It tells me such a lot. [She had just been painted by Philip de Laszlo in his characteristic romantic style]. It tells me that you have come thro a lot of hard hours, and that you have conquered. It says that thro it all you have *NEVER* gone hard, but remained a tender-hearted great lover. It

[58]Maude to Dick Sheppard (n.d. probably 1927) SP.
[59]Nancy Browne to Maude (24 Jan., 12 Jan. 1938) Fawcett 220.

says that you 'see' . . . . You have the eye of the seer. And you have the courage of a Crusader. How all that is contained in your small, and sometimes frail body is a mystery.

And then, you are in the truest sense beautiful. You once said lately that you were old and plain. But no, my dear, there is a rare kind of beauty in your face. It moves me *VERY* much. Its the beauty that comes by such brave endurance coupled to much loving . . . . Being old and grandfatherly, I would like to pick you up in my arms and hold you very firmly. That would express me. But I am equally ready to sit at your feet, and to kneel to my God in thanksgiving.'[60]

'It isn't horrid to flirt with old men, is it?' she had said to Kathleen in their Oxford days, 'it makes them feel young and gay, poor old dears! I am sure I shall want young men to flirt with me, when I am an old woman!' But at sixty eight, Herbert Gray hardly fitted the bill.

Maude's feeling old and plain may have had something to do with the fact that her lameness got worse as time went on. She was very matter of fact about it; accepting the need to take a high stool for use in the pulpit of the various churches in which she was invited to preach, and accepting the services of Florence Hill, a devoted member of the Guild, to carry it. Florence, more than fifty years later, could not get over the enormous resourcefulness this dependency evoked in her. 'If it was something Maude needed, I could do it!' (Which included everything from learning to drive to working out how Maude and a chair could be got onto the plinth of Nelson's Column to address a meeting, and down again).[61] Because of her lameness, travelling abroad meant she had to have a travelling companion, Maude told Sheppard, and she could not easily afford to pay one. However, together with Marjorie Corbett Ashby she was back in India in 1935 for the All-India Women's Conference. Later that year she told Ursula Roberts, 'I am much lamer now than I used to be'. But this was in a context as far removed from foreign travel as could well be imagined. She had been asked to put her name to a statement from women who aspired to the priesthood and answered, 'Alas, I no longer wish for it. I wish intensely that it may be possible for others, but for me it can never be. There is the physical obstacle now: I am much lamer than I used to be, and doubt if it would be possible for me to celebrate Holy Communion.' More important, she admitted, was the fact that she had grown 'too far away from "orthodoxy" to make public profession of the 39 Articles'. 'I am so very sorry to fail you in this matter.'[62]

It had arisen through the publication of another report on the ministry of

---

[60]Herbert Gray to Maude (n.d., probably 1936) Fawcett 222, 5/2.
[61]Florence Hill to author (10 July 1984).
[62]Maude to Ursula Roberts (18 Dec. 1935) Fawcett. An Anglican priest is required to subscribe to the Articles promulgated in 1562 'for the establishing of consent touching true religion', but from 1865 what Hudson called 'a general assent' has sufficed.

Plate 10 Portrait of Maude Royden in doctoral gown by Philip de Laszlo, 1931.
Reproduced by permission of the Principal and Fellows of Lady Margaret Hall, Oxford.

women, the work this time of an Archbishops' Commission set up following the Lambeth Conference. Anglican members of Maude's Society for the Ministry of Women had the chance to be heard, as did members of the Anglican Group, and both societies were pleased to find that the report rejected the idea that women were disqualified from being priests on eternal theological grounds. Indeed, 'the Commissioners do not deny that a reunited Church may in the future have the power to contradict its past, and to declare that women can be priests.' But this was not followed through. The Society commented sharply on the 'grudging spirit and fumbling logic' which led the Commission to propose no change. It was accepted that the Church's tradition had always been that of a male priesthood,

> and with this tradition we believe that the general mind of the Church is still in accord, It is our conviction that this consensus of tradition and opinion is based on the will of God, and is . . . a sufficient witness to the guidance of the Holy Spirit.[63]

They went on, 'Other practical considerations have also carried great weight with us. We do not believe that the pastoral work of a priest could be satisfactorily combined with the responsibilities of a married woman . . . especially if she should also have . . . children.' The Society already had a subcommittee trying to think its way round this (and Maude had involved herself the previous year with Vera Kenmure, a Congregational minister who was pressed to resign when she had a baby.[64] On the main issue it judged the Commissioners 'timid, vague, vacillating and inconsistent' – with the shining exception of the Dean of St Paul's who had signed the report with the reservation that he did not think women should be barred from the priesthood.

'If we were faced,' the *Church Times* commented, 'by a great body of devoted women who had become ministers *in all but name* . . . the situation would be different.' It was this fallacy which Ursula Roberts and the few others who signed her letter felt they must expose.

> It is clear that Churchwomen, even if they wished to, cannot become ministers in all but name. They cannot first administer the Eucharist, and, after they have shown an aptitude, ask for the Church's authorisation. We must . . . suppose the writer . . . to have had in mind an unofficial and a pastoral ministry. But it is definitely to the priestly functions (along with the pastoral) that some of us believe that God is calling us.

[63]'The Ministry of Women', *Church Times* (6 Dec. 1935). The Commission recommended a deaconess order, to be recognised as a Holy Order and to carry such privileges as a special seat in church and special place in processions but not to be equivalent to the male diaconate.
[64]The Rev. Vera Kenmure became minister of Partick Congregational Church, Glasgow, in 1928. Her subsequent marriage was accepted by the majority of her congregation but the birth of her first child in 1933 aroused such hostility that she left Partick and started a new church in Glasgow.

She added, 'We want to be ministers in name because we want to be ministers in fact.[65]

None of those who signed had Maude's experience of trying to be a minister 'in all but name', and there must have been disappointment that her scruples prevented her from signing. She herself felt bound to explain,

> I have never said these things in public as I don't want to behave like a peevish child who 'won't play', and my desire that (Anglican) orders should be open to women is as strong as ever. Perhaps you will feel that I ought to say it now, as the absence of my signature . . . may be misunderstood?

Ursula Roberts did not press for that and Maude seems grateful for her understanding.

> I do not think that anything now will change my mind, because it is not so much the *mind* that is changed, as the way of life. I have identified myself so much with people who are outside the churches or, if still inside, yet without very live interest. It is, I think, partly a question of being *forced* into another vocation than that which I believed and still believe was mine. One simply can't go on *waiting* for a vocation which does not come, while life goes on, and one must work while it is day.[66]

'I no longer wish to change,' she admits.

> I should feel I had deserted those whom God gave me to serve . . . if I were to become ordained into the ministry of any Church. Can you understand this, I wonder? I would perhaps struggle against it if it were not that I grow old, and also that I find it more and more difficult to accept what the Church of England demands.

She was glad no public recantation seemed called for as such a thing might dishearten others who did not understand that her own desire that women be ordained was as strong as ever.

Two things she does not mention but which helped to drive her 'into another way of life' at this time were the growing difficulty of running the Guildhouse and, as the international scene grew darker, her feeling that the main priority was peace.

The efforts made to pull up the Guildhouse finances after her illness had not succeeded. Subscriptions and collections had gone steadily down. The plain truth was that numbers were falling. In 1934 Maude suggested to Sheppard that, as she had 'now ceased to appeal to more than a very small congregation,' he might care to take charge of the Guildhouse, which could become a centre for peace work – as it was already, in a small way. 'No one can command the ear of the country as you do. And you would . . . at the Guildhouse be absolutely free to say and do anything that you chose.'[67]

[65]Letter, *Church Times* (20 Dec. 1935).
[66]Maude to Ursula Roberts (18 Dec. 1935); (4 Jan. 1936).
[67]Ellis Roberts, *H. R. L. Sheppard* (1942), 245.

He did not take this up. At a Guild meeting in October that year she gave a trenchant account of their problem. 'To go on just as we are is not possible.' And it was not simply a question of funds. 'The raising of money is not the point.' The point was that the Guild should do worthwhile work. If they did that, then the money would come – as it had, she said, in earlier days, when they raised a great deal for outside causes and had very seldom asked for themselves. 'I myself feel that we have chiefly lost in the appeal that we once had for the younger generation.' And when that happened,

an institution . . . may well say that its days are numbered because, however devoted and keen the older members are, as the years pass the old people pass also (including myself) and if the appeal of the Guildhouse is not to all generations it must come to an end.[68]

There followed a very painful debate on reorganisation and measures of economy. But apart from a cutting down of 'Five Quarters' (which, she thought, had suffered from the development of discussion programmes by the BBC) the big changes came in 1936, when Maude at length felt obliged to resign.

My reason is that I find the work of the Guildhouse and the work that I do for Peace outside the Guildhouse too much for my strength. . . . I have to choose; and in the present circumstances of this distracted world I feel that it is the Peace work to which I must give myself.[69]

Her work as minister ended in December; but in fact her last sermon in the well-loved building was preached in June the following year, since, by arrangement with the London County Council, the Guild retained some use until the lease ran out. It was thus in the summer of 1937 that she poured out her feelings to Martin Shaw.

That last Sunday at the Guildhouse was almost more than I could bear without bursting into tears, and I daren't speak to you – more than a few words – because I couldn't behave decently. No one tried to weep down my neck and I couldn't disgrace myself by weeping down yours. But I did want to. Everything that is lovely is lovely for ever, I know, but when the time comes for letting them pass into eternal things, it is hard to bear.

That building, redeemed from chocolate and buff decorations by Percy, and resounding to the last with your music, had become so terribly dear. And you yourself, beloved friend, have made yourself by all you did & were so unexpress-ibly dear, that I am bleeding, now that this part of our lives comes to an end. I know you will not cease to give me the delight of your friendship . . . . And never, in this world or the next, shall I cease to praise God for you & for letting me know you & have the joy of working with you. I know this *is* true & this *is* eternal, & I am not really resenting this present loss but rejoicing in my pos-sessions.

[68]*Guildhouse Monthly* (Nov. 1934) 254.
[69]ibid. (May 1936) 128, letter of April 1936.

Only one must be allowed to weep sometimes.[70]

'I wonder what will become of the people at the Guildhouse now?' asked an American whose pilgrimage to England in 1936 included not only cathedral cities and other historic shrines but Eccleston Square.[71] His impression, having seen a drab congregation brought to life by a remarkable pastor, seems to have been that they would lie down and die. This did not happen. In a modifed form, the Guild carried on for the next twenty years, first at 35 Gordon Square, later on in Great Ormond Street. Members (of whom 350 were still on the books in 1951) kept in touch through the *Guildhouse Fellowship*, a monthly which gave news of activities 'and of our Pastor in her work for international peace'. The group Maude had formed for meditation, the Little Company, also survived.

But the end of the Guildhouse was a terrible blow. Though the dream which she and Dearmer had shared of a guild in every city, reaching to people unreached by the churches, had passed long since, its passing had been scarcely noticed in the warmth of Eccleston Square. 'How I miss the Guildhouse!' people wrote now. 'How much your ministry meant to me!' 'I could not say what the Guildhouse has meant . . .' 'The life of the Guildhouse . . . a wonderful episode . . . .' Maude's personality had made it what it was, one writer concluded. As, at the start, another had predicted, 'Miss Royden will succeed, but her success will be the index of the power of her personality.' She had said once, 'We "saw a holy city, a new London" when we founded the Fellowship.'[72] Now she said, 'There is new work before us!' But her secretary, Daisy, felt no doubt that she experienced a great sense of failure.

There was little time to dwell on it, however. At the end of December 1936 she set out again for the USA at the invitation of American pacifists who launched the Emergency Peace Campaign. Peace work had been prominent in Eccleston Square up to the moment the doors closed. In 1935 the Guildhouse branch of the League of Nations Union had played its part in canvassing for the Peace Ballot. In 1936 it organized a Peace Week, entertaining numbers of foreign guests with community singing, refreshment and debate. More significant debate, of course, was going on then in Geneva itself about the invasion of Abyssinia. And unless the discussion in Eccleston Square ('Are Pacifists Fools?') remained very abstract it must have taken note of the bombs that were falling. For all that, the verdict was a confident no! Absolute pacifists are not fools: a view consistent with Maude's having recommended passive resistance the previous year to the Abyssinians, in the case of invasion.[73]

---

[70]Maude to Martin Shaw (15 June, 1937) Oberholzer copy made by courtesy of Mrs Martin Shaw.
[71]L. O. Bricker, 'Maude Royden' *The Christian Century* (24 June 1936).
[72]'The Future of the Fellowship' *Church Militant* supplement (July 1921).
[73]Ceadel, *Pacifism in Britain* 155.

In 1933, though, she had admitted 'I have really abandoned the attempt to be rigidly logical in my pacifism.' Faith still drew her to the absolute position, as it had in 1915 through the Fellowship of Reconciliation. But she was pragmatic as well: and this drew her to the League and sanctions. Non-military sanctions, at least. After some confusion she made this clear. 'I am afraid we do part company over Sanctions,' wrote Sheppard in May 1936, on the day he launched the Peace Pledge Union. 'I cannot think that you can impose sanctions unless ultimately you are prepared to back war, which our Movement will have nothing to do with.'[74] His movement invited a pledge on a postcard: 'I renounce war and never again will I support or sanction another.' War seemed to receive a tremendous check when a hundred thousand of these cards reached Sheppard. Maude, though, felt herself reduced to despair 'by the inclination of so many good pacifists to concentrate on purely negative matters. I am convinced,' she told Vera Brittain, 'that it is this attitude which makes the PPU have so little appeal to women.'[75]

It was a relief, perhaps, after a year in which high ideals were discredited in Europe to make the trip to the USA for the Emergency Peace Campaign. From across the Atlantic the emergency was seen as the risk of being dragged into another war, and American pacifist initiatives went well with the nation's galloping isolationism. It was eight years since Maude had been in the States and before setting out she sought Vera Brittain for the benefit of her more recent impressions. 'It is chiefly because of your love and understanding of American people that I want your help.'[76] A year later, she was offering Brittain her own impressions of the mood over there. She had found Americans 'tremendously keen' to build a new world in a warless hemisphere, and had warned them not to believe English speakers who tried to persuade them that going to war was right. 'It isn't,' she had affirmed in a broadcast, 'and it can't do anything but harm.'

> I wish you had not come in last time. If you hadn't, probably the war would have been a drawn battle. In any case, no one would have been in a position to *dictate* terms. We should have been saved from the Treaty of Versailles which has destroyed all we thought we were fighting for.[77]

[74]Maude to Dick Sheppard (22 May, 1936) Fawcett 220.
[75]Maude to Vera Brittain (30 March, 1939) Brittain Papers, McMaster University, Canada.
[76]ibid (26 Nov. 1936).
[77]ibid. (6 July 1938).

12

Maude at the End

No one will dare to associate failure with a life that justifies itself.
Maude Royden, memorial tribute to Jane Addams (1935)

Maude's peace-making in 1930 centred on the conflict in Palestine, where the Peace Army involved itelf for the first time in battle conditions: not by standing between Arabs and Jews but by sending two workers for 'practical peace service' (welfare, mainly) to an Arab village. Because of the risk of terrorist attack the authorities refused them permission to live there, but they lived in close touch with the villagers, as well as with the neighbouring kibbutz, Maude went out for a few weeks that spring; and in June, at a London conference organized by the Peace Army, took the line which she elaborated in *The Problem of Palestine* (published that year). Briefly, the problem of a state for the Jews (as opposed to a home for 'spiritual Zionists') seemed to her one for the world to solve, rather than the Arabs, 'for the things that are happening should touch the conscience of the whole world'.[1]

How well-informed she was on 'the things that were happening' under the Nazis is not clear. Presumably she read the kind of account that was published in the WIL news sheet as early as May 1933; and in 1937 when she crossed the Atlantic for the Emergency Peace Campaign she was struck, according to Daisy Dobson, by the great number of Jews on board. Daisy thought it was 'because of the Jews' that Maude went back on her pacifism later. In 1938, though, at the time of Munich, she was one of those who dug in deeper by rushing to join the Peace Pledge Union. Whether or not she felt, subconsciously, a need to shore up failing conviction, her view was that Chamberlain 'had given the world one more chance of a constructive peace and that the Peace Pledge Union was going to back him'. 'It is not too late to establish *Peace with Honour*,' she declared in a leaflet which the PPU published.

Let us ask for Justice for ALL. It is not just that Czecho-Slovakia should make

---

[1] 'Dr Royden's Speech at the Palestine Conference *Guildhouse Fellowship* (Sept. 1938), 'Mrs Pollard's Address at the Tea-Table Conference, July 10, 1938; *Guildhouse Fellowship* (Oct. 1938). One of the workers, Hugh Bingham, was killed (see Ceadel, *Pacifism in Britain* 96).

sacrifices alone. *It is not just to refuse a plebiscite to minorities who believe themselves oppressed.* What are we British to sacrifice for that Peace for which we have asked Czecho-Slovakia to sacrifice so much?[2]

While Maude's was only one of many conversions to the PPU at this time, in her case there was the painful duty, as she felt, to break her long connection with the non-pacifist League of Nations Union (of which Kathleen was soon to become vice chairman). She was resigning, she told Lord Cecil, on the grounds 'that I feel more and more strongly the absolute stupidity of war and have felt bound to join the Peace Pledge Union'.[3] She had scarcely joined, though, when she formed the conclusion that the PPU spent more of its time denouncing the government's air raid precautions than on real peace work. 'Once more that negativism which has been the curse of pacifism descended like a blight upon us.' Within twelve months she resigned her membership, admitting that she ought never to have joined.[4]

'When we make mistakes we will each believe – will we not – that the other acted from the best motives?' she had written to Kathleen in their Oxford days. 'Can you put so much trust in me, dear Kathleen, not only now, but through all the changes and chances of this troublesome world?' The changes and chances on the eve of war certainly made no rift between them. At bottom they had pursued the same end; or as Kathleen said in old age, 'we have stood beside each other in so many of the changing scenes of life'. 'You are my oldest friend,' Maude answered,

> except Evelyn who was at LMH one term earlier . . . . How much we have seen of life together and how deep such an experience of friendship goes! I think we have never been estranged or exasperated by one another, as even very good friends sometimes are, however we may have diverged in our views – and that I think was only on the question of pacifism. Nothing has ever come between us and we have shared a knowledge of each other's griefs as well as joys. 'I thank my God on every remembrance of you.'[5]

But if her friendship with Kathleen did not suffer during the terrible countdown to war, Maude's standing with some of her pacifist friends was affected in 1940 when she went back on pacifism. 'The mere renunciation of war is not enough,' Maude wrote in 1940, of her own changed position. That had been the message of *The Great Adventure*. But, as she explained, 'I believed then that there was nothing in the world worse than war. This is the only point on which I have now changed my mind.'

---

[2]*Peace with Honour* (n.d.) And see Ceadel, *Pacifism in Britain* 277–8.
[3]ibid. 277
[4]Maude Royden, 'I was a pacifist' *Guildhouse Fellowship*, July 1940 (the same article appeared in the *Sunday Dispatch* (16 June 1940); Ceadel, *Pacifism in Britain* 294.
[5]Kathleen to Maude (30 June 1949) Fawcett 222; Maude to Kathleen (4 July 1940) Fawcett KDC/H1/1–8.

I BELIEVE NOW THAT NAZI-ISM IS WORSE THAN WAR, IT IS MORE HIDEOUSLY CRUEL, MORE BLIND, MORE EVIL – AND MORE IMPORTANT. I am still a pacifist in that I believe . . . that spiritual power is the right weapon . . . . The tragedy of pacifism is that it has left the great mass of the unconverted under the impression that the use of spiritual power is simply 'doing nothing'.

'In 20 years of so-called peace, we pacifists have not found an answer to that'. In 20 years we have not shown the world a better way. She recalled the venture of the Peace Army.

I shall always think this failure of pacifists at least to *try* to make an offering for peace which should be more dangerous and more difficult than war was the measure of our failure to realise the emptiness of a mere refusal to fight.[6]

Her change of heart was shocking to some fellow pacifists. Sybil Thorndike (who became a sponsor of the PPU after war had begun) paid generous tribute on Maude's death to her courage in publicly admitting the change, but in an interview a few years later could not hide her own disappointment. Vera Brittain (in pacifist terms 'an undismayed believer right to the end') saw Maude's pacifism as shaky in retrospect, even during the First World War, and attributed her vacillation to an incomplete grasp of Christianity. The Rev. Constance Coltman looked back in old age to Maude in the First War, and especially to Hinckley. 'Then in 1939, bang went her pacifism! Some people felt, "What's the use of that woman"?'[7]

In 1941 at the height of the blitz and only a few months before she crossed the Atlantic for yet another tour in the USA Maude attempted to explain her volte-face and Britain's position to the Americans, whom on her last visit she had urged against war. To many British people, she said, the fear that their children could be brought up Nazis was worse, even, than the fear of death. 'Will you Americans, vowed as you are to freedom . . . look for a moment at your own children and ask . . . what so dreadful a threat would mean to them?'[8] When she arrived in the States that December she met Richard Roberts, now old and ill, founder of the Fellowship of Reconciliation. 'I asked him if he detested me for being a back-slider about Pacifism, and he took my hand and said, "You are *not* a back-slider, or only as I am too".'[9]

Her visit this time, at the invitation of the Federal Council of Churches, chanced to coincide with the attack on Pearl Harbour. She encountered a people in shock. 'I want you to know,' wrote Daisy Dobson, who was with

[6]Royden, 'I was a pacifist.'

[7]Sybil Thorndike 'In Memoriam Maude Royden', *Guildhouse Fellowship* (Sept. 1956). Her changed views were expressed to Emil Oberholzer (23 June 1966). For Vera Brittain, see Ceadel *Pacifism in Britain* 294 and Brittain *The Rebel Passion* 75. Constance Coltman gave her views to Emil Oberholzer.

[8]Maude Royden 'What Should a Briton Do?' *Christian Century* (16 April 1941) 522.

[9]Maude to Evelyn (18 Dec. 1941) Fawcett 221 'United States Visit 1941–2'.

her, in a letter to the Fellowship, 'that AMR is *needed* here.'[10] It would be hard to express more neatly a major element in Maude's appeal. She gave, as she had always given, a sense of stillness at the heart of the storm. People expressed this in different ways. After an earlier American visit a minister from Pittsburgh had written to her, 'To you life is a tightrope, to walk it is thrilling, but it is securely anchored at the ends.'[11] For many Americans who heard her now the anchors had been torn loose at Pearl Harbour. 'Some of us have heard you . . . and felt a new steadiness because you could bear not to be sure,' wrote a woman who worked with Jung in New York. Maude's own hope was that her mission would emphasise 'the spiritual significance of the catastrophic changes through which the world is passing'. As one minister put it, where others asked, 'Who is going to win the war?' Or even, 'Will America stay in the peace?' She asked, 'Have we the spirit of peace? Is there any spirit which could be said to be the foundation of the peace to come?'[12]

The tour (mostly in the East and in Canada) turned out as gruelling as anything yet. But it was successful – even glamorous at moments (lunch with the British Ambassador in Washington; an invitation from Princess Alice; tea with the novelist, Pearl Buck). It also offered the bizarre experience of plentiful and delicious food. Maude wrote back to Evelyn insisting that for once she must suppress her tendency to think of others and take full advantage of anything that came in American parcels.

> Don't keep it or share it with everyone! It is for you – not to gnaw secretly in your room, but not to have all the nicest things taken out and sent to Helen! And not to be hoarded for me. I have lived in luxury here all this winter.

When she wrote home she longed for home, 'austerities or no austerities'. 'Darling Evelina,' she had written, as the train pulled out at the start,

> The moment you had gone I wanted you back. But the train started very punctually and then I read your dear letter. Thank you, Beloved. I too feel that we have been much blessed in our friendship, and perhaps we have many happy years to come. I saw the wall-flowers in Hud's garden planted for next Spring, and I feel, now that we have started we are starting to come back! Already 1½ hours have gone![13]

She was away four months altogether. 'It is not true,' she wrote of Hudson later on to another friend, 'that he wants or has ever wanted to monopolise me. He has always done all in his power to help me on. Even as lately as 1940 he *wanted* me to go to America, though he knew the dangers and we both realised that we might not see each other again.'[14] Hudson was

[10] *Guildhouse Fellowship* (Feb. 1942).
[11] Walter J. Millard to Maude (7 Feb. 1928) Fawcett 222, 5/2.
[12] *Guildhouse Fellowship* (May 1942).
[13] Maude to Evelyn (24 Jan. 1942; 6 Oct. 1941) Fawcett 221.
[14] TFC 101.

eighty-two when she went. 'If he has sometimes seemed inconsiderate in small matters,' she told the same friend, 'I ask you to consider that Effie's growing happiness . . . her really happy old age, has been bought at a price: the price has been *his* old age, with periods of intense depression and physical exhaustion.' For Hudson, then, these four months were no small thing.

Maude came back in February 1942 to a life at home that was increasingly restricted. In the early days of the war she had volunteered for ambulance duty, (not to drive an ambulance, which would have been beyond her, but to drive an accompanying car which could take messages during an air raid). She liked the idea. But her own mobility varied with her rheumatism and lameness. At times during her American visit she was only able to walk with two sticks and a wheelchair met her at railway stations. Wartime England was worse than that. There were few wheel chairs, porters, taxis, or train seats 'even if travelling first class'. Practically immobilised in rural Kent, she applied for an extra petrol ration and carried out preaching engagements each month, with occasional special assignments: a retreat for the Little Company at Jordans, a baby baptised for old Guildhousites, and Helen's wedding. In September 1940, in Herbert Gray's church in Golden Square and to an accompaniment of air raid sirens, Maude married Helen to Donald Newman, a young man starting his teaching career, whom from the first she liked very much.

But as she got lamer even home life was difficult, while lack of petrol meant her drives with Hudson were limited to shopping expeditions once a week. 'What a miracle it was that we were neighbours!' Yet the effort of walking from one house to the other gradually became too much for him.

> There is something heart-rending about the gradual loss of physical strength in one we love, especially one who had been superbly strong . . . . It was anguish to him to realise that he had no longer strength enough to lift me off my feet or even, at last, to see me across our two small gardens in the evening . . . . Still his mind retained its extraordinary grip and he not only read but planned to write.

He could not start, though. 'He had written too little and spoken too much to be at ease with a pen . . . . The faculty had gone.'[15]

The City Temple and the Guildhouse were bombed. A bomb fell on the hedge between their gardens. Their part of Kent was known as 'bomb alley' and Hudson's deafness did not prevent his hearing the planes go overhead. It also brought him a new anxiety. 'What *shall* I do when I can't hear your voice?' ('How well I understand your dear husband's fear,' wrote a woman who read this in *A Threefold Cord*. 'It was just your *voice* only that often helped me')[16] But for all their worries and the horrors of war they had some lovely days, says Maude. 'Would you like to be called light-hearted?' he

[15] TFC 92–3.
[16] Miss Annie Lakeman to Maude (18 July 1948) Fawcett 221, 3/3.

asked. She said that nobody could feel light-hearted in a world so agonised as this. Hudson insisted that there was, for all that, a kind of 'noble' light-heartedness. 'This light-heartedness was still sometimes ours.'[17]

Nineteen-forty-four opened in style with a letter from her brother Tom: 'I thought it would give you a good laugh to think that after all these years I should have become a Lord.' But both Hudson and Effie were ill; and Effie died in the February. The wider implications took some time to sink in. For one thing, Hudson's own death seemed likely. 'The worst might happen at any time,' his doctor had written at the end of December, giving bleak reports of his heart. In the summer he revived, however, and was back in his garden, planning for spring and for the future 'after the war'. At first, says Maude, through their ingrained habit of thinking of life as lived always by three, it didn't occur to either of them that there was now nothing to prevent their marriage. 'After a little while, however, I realised it with a sense of shock.'[18]

'I can't explain why we so hunger for a day . . . in which we might call each other "husband" – "wife",' she told a friend who was opposed to the idea. 'I can only ask you to believe that we do desire it, and I as much as he.'[19] By her own account, though, she thought more than he of how friends would react. Daisy disapproved; she had never cared for Hudson and perhaps thought nobody good enough for Maude, certainly not a husband of eighty-five.[20] And Evelyn? Evelyn could never be opposed to anything she thought would make Maude happy. Apart from that, her own friendship with Hudson stretched right back to Extension days. Evelyn now suffered badly from arthritis and Maude and Hudson were both resolved that her life should not be upset by the change. 'I am at present living in two houses!' Maude wrote after the wedding to a sister. 'I can't leave this one as long as Evelyn Gunter is so crippled.' All the same, in Helen's opinion, Evelyn at that time seemed 'absolutely lost'.

The great anxiety was Hudson's heart. The Bishop of Rochester conducted the service gently and briefly in Weald parish church. There were nine people present. 'I felt somehow as though all of us there had been taken apart for a while,' wrote one, 'and were truly in the Kingdom of Heaven.' 'There was to my mind such a strong sense of the presence of eternal things,' said another. 'It seemed to me, while I listened to you and Hudson uttering those lovely ancient vows, that nothing could really hurt or trouble love, that death could not really part you and him nor any lovers.' The writer went on, 'I believe you don't mind a bit about being lame compared to this lovely joy . . . . Am I right?'[21] The following day they were besieged by the press. But as Maude had not yet given her hostage to fortune in the

[17] TFC 94.
[18] TFC 99.
[19] TFC 101.
[20] Dr Sylvia Chapman to author (3 April 1986).
[21] Dr Sybil Pratt (n.d.) Fawcett 221, 3/1 'Letters on our Marriage'; TFC 108.

shape of *A Threefold Cord*, there was as yet no banner headline 'The Other Woman waited for 43 years'.[22]

Hudson nearly died on their wedding day evening. 'I could not bear it . . . . I cried out to him not to go, not to leave me, and even at that hour my voice reached him. He heard . . . and came back from the shadow of death.'[23] After that he again recovered sufficiently to be out in his garden and promise her, joking, that he would try to rival those nonagenarians whose tardy deaths appeared in the *Times*. 'When your dear husband told me that he wanted to marry you,' Hudson's doctor said later to Maude, 'I knew at once from the tone of his voice that it was the one thing which would give him happiness.'[24] And it seemed to. He said contentedly, 'I shall never be jealous again, of your friends or your work or *anything*; for, after all, you did marry me.'[25] They had been married two months when he died.

'Why do people ever want to deny work to women? How can suffering be borne without it?' Maude wrote this in reference to the early days of her relationship with Hudson, when she had plunged into suffrage work; but it could as well have been written of the end. 'Oh blessed work!' She was helped by her commitment to the Fellowship and the Little Company, and other preaching and speaking engagements. She also began at about this time to establish herself as a broadcaster. But the work she really seized on after Hudson's death was writing the story of the relationship between herself and Hudson and Effie, which took shape as *A Threefold Cord*. 'Anyone who begins it will read it through', wrote the *Manchester Guardian's* reviewer – which is something short of saying, like Florence Hill, that people would fight one day for first editions – but yet a tribute. It is not great writing. Maude's literary powers did not match her oratory, as she well knew. Her style has dated. But *A Threefold Cord* can still grip the reader. 'Book came stop read the first time in two sittings stop' wired one of the earliest from Toronto. It is moving, 'true', and perceptibly erotic. Here, in real life, is that combination of strong passion and strong principle which works to such effect in *Jane Eyre*. 'A moving love story, as romantic in its way, as that of the Brownings,' said the *Christian Science Monitor*; 'one of the world's great love stories' (*News Chronicle*); 'Beatrice and Dante' (*Socialist Leader*); 'this courageous and beautiful book' (Vera Brittain in *Peace News*). She meant it was courageous to publish a story which might be open to misrepresentation. 'Her book is bound to cause acute controversy' wrote the reviewer for the *News of the World*. Or, as one American paper said, 'Skeptics won't believe it.'

Many of those to whom she showed the manuscript – including Daisy – thought it should not be published. The Bishop who had taken the marriage

[22] *Star* (24 Nov. 1958) 14.
[23] TFC 112.
[24] Dr Moseley to Maude (1 Dec. 1947) Fawcett 221, 3/3.
[25] TFC 112.

service advised her strongly against publication. He thought people would assume she had been Hudson's mistress, and he took a critical view of Effie. 'You will never be able to explain her . . . . It was a wrong and selfish act to marry a man for his protection, while unable and unwilling to give him the rights of married love.' Would the book help people? he asked.

Quite definitely No! It may incite some who have an affair to go on with it – on your recommendation; but without your and his background and Christian faith to uphold them . . . . Then also, other people cannot hope to have the third angle in the triangle – a person of neuter gender, as happened with you.

The absence in the book of anything that hints that Maude herself ever looked on Effie as a person of neuter gender casts warm light on their relationship. The Bishop, however, was more concerned to wonder why she had written the story. It was, he thought, the product of a natural possessiveness and seemed to say 'I want the world to know, and so does he, that we were each other's all the time.'[26]

He pressed Maude earnestly to think again, and, instead, write a 'Life' of Hudson, 'rather than a monograph on your part in it'. In answer, she may have made a few small changes, but she was determined on publication. He was right that she wanted the world to know. She also did want to 'explain' Effie and had the kind of sympathy to do it (she was one of the few of Sheppard's friends who showed real sympathy for his wife Alison, who broke up her marriage with Maude's 'beloved Dick').[27]

When the book came out she was swamped with letters, some 200 of which survive.[28] They are from friends, acquaintances and strangers and are mostly highly approving (she may not have kept the hostile ones). 'A true work of art,' wrote Herbert Gray, in his usual ecstatic vein. 'I believe this book will live as one of the unique and lovely things in our literature.' 'A courageous and beautiful book,' said Sybil Thorndike, 'I think so many people must be helped by it.' 'Best and dearest of friends,' wrote Kathleen, 'Your book came yesterday and has brought me great joy and a feeling of being very near to you. It is almost a holy book . . . and I do reverence you for writing it.' Martin Shaw thought that she must be gratified 'by the reception of what will take its place as one of the world's great love stories'. Abelard and Heloïse are much cited. 'I call it an EPIC and do not believe that is an exaggeration,' writes one. Another calls it an epic poem. One woman sent her a poem about it. A retired Army chaplain proposed marriage. At least one friend was surprised to discover something that she had never dreamed of ('never . . . did I know you had this in your life. You must have so conducted your life that all breath of innuendos passed you by'); while

[26]Christopher Chavasse, Bishop of Rochester to Maude (20 Dec. 1946) Fawcett 221.
[27]Alison Sheppard wrote to Maude (11 Nov. 1937) after Dick's death, 'I think it was extraordinarily generous of you to write. I know a little what Dick's friends think of me and I do not blame them.' Fawcett 220.
[28]These letters are in folder 3/3 in Fawcett 221.

another had the pleasure of confirming something that she felt she had always known ('I guessed that you loved Mr Hudson Shaw . . . once when I was alone with you, you spoke to him on the phone, and I saw your face and heard your voice').

Many of the writers share the Bishop's concern over contemporary moral standards but not his conclusion: they are glad she has published, thrilled to see morality fighting back. 'Oh, what a victory – what an example!' 'One is thankful to know what is possible to great souls, especially in view of the moral laxity of our time.' 'God knows one wants something to anchor to in these days.' 'My own sister,' writes one friend, 'says it is *impossible* to love and live together without the physical contact . . . I said "wait until you read the book."' One or two people thought it removed the nasty taste left by current writing. 'It is the more valuable,' wrote Charles Raven,' because it comes just after a novel written by a colleague which made me feel dirty and ashamed.'

In a very admiring review, Vera Brittain wrote, 'Life today is so bewildering, especially for the young, that those who can help them by sharing the heights and depths of experience have surely an obligation to do so.' But how many of the young read *A Threefold Cord*? The letters have a ring of middle age, of people saddened and ill at ease in the moral climate of the 1940s, or, in some cases, cruelly trapped between the standards of two generations. 'My life too is a Threefold Cord.' 'I myself have come to love someone who is unattainable.' 'I love a man married to a hopeless invalid.' The book confirms and uplifts them in their struggle. When one woman puts a specific question: 'I cannot quite realise where to place the physical boundary of passionate love,' Maude's reply is firm but unspecific.

> To have a passionate love for someone for whose sake you must never overstep the . . . moral code . . . is one of the hardest paths that human beings can follow. It means that while you . . . long to express that love on the physical as well as the mental and spiritual planes you must never do so . . . . And to be sure that you will never do so you must neither indulge in self-pity . . . nor must you allow your thoughts to dwell on what is forbidden.[29]

One of the letter writers admitted, 'It is difficult to realise that you too are growing old. You are associated in my mind with youth – with crowds of young people hearing you preach . . . with suffrage . . . . If you were announced to speak we rushed to hear you.' Maude was seventy-one when the book came out, and Sybil Thorndike, who – as we saw – added to the chorus of praise at the time, looked on it with distaste in her own old age as the work of someone 'old, feeble, tired' and said she preferred to think of Maude as she had been in the 1920s.[30] In fact, like Sybil Thorndike herself, Maude stuck fast, right up to the end, to the commitments of her earlier years.

[29]Maude to Miss Pickard (9 Feb. 1948) Fawcett 221 3/3.
[30]Dame Sybil Thorndike Oberholzer interview

'I was born a woman and I can't get over it,' she had said gaily in 1922, speaking for Lady Astor's election. It was still true. She never lost her eye for the devious workings of the double standard and in 1944 was incensed by a report on the morals of women in the forces. 'If we are to make these enquiries, why is there no report on the morals of men in the forces?'[31] She retained her faith in the ministry of women, and in 1944 a wartime development gave some promise of change to come. From early in the war the colony of Hong Kong had been under Japanese occupation and a number of Anglicans there were deprived of any chance to receive the sacraments. In 1944, Dr R. V. Hall, the Bishop of Hong Kong, ordained to the priesthood a deaconess, Miss Lei Tim Oi, 'Until we know more,' Maude wrote to the Fellowship,

> our duty lies in prayer for the Bishop and even more for the woman he has ordained. The path of the pioneer is never an easy one, and I cannot refrain from thanking God for her courage and devotion; for the noble ministry she must have given to the Church in Hong Kong thus to have her vocation recognised by its Bishop; and for that vocation itself . . . . 'readers . . . who do not share my hope for the ordination of women to the priesthood (and I think there may be some) will forgive me for saying how great is my joy in this event'.[32]

'There is no question that Lei Tim Oi has the gift of priesthood,' said Dr Hall, preaching in London in 1945. 'The only thing that remains is, is it going to be possible to ordain women with these obvious gifts and calling to the ministry? I am myself convinced that it is right.'[33] But his fellow bishops were not convinced. The Episcopalian bishops in China pressed him to ask for her resignation; which he did in 1946, and she complied.

How could ordination be 'resigned'? asked Maude (who had sent a statement on the case to Bishop Tzu Kao Shen of Shensi). Was it not an indelible sacrament? 'I should like to hear their explanation,' she wrote in a letter to Lei Tim Oi. 'Perhaps I may express a special sympathy with you because I have myself felt the call . . . to the priesthood and . . . been refused. When I heard of your ordination . . . my heart leapt with joy.'[34] In her answer the Chinese priest explained that, in effect, the choice had been between her own resignation and Dr Hall's; and that she had not felt she could force that prospect upon the man who had so bravely ordained her. Her congregation had been deeply shocked.

> There was a great reaction on the part of our church members after they had listened to the speech made by our Bishop . . . . They understood how hard for the Bishop to stand for the bitterness therefore they were very sorry for him . . . . They noticed quite clear that our Bishop used to respect the people in

[31]*Guildhouse Fellowship* (Feb. 1944).
[32]ibid. (Dec. 1944).
[33]ibid. (May 1946).
[34]Quoted, *Guildhouse Fellowship* (May 1946) Lei Tim Oi resigned her work as a priest; not her orders.

the East as well as in the West. He shows no colour-line at all because he cares
nothing about there is no woman priest in his own country . . . . They said that
he is really a Bishop with Christian spirit.

Women came up to comfort her afterwards. And 'one of our girl choir
members whose age is thirteen, when she took off her white gown after that
service she ran straight to her mother and put the following question to her:
"Why does God make women?" '[35]

No comparable challenge faced the Church of England in the postwar
years. The public, as Maude said to Ursula Roberts, was 'singularly
uninterested' in women's ordination. She herself made a special appeal to
try and raise the numbers of the Anglican Group so that it might exert
effective pressure on the Lambeth Conference in 1948. There was a small
breakthrough in 1947 when Lord Stansgate, at the Air Ministry, secured the
appointment of the Rev. Elsie Chamberlain, a Congregationalist, as an
RAF chaplain. Through her contact with Lady Stansgate (a keen supporter
of the ministry of women) Maude seems to have played some part in this.
But no similar Anglican appointment followed. 'The Arch (Cantuar) and
the Bishop of London are both anti-feminist to an astonishing degree,' she
told her sister Mary.

To a conference of the Modern Churchmen's Union that autumn she
gave an address on women's ordination which made yet again the case for
spiritual equality and dwelt yet again on the nature of vocation.

> It is sometimes urged that other vocations are open to those of us who believe that
> we should have been ordained priests . . . . All this is true but entirely irrel-
> evant . . . . You would not tell a musician that he had better paint pictures.[36]

Though it was over ten years now since she had given up her Guildhouse
ministry she had not escaped from the 'hampering frustrations' of a lay-
woman who could not be ordained. People still wanted her to hear confessions. To one woman she explained how reluctant she was. Not because she
felt that her current way of life was out of keeping with that of a minister
('Indeed, I give more time to prayer than I did when I was more employed')
but because she felt completely unworthy 'and I have not the grace of Holy
Orders nor the authority given to a priest by his Church.'[37]

In a sense the pastoral side of her ministry was maintained through the
medium of broadcasting. It was Sheppard in the early twenties who had
pioneered the religious broadcast – 'a travesty of Christian worship' to
some but, in his hands, a lifeline to thousands. Indeed, at one low point in
1925 Maude tried to cheer him up with the thought that by this means he
had spoken 'to more people . . . . than that dreadful Wesley, with the
constitution of a horse, did in all his long and misspent life!'[38] As for herself,

[35]*Guildhouse Fellowship* (October 1946).
[36]*Guildhouse Fellowship* (Nov. 1947).
[37]Maude to unnamed recipient (11 Nov. 1947) Fawcett 223 (1).
[38](15 Nov. 1925) SP.

her first broadcast in England (she broadcast during her trips abroad, especially in America and Australia) seems to have taken place in 1932 and bore the appropriate title, 'Hope'. There were other scattered occasions in the thirties, a few broadcast services during the war, a series on 'Suffering' in 1946 and later on talks for Woman's Hour. Her radio fans included many of those who were professionally involved in the broadcasts. 'I have been listening to your talk . . . this afternoon and have been very moved – here in the continuity studio of Light Programme,' wrote one man on a Christmas card. Stuart Hibberd, who usually announced her, became one of her admirers and often went early into the studio for the chance of talking to her. 'When I hear your voice I forget that I am blind,' Maude had once been told, and it was partly her voice that made her one of the most popular speakers on the BBC's Silver Lining programme when it was launched in the 1950s: that, and her warm, straightforward style, her touches of humour, her naturalness. Many years before, a troubled young woman in her congregation in Eccleston Square had written, 'You are the only person I can even bear to hear talk about God because you do it so naturally.'

Her radio listeners, like those at the Guildhouse, were some of them Christian and some not. They liked the feeling that she felt God with her but was not constantly dragging Him in. Fan mail mounted. 'Listening to Dr Maude Royden's broadcast,' one man wrote to the BBC,' I anew realised the enormity of the decree which bans women from ordination in the Church of England. This great and devout soul has however her own Diocese – the English-speaking world.' And he included a poem:

> Again that golden voice
> That consecrated heart is speaking
> My inward spirit must rejoice
> Here's end of seeking.
>
> Of life and death and mystery
> She holds the key
> The meaning of all history
> Makes plain to see.
>
> There's many a priest
> Many who wear the cope
> Who have not in the least
> Her visionary scope.
>
> And yet man's law
> Has locked the church's door
> Insensate to the awe
> And ecstasy of hearts that soar.[39]

Others were reminded of a shared past. 'Thank you for your Silver Lining talk yesterday,' wrote one old lady.

[39] W. R. Burns (14 Aug. 1944) Fawcett 222, 5/2.

It has helped me enormously to clearer thinking . . . . It's lovely to hear your dear voice on the Radio for it was my privilege to speak with you sometimes in the old 'Suffrage Days' . . . and when you came to speak at a League of Nations meeting it was my joy to propose a vote of thanks to you . . . . At 76 . . . I've had to give up speaking and all public work and I *do* miss it! . . . Goodbye, dear valiant Pioneer and may I wish you a happy Christmas.[40]

But could Maude see herself any longer in these reflections of her public face? The mood that comes across from her jottings in the old notebooks where she records the spiritual struggle of these last years often seems to approach despair.[41] 'This Xmas has unequalled chill and gloom' she writes in 1953, 'with . . . Evelyn G in such torment and I so puzzled and down-hearted.' Being puzzled was something she often admitted. Indeed, it had always been part of her appeal that she did not claim to know all the answers. When she spoke of 'the steep hill of old age' she did not pretend that the ascent was easy. When she spoke of pain she began by admitting. 'I have always dreaded physical pain', and when she spoke of failure, 'Can anyone always escape the desolating sense of failure?' For all that, people gained an impression that she herself had bottomed the pit. 'She has looked at the Medusa head of the world's suffering,' a journalist wrote once, 'and it has not turned her to stone.' Yet in these tension-ridden Cold War years Maude noted, 'Today the news terrifies me.' 'As for the prospect of war, invasion and persecution by Communists, I don't know how to face it.' And again, 'This morning waking early I have lain in a state of terror at the cruelty of men and the horror of torture and the fear they . . . inflict on one another.' At the time of the Korean War she wrote to Kathleen, 'What a world to end one's life in, when one has given the best part of it to work for peace, as you have and, in a lesser degree, I.'[42]

She felt she was losing the struggle with old age and was agonised by the struggles of her friends. Evelyn had become so crippled with arthritis that as far back as 1945 she had to leave their cottage and join her sisters in a bungalow in Hertfordshire. She faced her problems with the greatest courage. 'My dear, don't think I am ill because I do not write this myself,' she told Maude in a letter written for her by a friend a year or so before her death in 1954. She was, said Kathleen, 'the least self-centred and . . . most completely unselfish person'. Another friend saw in her, right to the end, 'the same young ardent Victorian girl she had once been, full of spirit and the capacity for enjoyment'. 'Yes, we have been "we three" for many years,' wrote Maude to Kathleen after the funeral. 'It is however about 10 years since Evelyn's long martyrdom began and I thank God that it is over.'[43]

[40] Mildred B. Shaw to Maude (19 Dec. 1952) Fawcett 222, 5/2.

[41] Three of the notebooks are in Fawcett 225; the fourth, lent by Helen Blackstone. It is impossible to give page references.

[42] Maude to Kathleen (10 Jan. 1951) Fawcett KDC/H1/1–8.

[43] Maude to Kathleen (20 Jan. 1954) Fawcett KDC/H1/1–8.

She herself had left Kent in 1952 and gone to a house in Golders Green. 'Come and see me,' she wrote brightly to the Fellowship, 'if you don't mind shouting at one who is deaf.' But in her notebook she searches in vain for the spiritual meaning of 'deafness, blindness, lameness, old age and less money – Inability to drive my car – Less writing – Long life – The loss of friends.' Thoughts that were never quite conquered return. 'I can't even now be glad that I am lame. I would still rather have had the joy of an efficient body than the wisdom of limitations and lameness. God pity and forgive me. Amen.'

Her conviction that disease was created by man, since no God of Love could will it, naturally drew her to spiritual healing. The Little Company had tried this (unsuccessfully) and Maude in the thirties helped to launch in England the American healer, William Macmillan, who saw his first patients in the Guildhouse vestry.[44] In one of her letters to Dick Sheppard (who had also supported Macmillan) she laments that the prayers of all his friends seem to bring him no better health; adding, 'We must pray wrong, I suppose.' In her private notes there are many references to the nature of prayer and the meaning of illness. 'Since I am awaiting spiritual healing,' she writes in 1953, 'I think I may concentrate on the thought that He made my *body* to express His own thought. He can't therefore will it to be defective . . . and must "will" its healing when it is imperfect.'

In March she wrote that she was greatly cheered. 'Last night in very depressing circumstances I heard a voice saying that I would get well.' Later she went to the Walsingham shrine, asking to be cured of her deafness. She also consulted 'Mac' [Macmillan]. 'I believe less and less in drugs, more and more in spiritual healing.' Her spirits rise. In May she notes 'The 3rd time I have dreamed I was healed.' And later, 'much conspires to help me. That I was able to broadcast, that my eyes are better, the pain in my side gone, the prayers of my friends and many others, the use of my voice, experiences of cures of people having "incurable" ills (which mine is not).' On this question of spiritual healing she was at variance with her confessor. The death in 1946 of Father Andrew, the East End priest who was reckoned as near a saint as could be met with in his generation, had deprived Maude and many others of a remarkable friend and guide.[45] Her confessor now, through these difficult years, was well-known but unremarkable: the Rev. Reginald Somerset Ward. 'I keep always on my mantelpiece the picture of a signpost on a . . . moor', he wrote, 'to remind me of the true nature of my work which is to stand and point but not to push.' As it happened he did not point in the direction Maude wanted to go, since he could not accept 'that our Lord heals all diseases if there is enough faith'.

[44]See 'William Macmillan: The Reluctant Healer' in Gloria G. Fromm (ed.), *Essays in Biography* (1986).
[45]Father Andrew (Ernest Hardy 1869–1946) was one of the founders of the Society of the Divine Compassion, a community which took up a life of harsh poverty and utter devotion to the poor.

Rightly or wrongly I am little concerned (save in my human sympathy) with your bodily ailment compared with my concern about the hidden poison of bitterness which might prevent the complete healing of the soul. . . . It is the shifting of the sense of value from ourselves to God which frees us from fear.[46]

This is the shift that, according to her notebooks, Maude was always trying, and failing, to make. Alongside the struggle with fear and disappointment is the unceasing search for humility. Writing in hospital in 1954 she notes 'My 1st thought on hearing the noise of the drill outside was for myself and my own suffering, then for my fellow patients; last for the workmen who are, I believe, often made deaf and nervy by the strain of the work.' A few days later she is slightly encouraged.

I am beginning to learn what it means to love my neighbour as myself. I had to choose between ringing for breakfast or waiting in great discomfort while others were served because I had been forgotten. I waited what seemed hours but was really only an hour and then rang.

But such comparatively bright spots are rare. Again and again, like the lash of a penitent, come her admissions of conceit and selfishness and of that special sin of the vain, the seeking for inferiority in others. In 1951 she castigates her 'hateful habit of criticism based on conceit and a desire to find people inferior to myself'. 'It seems to me now that I have never been moved by love at all.' And, three years later: 'You still think of yourself too highly. . . . You take evil pleasure in denigrating. It is your first response. And you take pleasure in praise and in any good you do becoming known.' 'Last night I couldn't sleep for wounded vanity,' she writes (again in 1951) 'lamenting my small congregation and my own gaucherie. . . . I want to be admired and liked not obscure and clumsy.' And a little further on she speaks of herself as 'wallowing in egotistic and conceited thoughts without even trying to stop it because I enjoyed my success so much'.

'"I have fought the good fight; I have finished my course". . . . Shall we be able to say that, do you think?' she had asked Kathleen long ago, when the end of their course was unbelievably remote. Now she looked on her work as a failure. 'How unreal much of my speaking and thinking has been! Here is cause for humility indeed.' 'All my crusades I preached beyond my experience. I think this is why I cannot reach that experience now.' 'It is very good for us,' wrote Somerset Ward, 'to accept the inward loss of reputation and the denial of self will.' He thought her approach to intercession was twisted, since it 'stresses out of all reason the importance of your part'.[47]

There are a number of entries in the notebooks which concern Maude's relationships with other people and record remorse, regret, at what she sees as her failure towards them. It is not here, though, that she reflects on the

---

[46]Reginald Somerset Ward to Maude (28 July 1949) Fawcett 223 (1)
[47]ibid. (1 Feb. 1950; 30 Sept. 1949) Fawcett 223 (1)

most striking failure in her personal life. 'I know well that there is a gulf between Helen and me,' she had written to Donald, Helen's husband, in the summer of 1948. 'You . . . who are so extraordinarily wise and understanding, might . . . have made a bridge between us. I know you have tried and I am deeply grateful.' Then she says as she had said to others,

I often wonder whether I was wrong to adopt a child who could not be the *first* claim on my time and strength. I have put my work first and only ventured to adopt Helen because I beleived I could give her something better than a home with a capital H, especially as I had Aunt to make for her a home with a small one! That I couldn't give her a perfect home I well knew, for it takes 2 people – a husband and wife – to do that; but Helen couldn't have had that in any case.

And there were great natural differences.

I have always thought it *extra* unlucky that Helen and I had nothing in common – nothing at all. . . . We are very far apart and I blame myself because as I had the start of her by 41 years, I should have done better.[48]

Whether doing better was ever an option on either side is the real question. Kathleen, in a memorial address, spoke of Maude as 'a great lover and giver'; and this is witnessed time and again in the remembrance of those who had from her whatever it was that kept them going: time, sympathy, prayer, appreciation, advice, understanding – sometimes money – love, in fact, in various forms. 'How can I thank you doctor dear for that little personal word of comfort?' 'Dear Madam, I was very grateful and relieved by your sympathetic letter. I thought perhaps you would not reply.' There were many such; and poems, even ('Of One who always understands, I'll sing the praise with tongue and pen'). Perhaps Maude failed to understand Helen through her own need to be understood: the eighth child and sixth daughter, however much loved, still short of love. As to that, her letter to Donald scarcely indicates her own feelings. But after her death, Tom Royden's widow, in the course of condolences to Helen, wrote that she liked to think of Maude reunited with Tom and three of her sisters, 'though I somehow don't think her family meant nearly as much to her as you did'.[49]

'As to the future, I feel rather hopeless,' Maude had told Donald in 1948.

I am 71 – have hardly ever found that, in problems of human relationship, explanations are any use . . . they make things positively worse. . . . Perhaps Helen and I may some day be closer than we are now. I hope so most earnestly, for my failure to win her affection is a wound in my heart, and perhaps she also wishes it were otherwise.

Helen and Maude were never closer, though they could never be described

---

[48]Maude to Donald Newman (12 June 1948) copied by Emil Oberholzer.
[49]Quenelda, Lady Royden, to Helen Blackstone (31 July 1956) Fawcett 223 (4).

as estranged. Maude was delighted with Helen's children and proud to be able to christen them. But in 1950, when Helen was told that Donald had multiple sclerosis, the relationship between them was not such that Maude was able to be of much comfort. He died in 1964.

Maude herself died in her eightieth year on 30 July, 1956. She evidently tried to take to heart one observation of Somerset Ward: 'A failure on our part to accept the limitations of old age involves labour and difficulty for those who care for us', for her old friend and housekeeper, Ethel, who looked after her again when she moved back to London, found her very patient in her last illness. And another friend, who did typing for her, remembered Maude in these final months of enforced dependence on others, 'bearing everything with high-hearted courage and never a complaint or moan'.[50]

There were still many friends and helpers. Daisy Dobson, who lived quite near, made herself again into Maude's right hand. Her impression is that Maude was not unhappy in her small house in Hampstead at the end of her life, but it is really impossible to tell. 'Today, I confess I am dwelling chiefly on the lovely things we have enjoyed together,' she wrote to Kathleen in 1955, 'Coverack and Pella and LMH [where the two of them had spent a week a few years previously as guests of the college] – and our journey to Parma and Piacenza, when the waiter compared us to *due colombine*.'

Her magnetism – that personal aura which so many people tried to put into words – was very little dimmed until the last few weeks. A friend had once likened it to the Indian *Brahmacharya* – the love that is still in God, 'and the bearer of that love has a radiance for others'. Another wrote after Kathleen had broadcast on Maude in Australia in 1954 about her own first meeting with Maude in England.

> When we were shown into her study she was sitting at her desk, and I shall never forget the sense that we both had as she got up and came towards us, of being in the presence of the most extraordinary spiritual quality.[51]

A nurse in a hospital where she went for treatment marvelled that though, asleep in bed, she was just like any other old lady, immediately she opened her eyes 'the whole room was filled with her personality'.[52] This changed at last. Ten days before she died Daisy Dobson wrote to Maude's sister Mary:

[50]Mrs Fordham to Kathleen Courtney (4 Oct. 1956) Fawcett KDC/H5/1–41. Maude, it seems, had done everything possible to help the Fordhams with their handicapped son.
[51]Catherine King (Australian Broadcasting Commission) to Kathleen Courtney (18 Feb. 1954) Fawcett KDC/H2.
[52]Florence Hill to author.

I am sorry you feel so cut off from AMR I think most people feel the same. She seems in a way shut off from everyone and it creates rather a difficult situation. AMR has not been seeing anyone for weeks [and] . . . she does not seem to *mind* not seeing them.

I think she has been very deeply disappointed that she has not been cured by spiritual healing. For very many months she believed she would be, and has had a healer coming to her each week. . . . AMR does not take into account that she is nearly eighty and has worked very hard most of her life. She says that the Gospels are full of stories of healing and why shouldn't she be healed? Now, I think she has come to the conclusion that physical healing is not for her, and she told me some weeks ago that she was coming to the end. . . . She has been facing up to the whole situation during the last few months and has in a sense withdrawn into herself. I don't know whether I am making you understand at all what I mean. You say that AMR does not 'say anything' even when she does write, and I think she does not 'say anything' to anyone. But I think she is happy and has accepted the fact that she will not receive physical healing.[53]

'After her death,' said Daisy years later, 'it was almost as though no trace remained. She was an irreplaceable personality, you see. She had to *be* there.'[54] There were numerous obituaries. Kathleen Courtney, whose sense of loss was acute for the eighteen years she survived, spoke vividly and movingly about her friend at the memorial service in St Botolph's and in a broadcast for Woman's Hour. 'I echo the cry of one who loved her much,' wrote Edith Picton–Tubervill, herself over eighty: "Maude is alive, it is we who are dead."'[55]

[53]Daisy Dobson to Mary Royden (20 July 1976) Fawcett 222, 5/2.
[54]Daisy Dobson in conversation with Sybil Oldfield.
[55]*Times*, (3 Aug. 1956).

Index